THE FLIGHT OF THE MANGO FLOWERS:

A MEMOIR OF OUR WAY OUT OF THE COLD WAR.

A TESTIMONY OF PEDRO PANES AND THE EARLY CUBAN EXODUS.

by

Antonio María Gordon

DORRANCE
PUBLISHING CO
EST. 1920
PITTSBURGH, PENNSYLVANIA 15238

Dorrance Publishing Co
585 Alpha Drive
Pittsburgh, PA 15238
Visit our website at *www.dorrancebookstore.com*

ISBN: 978-1-4809-2563-2
eISBN: 978-1-4809-2333-1

Dedication

To my parents and all Cuban parents who sent their young children and adolescents to an uncertain future in care of the Catholic Church and the United States of America to spare them being devoured by the evil of their time, Communism.

To my peers, both in Cuba and in the United States, who have died prematurely so that their hopes and aspirations for a better world would not be forgotten.

And, to all the living Pedro Pans to remind them that we may still be instrumental in the resolution of the issues that still divide Cuba and the United States, despite the end of the Cold War in 1989.

Contents

Acknowledgements

Although the island of Cuba has been rather close to the Florida peninsula as has been noted ever since the first maps of the region were produced in the fifteenth century, Cubans had never massively migrated off their island to the north until very recently. In fact, Cubans on their way to Florida were news worthy since the summer of 1959 when the United States Coast Guard rescued a boat load of refugees off Dry Tortugas. That was the beginning of the first Cuban migration during the Cold War, in which approximately 250,000 Cubans arrived in the United States from January 1959 until the nuclear missile crisis cut off all flights between the island and the U.S. in October 1962.

The largest migration of school age children in the Western Hemisphere occurred at that time in what has been termed Operation Pedro Pan. The Pedro Pans were more than 14,000 Cuban children and adolescents who were sent to the United States alone to be cared for or resettled by the Roman Catholic Church. Most of the children who left Cuba under the auspices of the Catholic Church were cared for by friends or relatives of the children in question, who had already sought refuge in the States. The Church was also involved in the boarding and housing of more than 8,000 unaccompanied young children and adolescents, who were cared for in camps, orphanages, and boarding schools for months to years because they had no one else to take care of them.

Two other major migrations occurred out of Cuba during the Cold War. The Freedom Flights brought out of the island nearly 300,000 Cubans from 1965 until 1973, and in 1980 the Mariel Boatlift resulted in the migration of 125,000 Cubans into the United States. Although these have been the major massive migrations out of Cuba during the Cold War, many more thousands have also escaped in small numbers.

I arrived in the United States alone during Operation Pedro Pan, becoming one of the thousands of unaccompanied children in care of the Church. This memoir has been in the making for more than fifty years. It began the first time I read and stored the more than 300 letters I received during my first two years in exile. These letters have allowed me to tell the story at this time. I thank first all those who wrote to me regularly from Cuba and from various points in the United States. They provided me unknowingly with a lifeline to the life that I was leaving behind forever. I am first and most grateful to my immediate family, relatives, school friends, neighborhood peers, and teachers. Without their concerns and support as expressed in their letters, I feel that my life would have been very different and this work would have never been able to come to life.

Once I began writing, I found the encouragement and assistance of two friends extremely important. Firstly, I express my gratitude to my friend María E. Vidaña, who assisted me in organizing the letters which have served as the backbone of this memoir. She also read several chapters of the manuscript in their first draft and made important recommendations that have made the material more amenable for current day readers. María also assisted me with the leg work necessary to collect the information I needed to complete this project.

Secondly, I want to thank my friend Sal Castaner, who took the time to review the entire first draft of the manuscript. He clearly noted after that exposure to my writing that I did well in becoming a physician because the future would not have been bright if I had become a writer.

My children Tony, Maribel, and Cecilia have also been very interested and instrumental in the writing of this book. All of them have been encouraging me to finish it so they can appreciate some of the complex history through which our family lived during the Cuban revolution and early years of exile in the United States. I do not want to forget, in this context, my nephew Alex Perez, the son of Muñeca and Eduardo, whom the reader will meet in the body of this work. Alex was born in Wilmington, Delaware and currently lives in Colorado where he and his wife, Lisa, have bought a farm and live there with their children Alex and Andy. My nephew read the first draft of the entire book and wrote back to me with encouragement. He also noted, "I see your book and your story much like I see the chickens I have running around my backyard these days. This time of the year in Colorado, the chickens tend to molt due to the change in seasons. The meat and the bones are good and solid, but the birds look disheveled and out of sorts. With a little grooming and more time, they will regain their eye-catching plumage and be as good outside as they are inside."

This is not the first book published on the memories of the Pedro Pan children. One of my peers while I was in the Unaccompanied Cuban Children Program, Jose

Ignacio Ramirez, wrote about his memories several years ago. Ignacio introduced me to the curator of Barry University's Pedro Pan Collection, Mrs. Ximena Valdivia. Mrs. Valdivia's assistance in my work has been invaluable because she received me with open arms at the Barry University Library and made available to me a number of works that are not in print about Operation Pedro Pan. Most important among them, was the booklet written by Mr. Thomas J. Aglio and distributed at the 50th Anniversary Reunion of the Pedro Pans in Miami Beach in 2011. I have used extended quotes from Mr. Aglio's booklet in this memoir. Mrs. Valdivia also directed me to the archive of *The Voice*, the newspaper of the Archdiocese of Miami, located at St. Thomas University in Miami. The latter institution is now an archdiocesan university, but it was founded in 1961 as Biscayne College by the Augustinian Fathers at the time when their Catholic university in Havana, Universidad de Santo Tomás de Villanueva was confiscated and closed during the revolution. *The Voice* collected many stories dealing with the Cuban refugees, their struggles, and the assistance that was being made available to them through the Catholic Church, the State of Florida, the federal government, and private institutions during the early 1960s. In this context, I want to also thank the staff at the Catholic Charities office of the Archdiocese of Miami at Wilton Manors in Fort Lauderdale, Florida, for their assistance when I reviewed my own Pedro Pan file.

The Cuban Heritage Collection of the University of Miami provided me, through the generosity of Mrs. María Estorino, a great deal of material on Operation Pedro Pan and the Unaccompanied Cuban Children Program. Access to original documents, manuscripts from individuals who worked with the Cuban children and photographs of the facilities in Florida City and Opa-Locka were most helpful to me in the reconstruction of this memoir. Finally, I want to express my gratitude to Mickey Garrote for his extremely valuable assistance in locating various sources of information on this subject at the Main Miami-Dade Public Library.

I attended two high schools, one in Havana, Cuba and one in Jacksonville, Florida. My school in Havana does not exist anymore, but the religious congregation that founded it and ran it, the Marist Brothers of the Schools, does. Brother Rafael Martin, FMS, presently retired at the Marist House at Christopher Columbus High School in Miami, Florida has organized an archive of Cuban *maristas* yearbooks, which is kept in Guatemala City. Brother Rafael directed me to contact Brother José Antonio López, FMS, in Guatemala. Brother José Antonio was extremely interested in my project and searched through the yearbooks in the Cuban collection. Through his assistance, I have been able to use historical photos published more than fifty-five years ago.

My second high school, Bishop Kenny, played a pivotal role in my growth and development during my adolescence. It also deserves my gratitude. The Office of Alumni Relations and, in particular, Mrs. Dorothy Gripps, not only took my phone calls, but also welcomed me at the school and made available to me all the pertinent material in the school library and the records kept in her office for the graduating class of 1961. Without the hospitality and assistance of the current Bishop Kenny High School staff, I would not have been able to review the yearbooks, list of graduates, arrangements for the graduation ceremony, and many details without which this memoir would be incomplete.

A picture is worth one thousand words, according to the proverb. Therefore, I also need to thank Mr. José A. Fernández for working with me to select, preserve, scan, and touch up a number of images from fifty-four years ago. José also drew the map of Havana in order to orient the readers to the various locations in the city mentioned in the book. I also recognize with gratitude the excellent and professional work done by my cousin Manuel Buznego in photographing various memorabilia of those years in my possession and restoring images from various sources, including a couple of short 8 mm films.

Finally, I want to thank Ms. Devon Victoria Smith, a professional proofreader and copy editor, who came into my radar through one of my Cuban neighborhood friends about whom I write in this book. For the sake of the metaphor advanced by my nephew Alex, Mrs. Smith does not consider herself an expert in chicken's aesthetics. However, Devon has reviewed carefully the original manuscript and turned it into a readable personal story with insights into the Cuban revolution, the Cold War, and the ongoing Cuban-American *diferendo*, which may be coming to an end as living conditions in Cuba continue to deteriorate, the regime's repression results in an increasing number of injured and arrested Cubans, and the United States strives to resume and normalize diplomatic relations with Cuba.

June 20, 2015
United Nations World Refuge Day 2015
Miami, Florida
Antonio María Gordon

Introduction

"Refugees are people whose lives have been torn apart when violence arrives on their doorsteps or when they are persecuted for their religious or political beliefs. Refugees are driven from their homes and communities by factors outside their control. It happens so fast. Quite literally, refugees are people running for their lives. Voiceless and without an advocate, most often grabbing only the things they can carry, refugees are the world's most vulnerable people."

–The United Nations Refugee Agency

This is a memoir of my world and my life in the early 1960s. I was born to a middle class, professional family in Havana, Cuba. As I was turning fifteen years old, I noticed that, as I was changing, the entire world around me was also changing. My memories of those difficult years are based in great measure on my own personal recollections and the content, views, and impressions of relatives, friends, and teachers that have remained recorded in more than 300 letters written to me during that period of time. Frankly, I would consider my own personal reminiscences alone to be insufficient to illuminate this very complex period of time in my life. I feel, therefore, that the points of view expressed here in *The Flight of the Mango Flowers* are the consensus and end product of the grapevine of the community where I was developing. Essentially, these are my recollections, impressions, feelings, fears, goals, and also those of my school classmates and teachers at the Marist school (located a few blocks away from the Plaza Cívica which later became known as Plaza de la Revolución in Havana), my family, and some of my friends and neighbors.

The period of time between 1960 and 1962 was a memorable one, not only for Cubans, but for the entire world. It should be remembered that at the climax of this period of time, the world faced the Cuban Missile Crisis. After years of Cold War public posturing and rhetoric, and secret dealings and accords, finally, in October 1962 the real, credible fear of a global, nuclear holocaust was triggered when news was made public of the presence on Cuban soil of Soviet intermediate range missiles capable of transporting nuclear bombs targeting North America. Obviously, if such an attack would have taken place, it would have resulted in a nuclear counterattack by the United States and multiple, worldwide, nuclear explosions with devastating effects, not only for humanity, but also for the environment and planet Earth.

Why should our memories be considered important? This memoir deals with many issues that should be brought forth and discussed openly, not only for our sakes, the Cubans who were at the time experiencing the beginning of the Cuban Revolution, but for the world at large. The Cuban Revolution was a major socio-political and economic process that changed Cuba and has become a subject of continued study for anyone interested in geopolitics, history, humanity, the Cold War, Cuban-American affairs, and issues dealing with immigrant children.

The changes brought upon Cubans by the Cuban Revolution were extensive and radical. They affected all Cubans and involved all spheres of life, from the neighborhood to the work place, the school to the public playgrounds. It was a change through which each and every Cuban family was to find itself divided. Children and adolescents were no exception. Since very early in the revolutionary process, Cuban children began to be sent to the United States in what was later to be known as Operation Pedro Pan. Other Cuban children were to find refuge in Spain and Mexico.

In part, because Operation Pedro Pan was clandestine and the complexities of everything that has to do with the Cuban Revolution, almost half a century after the fact a number of important questions regarding this period remain unanswered. For example:

- What was the real situation in Havana that caused parents to send their children alone to the United States and Spain?
- Why was Operation Pedro Pan kept a secret from its inception?
- How successful were the Americans and the Catholic Church in keeping Operation Pedro Pan and the Unaccompanied Cuban Children Program secret?
- Since the Catholic Church played a central role in the migration and resettlement of Cuban children, what was the situation of the Catholic Church in Florida in the early 1960s?

- How was the migration of more than 14,000 Cuban children and youngsters accepted by Americans, in general?
- How well did Operation Pedro Pan and the Unaccompanied Cuban Children Program actually do in providing a safe haven for Cuban children?
- Was Operation Pedro Pan a monstrous crime?
- Are the children of Operation Pedro Pan or the Unaccompanied Cuban Children Program mostly grateful or resentful?
- Were the various institutions involved in Operation Pedro Pan— the Catholic Welfare Bureau, U.S. State Department, Central Intelligence Agency (CIA), Havana American Chamber of Commerce—and the Cuban government communicating in any way?
- Was the issue of the "*Patria Potestad*," a presumed revolutionary law through which Cuban parents were to relinquish to the Revolution their right to safeguard and guide their children, a highly influential issue in the consideration of Cuban parents' decision to let their children come alone to the U.S.?
- Was Operation Pedro Pan a humanitarian operation or a political manipulation?

At the root of all of these questions, and as a result of the social and political forces that embattled the Cuban people during the early phase of the Cuban Revolution, all Cuban families were divided. How were Cubans divided? The divisions were between revolutionaries and counter-revolutionaries; those who had fought against Fulgencio Batista and those who stood on the sidelines; those who stayed on the island of Cuba and those who departed; those who were sent to prison and those who were not; those who were practicing Roman Catholics and those who were not; those who believed in God and those who did not; those who died and those who lived. The reader should get the point. In fact, it may be reasonable to suggest that this issue may be used to test if an individual or a family was Cuban or not at this time. This may be a test of Cubanhood: to have survived, even divided, after being submitted to an overwhelmingly strong, divisive stress. Some have survived and remained united to their own family, peer group, or community while others have not. All Cubans who dare inquire about their families' fate during that period of time are bound to find division in the fabric of their families through one or another of these complex issues—ideology, politics, religion, socio-economic issues, geopolitical alliances, and divergent concepts of zealotry, oppression, free-dom, and democracy—fueled by ignorance, fanaticism, misinformation, envy, hate, fear, terror, and remembrances of earlier strife in Cuba and Spain in the 1930s.

This is not by far the first book on this general subject matter. Some authors have written their personal accounts, in which the author describes his or her feelings in connection with the day-to-day history of their lives and the process of the revolution. Professor Carlos Eire of Yale University came to the United States through Operation Pedro Pan. He has described his feelings and perceptions as a preteen boy of this time in his award-winning work *Waiting for Snow in Havana*.(1) The reader will not find in my work the raw, personal emotions that have made Eire's work a must for anyone interested in this period of time in Cuba. In *The Flight of the Mango Flowers*, the reader will find written observations, impressions, fears, and goals of multiple observers as they were recorded during those difficult days. In short, the reader will more likely be exposed through this work to a more global and balanced description of what did occur back then. This book provides the perspective of an adolescent in the context of the memories, records, and observations of the community in which he was developing.

Another personal account of a Cuban teenager has been published by José Ignacio Ramírez. I met Ignacio in February 1961 at Camp St. John near Jacksonville, Florida. He also arrived in the United States, like Erie, through Operation Pedro Pan after being cared for in several facilities in the Miami area. He was—like me—one of the first to arrive at that Camp. This summer youth camp of the Diocese of St. Augustine became a boarding facility for unaccompanied Cuban adolescents. In his published chronicle, *Defining Moments*,(2) he describes his personal experience, issues, and feelings during his departure from Cuba through Operation Pedro Pan and the Unaccompanied Cuban Children Program. An important part of his testimony deals with his impressions and feelings upon his return to Cuba in the 1990s in search of closure to some of the many questions that had been left unanswered in his life. Ignacio, in my opinion, has done a great service in showing all concerned that, despite years of misunderstandings and absence from Cuba, it is possible to rekindle friendships and accomplish peace—at least at the personal level—among Cubans who had been divided by one or more of the issues and divisional axes that shattered our realities during the Cuban Revolution.

Others have looked at the subject matter more academically—but always incorporating into their work their own personal experiences and issues—and gone into the literature of displaced children, and also the archives of the United States government, the National Archives, and the Central Intelligence Agency. It has been important to undertake such extensive work because many of the questions raised during this era and the Cuban exodus of the early 1960s are still unanswered. In order to find answers to the many questions that have arisen from this period of time, one must look wherever valid information may be found. Obviously, this approach has been fruitful, but since many of the questions still remain unanswered, the search for answers to unresolved issues must be encouraged in the future.

Most of the lingering queries cannot be answered by the memories or experiences of any one of us who lived through those times, through those changes, through the revolution, and the early years of exile more than fifty years ago. The answers must be sought in official documentation on both sides of the Florida Straits, both sides of the Atlantic Ocean and in the centers of power that were in place at this period of time. In the latter regard, the work that has, in my opinion, excelled in terms of investigation and documentation is that of Professor María de los Angeles Torres of the University of Illinois at Chicago, *The Lost Apple*.(3) Her work should not be confused with an American-made film of the same title, in which the reception of young children is described in the early 1960s from the perspective of those housed in one of the reception centers in Florida City, the social workers, priests, and nuns working there, and obviously the American authorities.(4) The entire film is not very long and can be viewed on YouTube. I strongly recommend it to those readers who have not seen it, because it will make them familiar with some of the vocabulary of Operation Pedro Pan.

Other authors who have focused on the general issues of the Cuban children's exodus have also provided invaluable statistics, demographics, and surveys, without which any student of these matters would be shortchanged. The works of María Cristina García in *Havana USA*(5) and Professor Felix Masud-Piloto of Florida State University and presently of DePaul University in his *From Welcome Exiles to Illegal Immigrants*(6) have disclosed important historical and sociological data on this subject. Finally, one of the most useful resources on this subject is *Operación Pedro Pan*(7) by Yvonne M. Conde. Before leaving the matter of important resources, I should mention that most of the literature available on Operation Pedro Pan has been published in English. The work of Yvonne M. Conde is an exception, for it has been appropriately published in both English and Spanish.(8)

At least one book on Operation Pedro Pan has been published in Cuba. The title of it is almost identical to the work of Yvonne M. Conde, but the contents are not. The work published in Cuba, authored by Ramon Torreira Crespo and José Buajasán Marrawi, is entitled *Operación Pedro Pan: Un Caso de Guerra Psicológica Contra Cuba*.(9) It purports to be an indispensable book and it begins with a couple of quotes from the New Testament. Unfortunately, the book is replete with fabrications and misrepresentation of the facts. I found the work unsuitable for shedding light on this period of Cuban history and assisting researchers and readers in achieving an understanding of this complex era. If anything, the work of Torreira Crespo and Buajasán Marrawi will remain as an example of the fanatical and fossilized arguments with which the revolutionary authorities explained the destruction of Cuban families. Furthermore, the Cuban version of *Operación Pedro Pan* is, in my opinion, not useful with regard to the understanding and reconciliation of Cubans. Eventually, the divisions that have emerged and continue to emerge in all Cuban families as a result of the Cuban Revolution must come to an understanding and acceptance if the Cuban nation is to go on living.

These are by far not the only works on this subject matter. There are other books, films, a few graduate dissertations, and other sources that have been consulted and used in the writing of this work and will be referenced herein. Despite the fact that multiple publications have already been provided for the public to get an idea of what actually occurred during this era, there are still many issues and questions that remain unexplored or unsatisfactorily answered. Therefore, there is a need to expand our collective experience, shed light where no one has provided an insight before, and enrich the literature covering this important epoch.

This book begins with a summary of key events in the history of Cuba in the first half of the twentieth century because I feel that the reader should appreciate that period of time before entering into the substance of the collective memoir that follows. I feel that this will be most useful in order to appreciate the background of the testimonies and opinions expressed beginning in September 1960, when I was in the fourth year of the Cuban *bachillerato*, a secondary education course of study leading to a university career. The course of events will take the reader to what was happening in both Havana and Miami during that fall semester and into the Christmas holidays.

In January 1961, I departed from Havana and from that time onward, I share with the reader some of the letters or segments thereof that I received during 1961 and 1962. I kept all letters and have read them more than once in order to place myself at that particular point in time. The process has not been easy, and many times I have had to stop working on account of the fact that I felt as if I were reliving those times.

I kept the letters because I knew that I was going through a very important period of time in my life. I did not know back then that I would ever be writing this memoir at this time. However, I kept the letters rolled up and bound by rubber bands. I felt, unconsciously perhaps, back then in 1961 that I was going to read them again. The letters have accompanied me through my migrations in the United States from Florida to Vermont; from Vermont to New Jersey; New Jersey to South Florida; Florida to Ohio; Ohio to Central Florida; Central Florida to Miami; Miami to Fort Lauderdale; Fort Lauderdale to Coral Gables; Coral Gables to Tallahassee; Tallahassee to Atlanta, Georgia, and finally from the latter to Miami and then through at least six residential changes in the Miami area. It is a miracle that the letters have survived and remain intact and readable.

Actually, it was not until May 1980 that I decided to go back to the letters and review them carefully. By that time, I had been trained to be an American physician and the thought came to me while doing volunteer work at the Immigration and Naturalization Service Station set up at Tamiami Park and Opa-Locka in May 1980. I was examining Cuban immigrants who had arrived in the United States through the famous Mariel Boatlift. At that time, more than 125,000 Cubans arrived through the *Puente Marítimo Del Mariel*. I identified with the families of newly-arrived Cuban refugees going through my examining booth and that caused me to go back to the letters.

The public opinion in the Cuban community in South Florida was not the most favorable one with regard to these new refugees. Soon after they arrived here, there were racial riots in Northwest Miami on account of African-American community issues not directly related to the Mariel Boatlift. There was also, soon after the arrival of the *Marielitos*, an increase in violence in Dade County.(10) *Marielitos* were often blamed for those negative statistics. Soon thereafter, the major cinematic production of *Scarface* was released and became popular. Through this film, public opinion was validated and confirmed in its previous impression regarding the "negative nature of Cuban refugees."

The *Marielitos* were thought to be the products of the recently approved trips to the island under the administration of U.S. President Jimmy Carter. Some would like to belittle the efforts of President Carter as something negative, since he was thought to be unjustifiably soft on the Cuban regime. I write unjustifiably because there have been a grand total of eleven American presidents dealing with the Cuban issue since 1959, and none has accomplished anything final, despite a number of implicit and explicit promises. The Cuban issue may be front page news again, but it is still as unsatisfactorily unresolved as it ever was.

But going back to the arriving *Marielitos*, I volunteered to perform immigration physicals at the Opa-Locka Blimp Hangar, where an Immigration and Naturalization Service Station had been organized and refugees were being processed.

It was there that I saw in their faces, their histories, and their ambitions, the reflection of my own situation in 1961, my own uncertainty, my own aspirations of the Pedro Pan years and early exile. I decided then that I had to share the story that I had kept in my stowed-away letters because that story would reveal that the migration through which I came to the United States was not that much different from that one of the *Marielitos* I examined. I felt at one with them and that was useful to my own psyche. I trust that this work is useful to our collective psyche in and outside of Cuba.

On a larger scale, I feel that this work will add understanding of what we experienced and readers in general and Cubans in particular will be able to look at these events from a wider perspective than they had been privileged to share in the past. May the reader find in this work useful information, analysis, and stories with which to go on inquiring about our common history, our Cuban roots, and our destiny on planet Earth. And, may these memories help those in public office and social welfare agencies to deal with migrations of children and youngsters more transparently, humanely, and more effectively. Before turning our attention to the actual "flight" of all of us who left Cuba at the spring of our lives, it is necessary to review our roots so that we can appreciate better these dilemmas.

In the spring, mango trees are gorgeous
And full of flowers in their branches.
Depending on the environment,
Whatever winds are prevailing.
Some flowers are blown off trees.
Some land by the mother tree,
While others land far, far away.
Some, are never seen again, lost forever.

CHAPTER 1

BACKGROUND: ON CUBA, THE UNITED STATES, AND THE CUBAN REVOLUTION

"In order to know a country,
One must study all its aspects,
Expressions, its elements,
Its apostles, its poets,
And its bandits."
-Jose Martí

Although the island of Cuba was originally discovered by Christopher Columbus on his first voyage in 1492, contemporary Cuba has become known during the past half century by the entire planet because of the migration of its people and the role Cuba has played in world politics and intrigue.

From the outset, this is obviously a complex subject. Consider, for example, the views of anything dealing with Cuba from the perspective of any two different observers. The views are bound to be rather different if one observer has learned about Cuba in Miami and the other one in Luanda. And, to complicate matters worse, suppose both observers learned about Cuba in Miami, but one made his observations in May 1961—just after the fiasco of the Bay of Pigs Invasion—and the other one in May 1980—as the *Mariel* exodus was arriving en masse in South Florida. Their impressions are bound to be rather different as a function of the popular sentiment in the various communities that make up the mosaic that is Miami-Dade County, and the changing sociopolitical environment.

In fact, the global awareness about Cuba and anything that is said to be Cuban has obviously been due to multiple factors. At the center of all of them, on the one hand, is the massive emigration of Cuba's population through involuntary and voluntary migrations. On the other hand, there are the engagements abroad of those who, while working with and for the Cuban government, have provided on multiple continents everything from military support to political influence, sports to artistic performances, and health services to education. In short, in one way or the other, Cubans have become integrated into the fabric of most regions and countries of the world.

No one would argue that some of the global exposure to Cubans has occurred through the anti-Castro activities of Cubans escaping from the island and its totalitarian, communist regime. But there are also tourists who have actually visited Cuba in the last fifty-five years.(1) Most of them should have realized that they were visiting a highly-controlled society under a totalitarian regime of government. For most of those who have actually met Cubans in Cuba, not in Hialeah[1] or in Angola, Cuba appeared to be a theme park where a commendable production and performance led most tourists to arrive at the predictable conclusion: Cuban communism and the achievements of the Cuban revolution have been for the betterment of all the people, especially the most humble. That is, provided that the visiting observer did not ask "too many" questions or did not set his eyes beyond the invisible fences "protecting" Cubans. If the tourists go beyond the theme park atmosphere of Old Havana, they will discover the miserable conditions under which most Cubans on the island subsist on less than $8 a month.

Many others have made acquaintance with Cubans because they encountered Cubans working and serving the Castro regime outside of Cuba in one capacity or another, from health services to education to the worlds of sports and entertainment in various countries I have met patients that have been extremely grateful for the health services provided to their children in Guyana by Cuban physicians and healthcare workers sent there through Cuba's MINSAP (Ministry of Public Health). Although the health personnel and physicians involved in these international missions do impart humanitarian and professional medical services, the Cuban regime has been said to garnish up to $2 billion per year from these activities. It should also be mentioned in this context that many Cubans engaged in service and work outside of Cuba on contracts negotiated through the Cuban communist government have not always been true to the Cuban Revolution. In fact, an appreciable number of them have taken those opportunities to work outside Cuba to seek political asylum in places as different as Zimbabwe and France.

Essentially, while during the first half of the twentieth century it may have been

---

[1] Hialeah has the highest percentage of Cuban and Cuban American residents of any city in the United States, at 74% of the population, making the island's immigrants and exiles a distinctive and prominent feature of the city's culture.

easy to find someone in the world who did not know any Cubans or even know where Cuba was exactly geographically located(2), as a consequence of the Cuban Revolution, by the end of the twentieth century, Cuba had become—for better or for worse—known to most people in the world. The historical process commonly referred to as the Cuban Revolution needs to be given credit for making Cuba known throughout the planet. Most experts place the beginning of the Cuban Revolution in the aftermath of the coup d'état carried out by Fulgencio Batista on March 10, 1952 in Havana. While some writers and students of Cuba have claimed that Cuba has always been in a revolution(3), the reality of our short history provides evidence to the contrary.(4)

The influence of the United States, hereafter simply mentioned as American influence, has permeated Cuban history since long before the Cuban Revolution.(5) In fact, most experts agree that American influence has been evident in Cuba since the middle of the nineteenth century. The great fear of Jose Martí and most Cuban thinkers of the nineteenth century dealt with the fact that Cuba was at risk of becoming American, literally being swallowed up by the United States due to its proximity and its growing economic ties with the giant to the north. Just consider this fact: Spanish colonial currency used on the island of Cuba in the 1890s was printed in New York, not in Madrid. Who could deny that Cuba's economy was highly influenced by the United States?

Spanish colonial currency circulating in the Island of Cuba in the 1890s was printed in the United Stated of America.

Cuban nationality was forged during the nineteenth century. The idea of Cuban independence grew through those 100 years. On my father's side of the family, my great-great-grandfather arrived in Havana in the first half of the nineteenth century, set up himself as a businessman, and married a Cuban girl from one of the original families who had settled Havana in the 1500s. The couple of Antonio Gordon and María del Carmen Acosta had two children, a boy and a girl. The boy was my great-grandfather, also named Antonio Gordon.(6) My great-great-grandfather died in Havana of tuberculosis and in his last will and testament, ordered that his children be educated in Spain. His young widow took the children to Cadiz, where she enrolled them in school. Unfortunately, María del Carmen was also struck by tuberculosis and died in Spain. The two orphans were then sent back to Havana. The children must have found the returning transatlantic voyage to Cuba long and definitely uncertain. When they arrived in Havana, they were cared for by the family of Gonzalo Alonso Soler and Merced Poey Aloy, who had been friends of the Gordons. Gonzalo took care of the Gordon children as if they were his own. His wife was the sister of Felipe Poey, Cuba's pioneer in natural sciences.

A few years later, my great-grandfather's sister also died of tuberculosis. By that time, my namesake had already decided to study medicine. He was placed in the Colegio El Salvador, a famous school in Havana founded by Don José de la Luz y Caballero, one of the pioneers of Cuban education and pedagogy. My great-grandfather was completing his secondary education when Cuba's longest war for independence broke out. He was then sent to Cartagena de Indias in Colombia, where he had relatives on his father's side. He went on studying there.

Although there had been rebellions in Cuba since the 1820s, it was not until October 10, 1868 that the Guerra de los Diez Años (Ten Years' War) began after the Cuban Declaration of Independence was proclaimed in La Demajagua in eastern Cuba.(7) The Ten Years' War began at a time when there was a governing *junta* in Madrid and it was not immediately obvious to the American press—attentive apparently solely to the situation in Spain—what exactly was going on in Eastern Cuba where Carlos Manuel de Céspedes declared Cuban independence and freed his slaves. Soon thereafter, the war began and the sugar mill La Demajagua where the rebellion erupted was demolished. By January 1869, the entire city of Bayamo was burned by its Cuban inhabitants before they would surrender it to the Spanish troops.

My mother's side of my family had settled a few kilometers from La Demajagua decades before the war. When the Ten Years' War broke out, their property was confiscated and they sought refuge in Jamaica, where they arrived by boat. My grandfather, Gabino Palomino, was born there while his family was in exile. It was not until the late 1870s that my mother's side of the family returned to their farm in Calicito, near La Demajagua.

Neither the Cuban Declaration of Independence, nor the burning of Bayamo were deemed worthy to appear in the American media. The *New York Times* did not report either of these events. Its coverage of those years of Cuba centered on maintaining in good terms the relationship of the United States with Spain. However, the *New York Times* did report and denounce the killing by firing squad of eight medical students by the Spanish volunteers in Havana on November 27, 1871.(8) It should be mentioned that the latter was one of the main events that served to define the Cuban nationality. Up to that time, Spanish propaganda had claimed that the Cuban insurgents were all Afro-Cubans. However, all eight medical students who were shot by that firing squad, *paredón*, were white Cubans. They were executed after a biased military court found all of them guilty of defacing the tomb of a Spanish journalist and activist.(9) The military court was fearful of finding the medical students innocent. A crowd of Spanish volunteers outside the courtroom shouted, "Death to the traitors." At one point in time during the proceedings, the court found three students guilty and the Spanish volunteers shouted, again, "Death to the traitors." Then the court, having no legal grounds or evidence to go on with the trial, began to select students from a lottery until there were eight who were to be shot at the *paredón*. That is how many lives it took to appease the Spanish volunteers, eight Cuban lives.

The presence of this event in the American press at the time may be related to the brutality of the entire process, in which innocent youngsters were killed to satisfy the anger of the Spanish populace in Havana against the growing feeling of nationhood felt by Cubans. However, this atrocity was of American interest for two reasons. First, there were a couple of American citizens who were studying medicine and were in that particular first-year class in Havana at the time. The American consul in Havana intervened on their behalf and they were not tried, their names were not included in the lottery to select who was going to be sent to the firing squad, and, therefore, the Americans were not condemned to prison terms of four to six years forced labor, as all the remaining thirty-five Cuban students were. It should be mentioned here that when the eight Cuban medical students were killed in Havana, the United States dispatched three warships to Havana in order to protect American interests on the island.(9) The second reason had to do with growing American business ties with the Spanish on the island of Cuba. American press at the time reported on anything that had to do with the stability of those regions where Americans had a presence and investments. At the time, the relationship between Spain and the United States was very favorable.

The Cuban Gordons were directly affected by the medical students' demise. My great-grandfather had come back to Havana from Cartagena de Indias, where he had obtained a medical degree. My great-grandmother, María del Carmen Bermúdez, was the sister of Anacleto and Esteban Bermúdez. Both brothers had entered the University of Havana School of Medicine in the fall of 1871. Anacleto was one of the eight students shot in the *paredón* and Esteban was sentenced to six years of forced labor.

Meanwhile, the official policy of the United States at the time of the Ten Years' War was on the side of Spain. This is understandable, since the United States was recovering from the American Civil War (1861-1865). The situation proved quite different during the second major war of independence in Cuba, at the end of the nineteenth century. The United States intervened in the last Cuban War of Independence (1895-1898) after the cruiser the *USS Maine* exploded and sank in Havana harbor on February 15, 1895.(10) The war ship had been sent to Havana to protect the interests of the American community in the city as the Cuban War of independence was coming to its final phase under the draconian measures imposed by the last Spanish governor of the island, Valeriano Weyler.(11) The forces responsible for the explosion of the *USS Maine* have never been fully determined to the satisfaction of all parties. An American commission found that the explosion had occurred from the outside of the vessel. A Spanish commission concluded that the explosion had occurred from inside the ship. The fact is that the ship exploded, the explosion led to its sinking, and the sinking served as the catalyst that brought the United States into war with Spain. The remains of the *USS Maine* are presently at Arlington National Cemetery near Washington, DC, and at the United States Naval Academy in Annapolis, Maryland.

In the archives of American military history, the war with Spain brought about on account of Cuba, was the most noble one ever fought by this country. An American military physician wrote in 1898:

"For a fifth time our nation is face to face with a war, the gravity of which it is impossible to estimate at the present time. The first brought us our liberty and independence; the second established our reputation on the sea; the third taught our Mexican neighbor respect for our country; the fourth saved the Union; and the fifth, which is now being waged, was provoked in the cause of humanity."(12)

Humanity, we should add, in the form of Cuban misery and blood. The United States declared war on Spain in June 1898. The war known in the United States as the Spanish-American War is known to Cubans as *Guerra Hispano-Cubano-Americana* (the Hispanic-Cuban-American War). It was a short war lasting less than 3 months in which the American forces prevailed since they had the sea power and the Cuban *mambises* or insurgents were initially their boots on the ground. It ended with the Treaty of Paris, in which Spain and the United States were the only signatories, whereby Cuba, the Philippines, and Puerto Rico became American territories.

The first American intervention followed the peace treaty governing Cuba from 1898 until 1902. The new Cuban Republic was inaugurated on May 20, 1902 and only accepted into the community of nations under the supervision of the United States as clearly documented in the Cuban Constitution of 1901 by the Platt Amendment with its territorial, political, military, economic, and health statues and provisions.(13) Consequently, it is not surprising that most of the world understood Cuba to be a kind of American protectorate in the beginning of the twentieth century. One important positive aspect of the first American intervention was that it successfully fought corruption in public administration.(13) Corruption was, until then, part and parcel of the Spanish colonial regime in Cuba.

The first Cuban administration of Tomas de Estrada Palma governed following pretty much the patterns established by the first American intervention. At the conclusion of Estrada Palma's term, the Cuban government had a surplus of $24 million.(14) At the time when general elections were about to take place, revolts erupted in various places on the island and the first Cuban president requested, utilizing the Platt Amendment clauses, a second American intervention. The second American intervention under Charles Magoon was not as transparent and clean as the first intervention in terms of cleaning up corruption.(14) Magoon governed Cuba from 1906 until 1909, at which time President Miguel Mariano Gómez was elected. By then, however, corruption again plagued Cuban public administration.

The Cuban political process went on through various presidents and administrations during which there were minor incursions into Cuban territory by the U.S. armed forces to quell disputes or revolts, usually in the context of some sugar mill or American enterprise.(15) Then, during the first presidency of Gerardo Machado (1925-1928), a special legislation was proposed *a sota voce* initially and then openly, the so called *Prorroga de Poderes*, through which an exception would be made to the Cuban Constitution of 1901 and President Machado would be able to be re-elected for a second term in office.(16) The *Prorroga de Poderes* took place, despite appreciable opposition from various political and civic groups. The second term of Machado's presidency soon became a reality and it coincided with the Great Depression that affected the entire world.(17)

To the ongoing political unrest on the island resulting from the re-election of Machado, economic and social unrest followed. The political irregularities inherent in Machado's second term in office led to a national situation, in which Machado did not complete his second term in office. By 1932, a revolution against Machado was already feared, not only in Cuba, but also in Washington.(18) Details of that process can be reviewed in the works of Phillips(19) and Carrillo.(20) Suffice it to mention, there were street demonstrations by the students of the University of Havana—violence, torture, imprisonments, and innumerable deaths. The memories of what later was called the 1930s Cuban Revolution were still vivid thirty years later in 1960 in the minds of many Cubans who had lived through them or heard of them firsthand.

In view of the deteriorating situation in Cuba, while the Platt Amendment was still on the books, the United States appointed as Special Ambassador (*Embajador Plenipotenciario*) Mr. Benjamin Sumner Wells to serve as mediator between all Cuban factions and to prevent another American intervention during the crisis.(21) Sumner Wells was a Harvard graduate who had served in the Foreign Service of the United States in Argentina in the 1920s. He was also well connected with the popular American President Franklin Delano Roosevelt and his wife Eleanor.

In 1933, although there was no open American intervention, American interests were well represented in the person of Wells. The latter was known to have a great influence on the outcome of the 1930's Cuban Revolution, including the exit of Machado by plane to Miami and its aftermath.(22) While the student movement got their former professor Ramon Grau San Martín to be the provisional president after Machado's departure, lack of diplomatic recognition from Washington dictated that someone else be installed in Havana. It was then that Fulgencio Batista, a Cuban Army sergeant, led the soldiers and non-commissioned officers in a revolt against the officers of the Cuban Army.(23) The officers lost the battle after they had garrisoned at the Hotel Nacional de Cuba on the *Malecón* sea side drive and 23rd Street in the *Vedado* section of Havana. Batista suggested another provisional president and he became the de facto strong man of Cuba from then until 1940. In the process, Batista rose from a sergeant to colonel. He became an American darling.

The thirties were a particularly hard time for my family. My great-grandfather died in 1917 from a massive heart attack and his wealth was divided between his two children and his second wife María Josefa Huguet. My grandfather, Ramón, worked for the Cuban Ministry of Health. During the depression, he was not able to collect the rent from the properties he inherited from my great-grandfather. My grandmother Amparo turned her hobby of sewing into a business to balance the family budget. Ramón and Amparo had four children, Antonio—my dad—Ramón, Carmen, and Ofelia. My father was already in the second year of medical school at the University of Havana in 1930. My uncle Ramón had finished his secondary education and was also expected to enter the university. There was talk in the family of sending them both to study abroad to New Orleans or perhaps to Paris. In fact, many well-to-do Cuban families opted at that time of unrest at the University of Havana in favor of sending their children to school abroad. The Gordons were not able to, however. Their economic situation could have allowed them to send one of the two brothers to a foreign university, but not both. Therefore, according to my grandmother Amparo's story, neither of them went. Antonio, my dad, entered the Cuban military as a medical student and my uncle Ramón organized a neighborhood school in one of the properties the family owned where there were rooms vacant.

By 1936 a notable jurist who was a veteran of the Cuban War of Independence, Federico Laredo Bru, organized the constitutional assembly which led to the writing of a new constitution ratified in 1940. That year, Cuba had a fair and transparent election under a more progressive constitution, the Constitution of 1940, which embodied Cuba's time-honored political and social philosophy. The new Cuban Magna Carta reflected a strong desire to promote national autonomy and social commitment unlike the Cuban constitution prepared after the *Guerra Hispano Cubano Americana* under American guidance. The Cuban Magna Carta of 1940 explicitly guaranteed rights to employment, minimum acceptable standards for working conditions, property ownership, education, and social security. Although most democratic Cubans claim that the Constitution of 1940 was so ahead of its time that it may even serve Cuba in the twenty-first century and beyond, it should be noted that some experts who have studied it point out that some of the provisions in it are either unreasonable or impractical requiring a review and update.(24) Essentially, they point out that the Constitution of 1940 was the product of a compromise between political factions from the left and right. Under this new constitution, the republic had three consecutive elected presidents. Free elections were carried out in 1940, 1944, and 1948. In 1944, Fulgencio Batista, who had been democratically elected in 1940, relinquished power to Ramon Grau San Martín. The latter relinquished power to Carlos Prío Socarrás in 1948.

The third constitutional president of this period did not relinquish power after the democratic elections, which were to take place on June 1, 1952. Carlos Prío Socarrás was ousted in a coup d'état by Fulgencio Batista, who was a candidate for president along with at least two other contenders, Roberto Agramonte and Carlos Hevia.(25) The Platt Amendment had already been negotiated out of existence in

1934, derogated. Batista's second coup d'état broke the constitutional order and government precisely eighty-three days before the presidential election was to occur, on Sunday, June 1, 1952. In fact, the Batista coup d'état occurred on the day when the deadline to close the presidential nominations was to occur. It turned out that it was the deadline when the constitutional order expired.

However, aside from greed, perhaps, American undercover activities, underworld, and mafia suggestions that could not be refused by Batista or other issues may have been behind Batista's coup. Some historians have advanced purported reasons for Batista's coup d'état. These are the main publically recognized reasons:(25)

- Debugging the politics and public administration of Cuba.
- Elimination of administrative and political corruption.
- Effectively fighting gangsters.
- Declaring illegal the communist party.
- Re-establishment of close diplomatic ties with Franco's Spain.
- Breaking of diplomatic relations with the USSR.

The United States government pretty much certified that there was "no outside country behind the Batista coup."(26) At the time there was a great campaign going on to detect, capture, and imprison communists or those thought-to-be communists in government and society in the United States.(27) The zeal of U.S. Senator Joseph McCarthy and his Committee on Anti-American Activities is well known. Although Carlos Prío Socarrás was not a communist, it has been suggested by some that the Batista coup d'état may have been—at least in part—inspired by the ferocious anti-communism of the McCarthy era in the United States. Declassified records from the American Embassy in Havana do not support such a hypothesis.(28) However, it is known that not all State Department records dealing with Cuba from that era have been declassified.(29)

Early in the morning on March 10, 1952, when informed about the coup d'état, Carlos Prío Socarrás also received a call from the military chief of the garrison at Matanzas, sixty miles east of Havana. Colonel Eduardo Martín Elena had learned about the coup d'état in the early morning hours of the same day. He gathered all the Matanzas Cuban Army regiment and spoke to the troops and officers to let them know that there had been a coup in Columbia, the central Cuban Army installation in Havana, and that he had been wired to support it, but that he opposed the coup. It can be assumed that other provincial regimental commanders were notified in a similar manner. The conspirators did not seem to have men on the ground in the provinces. Martín Elena called on the officers and soldiers under his command to fight the Batista forces with him and to preserve the constitutional order.(30)

Prío Socarrás is said to have gotten into his car and asked to be driven to Matanzas. In the meantime, the military commander of the Oriente garrison, Colonel Manuel Alvarez Margolles, also pledged to fight to uphold the Constitution of 1940. The Batista forces, upon entering Columbia, had launched several military planes to fly over the provincial capitals and signal the coup for the urban population and the major army garrisons. Despite the fact that the conspirators had occupied and taken control of all radio and news outlets in Havana, there were student and popular demonstrations against the coup in Havana, Matanzas, and Santa Clara. The University of Havana students came out in support of defending the Constitution. Some historians point out that the *Directorio Revolucionario Estudiantil* was immediately regrouped and had the entire support from the students of the *Federación Estudiantil Universitaria* (FEU), the politically active student body organization at the University of Havana.(31)

For reasons that no one has explained satisfactorily, Carlos Prío Socarrás did not reach Matanzas from where he was to lead the resistance against Batista, the coup d'état, and the gross infringement of the constitutional order. Instead, he changed course, returned to Havana and went into the embassy of Mexico in the Cuban capital where he sought and received political asylum.

It is true that for most Cubans, the change in government in March 1952 went through almost unnoticed. But months later, the forces that opposed Batista's coup d'état gathered in Montreal, Canada on June 1, the day the elections of 1952 would have taken place in Cuba had it not been for the coup.(32) The meeting was going to be held in New York City, but some of the Batista opposition members could not get an American visa, presumably on account of the anti-communist sentiment in the United States at the time. Therefore, the politicians gathered in Montreal, Canada. The representatives of the various political parties of that era agreed to work together, organize all opposing forces and prepare an invasion of the island to restore the constitutional order.

The invasion proposed by the Montreal attendees did not occur. In the meantime, independently, the figure of Fidel Castro appeared in Cuban history. Fidel had been born out of wedlock in Oriente province, schooled in Catholic boarding schools in Santiago de Cuba and Havana, and become active in national politics while attending the University of Havana School of Law. I have known two individuals who were in Fidel's class at the University of Havana. Both of them remember vividly how he was always accompanied by a group of gangster-looking guys. Fidel entered each classroom with a 45-caliber gun and placed it on his desk to remind everyone, including the professor, that he was determined to do what he pleased.

A few years after graduating from the university with a law degree, Fidel organized an attack on the Oriente provincial Cuban Army's regiment, the Cuartel Moncada on July 26, 1953.(33) The attack was a military failure but Castro, in due time, turned it into a political victory. Castro himself was sentenced to six years in prison. By 1955, he and all other imprisoned members of the 26th of July Movement were pardoned by Batista, who had conducted rigged elections in 1954. They were released from the Presidio Modelo on the Isle of Pines(34) and arrived at Batabanó by boat, and then into Havana by train. Castro was already known by many political activists and he was received as a hero at the Havana train station. They all pledged to continue the fight against Batista.

In a matter of months, Fidel Castro himself was in New York City. There was talk of his taking up law at Columbia University. Instead, he gathered financial support—at least some of it from Carlos Prío Socarrás—and traveled to Mexico, where he organized and trained the fighters for the Granma yacht expedition that took him to Cuba's southeast at Playa de las Coloradas on December 2, 1956. Most of the eighty-two invaders who reached Cuba's coast on the Granma were killed or captured. Fidel Castro and a dozen others survived and took refuge in the Sierra Maestra Mountain Range in southeastern Cuba.

Castro's forces and their views on the struggle against Batista became worldwide news when the *New York Times* published four articles by Herbert Matthews in February 1957.(35) While the Batista regime had claimed that Castro's forces were disbanded after reaching Cuban soil and Castro himself had been killed, the leader of America's newspapers showed the world otherwise. In Matthews' articles, Castro was photographed alive and his proposed program of government was presented as entirely democratic and fair. After that, the popularity of Castro in and outside of Cuba surged. Supplies and war materials began to flow into the Sierra Maestra Mountains. Pedro Díaz Lanz, who later on would be Castro's personal pilot, flew missions from Central America and Florida with supplies, ammunition, and weapons to Castro's forces.

Other anti-Batista forces began to take aim at his dictatorial regime. On March 13, 1957, the *Directorio Revolucionario Estudiantil* organized an attack on the presidential palace in Havana to kill Batista in his own office.(36) The attack failed because Batista was not where he was expected to be at the time. Many students were killed in this attempt to oust Batista, including the leader of the *Directorio* and the FEU, José Antonio Echevarría.

Opposition against Batista grew. In April 1957, an Army rebellion was thwarted.(37) The leader had been Colonel Ramón Barquín. He was a respected, career military officer who had trained both in Cuba and in the United States. At the time of his attempt to oust Batista, he was the Cuban military attaché in Washington. The revolt never got started. It was picked up by the *Servicio de Inteligencia Militar* (SIM), Batista's security apparatus. All of the conspirators and the other officers involved in the movement were court martialed and sentenced to jail terms at the Isle of Pines.

In September, 1957 another attempt to oust Batista was organized by the civilian opposition and the military.(37) The revolt failed, despite the fact that a battle was fought in the city of Cienfuegos. My father was part of this conspiracy as one of the operatives who passed information from military commanders to the political wing of the revolt. He was court martialed in October 1957 and sentenced to one year of prison.

After these two military and civic attempts to bring down the Batista regime, a very serious attempt was made by Cosme de la Torriente and other civil society leaders to bring all opposing parties and hostilities to a peaceful transition to democratic rule. Despite all efforts, no agreement was reached.

In the fall of 1958, most organizations involved in the fight against the Batista dictatorship met in Caracas, Venezuela.(38) An agreement was reached by the representatives gathered there. The following table lists the organizations from a wide spectrum of political thought which arrived at an agreement in Venezuela:

Table I - The Pact of Caracas by Anti-Batista Organizations. (39)
Amplio Frente Cívico Revolucionario
Movimiento 26 de Julio
Directorio Revolucionario Estudiantil
Partido de la Revolución Cubana (PRC)
Partido del Pueblo Libre
Partido Ortodoxo
Organización de los Auténticos
Demócratas-Abstencionistas
Grupo de los Antiguos Militares
Grupo de Montecristi
Federación Estudiantil Universitaria
Movimiento de Resistencia Cívica.

The anti-Batista forces agreed to:

- First, continue the common strategy of armed insurrection in the struggle to overthrow the Batista tyranny.
- Second, form in our country, after the fall of the tyranny, a provisional government with members from all opposition fronts, so that the constitutional order would be reestablished as soon as possible.
- Third, propose that such brief government would have a minimum program of government support for these points:

  -To ensure punishment of the guilty,
  -Secure order in society,
  -Preserve the peace,
  -Guarantee freedom, and
  -Encourage the economic, social, and institutional progress of the Cuban people during the transition to constitutional government.

Batista had already exhausted all civilian and political attempts to reform his regime by 1958. His last attempt had been to organize a general election, in which most of the opposition did not take part because of the likelihood of fraud. What remained of the Cuban Constitutional Army was not willing to fight for the dictatorship. It was demoralized by corruption in the higher ranks and the fact that many of their officers had been jailed for conspiring to bring back the Constitution of 1940.

By September 1958, the United States removed Batista publicly from its list of favorites. An arms and ammunition embargo was declared by Washington against the Batista regime.(39) From then onward, the Batista regime would not be able to buy weapons or ammunition in the United States. The final stand of what became known as "Batista's Army" occurred in Santa Clara in central Cuba where Camilo Cienfuegos and Ernesto "Che" Guevara took command of that provincial capital.(40)

By then, it was no secret that Batista and his regime were in trouble. The *New York Times* published a signed dispatch from December 31, 1958, in which the American Assistant Secretary for Inter-American Affairs, Roy R. Rubottom Jr., reported to a Senate Foreign Relations sub-committee behind closed doors on the grave situation of General Batista in Havana.(41) Rubottom explained, according to the *New York Times*, that if Santa Clara fell, Batista's government would collapse. A few hours later, it was American Ambassador to Cuba, Earl T. Smith, who delivered the final "order" to Batista on December 31, 1958: "My president asks that you leave the island" were the words voiced by Ambassador Smith to Batista who took him literally and convened his close associates from his regime to inform them of his plans to abandon Cuba. Anyone escaping with the dictator could bring their immediate family and limited luggage. They were on the run. Batista, like Machado before him in the 1930s, left power on the strong suggestion and advice of someone representing the United States government. The exit of Batista occurred in the early hours of January 1, 1959. Several airplanes were noted leaving the airfield at the Columbia Military Base from 1 to 2 A.M.(42)

Various observers have reported to me that Batista left shortly after midnight or, perhaps, a little later. His departure appeared to be more unexpected than the departure from Cuba of most children of Operation Pedro Pan.(43) Several planes departed, but not all of them were flying to the same destination. Some of Batista's relatives landed in Jacksonville, Florida while others landed in New Orleans, Louisiana.(44) It has been claimed by a source that was, at the time, married to one of Batista's relatives, that in the escape Batista's plane flew first to Tampa, Florida where he was denied permission to disembark by the American authorities. He then flew to New Orleans where, again, he was denied permission to disembark. It was only then that he flew to the Dominican Republic, where Dominican Dictator Rafael Leonidas Trujillo allowed him to disembark, after paying a substantial amount of money and under the proviso that he would not stay in the Dominican Republic for long. The source, who claims to have known these unpublished details of Batista's exit, knew these facts from direct sources. He defends his points, arguing the fact that considering the time of departure of the several airplanes from Havana, Batista could not have arrived in Santo Domingo after dawn, as widely reported by the press, if he had flown directly from Havana to Santo Domingo.

The two individuals left in place by Batista did not last in power but a day or less. They were General Eulogio Cantillo, who had been negotiating terms of surrender with Castro in the latter weeks of 1958 and Carlos M. Piedra, the head of the Cuban Supreme Court.(45) The latter, by the Constitution of 1940, should have been acting president in the absence of the president and the vice president.

The revolutionary forces ordered a general strike until the new provisional government was in place and recognized. The agreed upon and signed Pact of Caracas was apparently a factor in the diversity of political and ideological aspects of the first revolutionary cabinet.

On January 3, 1959, Manuel Urrutia Lleó was sworn in as provisional president. Urrutia had been the dissenting voice and vote in the tribunal where Fidel Castro was tried after the attack on the Moncada Army Barracks in 1953. By January 5, the council of ministers, the cabinet, was announced and the ministers sworn in by Urrutia. Out of thirteen ministers, there were three known communists. In the next few years, however, none of the original ministers were in the office they occupied in January 1959.(46) Six ministers became counter-revolutionaries. Of these, five went into exile and one was tried in a mock trial and then killed by a firing squad, *paredón*. He was Humberto Sorí Marín, a young lawyer who was said to have been the "legal brains of the rebel army" and had served in that first cabinet as minister of agriculture. Of the remaining ministers who were not known publicly to be counter-revolutionaries, two died in accidents and one committed suicide.

The nature of the contest, in which Cubans were to go on taking sides, was beginning to be defined soon after the very beginning of 1959. The latter date has been taken as the "triumph of the revolution" but, in fact, it was the triumph of Fidel Castro. For the Cuban people—although we did not know it then—it was just a necessary change in tactics and strategy: The Cuban strife was to go on and become entangled in the Cold War. It was a contest between communism and democracy. As opposition to the communists began to emerge, it was noted in retrospect, that American CIA agents were on site in Cuba to offer their assistance to the Cuban anti-communist movements and forces. It was only logical to incorporate the assistance of the Americans, since at the time it was a world of two poles—the American and the Soviet Union—democracy and respect for human rights versus communism and serfdom.

The fate of a dear friend of mine will serve to illustrate for the reader the degree of infiltration that existed in the anti-communist forces of the Underground. My friend, María E., was a young woman who was working against the communists through a workers' movement with her young husband. They had been newlywed months before they got fully into the anti-Castro movement. Their group had been organizing an assassination plot to kill Fidel Castro.(47) She related to me confidentially that the CIA infiltrated her group. The assault failed. Castro was not physically where he was supposed to have been. A few days after the assault was to occur, all members of the group were arrested and jailed. María's husband was sentenced to death by *paredón*. She was sentenced to thirty years in prison and had her first and only son while in seclusion at the revolutionary women's prison in Guanajay. She eventually arrived in the United States in the 1970s after U.S. President Jimmy

Carter intervened on behalf of Cuban political prisoners. She was my patient during most of her life thereafter.

Cuban secret services were also infiltrating the anti-Castro movements. Castro, from the outset, organized a very sophisticated and successful network of spies with the assistance of the East German Stasi agency. In short, it is the opinion of most experts that at this pivotal time in the history of Cuba, the anti-communist movement and forces of the Underground were thoroughly infiltrated and spied upon by both CIA elements and Cuban security forces.

The fate of freedom-loving Cubans, obviously, was truly out of their hands. It did not matter if there were representatives from twelve anti-Batista organizations in the initial revolutionary government cabinet and only one of those organizations was heavily infiltrated by communists, the July 26 movement. It did not matter if there were only three communist ministers in the initial revolutionary cabinet out of thirteen ministers. The future of the Underground and the anti-communist movement was doomed, but not one of us or those in the Underground or the movements themselves knew it back then.

Marist School outing to Jibacoa on April 20, 1960
(Left to right) Rafael Castellanos, Alberto Ramos Izquierdo, Juan González, Zenón Arribál-
zaga, Antonio Gordon, Juan Pella, Luis Faura, Arturo Novoa, Lorenzo Lorenzo, Manuel Re-
villa, and Brother Balbino, FMS

CHAPTER 2

HAVANA 1960: FROM CIVIL STRIFE TO CIVIL WAR

"Juventud, porvenir de la Patria,
Juventud, porvenir de la Fe.
El futuro descansa en tus brazos,
Tus espaldas serán su sostén.
Con la Estrella y la Cruz como emblema,
Ha de ser nuestra marcha triunfal.
Viva Cuba creyente y dichosa,
Viva Cristo monarca ideal.
Adelante es el grito de guerra
Adelante cual fuerza de paz
La doctrina de Cristo se encierra
En el dulce mandato de amar."

-Chorus of the Hymn of the Cuban Catholic Youth Organization [2]
(*Himno de la Juventud Estudiantil Católica de Cuba*)

When the summer of 1960 came to an end, as all things do on this earth, there were signs of distress for all of us in Havana. Our last outing as a class had been in April, when we went out to Jibacoa on the coast east of Havana with our third year of *bachillerato* head teacher, Brother Balbino. Since the beginning of the year, signs of growing concern had been experienced by most Cuban families. My family was no exception. In January 1960, our family took a trip to central Cuba to Sancti Spiritus. My cousin Emilito had graduated from the Universidad de Villanueva with a degree in architecture. He had a job at the Ministry of Public Works and he was getting

---

[2] "Youth, the future of the fatherland, Youth, the future of the faith. The future lies in our arms, Your backbone will be our support. With the star and the cross as our emblem, This will be our triumphal march. Long live Cuba, faithful and happy. Long live Christ the ideal king, Forward is our cry in the struggle. Forward like a peaceful force, The doctrine of Christ is contained in the sweet command to love."

married in Sancti Spiritus, which was the hometown of his bride to be, María Ofelia, whom he had met at the University. My side of the family went to the wedding in two cars, my uncle Ramón's and my dad's. We drove through the Vía Blanca on the north coast of the former Havana province toward the east and reached the city of Matanzas in about an hour. We drove through the city and after we had passed the Matanzas Bay, we stopped at a bakery on the right-hand side of the road to have some refreshments and rest. My grandmother, Amparo, who was already in her 70s, was riding in one of the cars. Emilito had been her first grandson, the product of the love between her daughter Carmen and her husband, Emilio.

While everyone stretched their legs and rested at the bakery, I stood outside in the parking lot facing the highway and began taking 8 mm movies of the bay on the other side of the road. I had taken with me my Brownie movie camera in order to have a film record of Emilito's wedding. Another cousin, Manolo, had given me the Brownie camera for my thirteenth birthday.

After they had finished inside the bakery, we all got into our respective cars and resumed our trip on the "Carretera Central," Cuba's central highway, which was built during Machado's presidency. About fifteen minutes had passed when we noticed that we were being followed by a number of military jeeps teaming with armed soldiers who were signaling us to stop. We stopped. They were armed with pistols and rifles. My dad took the initiative and walked up to meet the leader of the group of rebel army soldiers. He asked, "What is the matter?" They informed him that someone in our group had been taking photographs of military cargo being unloaded in Matanzas and no one was allowed to take pictures of those highly sensitive installations and maneuvers. They explained that this was a very sensitive issue and they were concerned about counter-revolutionaries and espionage in the area. They wanted to know who it was who had taken pictures and what else was going on.

My dad did not know at that point that I had been taking movies outside the bakery. So, the word went around the occupants of both cars. Who has been taking pictures? I confessed. I came out and told my dad and the soldiers that I had taken movies, some panoramic views of the Matanzas Bay from outside the bakery. Immediately, they wanted to take my camera with them. Then my father identified himself as a physician of the military hospital in Columbia, the army headquarters. He had some identification documents with him. He reassured them that we were not counter-revolutionaries or spies and I was only taking home movies on the way to the wedding of my cousin in Sancti Spiritus. Obviously, he explained, I had no military or strategic interest whatsoever. I was a child. They must have looked at

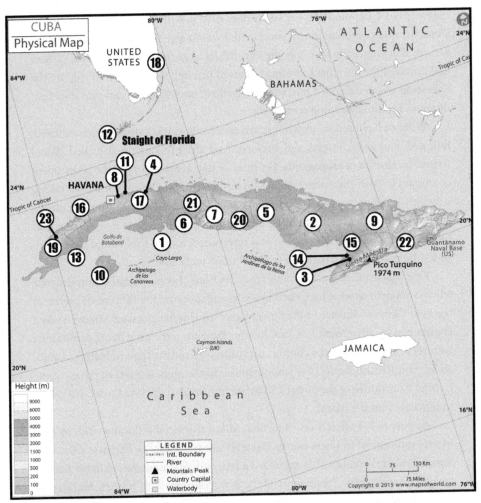

Map Legend

1. Bay of Pigs 2. Camagüey 3. Calicito 4. Camarioca 5. Ciego de Avila 6. Cienfuegos
7. Escambray Mountains 8. Guanabo 9. Holguin 10. Isle of Pines 11. Jaruco 12. Key West, FL
13. La Coloma 14. La Demajagua 15. Manzanillo 16. Mariel 17. Matanzas 18. Miami, FL
19. Pinar del Rio 20. Sancti Spiritus 21. Santa Clara 22. Santiago de Cuba 23. Viñales

Map of Cuba and the Northwestern Caribbean

me again and agreed that I did not appear to be a mature spy or anything of that nature. They continued to speak to my dad. After a while of back and forth discussions, my dad's negotiation was successful; I was to give them the film, but not the camera. They agreed to take only the film and let us go free. So, I opened the camera and unrolled the film that had already passed through the lens and rolled into the collecting reel and handed it to them. We all got back into our cars and the expedition to Emilito's wedding continued.

Without having done anything particularly dangerous, we had been watched, followed, stopped, charged, and stressed. And all of this by the so-called "Rebel Army," another bit of propaganda. For three or four years after 1959 the government continued to label their army "Rebel" as if it was fighting for freedom, not taking it away from us. It was the Underground, anti-Castro, and anti-communist organizations who were actually fighting for freedom and justice. As it was, if my dad had not had a military connection and intervened, maybe they would have taken us to Matanzas for interrogation or God knows what else!

Our Matanzas delay, although scary, had only been a minor inconvenience when compared to what happened to some students after the February 4 arrival of the First Deputy Minister of the Soviet Union in Havana. Anastas Mikoyan was a communist by all accounts. In fact, he may have been the only living communist who served under all three communist leaders up to that time in history: Lenin, Stalin, and Khrushchev.[1] He was obviously in the highest levels of power of the Central Committee of the Soviet Union and the head of the first Soviet delegation to officially visit the island.

As part of his official visit to Cuba, Mikoyan placed a floral wreath by Jose Martí's monument in his honor in Havana's Central Park.[1] The new *Directorio Revolucionario Estudiantil*[2] organized a reparatory demonstration in the park to counteract and protest the presence of the Soviet minister who, by then, had already departed. Mikoyan had left the park and went on to the Palace of Fine Arts just behind the Presidential Palace to open the first Soviet Union Exhibition in Cuba.[2] Meanwhile, at Central Park in the aftermath of Mikoyan's visit, university and high school students gathered, marched, and placed another floral wreath at the foot of Martí's monument.[2] While the students were demonstrating in Havana's Central Park, a fight broke out between them and some bystanders. Almost immediately, the revolutionary police and state security personnel arrived on the scene. Some shots were fired into the air and several people were wounded. Many students were incarcerated at that time.

The Havana Central Park anti-communist demonstration may appear remi-

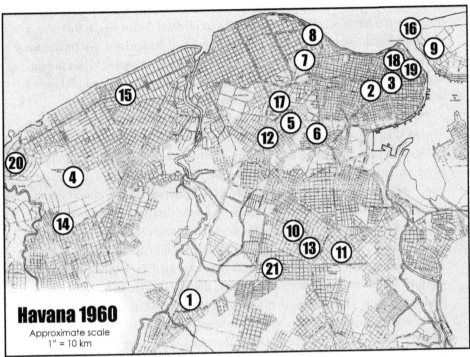

Map Legend

1. Altahabana 2. Capitol 3. Central Park 4. Columbia Military Camp 5. El Cerro Neighborhood
6. Havana Stadium 7. Havana University 8. Hotel Nacional 9. La Cabaña Prison 10. La Vibora
Neighborhood 11. Lawton Neighborhood 12. Marist School at Centro Civico/Cerro 13. Marist
School at La Vibora 14. Military Hospital 15. Miramar Neighborhood 16. El Morro Castle
17. Plaza Civica Jose Marti 18. Prado Boulevard 19. Presidential Palace 20. Villanueva University
21. Villa Marista.

Map of Havana

niscent of the Machado era when students demonstrated against a dictatorial government. However, in February 1960, the students demonstrating against the government in power were both university and secondary school students. There was also another difference. The government security forces acted quickly to drown the protest and took into detention many students. While in Machado's and Batista's time, an incarceration of this type had a serious physical dimension, at this time, a psychological dimension was added to the experience. It consisted, systematically, of mock executions, sleep deprivation, and intense interrogations. When the students were released in a matter of days, they were more fearful and prejudiced against the government than when they went into detention.

On March 9, the Belgian ship *La Coubre* exploded in Havana harbor, resulting in more than 75 people dead and up to 200 wounded.(3) Two explosions occurred and some experts have suggested that the explosions were the result of CIA operatives working undercover.(3) It may have been an accidental explosion, however. Either way, the Castro regime could not and did not pass up this opportunity to blame the United States, directly or indirectly, for the disaster and the victims. The next day, there was a parade to honor the dead and formally blame the United States for the explosion. Washington denied any participation in the *La Coubre* incident.

There have only been two ships that have exploded in Havana harbor. One was the *USS Maine* on February 15, 1898 and now *La Coubre*. The *USS Maine* exploded and sank. The 1898 incident was the turning point that caused the declaration of war by the United States against the Spanish Empire. We had learned these historical details in our third year of the Cuban *bachillerato* History of Cuba course by Dr. Manuel García Iglesias. The second ship to explode in Havana harbor was not something of historical interest, yet. Neither we, nor anyone else, had learned about *La Coubre* in Cuban history courses. No, it was an explosion that we had seen and heard. We felt the trembling and then we saw the slowly rising plume of dark smoke. We saw it from the third floor of the Marist School near the Plaza Cívica in Havana. Dr. García Iglesias was not teaching at that time. Brother Balbino was conducting the class.

The class stopped when we heard the first explosion and felt a brief tremor. Then we saw the column of black smoke rise from the north-northeast direction from our vantage point. At the time, we obviously did not know what had occurred. When the news began to circulate about the location of the disaster, we did not know who was responsible for the explosion of *La Coubre*. But discussion immediately began among us with the idea that it could have been an accident or the Underground forces may conceivably have been involved. We did not dis-

Dr. Manuel García Iglesias taught History of Cuba, Civics, and Literature at the Marist School near the Plaza Cívica.

cuss this other side of the issue then. However, if the Cuban Underground was involved, the CIA was likely infiltrating the conspirators and the Americans would have known of this plan ahead to time. And, what about the G-2, Castro's State Security apparatus? Why didn't they discover the conspirators and prevent the explosion? No one may ever know. An accidental explosion, however, may have been used by Castro to score political points and blame the United States for another "attack."

It was also in March of 1960 that U.S. President Dwight D. Eisenhower ordered the organization and funding of an invading force composed of Cuban exiles, with the express purpose of bringing down the revolutionary government of Fidel Castro.(4) If you were in Havana, you could not help but notice that the sides in the Cuban strife were already becoming clearly delineated, not only in our own neighborhoods and classrooms, but also among the major world powers at the time, the Americans and the Soviets.(5) The world power to the north was also posturing to take sides against the Castro regime. It was understood as something natural and expected, since there were only two political poles at the time in the world of the Cold War, the USA and the USSR.

On June 29, American and British oil refineries were confiscated by the Castro regime.(6) It was argued by the revolutionary authorities that the refineries were not willing to process Soviet oil. Therefore, the refineries were nationalized. The road toward complete control of the economy led next to Cuba's major exporting crop—sugar. On August 6, all American-owned sugar mills and other businesses were nationalized and confiscated by the revolutionary government.(6)

That summer, the presence of the Rebel Army and Fidel Castro was also noticed in the Gran Estadio de La Habana, Havana's baseball stadium, which has been since remodeled and re-baptized as Estadio Latinoamericano. In an International Baseball League (AAA) game, in which the Cuban Sugar Kings were playing against the Rochester Red Wings, two of the ball players were wounded by stray bullets in a long game that began on July 25. The game had gone past midnight on extra-innings and when the clock marked midnight and the 26th of July arrived, there were demonstrations in the streets of Havana and shots were fired into the air. One player from each team was wounded.(7) Later on in the season, the Sugar Kings were playing the Minneapolis Millers in September. Castro made it a point to go to the stadium for every single game of that series, always entering through the gate in centerfield with an entourage of soldiers and Rebel Army security personnel. At one point, there were some 30,000 fans in the stadium full to capacity, and more than 3,000 armed soldiers. Eventually, the series went to seven games and the Cuban team won the last game by a score of 3 to 2. The winning run came on a hit from Dan Morejón.(8) Some of the Millers' players on the bench commented at the end of the game that they were lucky to be able to leave Cuba with their skins intact!

The reader should be able to appreciate the general situation and reality of Cuban society as the time got closer for us to begin school again. As I noted earlier, my cousin Emilito had been working for the revolutionary government in the Ministry of Public Works after he graduated from architecture school. At that point in his early career, he found himself being harassed and accused of being a counter-revolutionary by some of his fellow workers in the architecture department. Immediately, the thought of getting out of Cuba came up. The *Diario de la Marina*, one of the oldest newspapers in Cuba, where his father Emilio had worked for years as a sports journalist, was confiscated in May 1960. Therefore, from that time on, Uncle Emilio had become an employee of a revolutionary government entity. Emilito had an American visa, but his wife did not. After arriving at a consensus between themselves, my Uncle Emilio, Emilito, and María Ofelia decided to temporarily leave Havana. They traveled to Spain, where Emilito would take a post-graduate course in architecture in Madrid. Uncle Emilio had connections in the Spanish Embassy. In a matter of weeks, Emilito and María Ofelia left Cuba on the steamship *Covadonga* accompanied by my Uncle Emilio. Uncle Emilio's wife—my aunt Carmen—and his daughter Muñeca remained in Havana but soon thereafter traveled to Tampa, Florida. Muñeca at the time of Emilito's departure was still a student at the Universidad de Villanueva. Uncle Emilio's official reason for leaving Havana had to do with going to Spain to report on soccer and investigate the ways of adapting soccer to the Cuban mentality and sports culture.

When the school year began for me and my classmates in September 1960, we learned that there were two new courses in the curriculum established by the revolutionary government for the fourth year of the Cuban *bachillerato*. In the old curriculum, during the fourth year, there had been a course on Political Economy (Economia Política). This course was changed to one entitled Economía Política y Agraria. All of a sudden, it seemed that everything in Cuba had turned revolutionary and agrarian. There was no textbook for these new courses. Discussions during the class involved reading newspaper articles and the class was expected to carry out one excursion to an agrarian facility. A second course involved student government, and did not have a text either. It was supposed to deal with the role that students play in the various facets of the Cuban Revolution.

The first revolutionary law of agrarian reform had already been decreed and passed by the council of ministers, the cabinet, in 1959.(9) It could not have been passed through a congress because there was no congress. Laws at this time during the revolution were the result of Fidel Castro's initiatives, sometimes based on issues that he had discussed in *La Historia Me Absolvera*,(10) his published discourse from the trial against him for the events that marked the beginning of the armed struggle against the Fulgencio Batista dictatorship after the coup d'état of March 10, 1952. The failed attack by Castro's forces on the Cuban Constitutional Army's provincial headquarters in Santiago de Cuba, the Cuartel Moncada, occurred on July 26, 1953.

Since Castro was a lawyer, he assumed his own defense in the trial. His defense speech was turned into a book entitled *La Historia Me Absolvera*. In it, Castro described the reasons for the attack centered on the coup d'état and the need to re-establish the constitutional order according to the Constitution of 1940. He detailed the injuries and deaths resulting from the attack, and proposed a revolutionary plan to deal with the future of Cuba. He used available data on the average ratio of injured to dead soldiers from battles during the Cuban War of Independence from 1895 until 1898 to strongly suggest that Batista's forces had tortured and massacred Castro's forces after the battle. The expected ratio of injured to dead was inverted at the Moncada attack. There were very few attackers injured for the number of dead reported suggesting that many attackers were not killed in battle and may have been shot after being captured.

However, it should also be pointed out that Castro held back some crucial facts in his discourse that have now been well documented. That is, that Castro's forces massacred untold numbers of Cuban army personnel, particularly those who were interned in the Military Hospital adjacent to the Cuartel Moncada. Castro's rebels stormed the military hospital during their escape from the Moncada headquarters, seeking a hiding place to avoid being captured, at which point they slaughtered patients with impunity. The attackers also, during their retreat, knocked on the houses of non-commissioned officers and killed whoever opened the door.

Returning to *La Historia Me Absolvera*, in terms of sociopolitical issues, Castro proposed an agrarian reform that would purchase lands from large land owners (*latifundistas*) whose lands were not being cultivated and were unproductive. The revolutionary government would then, after purchasing the uncultivated lands, issue them to the landless farmers who would, in turn, cultivate the lands. This would create the wealth with which education and health care were to reach all Cubans, including those in the most distant rural areas.

We did not know it back then, but in 1946, Lowry Nelson—a rural sociologist who, at the time, worked at the University of Minnesota—went to Cuba to study the rural conditions and life on the island.(11) He traveled throughout the entire island and surveyed a number of agrarian facilities with an aide and translator provided by the government of President Ramón Grau San Martín. He concluded that the rural conditions in Cuba at the time were not very different from some of the conditions he found in Mississippi and Alabama. However, one issue was clear to Nelson, and he proposed that it be addressed without delay. He recommended that roads and electric power be provided to Cuban agricultural and rural communities. Nelson postulated that when roads and electric power were available to the Cuban *campesinos,* more commerce and support personnel for schools and health facilities could be expected to follow.

During the 1959-1960 academic year there had been frequent campaigns in our school to raise funds and help for the agrarian reform. We finished our campaign on time in 1959, donating a tractor to the revolutionary government for the agrarian reform. An alumnus of the Marist schools in Cuba who was, at that time, the minister of agriculture in the original revolutionary government, Humberto Sorí Marín, received the tractor on behalf of the National Revolutionary Institute for Agrarian Reform (INRA).

A couple of months after Sorí Marín received our donation, he resigned from his Ministry of Agriculture post in May, 1959.(12) He was not a communist, and immediately after his resignation, went to work in the anti-Castro movement in the Underground. From then until his death, he worked against the communist infiltration in the revolutionary government. He landed with others near Havana before the Bay of Pigs Invasion and was captured in March 1961 by Cuban State Security. He was jailed and was shot to death at the now infamous *paredón.*

With the enactment of the Law of Agrarian Reform, a number of agrarian cooperatives had been organized, presumably in the lands where nothing had been cultivated before. The revolution was interested in showing its early accomplishments to the entire world. It was back then that arrangements were already in the making for American college students to travel to Cuba to observe firsthand the progress of the revolution through the Agrarian Reform.(13)

Since we had been asked in the new course, *Economía Política y Agraria,* to visit an agrarian cooperative to determine what was going on in the new Cuban countryside as a result of the Agrarian Reform of the revolutionary government, we did exactly that. I was able to help arrange for our excursion to a newly organized agrarian cooperative in the vicinity of Caimito, southwest of Havana. On the agreed upon date, we were driven to the cooperative by our parents. Some of my twenty-five classmates did not make it to the cooperative. No one knew whether the absence of some of the students was related to personal issues, incipient fear

Rebel Army Commander Humberto Sorí Marín. He was a Marist alumnus and received our school's contribution to the Instituto Nacional de Reforma Agraria (INRA) (National Institute for Agrarian Reform) at the school yard.

A group of students gathered around the Ferguson tractor donated by the student body of our Marist School to the Agrarian Reform in 1959.

even that early in the revolutionary process, ideological issues, or transportation issues. However, we were able to muster about a third of the class to attend.

To our surprise, the agrarian cooperative we visited was not the result of the acquisition of land that had been uncultivated. The cooperative had been organized on a farm that had been confiscated without any monetary compensation from a former Batista regime officer. We were not able, although we tried, to draw an organogram of the personnel who worked on the farm. It was not evident who did what, who directed who, or who answered to whom. We were able to examine some of the equipment, though. To our astonishment, a couple of American tractors, much like the one our school had donated to the Agrarian Reform, stood in a clearing to the side of the entrance of the farm with their hoods up, appearing to be under repair. We asked about what had happened to the tractors and learned that some other tractors had broken down and they had used those two tractors for parts to keep the other tractors in the cooperative running. We did not see the other tractors, the ones that were working. We also inquired about the production of the farm. We learned from some of the agricultural workers that the farm had actually produced nothing for several months after it was confiscated and organized into an Agrarian Reform cooperative in the summer of 1959.

These firsthand impressions served as the background for the topics on which the classroom discussion was going to center during the coming weeks in the fourth year of our Cuban *bachillerato*. The group who had visited the farm became the most fervent opponents of the manner in which the Agrarian Reform was being conducted. Our visit to the cooperative had been an eye-opener, through which we saw that anything dealing with both the Agrarian Reform and the revolutionary government was not functioning correctly. I venture to conclude that if anyone who visited the farm had not been aware of the irregularities, propaganda, and manipulations of the revolutionary government before the visit, they were convinced afterwards that not everything was transparent, proceeding according to what had been promised, and definitely not going well.

As early as the middle of 1959, the student body was beginning to be divided into two fairly well defined groups. But by then, the divisions were more obvious. In one group, we were ready to defend that the actual spirit of the revolution against Batista and the Agrarian Reform had not been honored or followed since the farm land where the cooperative we visited was formed had already been cultivated and productive before the revolution. Secondly, we argued, the farm was seemingly disorganized and at least some of its workers noted that nothing was being produced since it was confiscated. On the other side, the group favoring the revolutionary government point of view at the time argued that the farm was confiscated from a "war criminal" and the revolutionary government had used it to form a cooperative with the workers that used to be exploited on it. They also argued that without such action, the farm would have been uncultivated and fruitless. Obviously, we argued that the land was now cultivated, but fruitless. In terms of the organization of the cooperative and the newly acquired broken agricultural equipment, they argued that the Americans had placed an embargo on Cuba starting at about that time in 1960. They suggested that tractor parts could not be obtained and some tractors had to be "cannibalized."

The debates were lively in the classroom, but most of us did not argue outside the school for fear of becoming known as counter-revolutionaries. Out of the twenty-five students in my class, one of us had enrolled already in the *Milicias Nacionales Revolucionarias* and had the guts to come to school on occasions with the uniform of the *Milicias*, a light-blue, cotton twill textile shirt, olive green fatigue pants, a black beret and, yes, black boots on his feet. At the time, maybe up to a third of the class favored the revolution's point of view in public. There was another student who was very well respected and reliable, Luis de la Cruz, who was definitely in the group favoring the revolution's point of view, but he was very quiet and did not like to argue. He had already been active during the summer of 1960 in the countryside in the literacy campaign of the revolutionary government, which would spread through the entire Cuban society later on. He came back from Eastern Cuba in the area of Las Tunas convinced that the countryside needed the help.

Luis de la Cruz, Marist School Yearbook, 1959

Our classmate turned *alfabetizador*[3] had arrived at a conclusion similar to that of Professor Lowry Nelson, the need to provide roads and electricity. In fact, most students in my class, myself included, agreed that the *campesinos* and the countryside needed help with literacy and education. However, the provision of transportation and power was outside our possibilities as students. A truly progressive revolution may have approached the problems of rural Cuba at the time differently. However, in our classroom, it was obvious that the two sides in the ongoing strife and an incipient civil war were beginning to become better defined. We did not know what a civil war was because none of us had been in a civil war. But back then, we were aware of the tensions at home, school, and in the national arena, particularly along ideological lines. In retrospect, a civil war was brewing and each side seemed to have the support of each one of the global poles of power at the time—the Soviet Union and the United States.

We noted that the Marist brother who served as our main teacher, Brother Teodoro Fernández, FMS, did not make any comments on behalf of one side or the other during our discussions in either student government or the new course on *Economía Política y Agraria*. Years later, we found out that the Church had been warned that there would be spies in the classrooms who would note the attitude of the clergy and religious men and women in regard to the revolution in order to have an excuse to label them counter-revolutionary and confiscate the schools.(14) I should not get ahead of the story, but eventually it did not matter if Brother Teodoro expressed himself on one side or the other or none. The school was to be closed and confiscated.

The other new course in the curriculum was student government. Each classroom was to elect a council of three representatives and a president. These leaders would run the classroom student government; discuss the issues in the classroom, the school, and their neighborhoods; propose revolutionary changes; and participate in the official campaigns of the revolutionary government. It was during one of these student government sessions that the first student from our group came to school without the Marist school's uniform—khaki pants and bright blue shirt with a white tie. Cosme Damian del Peso came in with his militia uniform, boots and all.

During the first day, the officers of the student government class were elected. I was elected the president of the council. I was very surprised, because I had never been elected to be the head of anything in school. However, I noted that the individual who was the natural leader of the class was perceived to be either on the ideological fence or still attempting to argue in favor of the case presented by the revolutionary government. I also thought that, perhaps, those appearances had to

---

[3] Someone who taught the ABCs in the literacy campaign.

do with the fact that he was related—although distantly—to the revolutionary Minister of Education. At the end of that day, however, I understood that classroom election—and still see it in the same light now—as a small referendum on the revolution, voted on by the twenty-five students in our fourth year of the Cuban *bachillerato*. At that time, our classroom was favoring, slightly, the counter-revolution, not Castro's revolution; the sides for the upcoming civil war were better defined.

By the fall of 1960, there were clear indications that the revolutionary government of Fidel Castro was pointing its military establishment and rhetoric against Catholic schools. (15) There were 275 Catholic schools, at that time, in Cuba. Some were subsidized by the Church, so the tuition and materials were free. At other schools, tuition was required. However, even in those schools, tuition was affordable even for low-middle class families. According to the Institute of Cuban and Cuban American Studies (ICCAS) of the University of Miami, Cuba was one of the richest underdeveloped countries in the world with Gross National Product to per-capita income ratio yielding in the mid 1950s an estimated yearly income of 360 pesos per person. The Cuban peso at the time was exchanged at the same rate as the American dollar. The island had the third-highest per capita income in Latin America and its middle middle class was about a third of the population according to ICCAS data. The Marist schools began tuition in *Pre Primario* (a kind of kindergarten) and first grade at about six Cuban pesos per month. The tuition went up steadily as the school grades progressed up to about fifteen pesos monthly in the last years of the Cuban *bachillerato*. There were more expensive Catholic schools and also less expensive ones on the island.

On the sidewalk opposite our Marist school on the *Avenida Independencia* near the Plaza Cívica, a couple of anti-aircraft machine guns were set up sometime in October 1960. The weapons were of the Soviet-built ZPU-4 anti-aircraft machine gun type. These battle stations were manned at all hours of the day and night by shifts of the newly organized *Milicias Nacionales Revolucionarias*. It will be recalled that earlier in 1960, Soviet Vice President Anastas Mikoyan visited Havana and signed a number of commercial and defense agreements. By the end of the same year, some of the fruits of the newly-formed alliance of the Castro revolution were literally in full view in front of us, not in any exhibit or exposition!

Since his defection from the Revolutionary Air Force on June 29, 1959, Commander Pedro Luis Díaz Lanz had become engaged in anti-Castro activities. Díaz Lanz was the chief pilot who flew supplies and weapons into the Sierra Maestra during the arms struggle against the Batista tyranny. After he defected, he flew over Havana in the fall of 1959 in what was described as "a B26 bomber, dropping anti-

Castro leaflets." Castro's forces fired on Díaz Lanz's plane, but failed to bring it down. Instead, the gunfire caused a number of injuries on the ground as bystanders came out to get the leaflets and take a look at the plane. Paradoxically, Díaz Lanz had also been a pilot in the past for one of the Cuban airlines, Q Airways. Interestingly, it was one of the Q Airways' DC-3s that I eventually boarded and arrived aboard in the United States.

The dropping of leaflets with information and propaganda from an enemy airplane was a practice used during the Spanish Civil War (1936-1939). During that conflict, a few days after dropping leaflets, German and Italian war planes bombed Guernica and other cities and towns of the Basque Country in northern Spain. (16) The cultural proximity of Cuba to Spain and the presence in Cuba, at that time, of many survivors and refugees of the Spanish conflict between Communism and Fascism, provided the people of Cuba with ample background to be not only terrorized, but awaiting some sort of bombardment or invasion at any time.

If the revolutionary anti-aircraft machine guns would have been placed along the shoreline of Havana, the famous *Malecón*, also known officially as Antonio Maceo Avenue, it would have been easier to agree with the stated intentions of the authorities that the battle stations were there to protect the revolution from foreign aggressors. However, the battle stations were systematically placed in close vicinity to the major Catholic schools—the Jesuit's *Colegio de Belén*, the Christian Brothers' *Colegios de La Salle*, the Priarist Fathers' *Escuelas Pías*, and the Marist brothers' schools, the *Colegios Champagnat*.

The rhetoric against Catholic education stepped up when Castro himself labeled the only Catholic university in Cuba, Universidad de Santo Tomas de Villanueva, a "university pro Yankee." (17) A high church official was quoted by the press at the time as predicting that the Catholic university would be closed by the middle of 1961. Indeed, the Catholic university had been founded by mostly American Augustinian priests in 1946. Until 1959, the president of the university had been an American Augustinian, Father John Kelly, OSA. It was not until after the triumph of the revolution that a Cuban, Auxiliary Bishop of Havana Eduardo Boza Masvidal, was elevated to president of the Universidad Católica de Santo Tomás de Villanueva. At the time, an official label of being pro-American or pro-Yankee was a serious insult in Havana. In a world of two poles, the American and the Soviet, if you were on the "wrong pole," you were anathema. That "pro-Yankee" label was equivalent to being anti-communist. Church officials and everyone connected with the Catholic university, including religious faculty (approximately 120), lay faculty (more than 100 in total), and nearly 1,000 students and their families were all concerned. My cousin Muñeca was still a student at Villanueva in the School of Education. The concerns were also felt in all other Catholic schools and circles.

The students from the University of Havana were also very active in the political and social reaction against the Castro regime. They had already demonstrated and had taken sides in the ongoing strife and the incipient civil war. Even before the visit of Anastas Mikoyan in February 1960, the *Directorio Revolucionario Estudiantil* had been organized to take part against the new dictatorship of Fidel Castro. The *Directorio* had been instrumental in the fight against the Batista dictatorship. As the reader will recall, its leader at the time, José Antonio Echevarría, was killed near the University of Havana in the aftermath of the attack on the presidential palace on March 13, 1957. The new leaders of the *Directorio* in 1960 were Alberto Mueller and Manuel Salvat, among others. The sides for a civil war were also being defined in the public Cuban universities.

Fidel Castro was not the only one incriminating the Catholic schools in the counter-revolution and anti-Castro efforts. In 1960, or about that time, the minister of education, Armando Hart Dávalos, said, "The public schools are trying to form a man without prejudice or fears. The private schools, in particular the Catholic institutions, are trying to create another type of man full of prejudice and falsehood." (18) In the terms used by the revolutionary education minister, the strife was not between communism and democracy. Instead, it was to be understood as a struggle between two conceptions of man, one free from prejudice and fear, and the other one consumed by prejudice and fear. The minister of education was right; we were fearful. The problem in his views and ours was simple. We did not think that the educational experience, which we had enjoyed for years, was responsible for the fear. We thought that it was actually the revolutionary government and its policies that were responsible for generating and spreading a climate of terror and fear in Cuba.

President Urrutia had been deposed in July 1959 by Castro himself. The currently-appointed Cuban President Osvadlo Dorticós summed up the points made by his minister of education by stating that the Cuban Catholic schools were teaching that the revolution was a communist movement. He labeled the latter "a crime against our country." (18) As the year ended, a high Soviet official, Leonid Brezhnev, who would become the USSR Communist Party leader years later, was reported to have sent a note to Cuban President Osvaldo Dorticós, reassuring him that the Cuban people had the total support of the Soviet people. (19)

There is no doubt that life in Cuba, in the fall of 1960, had turned into a dangerous military and political puzzle: That is, an ongoing revolution. Although the students at the University of Havana had been known to be active in national politics since the era of Machado in the 1930s; at this time, in 1960, teenage and younger students from all walks of life, from all types of schools, private and public, religious or non-denominational, were already politicized and, in some cases, militarized in the *Milicias*. The stage was clearly set. The Cuban revolution and government were turning rapidly into what was to be a communist, totalitarian regime controlling all aspects of Cuban society. It was also evident that not everyone was in agreement with the revolutionary government's priorities and practices. Hence, the elements for a civil war were in place.

CHAPTER 3

ACROSS THE STRAITS OF FLORIDA: ANOTHER CUBA EMERGES

"Milicianos, adelante. Milicianos, a marchar. Solo tenemos un ideal. Salvar a Cuba y su libertad. No somos uno, no somos dos. Somos un pueblo junto a Fidel." (Chorus of a hymn of the *"Milicia Nacional Revolucionaria"*)[4]

While in Havana, there was a great deal of concern about the communist and dictatorial direction that the revolution was taking; in Miami in 1960, there was already a complementary process going on. However, the center of attention of the Cuban issue in Miami was not communism. By then, the era of McCarthyism, anti-communism, and anti-American activities was already gone. The two main aspects of the Cuban issue at that time in Miami were the management and resettlement of exiles and the organization of anti-Castro forces that would participate in the incipient civil war on the island.

Some Cubans began to seek political asylum in Miami right after the triumph of the revolution on January 1, 1959. Indeed, some Cuban families, who foresaw the beginning of the end of the Batista regime, and still had vivid memories of the horrendous violence that erupted in Havana in the aftermath of the downfall of Gerardo Machado in August 1933, left Havana days before the end of 1958. The particular family I have in mind when I write these lines was fortunate in that their father had the experience of having been an activist and fighter in the first *Directorio Revolucionario Estudiantil* during the 1930s. After the political and social upheavals of that bygone era, the father had become a prominent lawyer and by 1958, he had the means with which to take his family out of Cuba to safeguard them from

---

[4] "Militia men and women ahead. Militia men and women to march. We only have one ideal. To save Cuba and its freedom. We are not one, we are not two. We are a people with Fidel."

any violence or serious disruption in their lives while major changes occurred in the country. He was intelligent and well connected with the Batista regime hierarchy and foresaw that something important was going to occur. Therefore, he thought that he was sending his wife, children, and their nanny to Miami Beach for a couple of weeks. I am sure that he meant to spare them the violence, looting, and lynching that followed the exit of Machado from Havana. At that time, in one notorious case, the brutal chief of police, Antonio Aicierte, was cornered by revolutionaries, shot to death, and buried.(1) A few days later, the university students discovered the tomb, removed the cadaver, and took it to the University of Havana campus. There, they hung the lifeless body of the well-known assassin and burned it as part of a rally of the anti-Machado forces.

All Cubans who left Cuba beginning on January 1, 1959, have been labeled in one way or another by the official Castro propaganda. The first set of Cubans to leave the island on account of the revolution was labeled "War Criminals." I daresay that some may have indeed been war criminals. For example, a notorious Cuban army intelligence officer, Irenaldo García Baez, was walking the streets of Miami, obviously in civilian clothing, in January 1961. I saw him myself. He and his family had left the island in the very first wave of exiles–aboard the planes in which Batista left from the military airport in Camp Columbia. García Baez' father, Pilar García, had been another notorious villain of the Batista regime. After they arrived in Miami, their family had opened a restaurant, El Castillo de Jagua. Both García Baez and his father were well known to have tortured many Cubans while they served the Batista regime in more than one capacity through seven years of tyranny.(2) Irenaldo was a high officer in the *Servicio de Inteligencia Militar* (SIM, Military Intelligence Service) in 1957.

My personal experience with the SIM occurred through my father. He was detained by the SIM during the aftermath of the September 5, 1957 uprising of the Cuban Air Force and Navy in the second attempt of the Cuban military to take down the Batista dictatorship. This uprising had been organized in association with elements of the civil society and political parties, in particular, the *Auténtico* Party. The opposition was attempting to topple the Batista regime and reinstitute the republic under the Constitution of 1940.

My father was detained for four weeks at the SIM before being brought into a court martial. The SIM headquarters were not entirely foreign to him. The intelligence and torture agency of Batista's regime was located just in front and to the south of the Carlos J. Finlay Military Hospital in Havana's Camp Columbia in what had been the *Clínica 4 de Septiembre* in the late thirties and early forties. My father recalled that some of his fellow detainees were submitted to a common practice at the SIM. The detainees who were being tortured in order to get more information out of them were taken to the nearby military airfield blindfolded to fly them in DC-3 aircrafts. Once in the air, the prisoner would be placed near an open exit door and the blindfold would be removed. While the door was open, García Baez and his staff would interrogate the prisoner and threaten to push them off the flying aircraft if they did not provide the information requested by their inquisitive torturers. The flight course usually took the aircraft to the province of *Pinar del Río* in Western Cuba over the *Sierra de los Organos* Mountains. It should not be surprising then, that in the fall of 1960, arsonists placed an explosive device in the bathroom of the restaurant owned by García Baez and his family and the entire place caught fire.(3)

Obviously, the Cuban issue in Miami was revealed not only in the news coming out of Cuba, but also in the violence exercised against certain enemies of the revolution. It is true that most of the news related to the Cuban exiles at the time in Miami had to do with surviving in a foreign country and liberating the homeland left behind. But, who were the perpetrators of such violence as noted against El Castillo de Jagua? Who was behind those other forces? Was it anti-Castro forces? Probably not, because if all movements were infiltrated on the island by the CIA and the Cuban state security apparatus, why would one expect the CIA to allow such violence on American soil? But, could Castro forces have brought the violence to Miami? Could undercover Castro forces have been responsible for the bombing of El Castillo de Jagua? Well, García Baez had been sentenced in revolutionary courts in Cuba to death forty-two times by Castro's military-revolutionary tribunals.(3) Could it be that Castro's forces were trying to execute in Miami the man they had sentenced in the Cuban revolutionary courts? Perhaps, but we may never know for sure. The arsonists were never found by the authorities in Miami. It should be mentioned here that since then, there have been a number of arsons and crimes, including homicides against prominent Cuban exiles, for which no one has been arrested or found guilty. The last of these mysterious attacks occurred during the aftermath of the visit of Pope Benedict XVI to Cuba in 2012. A travel agency that organized trips to Cuba was burnt to the ground on Ponce de Leon Boulevard in Coral Gables near Little Havana's *Calle 8.* Who was responsible for that? Nobody knows!

Going back to the Cubans, who were seeking asylum in the United States right after the triumph of the revolution, there were many others who were not "War Criminals," but just average Cubans who had been part of the losing side in the fight against Batista. Some of them were seeking asylum in Miami because they had been employed in the Cuban army or worked for the police or an agency of the government, but they had not committed abuses, crimes, or atrocities. Many of these Cubans felt totally out of place in revolutionary Cuba. They may not have had a job, any prospects for any job, or faith in their future in Cuba under the revolution.

Among this first wave of Cubans who left the island, was a man we knew in our family as Luis Morejón. He had been guided and sometimes supported by my Uncle Emilio, who was not a supporter of the Batista regime, but had connections in it through which Morejón got a position as a policeman in Havana in the late fifties. Morejón lost his job with the police in January 1959 and left Cuba very soon after that. He settled in the Tampa area, where he married an Italian widow and began a new life as a truck driver. I dare to say that there were many more Morejóns than García Baezes in that first wave of exiles.

At any rate, there was a great deal of happiness in the hearts of the vast majority of Cubans on the island at the time of the Batista downfall.(4) Everyone expected the restoration of law and order, the resumption of the Constitution of 1940, and free and fair elections in a maximum of two years. Those had been the main points, promises, and reasons enunciated by the major anti-Batista organizations for toppling the regime. These were also specifically the promises of Fidel Castro himself, whose 26th of July Movement had been a signatory of the Pact of Caracas as noted in the Introduction. These were also the expectations of the civil society, the armed forces, the populace, and the national and international press corps on the island.

However, as history was evolving in front of our own eyes during the remainder of 1959 and by the middle of 1960, there were signs that another dictatorship, this time communist and totalitarian, was brewing on the island. By the fall of 1960, there were already an estimated 30,000 Cubans in exile in the Miami area.(5) Some children were among them. The first individuals who left Cuba from my own classroom were Luis Díaz and Manuel Revilla. Soon thereafter, in October 1960, my cousin Ramoncito was sent by his parents, without any explanation given or discussion openly in the family. He was sent to Miami to live with a friend of his father's from the Mantilla district of Havana. My uncle Ramón was a dentist who worked in a health dispensary, *La Casa de Socorros de Mantilla*, in the dental clinic. A friend of my uncle's went by the name of Lola. In Miami, Lola lived in a four-bedroom, one-story house on the corner of NW 8th Avenue and 2nd Street. She took into her home many Cubans seeking asylum, including my cousin Ramoncito. Lola also used to have a concession store in the Havana airport before she herself sought asylum in Miami. Therefore, among the Cubans residing in her house, there were some pilots who had flown for Cubana Airlines. Ramoncito had just turned

16 years old, but there were many others much older than him living in the Lola's four-bedroom house. Those arrangements became known by Miamians as a "*Cuban Barracones*" (for the word barracks).(6) In a similar house described in an article in the *Miami Herald* at that time, there were twenty-six Cubans boarding, most of them had fought against Batista, but had ended up in Castro's prisons during 1959. They had escaped the island by sea and were looking for a job or a way to go back to Cuba with a weapon to bring down the communist regime. In that particular Cuban barracks, there were only two Cubans working. All others were still looking for something to do.

Miamians were becoming aware of Cuban exiles very quickly. The *Miami Herald* assigned a staff writer, Juanita Greene, to cover the story of the Cubans in Miami. By the end of 1960, interestingly, Cubans were already formally labeled in the press as refugees, not simply exiles. From then on, the Cubans would live with two labels, one given to them by the Castro forces, the other by the American press and establishment—war criminals and *gusanos*[5] versus refugees. In Lola's "*Cuban Barracón*" there were at least four guys working. Once I got to Miami, I remember seeing them off to work as Lola reminded them to take a vitamin "because in this country, you have to work hard."

Juanita Greene published a set of four articles in the *Miami Herald* on the situation of Cuban refugees in Miami, beginning on November 28, 1960.(7) She met and reported on Napoleón Bécquer and his family, who were among the Cuban refugees featured in the initial *Herald* story.(8) Bécquer had been a wealthy man in Manzanillo, Oriente in Eastern Cuba before he joined the Castro guerrillas in the Sierra Maestra Mountains in 1958. He served in the Rebel Army immediately after January 1, 1959, but became convinced that the communists were taking control of the course of the revolution and the country was going in the direction of another dictatorship.

Bécquer was not the only one who noticed the communist infiltration in the Rebel Army. My father, as I noted earlier, had been involved in a Cuban republican army conspiracy to down the Batista dictatorship. He had been a prisoner during the balance of the dictatorship. A day after the triumph of the revolution, when his fellow officers were freed from prison, he returned to the Military Hospital in Havana and was reinstated into the medical service of the new army. One week later, I remember him coming home rather saddened. He explained that he had seen how the communists were taking over the Rebel Army. He did not speak of details,

---

[5] *Gusanos* means worms. The term was used to denounce counter-revolutionaries because they were "underground." Soon thereafter, it also came to refer to the duffle bags used as suitcases to leave the island.

but was convinced that his observations were accurate. For the next four to six months, he and I would argue about the true course of the revolution, social justice, the economy, discrimination, and more. Those arguments were a direct threat that could have led us to break off our father/son relationship. Thank God we never did! Why were we arguing? Because I was not convinced, yet—as he was—of the dictatorial turn of the new government. In my case, I was not convinced until the summer of 1959.

Going back to the story of Bécquer, he had spoken openly in Cuba about his feelings against communist practices and the indoctrination of the troops. These were practices that were instituted very early on in the course of the revolution. He was soon thereafter labeled as counter-revolutionary, taken prisoner, and jailed at the La Cabaña Military Prison just next to the Morro Castle in Havana. From there, he escaped and, through friends in the Cuban Navy, who were also defecting, arrived in Miami by boat months later. His wife and two children also left Cuba by boat several weeks later. Bécquer was working part-time when he was interviewed for the *Herald* story. His two children were already enrolled at the Allapatah Junior High School. The *Herald* reporter asked his 13-year-old son about what he was doing. The adolescent responded as follows: "The school is okay, but I'd rather go back to Cuba and fight." This 13-year-old adolescent had already taken sides in the civil war that was brewing on the island.

My cousin Ramoncito and Bécquer's son's situations were not unusual. By the end of 1960, there were more than 5,000 Cuban children in the Miami area.(9) In September 1960, the Dade County School Board estimated that out of 160,000 students in the county, there were 3,000 Cuban refugee children enrolled. The number of Cuban refugee children in the parochial schools posed an enormous challenge in parallel to a more impressive proportion. Again, as of September 1960, there were 2,500 Cuban children among the 18,000 students in the Diocese of Miami parochial schools. The parochial schools' situation was essentially, just by the numbers, seven times worse than that of the county public school system(10) in terms of how many new Cuban refugee students had to be educated.

At the time, it was estimated that from 1,000 to 1,500 Cubans of all ages were arriving weekly to Miami International Airport. The authorities had projected that by the end of 1961 there would be 100,000 Cubans in the Miami area.(11) These projections were rather alarming, considering the actual population of Miami and other South Florida cities at the time. The population of the city of Miami in 1960, according to the U.S. Census Bureau, was 291,688. Obviously, if in one year Cubans would amount to up to a third of Miami's population, something had to be done about this trend and quickly. Basic social services were needed to handle the increasing load of displaced persons and a program was proposed through which the newcomers would be able to travel and settle in communities other than Miami in the United States.

Since a large percentage of the Cubans fleeing the island were Catholic, the Diocese of Miami played an important role in those times. The Diocese of Miami was founded in 1958 by the Vatican.(12) Its first bishop was Bishop Coleman F. Carroll. From the time the State of Florida became incorporated into the United States in 1845, there had been only one Roman Catholic diocese in the state, the Diocese of St. Augustine. It was a historical diocese, the place where the first Catholic Church had been built in the United States.

Bishop Carroll seemed to have seen and understood the demographic trends of the times in South Florida. In 1959, he organized the *Centro Hispano Católico*(13) to help Cuban refugees find jobs, schooling, food rations, childcare, and attend to their spiritual needs. The *Centro*, as it became known, was located in downtown Miami adjacent to the Gesu Church, the first Roman Catholic Church in southern Florida, dating back to just before Miami became incorporated as a city in 1896.

Bishop Carroll placed an American nun, Sister Miriam, OP, from the Dominican order as the head of the *Centro Hispano Católico* in Miami soon after she arrived in exile from Havana in the fall of 1959. By the end of 1960 she was well known, not only at the *Centro*, but also in the Miami area. The *Miami News* selected her and five lay women for the "Outstanding Woman" award for Miami in 1960.(14) The story was carried in the New Year's edition of the daily paper on January 1, 1961. According to the *Miami News*, Sister Miriam had "brilliantly shouldered a burden assigned to her by Bishop Coleman F. Carroll of the Diocese of Miami." They continued to summarize what she and the *Centro* were doing as follows: "Not a day passes without an outpouring of sympathy to many Latin Americans in distress, especially Cuban refugees…There is a constant stream of bewildered, unhappy, hungry, uprooted people who appeal to the Center. Sister Miriam and her associates receive them kindly; listen, advise, and aid. Days are endless, filled with service that none appreciates as much as Cuban homeless, jobless, penniless refugees. Spiritual, professional, economic problems, insurmountable to some, are straightened out under wise counseling at the Catholic Latin Center."(14) At the time, considering the word usage in the *Miami News* article on the "Outstanding Woman of the Year in Miami," it is noted that the term "Latin American" and "Cuban refugee" may have been as interchangeable as Hispanic and Latin have turned out to be later on.

The *Centro* founded by Bishop Carroll served the exiles well. Sister Miriam had been assimilated by the Cubans as one of their own. Although Sister Miriam was born in Philadelphia, she served in the American Dominican's school for girls in Havana from 1946 until 1959. She was removed from the Havana school at about the time the rector of the Universidad Católica de Villanueva, Rev. John Joseph Kelly, OSA, was asked to leave the island on account of being an American priest. By "definition" this meant pro-Yankee and anti-communist, and, of course, counter-revolutionary. And counter-revolutionaries like him and Bécquer belonged in prison or in exile.

CHAPTER 4

BACK IN HAVANA: "THE TRAIN IS DOOMED"

*"The government, the State Department, called me
Christmas Eve 1960 to say they wanted to help some parents in
Cuba to send their children here, but needed a social agency like the
Church that could accept responsibility for children, and that we could have govern-
ment assistance in financial matters, that is, money and all that.
But they needed someone to sign and then I said 'yes'
I will sign the document and we helped depart from
Cuba and enter into this country more than 15 thousand children."*
-Father Bryan Walsh, in the Documentary *"Operación Pedro Pan: Volando de
Vuelta a Cuba"*

By the beginning of November 1960 in the Cuban capital, the school year was progressing despite the fact that, in my classroom at the Marist School near the Plaza
Cívica, there were already three students who had sort of disappeared, gone into
exile. They were no longer in the class. I only knew of the fate of one of them, my
cousin Ramoncito, who, as stated in the last chapter, had been sent to Miami independently to seek refuge in the home of a friend of his parents. The other two individuals, Manuel and Luis, must have made personal or familial arrangements
totally unknown to the rest of us. We did not know the why or the how they had
gone or how they were doing.

By that time and unbeknown to anyone I knew, the headmaster of the Ruston
Academy, James Baker, was already getting requests to help get children out of Cuba
from some of the parents of the students at his American school in Havana.(1) His
school had been in operation since the 1930s when Hiram Ruston founded it to
provide a taste of American education in Havana in the hope that some Cuban
children had plans, or could become interested in attending college or furthering
their schooling in the United States. After World War II, when Ruston himself died,

the school was left in the hands of Baker. By 1960, the school was well known and recognized, both in Cuba and the United States. About half of the student body was made up of children of diplomats from the American Embassy in Havana and other foreign delegations. The remainder of the student body was composed of children of Cuban families who were interested in getting their children, upon graduation from secondary school, into an American college or university. The school was bilingual and most classes were conducted in English.

According to testimony rendered by Baker himself(2), one of the first parents who asked about the need to get the students out of Havana on account of the growing social unrest and the likelihood of a civil war in Cuba was David Phillip Atlee. It may not have been known then, but it has been openly disclosed since then that he had worked as far back as the early 1950s as a Central Intelligence Agency (CIA) operative in Latin America and in Cuba. His children were students at Ruston. It is entirely possible that Atlee was involved in the anti-Castro movements in Havana and wanted to safeguard his children from any violence or harm. It was entirely reasonable for someone in his position to try to keep his family and children out of harm's way.

Many sources now report that the original idea for getting children out of Cuba to safety from the likely civil war was to save the children of individuals who were already organized in the fight against Castro and communism.(3) The initial idea for how to protect the children and what to do with them revolved around the possibility of organizing a school in Miami, where the children could continue their education while the civil war was fought in Havana.(4) Once the children were in a safe place, continuing their education, it was reasoned that the parents back in Havana would be able to dedicate themselves to the task of bringing down the Castro regime; that is, to the Cuban Civil War.

The idea of taking children to safety during an armed conflict was not new. When the Nazis began persecuting and incarcerating into concentration camps the Jewish population, many Jewish children were secretly sent out of Nazi Germany into various residential schools in France under the auspices of the *Organisation Pour La Santé et l'Education* (OSE).(5) Those schools and centers functioned as bilingual—French and German—schools, in which teachers and counselors trained and oriented the Jewish children as if their parents were going to live through the Second War II. That is, a great deal of effort was placed on maintaining the values of the parents who had sent their children out to safety. Unfortunately, most of their parents died in the concentrations camps. It is also worthwhile to note that some of those residential schools for Jewish children in France were bombed, attacked with chemical agents, and finally overrun by the Nazis when they entered France. Most of those children survived, but they never saw their parents again.

In the context of the various scenarios that could be considered to safeguard the children—keep them out of harm's way—and, at the same time, continue to provide support for their physical, emotional, and intellectual growth and development, one requirement was common to all of them: For the children to be moved from Havana to Miami, they all had to have an American visa, preferably a student visa. Obviously, that issue had to be taken up with the American Embassy in Havana and the State Department in Washington. And by then, the fall of 1960, the issue was *ipso facto*, going to have to be cleared in one way or another by the Cuban government. The government had already placed requirements and restrictions on the specific documentation required to depart from Cuba and how much money anyone could take out of Cuba. A number of Cuban government requirements, besides having a valid passport, were already enforced for departure from the island by any Cuban citizen.

It is understandable that while Baker was receiving all these requests in Havana, he was not sure how all of this would play out in the United States. Therefore, in late November 1960, Baker flew to Miami to find out.(5) He found that the local situation in Miami regarding unaccompanied Cuban children was already recognized as a formidable challenge. Reporter Juanita Greene had dedicated a full article in the *Miami Herald* to the Cuban children's issue. According to community leaders, just in terms of the educational needs, the situation of the Cuban children in Miami posed an insurmountable challenge to both the Dade County Public Schools and the parochial schools of the Diocese of Miami.

In this context, Mr. Baker met with Father Brian Walsh.(7) Father Walsh was the head of Catholic Charities for the Diocese of Miami. They discussed the need for a system, through which the Cuban children were to be assisted out of Havana and received in the Miami area. Remember, an exit from Havana required an American visa, preferably a student visa. A student visa required not only the involvement of the American embassy in Havana, but also an approved school(8) that would accept the student in question. At the time, they must not have had any particular existing school in mind that would be suitable for the proposed Cuban immigrant children. Otherwise, they would not have discussed the possibility of organizing a new school. Unfortunately, they did not think that they had time to set up that mechanism.(9) What was clear with regard to the requirements of the U.S. State Department was that the children had to have a visa. Furthermore, since the very beginning, American officials thought that the children would be coming without their parents. Therefore, they were in need of an established social service agency to accept the children upon their arrival on American soil.(10)

Initially, the agreement was to have Baker run the operation in Havana and Father Walsh its counterpart in Miami. It was, since its inception at the Ruston Academy and its connections in Miami, a secret operation. By definition already, it was an international, secret deal. Initially, and during most of its existence, it had no public name. However, by the end of 1960, it was already known to some as Operation Pedro Pan.(11)

In terms of the secrecy of Operation Pedro Pan and its name, it is worthwhile to note that eventually when Baker left Havana in January 1961, the Havana side of the operation was left in the hands of a British Embassy officer, Penny Powers, and two Cubans—Polita and Mongo Grau.(12) It is remarkable that even Polita Grau admitted much later that, while in Havana, she did not know the work she was doing to assist children to get off the island was named Operation Pedro Pan.(13) The term Operation Pedro Pan may have originated informally by some of the CIA operatives in Havana, but somehow, despite the lack of similarities in the travels to "Neverland" and going into exile, it stuck. Until his death, then Monsignor Walsh claimed that the name had been given to the operation of assisting children out of Cuba into safety by the press. Indeed, it was the *Cleveland Plain Dealer* in Ohio that first published the term Operation Pedro Pan in connection with the Cuban children's exodus in the spring of 1962.(11)

While Mr. Baker and Father Walsh were concerned about the secrecy and international intrigue around the Cuban children, at home in Havana, we were still visiting friends from time to time. It must have been at around the beginning of December, perhaps something to do with Cuban Doctor's Day, the birth date of Dr. Carlos J. Finlay on December 3, that we were invited to have a Sunday lunch at Joaquín's and Lily's place in the Fontanar area. Fontanar was located on the airport highway past Altahabana—where we lived—and before the town of Rancho Boyeros and the airport proper for Havana. My father Antonio, my mother María Luisa, and I were among the guests at Joaquín's place that day. We had known Joaquín's family for a long time. They were our neighbors on San Francisco Street in the Lawton neighborhood before they had moved to Fontanar, where they had a new home built in the late fifties.

To our surprise, there were in attendance at that luncheon several people we did not know. While my immediate attention turned to the daughters and son of Joaquín and his wife, Lily, the older folks sat down and began talking and munching on various treats while sipping a *mojito* or two. By the time lunch arrived, we all sat down at a long table, especially put together for the occasion on their patio. I remember my father was offered one of the seats at the head of the long table. At the other end, there was a man dressed in the olive-green uniform of the Rebel Army with various insignia. He was the patriarch of the other family invited that Sunday for lunch and was seated at the "opposite pole" of the table.

As the guests were eating, the issue of medicine and medical advances in the world became a topic of discussion. My father took one side of the issue, while at the other end of the long table, Comandante Fernando Flores Ibarra took the other side of the issue. It will be remembered that in 1960, there were only two poles in the world, the Soviet and the American poles. At that particular time, those two theoretical geopolitical poles had turned into two real poles in front of us—my father against Comandante Flores.

My father argued that American medicine was more advanced than Soviet medicine. He pointed out that already, in 1960, a cardiologist in New York could have an electrocardiogram tracing transmitted by telephone to Los Angeles for review by a colleague. Comandante Flores argued that this treatment was only for the rich classes. He pointed out that there were people dying from heart attacks in New York because they could not afford to go to the doctor. He went on to mention that the infant mortality in Mississippi was five times higher than what it was in Cuba. My father went on to share his experience with the medical equipment that had been part of the Soviet exhibit in February when Anastas Mikoyan, the Soviet Vice Premier, had visited Cuba. Back then, my dad and I and a group of my peers from the Marist School had visited the exhibit. As it turns out, the entire display of medical equipment in the Soviet exposition of 1960 had been donated to the Military Hospital. My father testified in front of Comandante Flores that the equipment, in great measure, was not functioning properly and that by the summer of 1960, the surgical instruments had all been discarded because of rust.

Comandante Flores mentioned as a possibility that the tropical weather in Cuba may have been a factor in the spoilage of the surgical equipment. The Comandante went on to discuss the importance of recognizing the equality of all men and women. My father went on to recognize that all human beings are not exactly the same biologically. He pointed out that the syndrome of sickle cell anemia is most common in persons with a genetic history of African or Mediterranean ancestry, whether they were actually black or not.

While all of these arguments were going on back and forth, most of the people at the table were not eating or enjoying themselves anymore. We were all looking to one end of the table or the other as the arguments flew between the poles. The arguments had escalated to the point that my mother appeared very upset. She later commented on our way home that she was very sorry that we had ever joined Joaquín's family on that particular occasion. I am not sure that we stayed for coffee or anything else. Somehow, my mother managed to have my father disengage from the situation and we left. Joaquín did come out with us to the car and tried to settle down my dad, who kept arguing about the medical issues discussed at the table. It was then that he asked Joaquín who exactly was this Comandante Flores. The three of us learned that he was assistant attorney general (*asistente al fiscal general*) of the revolutionary government. He was assigned to La Cabaña Prison, where he conducted numerous revolutionary trials, in which hundreds were sent to *el paredón*. Soon thereafter, in 1961, he acquired the nickname, *Charco de Sangre* (pool of blood). As it turned out, Flores had been a neighbor and a friend of Joaquín's since before the revolution. Here we have another sign of the division within Cuban families and friends. The division, it turned out, of the entire nation.

On our way home to Altahabana, while my father was being admonished by my mother to be more careful about what he discussed and with whom, I listened silently and was glad that I had not taken part in any discussions while at Joaquín's house.

At this point, I was already in agreement with my father on the fact that the revolution had turned communist and the Cuban government under Fidel Castro was dictatorial and verging on fully totalitarian. In fact, by then, without my mother's knowledge, my father was involved in an anti-Castro organization, the nature or name of which I never knew. However, I knew that he had hidden explosives and various guerrilla artifacts in the closet of what we called the *cuarto del medio* (the middle room), where we had an extra bed and storage for supplies for his medical office. I only found this out by accident, when I came across a box with what turned out to be the makings of a bomb in the closet. My friends and I were looking at names of medications and trying to figure out what chemicals were in them when we found the explosives in a box. When I asked my father about it, he said that it was something that his group of anti-Castro forces was preparing to place in a water plant. He asked me to keep the secret, and only now after fifty-five years, do I dare mention it. Here is another division. In the same household, in which all three agreed politically with the same fundamental issues, there was secrecy and a division of information.

Obviously, as part of the divisions that were evident in Havana already, there was a lot of mistrust. My father was using his own home to hide anti-government war materiel without any open discussion about it. In similar fashion, the information regarding the movement to spare Cuban children from the envisioned civil war was also officially clandestine, but by its nature and the desperate need to seek safe haven for the youngsters, its ways and means spread quickly to all who were interested.

As the information spread about the possibility of safeguarding children from the atrocities of a civil war and revolution, other Cuban parents—not only those who had students at the Ruston Academy—were privy to Operation Pedro Pan, although they did not know it by that name. In a matter of weeks and months, parents of students in all private schools, religious or non-religious, became aware of the possibility of sending their children out of Cuba and into a safe haven for the duration of the civil war.

At that time, the Cuban revolutionary government had already enacted regulations that prohibited Cubans from having American dollars. In fact, having American currency was punishable under revolutionary law. Cubans were only allowed to purchase a ticket to leave the country in American dollars that were supposed to be delivered to the travel agency or airline in the form of a United States money order for the exact amount of the ticket purchased. It should be pointed out that the need to have the purchase amount of the airline ticket in American dollars in the form of a U.S. money order was also enforced for tickets bought from Cuban airlines.

In order to leave Cuba, there was obviously the need to have a Cuban passport and an American visa if the traveler was going to the United States. But this was not all. Cubans were also, at that time, asked to obtain a departure document from the *Policía Nacional Revolucionaria* (PNR), or specifically from the *Departamento Técnico de Investigaciones de la PNR* (DIER), that is the technical department of the revolutionary national police. The document, known as a *vigencia,* was in the form of a yellowish card which certified that the bearer whose photograph appeared on it was allowed to leave the national territory of Cuba.

In summary, to depart from Cuba in 1960, anyone had to procure a passport, a visa, a U.S. money order and the *vigencia,* the special police permit to depart. Minors who were traveling alone also needed a notarized document, in which their parents gave permission for the minor to depart to wherever they were traveling.

At the time I am presently describing, the *vigencia* was the most limiting factor to anyone leaving Cuba, even if they had someone in the United States who would assist them by getting a U.S. money order for the amount of the ticket. While the *vigencia* was given to students without delay, it was withheld from parents, especially those parents who were involved in any of the professions, including the medical profession. Medical professionals had to have all of the requirements, same as everyone else, plus a certificate from the Ministry of Health attesting to the fact that they were allowed to depart from Cuba.

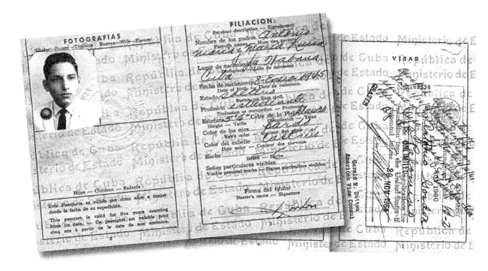

Author's Cuban passport and American tourist visa

OCTAVIO J. SMITH Y FOYO
ABOGADO Y NOTARIO
EMPEDRADO 217, HABANA

DOCTOR OCTAVIO JORGE SMITH Y FOYO, Abogado y Notario del Colegio y Distrito de esta Capital con fija residencia en la misma en Empedrado # 217, en esta Ciudad.

Doy Fé:De que en este acto comparecen ante mí, los Señores D .ANTONIO M.GORDON Y OSORIO,y Sra. MARIA LUISA PALOMINO Y QUESADA,naturales y ciudadanos de Cuba,mayores de edad,Médico y de su casa,casados entre sí,y vecinos de Calle C #651,Alta habana,los que debidamente instruidos por mí,el Notario,sobre el delito de perjurio y de las sanciones al mismo señaladas,juran solemnemente la certeza absoluta de los siguientes extremos.

A)Que se nombran y son de las generales consignadas en esta acta.

B)Que autorizan plenamente a su menor hijo nombrado ANTONIO MARIA RAMON ELADIO GORDON Y PALOMINO,de quince años de edad,estudiante y de su mismo domicilio,para que pueda salir de viaje, fuera del Territorio Nacional y trasladarse al extranjero y en especial a la Ciudad de Miami, Estados Unidos de Norte América y residir o habitar temporal o permanentemente en dicho lugar.

Leido íntegramente este documento por los comparecientes en uso de sus derechos,de ratifican en su contenido,en especial en la autorización y consentimiento concedido a su menor hijo de ambos,y firman conmigo,el Notario,que de ello de conocerlos por sus nombres y apellidos y sus demás generales por sus dichos,de todo lo expuesto doy fé.-En la Habana a 5 de E n e r o de 1961. Enmendado-Altahabana-Vale- Enmendado-Enero)Vale-

D .Antonio M.Gordon Osorio

María Luisa Palomino Quesada

Dr.Octavio J.Smith y Foyo

Affidavit prepared by a Cuban lawyer documenting the permission of parents for a child to leave the island alone

Arguments in our classroom at the Marist School near the *Plaza Cívica* in the month of December progressed to the point that the debates in the student council became more vigorous. The latest issue to be taken up was the Urban Reform. One of the students in the class, Roberto González, argued vehemently that his father, a male nurse, had invested since the early fifties in a couple of small houses. He rented them out and had planned that the income from his investment would help with his retirement and the university expenses of his children. Roberto's argument was very straightforward. He was representing a middle class family. Why should the revolutionary state, or any state for that matter, confiscate a property from its— up to that moment—legitimate owners? This question was particularly difficult to answer in a country where, at that time, there was no representative government or a parliament. The government was Fidel Castro and his cabinet.

What did the Urban Reform entail? The Urban Reform had nationalized all rental properties in Cuba. That is right. All properties that were being rented became the property of the revolutionary government. The rationale for such a law was that when you rent a property you are enslaving the occupants and they never become owners. Through the Urban Reform, the individuals living in any rented apartment, house, or dwelling, were from then on to pay 10% of their salary to the Urban Reform Ministry! So, Roberto's argument had to do with his family's livelihood. Everyone in the class agreed as Roberto had argued; his father did not steal those properties. In fact, he bought the lots of land one by one and then had the homes built by a friend of his who had a construction company. His father even labored himself to help build the houses.

By that time, there were not many in the class who were fervently in favor of the revolution. Perhaps, fortunately, Cosme, the one who became a *miliciano,* was not there that day. At the end of the period, the entire class was questioning why the houses had been confiscated.

No one dared raise the question of who would be in charge of maintaining those houses, apartments, and dwellings after they were confiscated. Not one of us thought back then that the entire city of Havana would look like a victim of a bombardment years later. But then, we were too young and inexperienced to know or to anticipate the long-term consequences of the revolutionary measures being imposed on us and Cuban society. In a certain way, however, we Cuban adolescents who were too young and immature were arguing, not from our own perspectives and observations, but from the perspectives of our parents and teachers, from whom we had learned the values and principles that at the time we defended as our own. Interestingly, despite the fact that we were in full adolescence trying to

Cosme del Peso, Marist School Yearbook, 1960

exert our own independence, most of us sought refuge in our families and their values when confronted with the radically changing culture on the island.

I do not know how my parents found out that we had discussed these Urban Reform issues in the classroom, but they did. It could have been because we were so loud that students in the classroom next door, the third year of the Cuban *bachillerato*, heard us arguing points back and forth. A couple of the third year students lived in Altahabana. Who knows! I do not know why, but to complicate matters, that night two police cruisers began circling the block where we lived. My mother saw the police cars and became very fearful that one of them was going to stop and request that I accompany them for interrogation. That had been the way in which the Batista military intelligence had arrested my dad on September 10, 1957, five days after the failed attempt to oust Batista by Naval and Air Force officers in connection with the *Auténtico* opposition party. My mother turned off the lights in the house and asked that I remain inside and silent. Our dog, Poppy, a Boston terrier, kept unusually quiet, as if he knew the seriousness of my situation. My father was not home at that time. Eventually, a few hours later, the police cars stopped going around our block.

My parents' patience with me was running very thin. I already had a passport. When my father came out of jail during the Batista regime in 1958, I got a new passport. My mother had her passport updated then and my dad's passport was lost. In fact, it was not until February of 1959 that he got his passport back when the revolutionary authorities were cleaning up the offices of the SIM. Irenaldo García Baez had retained my father's passport at the SIM. Even if we had wanted to, we could not have become exiles back then.

In preparation for the inevitable, we went to the American embassy and were interviewed by a consular officer by the name of Mr. Sutton. An American tourist visa was issued for each of us on November 29, 1960. By December, they were already, without telling me, arranging to get a U.S. money order from the United States. Remember that it was a time of secrecy and divisions within Cuban families. They knew, but I did not know, yet. It would not be until they had the money order that they took me to have my picture taken for the *vigencia*.

Sometime in the fall of 1960, a new *bola* was talked about in my family circle after it had made its rounds in Havana. I say a new *bola* because there were many such rumors that spread through the slopes of the city and from person to person like a ball or *bola* that comes down the street and keeps on rolling. The *bolas* were thought to be part of the psychological war that was being waged against the Cuban population by the Castro government. Some *bolas* were like an epidemic or some

Dic. 16 / 60
Fecha

AC- 10181 H.
Clave No.

30065 / 59
No. Expte. Ppte.

27865
No. Pasaporte

EL CIUDADANO: Antonio Maria Ramon Gordón y Palomino

de **15** años, empleado en Estudiante

y vecino de Calle C # 651. Rpto. Al-tahabana. Habana

está autorizado para abandonar el Territorio Nacional a su entera libertad. (Válido por un año, a partir fecha expedición).

Jefe Ngdo. Vigencias Pasaportes DTI (PNR)

VISTO BUENO: Jefe Dpto. Técnico Investigaciones (P.N.R.)

Vigencia - document issued by the Revolutionary Police required to leave the island sort of contagion that could hurt you or make you behave in a certain fashion so that you would not want to be struck by it. Some could even turn malignant. For example, if you reacted to a *bola* and it turned out that it was intended as a trap to capture those who in one way or another opposed the communist government, you were immediately caught and punished.

One *bola* that was circulating was extremely worrisome to families, and it did not get started out of thin air. It began with a written document purported to be a law that was already being readied by the revolutionary government for Fidel Castro's signature.(13) It will be recalled that there was no congress and revolutionary laws were prepared, written, and approved by the council of ministers, which was the revolutionary cabinet headed by Castro himself.(14)

The new law was labeled *patria potestad,* because it stipulated that the parents of minors would no longer be the ones who decided about schooling, nutrition, residence, and whatever else parents usually decide for their children. Instead, the state, in this case, the communist revolutionary state under Castro's rule, would be the first and most important deciding body on the schooling of all children, where they would live, and what and how their needs were to be met. It was argued that in this way, the children would be more prepared to face their future in the communist Cuban republic.

This proposed law was certain to take the entire country in the direction of communism. However, there were some issues that immediately caught the attention of some Cubans with regard to the veracity and validity of the new *bola* on the *patria potestad.* For one thing, the minister who presumably signed it was not in Cuba at the time that the *bola* began circulating in Havana. Since the minister was known to be in Japan at the time, some argued that he could not have signed the law, because the signature portion of the law stated that it was signed in Havana on a date in which he was known to not even be in the city. The second issue was more general and could be understood by most Cubans who were exposed to this *bola.* At the time, it was well known that there was a great deal of communist infiltration in the revolutionary government. In the fall of 1960, there was already a great deal of enmity toward the United States and anything American in the media and in government circles. It was also obvious that the revolutionary government was friendly toward the Soviet Union and communism. However, at that time, the revolution had not yet been declared publically to be a communist revolution. This made the *bola* seemed premature and therefore suspecious. The *patria potestad,* in the minds of many, would be the equivalent of declaring the revolutionary government a communist government.

In fact, it was not until much later, the day before the April 17, 1961 invasion, that Castro declared that he had been a communist and the revolution was a communist revolution. Therefore, in a way, the presumed new law jumped the gun on the important issue of declaring openly that the revolution was communist. In terms of the exodus of unaccompanied Cuban children, the Bay of Pigs Invasion and everything that surrounded it proved to be a watershed moment. The emergence of the *patria potestad bola* did not seem to have a marked effect on the actual departure of children out of Cuba.(15)

There is one important aspect of the Cuban reality lived by both parents and children during this phase of the revolution that has not been documented well enough. I refer to the fact that each set of parents, each one of the children, each family, had their own personal experience through which they individually were in a position to decide if they would send their children out of the country or not. Carlos Eire has said it in a most convincing manner, when he assumed the position of the parents and asked, "If I am traveling in a train that is doomed, do I throw my children to one side or the other of the train in order to give them a chance to survive? And what about if I know that if I throw them to the right they may have a chance to live, be free, and develop. And what about if I know that if I throw them to the left side they may survive, but only to be slaves of the state where they will develop."(16) In either direction, the question still remained as to when would parents be convinced enough that the "train was doomed?" Most Cuban parents decided to throw their children to the right side of the train to either the United States, Spain, or another Western country, although some 800 children were sent to Russia, most of them willingly. But that decision was not made on rumors, threats alone, or *bolas,* despite the fact that there was a psychological war going on as the violence increased in what turned out to be a truncated Cuban civil war. In my opinion and after knowing the details of many Pedro Pans and others who were sent to Spain and some to Mexico, that decision was invariably made when the personal situation of those parents and those families was such that it was obvious to them that it would be better for the children to "be thrown out of the train" than wait for the final catastrophe.

The case of Candy Sosa is worth remembering because it is a documented case where parents acted on their own situation and experiences. Candy was ten years old and back then she was sent to a corner *bodega* (grocery store) Havana neighborhood to buy some milk. While she was there, Fidel Castro and some of his entourage walked into the place. This was not unusual in 1959 and 1960. I remember seeing Castro and his men come into Altahabana where we lived at the time and standing in the outside yard of one of the houses on the corner of C Street and 10th

Street talking to the neighbors and admiring the quality of construction of the properties in that section of Havana. The neighborhood had been built by the San Martín brothers who had worked in Cuba's Ministry of Public Works in the 1940s under Carlos Prío Socorra's presidency. In fact, if there would have been no coup d'état in 1952, one of the San Martín brothers may have eventually been president of Cuba.

But going back to the *bodega* near Candy's house, the neighbors told Castro that Candy could sing and sing well. So Fidel picked her up and asked her to sing. Candy did sing a song and then Fidel said a few words pointing out that the future of Cuba depended on little girls like Candy. Then he left with his entourage. Candy thought that was the end of the experience.

A few hours afterwards, some armed men with Rebel Army green fatigues appeared in Candy's home. What happened next, Candy relates in this manner: "They had decided that they were going to send me to Russia to study to become an opera singer."(17) That is when her parents said, "No, she is not going anywhere!" Obviously, it took guts for her parents to say no to Castro's men when they knew that they could do something to Candy, even take her by force. Therefore, it was totally reasonable for her parents to "throw her off the train as soon as possible." Candy became one the many children sent to the United States by her parents via the Operation Pedro Pan.

One other point needs to be made regarding the *bola* of the *patria potestad*. The late Professor Juan Clark, a sociologist who specialized in the Cuban revolution and Cuban affairs, has explained that the revolutionary government did not have to have a law through which the state took the responsibility of the natural parents in the decision making process of anything that mattered to their children.(18) They did not need a law because they had a totalitarian state where, not only all the resources were in the hands of the revolutionary government, but all the schools and recreational facilities, as well. In a matter of a few years, for each student there was a cumulative student record composed of traditional school grades, plus ideological attitudes, political issues, work habits, and many other highly personal details.(19) That record would accompany each student from day one in the Cuban school system up to the time the student finished in a technical, vocational, or university program. The government had access to this and could do whatever it liked with the children. Therefore, regarding the *patria potestad*, what originally began as a *bola*, in due time turned out to be a matter of fact, but not in the form of a law. It was part of the fabric of the new and "revolutionary" system of government and of a "socialist" society. It was the Cuban version of totalitarian communism. The future of each Cuban was uncertain, but the country was doomed.

CHAPTER 5

1961: AÑO DE LA EDUCACIÓN

"The pattern of training is similar to that used by many totalitarian governments.
It includes indoctrination in schools, on radio and on television, and in the press;
also military training from 7 years of age; a hate campaign, this time directed
against the United States, the organization of work brigades of boys from 14 to 18;
and meetings and fiestas, all with a political purpose."
-Ruby Hart Phillips

Since January 1, 1959, each year in Cuba had had a goal, a reason to exist and a target to achieve. In that manner, 1959 was termed the Year of the Liberation. Then 1960 was named the Year of the Agrarian Reform. And, when 1961 rolled in, it was to become the "Year of Education."

There was not much in the way of enthusiasm during the Christmas holidays at the end of 1960 in Havana. Very few, if any, of the houses in Altahabana had any colored lights or other Christmas decorations up. The situation contrasted with the year before. In 1959, most houses had some sort of adornment for the holidays. My father added to our display on that year a rather large Cuban flag illuminated with a floodlight by the coconut tree in the middle of the front yard, along with multicolored lights and signs wishing passersby *Feliz Navidad*.

However, by the end of 1960, at least in the environs of our home, there was no joy in the season. It could not have been a happy season for some other families, since the first children that left Cuba via Operation Pedro Pan left the Havana airport on December 26, 1960.(1) I would be following fairly soon. I had a valid Cuban passport and a tourist visa, type B-1, issued by the American Embassy in Havana. My father and mother also had their passports and the same type of visa. In November 1960, we had all applied for the *vigencia*, the special police permit to leave the island. My mother and I obtained the *vigencia* on December 16, 1960. My father's was denied. When all of these issues were occurring in real time, I was not aware that both my father and mother had applied for the *vigencia,* but only my mother had gotten it. This pattern of ignoring an application or denying the expedition of the *vigencia* was not a random process. It was a malicious practice designed to divide the Cuban families who were seeking to find refuge outside Cuba. The bottom line always favored the departure of the children and adolescents, particularly if they were members of families in the middle class. The tearing apart of the Cuban social fabric was apparently on track, as the totalitarian communist forces secured their power over all aspects of life in the island.

Unbeknownst to me, my parents received a U.S. money order for $20 when my cousin Muñeca came back to Havana from Tampa. She had returned to take exams at the Universidad de Villanueva. While at the university, she obtained a recommendation letter for me from an officer of the Catholic university addressed to Sister Miriam in Miami at the *Centro Hispano Católico.* I had no idea who she was or what the *Centro* was. I was to deliver the letter to her myself upon my arrival in Miami.

Soon after the beginning of the New Year, the United States announced that it was breaking diplomatic relations with the revolutionary government of Cuba. On January 3, 1961(2), the American Embassy in Havana was closed. From then on, the Swiss Embassy would handle American affairs, translations, and certifications in Cuba. However, the Swiss were not to provide American visas or other consular services. The lack of an American Embassy in Havana to be able to issue American visas, especially student visas, immediately became a nightmare for James Baker and Father Brian Walsh and their secret Operation Pedro Pan.(3) It became a very serious issue, since all the children expected to leave Cuba had to have a visa in order to depart from Havana. If anyone had not obtained an American visa prior to the closing of the embassy, how could they be taken to a safe haven in the United States while the civil war was fought?

Fortunately, the impasse regarding the lack of American diplomatic representation in Cuba was solved rather quickly through connections between the U.S. State Department and Father Walsh in Miami.(4) The department agreed to provide the status of "visa waiver" to any child between the age of six and sixteen who wished to travel from Cuba to the United States in the care of Catholic Charities of the Diocese of Miami. This was a sort of safe conduct in a time of war in the form of a simple letter, in which Father Walsh stated that the bearer or designated traveler was issued a "visa waiver." That is, essentially, any Cuban national from the age of six to sixteen did not need a standard tourist or student visa to enter the United

UNIVERSIDAD CATOLICA
DE SANTO TOMAS DE VILLANUEVA
APARTADO NO. 6 · TELF. 89-1944
MARIANAO, HABANA, CUBA

12 de enero de 1961

Mi querida Sr. Miriam: El portador Antonio Gordon Palomino, 4to. año de
Bachillerato, tiene que trasladarse a ésa. Es un buen alumno, pertenece
a Acción Católica y responsable en todos los sentidos.

Todo lo que puedas hacer por él, te lo agradeceré grandemente.

Felicito ex corde a la The most outstanding woman of 1960 in Miami. No
a tí sino a Dios hay que dar las gracias.

Recuerdos a los Padres y a las Sisters,

P. Medina ora

Recommendation letter brought to the U.S. by the author

States. The Cuban government, although it had already put in place a number of hurdles for anyone wishing to leave the island, seemed to immediately accept the visa waivers and never questioned them. Presumably, Cuban authorities were not made aware of the program administered by Father Walsh, the secret Operation Pedro Pan. At the end of the day, the visa waivers for Cuban children were issued by Father Walsh through the authority given to him by the U. S. Department of State and the implied consent of the Castro government.

At this point in time, Cuban parents were not given *vigencias* as easily as their children, and also there was no way for a parent to be able to leave Cuba with a visa waiver from Father Walsh because of the age restriction. In fact, at that time, the U.S. State Department was very firm in that anyone between seventeen and eighteen years of age had to undergo a special screening, for fear that they might be Castro's spies. However, soon thereafter, the International Rescue Committee (IRC), with offices in various points in the United States, was authorized by the State Department to issue visa waivers for adults in Cuba who were seeking refuge in the United States. It should be mentioned here, that the IRC was revealed later on to have been operated by the CIA.(5)

Terrible *bolas* saying that Cuban children were going to be sent to the Soviet Union were spread in Havana in the fall of 1960. In January 1961, an interchange of Russian students for Cuban students was announced.(6) Some 800 to 1,000 Cuban children were to be sent to Russia during the initial phase of this exchange, as agreed upon by the U.S.S.R. and the revolutionary government of Fidel Castro.

But, going back to my situation, I had all documents necessary to depart except for the airplane ticket. No one knew the exact date of my departure until forty-eight hours earlier when the ticket became available. I was asked to keep the information as secret as possible. Only some of my closest friends at school knew of my plans to leave.

Very early in the morning on the day I left, Friday, January 13, 1961, as we were finishing packing my suitcase—only one suitcase was allowed per person departing Cuba—my father told me that he had hidden the amount of fifty dollars in American currency in the top inner cover of the suitcase. He reminded me that the revolutionary government did not allow anyone to have American currency, much less take it out of Cuba.

Everyone in Cuba was aware that since the early 1960s, the revolutionary government was confiscating any American currency or what they called *divisas*—exchangeable currency. My father proposed a plan; I would declare only six U.S. dollars as my capital leaving Cuba, hoping such a small amount would not be confiscated. It wasn't. Since I could not buy a ticket to Miami with the twenty dollars provided by the money order I had received, I was using the money order to leave Cuba to Key West on a Cuban airliner, Aerovias Q, on their routine flight from Havana to Key West. The price of the roundtrip ticket was exactly twenty dollars. I was to land in Key West and purchase a bus ticket in the Greyhound station in downtown Key West to travel to Miami. Once there, I was to telephone my cousin Ramoncito, who was residing at Lola's house.

I finished packing the suitcase, took my 8 mm Kodak Brownie Camera in one hand and my daily missal (a Catholic prayer book) in the other, and we were on our way. We arrived very early in the morning at the airport. The description of that last ride to leave home and parents behind has been offered by many of the Pedro Pans who have written their memories. My trip to the airport was in silence. My mother, I learned afterward, pretended that she did not know about the fifty-dollar contraband in my suitcase, but she did. When we got to the airport, everything seemed peaceful. As the morning progressed, more people arrived at the José Martí International Airport terminal. I remember being in the now famous or infamous *pescera*, a glass-encased room that separated the departing passengers on a given flight from their friends and relatives who were not leaving. There were several *pesceras,* which means fish tank in Spanish, located off the airport's main lobby on the first floor.

My *pescera* was occupied by passengers belonging to two flights. One flight was a Cubana Airlines flight to Mexico City. There were a number of Rebel Army officers in there, some of them *barbudos.* The words *barbudos* literally means "bearded men" in Spanish. The Rebel Army men came down from the Sierra Maestra Mountain Range with beards. At the time, in Cuba a *barbudo* was a revolutionary official. There was also the flight to Key West through Aeorvías Q. Those glass compartments were indeed *pesceras.* I felt that everyone was looking at me and I could not go anywhere. It was important to be patient, despite all the emotions and issues that were going through my head. As I was sometimes sitting and other times standing, I saw my parents on the other side of the glass. They appeared to be confident. I had no knowledge of what was going to occur next.

At that point, in the *pescera* contaminated by the Rebel Army, a man entered from the side of the tarmac and runway. He looked around. I recognized him as the physician who worked the medical station at the airport and a friend of my father's. His name was Dr. Martínez de la Cotera. He had been to our home a couple of times to talk about his trips up north in years past. To my surprise, he came directly toward me and extended his right arm to shake my hand. In his right hand

CUPON DE	R.T. Nº 241357	CUPON DE VUELO	R.T. Nº 241357

IDENTIFICACION
INTRANSFERIBLE

AEROVIAS "Q", S. A.

De ..HAN.. a ..KW..

Y REGRESO

Sr. ANTONIO GORDON

Importe Total ..$... 26.30

"NI TRANSFERIBLES"

Agencia: ....

No es válido para vuelos ni devoluciones.

"NO ENDOSABLE NI REFUNDABLE ONE CUBA"

AEROVIAS "Q", S. A.

De ..KW.. a ..HAN.. R

Válido solamente para un vuelo

Vuelo............ Fecha...............

Importe................ $.. 10.00

Agencia: ....

"NO ENDOSABLE NI CUBA"

La tenencia del presente billete, implica el conocimiento y la aceptación expresa de los términos y condiciones del Contrato, por el cual habrá de regirse el transporte, según consta archivado en la Comisión Nacional de Transportes y exhibido en las Oficinas del Porteador.

No es válido sin el sello oficial.

Round trip airline ticket Havana-Key West

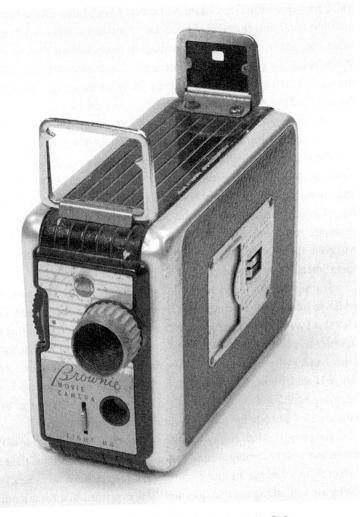

Brownie 8mm movie camera brought by the author in his flight.
Photograph by Manuel Buznego

he had a roll of something. He gave it to me in my right hand. I concealed it immediately; I suspected that it was American money. I had felt the texture of money and when I looked down and saw the green color of the papers that made up the roll, I confirmed my impression. As I greeted him, I transferred the money from my right hand into the right side pocket of my pants, where I left it for the time being. He spoke for a few seconds, perhaps minutes. I do not remember about what. When he left, I sat down, keeping either the Brownie camera or the daily missal on the side of my right thigh to obscure somewhat the bulge caused by the roll of money. I did not get up again until my flight was called:

"*Aerovías Q anuncia la salida del Vuelo 951 con destino a Cayo Hueso.*"

"Q Airways announces the departure of Flight 951 to Key West."

On my way to the plane, as I was departing the exit door from the *pescera*, a Rebel Army official was patting down every passenger. I showed him my camera and my missal and he did not bother me. As I climbed the stairway to the plane's door, I looked back to the see if anyone was up on the balcony, but I was not able to recognize anyone. As it turned out, three of my friends from the Marist school had gone there on that morning to see me depart. However, I did not recognize them when I looked back.

Throughout the weeks since I got my *vigencia* and then the money order with which to purchase the airline ticket, my feelings were rather mixed. On one hand, I felt that I was leaving family and friends behind, but rationalized that I was leaving in order to expedite, somehow, the return of normalcy to Cuban society. On the other hand, I felt excited about the fact that I was traveling alone into a new country, where I could, perhaps, make friends and experience life beyond adolescence before attaining adulthood. At the time when I boarded that airplane on that morning, January 13, I actually felt more adventurous than melancholic.

The plane was half empty. I took a window seat on the left side of the cabin. As the stewards were coming around making sure all passengers had their seatbelts on, one of them asked me if I knew who was going to pick me up in Key West. I asked, "Why are you asking me that question?" He explained that I was a minor and that by international travel regulations, any minor traveling alone would have to be picked up by a responsible adult at the point of arrival. I do not remember what I answered then, but he must have accepted it, because he let me stay on the plane.

As the trip got under way, I saw the area of Santa María del Mar beaches from about 20,000 feet. The plane left the island of Cuba just to the east of where the Cuban Medical Circle (*Círculo Médico Cubano*) club was located. It was there that I spent many a summer day, either playing baseball or at the beach or both.

I did not know it then, but I had departed from Cuba in a historic airplane, the DC-3. As it turns out, the first airline in Latin America to use DC-3s was *Cubana de Aviación*. They used the DC-3s to start their first scheduled international service from Havana to Miami in 1945, precisely the year I was born!

A little later during the flight, the flight attendant again came to me and inquired about who would pick me up at Key West. I told him that the person picking me up was in Miami. Then he gave me a form on which to write the name of the adult who would pick me up. I wrote down the name of my cousin, Ramón de Gordon, his address 779 NW 2 Street, Miami, Florida. I did not tell the attendant that my cousin also was only sixteen years old!

During the flight, I glanced around and the fifteen or so passengers en route seemed to be resting. While no one was walking in the aisle, I took the roll of money Dr. Martínez de la Cotera had given me out of my pocket and placed it inside the 8mm movie camera, it fit in the empty reel where film would go if I were taking movies. I closed it with difficulty, but it did close.

In less than forty minutes we arrived in Key West. The plane landed uneventfully. As I got out and climbed down from the cabin, I saw a uniformed guard standing by the gate where all passengers were filing past to get into the customs area. I approached the officer, a tall man with a military uniform and a hat like the ones worn by Boy Scout leaders. When one of the flight attendants saw that I was standing next to the American officer, he approached me and told me to forget about the requirement of having someone sign or be responsible for me. He signaled that everything was okay.

In the meantime, I had tried to tell the American officer that I was a Cuban refugee and requested to stay in the United States. I have no idea, however, how it sounded or what exactly I said, or what he understood. I do know, however, that the officer just calmly took me by the arm and walked me to the entrance of the customs area, left me there alone, and then stayed behind.

There was no problem whatsoever in the customs area and passport control. After I picked up my suitcase, I went off to the curb. A large taxi cab was going to downtown Key West. I had made the same trip with my parents back in 1954. Although the airport at Key West was different and new now, the general area was known to me from before. Many of the passengers from the Cuban flight were getting into the taxi. I asked for the Greyhound bus station and got a positive response that the taxi was going there. I went to give a tip to the African-American man who was putting my suitcase in the trunk of the vehicle. I did not know how much tip to give him. Then I tried to explain to him in English that "I was giving him a dollar because of the money situation in Cuba." Cuba had little to do with my tipping but the fact was that I gave him a dollar because I pulled that bill from my pocket. He signaled 'yes' with his head, and that was that.

In downtown Key West, I went next to the Greyhound bus station at a counter and asked for a hot dog, a Coca Cola, and some chips. I did not have to open my camera to pay for the lunch. It amounted to about two dollars.

The trip to Miami was uneventful. I took an aisle seat next to a slender woman who seemed to be an actress or a dancer, judging from her looks and attire. She did not talk to me and I did not talk to her. I had spoken enough English for one day, with the airport officer who wore the Boy Scouts type of hat, the taxi man, and the lunch stand attendant.

Upon arriving in Miami, I collected my suitcase and got to a public phone from which I called my cousin. He immediately recognized my voice on the telephone and came over to pick me up with someone who lived with him in Lola's *Cuban Barracón*. Lola welcomed me to her home for the night. I explained to her that I would be going on to Tampa in the next few days, or my Uncle Emilio would come and get me, since my instructions from home in Havana were to be with my Aunt Carmen and my Uncle Emilio. I am sure Lola did not want another unemployed Cuban in her "barracks."

That night I slept in the living room of Lola's house on a sofa bed. In the middle of the night, the sofa bed, for reasons unclear to me, closed its two panels so that for a time I was like a hot dog inside a bun. It did not occur to me that this had anything to do with my first American lunch. I got up and opened the sofa bed again, and thinking that it might occur again, I slept on one of the panels of the sofa, rather than in the middle. In the morning, which was a Saturday, my cousin took me for a walking tour of Miami. We repeated these outings several times during the rest of the weekend.

CHAPTER 6

KEEPING IN TOUCH: THE IMPORTANCE OF THE MAIL

"Hoy casi sin una despedida
Me alejo con el corazón deshecho
Se que es profunda la herida
Que me llevo grabada en el pecho."

"Today almost without a farewell
I leave with a broken heart
I know the wound's depth well
Engraved in my chest as I depart."
-José Azel[6]

It did not take very long for me to begin writing to my parents, relatives, and friends in Havana. From that time onward, and for the next several years, the mail was the most important instrument through which I could feel closer to them. This is the first letter I received after I had left Havana, a letter from my parents:

January 18, 1961
My dear son:

We received your letter and we see from it that you're all right. Here, we are okay. Since yesterday, according to Muñeca, the Marist students are on strike, as well as the students at Edison, and Our Lady of Lourdes. I do not know what is the issue or problem that led the students to go on strike.

---

[6]From Pedazos y Vacíos, a poetry book by José Azel a Pedro Pan child himself, Alexandria Library, Miami 2014, p 31.

Your friend Faura is preparing his papers to go to that country. He continues to do fine with his headaches.

The weather here has been fairly cold since yesterday. I can only imagine that over there the cold is more intense for you.

Muñeca is doing well. On the 29th, Pedroso will present her passport at the DIER for the "vigencia."

If you go to Miami with your uncle, do not forget to go and greet my relatives, the ones I told you about, who are living in there...

Give twenty of the candies you took there to your uncle Emilio.

A kiss from your mother and your father's blessing,

María Luisa and Antonio

The year of education in Cuba had been received by Cuban secondary school students in a most disrespectful manner—a call for a student strike. Muñeca was providing news to my dad about it. The striking students were from at least the various schools in the neighborhood of La Víbora. However, we can assume that other schools were also involved since the Marist School near the Plaza Cívica in El Cerro neighborhood was.(1) My father pretends in the letter that he does not know the "reason as to why the students called for and executed a strike." To appreciate these letters, the reader has to go back to that particular time and place where we were—Havana in civil strife and ongoing revolution in January 1961. There was no trust whatsoever that the mail was privileged. It was widely known that letters, particularly those to the United States, were opened at random, read, and analyzed to find out what was going on and who was writing what.

My classmate Lorenzo wrote a few days later with more detailed information about the student strike with which this memorable year was inaugurated. This is what Lorenzo wrote:

Havana, January 25, 1961
Dear friend:

I write this as I told you.

Last week we skipped classes on Wednesday afternoon, Thursday afternoon, and Friday morning because of the student strike. At our school we had distributed many leaflets announcing the strike. On Thursday morning, we placed a large Cuban flag in the physics

*room with a black bow from the DRE. We also distributed a lot of
information. The principal of the school threw students out of the
place.
In another school, there have been searches and many arrests including teachers, Marist Brothers.
I remain waiting for your reply as soon as possible after you receive
this letter.
Your friend and classmate goodbye,*

*J Izquierdo
PS. I enclose the last pastoral letter.*

From the handwriting and its content, I knew this letter was written and sent
to me by Lorenzo. What he means by "I write this as I told you" is that he had told
me that he was going to write using a pseudonym and would send secret messages
written underneath the stamps. Lorenzo was the most involved of my classmates
in the *Directorio Revolucionario Estudiantil* (DRE). He used a fake name and return
address so as not to be recognized by the censors reviewing the mail. This was his
first letter. The student strike was called by the *Directorio*. He also confirms that
there had been a search of the "other school," that is the Marist School at La Víbora.
I learned much later from the brothers who were at the school at La Víbora at that
time that the *milicianos* were searching for weapons and for a tunnel. They found
no weapons in the school. The tunnel they were looking for supposedly connected
the underground parts of the Marist School with the girls' school nearby, Our Lady
of Lourdes (*Nuestra Señora de Lourdes*). They did not find any such passage, tunnel,
or connection.

Catholic school students had further issues with the *milicia* forces, who were
reported to have cordoned off the main Franciscan church in Old Havana and intervened in the Jesuit seminary at El Calvario and the Franciscan seminary in Santiago de Las Vegas.(2) Since January 1959, the revolutionary government
intervened in houses, businesses, and other properties. First it was argued that the
properties confiscated had been stolen from the people by war criminals. Then
the American-owned businesses were intervened, that is confiscated. The government just took over the properties or businesses from anyone who was not a revolutionary. Then came the confiscation of some Catholic Church properties. These
three properties belonging to the Franciscan and Jesuit orders may have been the
first Church properties the revolution took over and closed. Also at that time, the

offices of the *Acción Católica Cubana* had been occupied by the revolutionary militia.(3)

Going back to my parents' first letter, Faura is another of my classmates at the Marist School. He appears in the photograph published in the 1959 yearbook by the tractor donated to the Agrarian Reform by the school; he is located at the back of the tractor, by the seat. He also lived in Altahabana. When I left, I entrusted the responsibility of running the mimeograph and publishing the leaflets and pamphlets for the anti-communist movement for our school to him. I kept on doing this until a week or so before I left Havana in charge of reproducing leaflets and announcements for the catholic youth organization at our Marist School near the Plaza Cívica since I entered my third year of *bachillerato* in September 1959. One of the first leaflets we placed in each desk of the *bachillerato* classes in 1959 read: *"Fidel nosotros de subimos y nosotros te bajamos."* (Fidel, we raised you and we will bring you down.) Regarding this responsibility, Faura used to say that the whole issue of "printing those documents was a headache." He did not have any head injury or actual headache. As it turned out, it was a "headache" because he did not feel that he could do the job from his home. When we discussed that issue, we agreed that the job would continue to be done from my home, where the equipment was set up. That is what my father is referring to when he writes about Faura's headaches. Interestingly, at that point, Faura appeared to have decided to escape from Havana as written, "He is getting his papers ready to go to that country." In Faura's case, it seems that he may have been more willing to depart once he felt the pressure of working for the anti-Castro movement as he did by printing the leaflets announcing student strikes and the like.

Back in Miami, I called Colonel Eduardo Martín Elena on my father's advice given to me before I left Havana; he had given me his telephone number. My father would refer to Martín Elena as *mis parientes en Miami*, his relatives in Miami, in his letters. I took care of some of my father's errands as soon as I could. Martín Elena was known to my father and, at that time, he was working in the anti-Castro movement. Obviously, I did not know this at the time. I told him that my father had asked me to call him. He recognized his name. Then he asked me about my age. I told him that I had just turned sixteen years old, and he immediately told me to try to get into some sort of school. He could not use me for anything dealing with what he was doing because of my age. He did not say what he was involved in, but I later learned that he was the officer in charge of recruiting young Cubans for the invasion of Cuba. Much later, I also learned that he resigned from that post in the Brigade 2506 at the end of January, 1961.

Faura had been photographed by the Agrarian Reform tractor in our school yard in 1959.
Marist School Yearbook, 1959

Martín Elena had been one of the Cuban Constitutional Army regimental commanders who on March 10, 1952, called President Carlos Prío Socarrás and told him that he did not accept the *coup d'état* perpetrated by Batista and other officers.(4) He pledged his services to the constitutional president. Early that morning, Colonel Martín Elena had assembled his troops at the Matanzas Goicuruía Regiment Number 4 headquarters and told them the same thing—that he did not accept the *coup d'état.* He then asked his troops to be on the alert for further orders.(5) As that day came to an end, the handful of high officers who offered to defend the Constitution of 1940 was left without leadership when Prío Socarrás sought diplomatic asylum in the Mexican Embassy in Havana.

According to my parents' first letter, Muñeca was said to be getting the last of the official government papers to be able to leave Cuba on January 29. Mr. Pedroso had a travel agency (Misiones Tours) located at Misiones Avenue near the presidential palace and was well known to the family. He is the one who sold us the ticket with which I traveled out of Cuba.

Also, I did not bring any "candies" into the United States. I did bring, as I have confessed earlier, extra money smuggled out of Cuba. Some of it was in the suitcase lining and the remainder had been given to me at the *pescera* in the Havana airport. My father wanted to be sure that I was not a financial burden on anyone here in the United States. He knew that my Uncle Emilio and Aunt Carmen had limited reserves and resources. I was asked to give them twenty dollars. I think I did.

Back on the streets of Miami, on Monday morning January 16, I dressed up in my sports jacket and walked down to the Gesu Church. Before I got to the church, I saw ambulating through downtown Miami, some of the personnel that I had seen working in the American Embassy in Havana. That was not the only observation that got my attention that morning. I experienced an eerie feeling when I saw, as I mentioned before, a high officer of the Batista regime's military intelligence (SIM). I recognized him immediately, Irenaldo García Baez. My father had been imprisoned by him back in 1957 during the revolution.

I walked as if I really knew downtown Miami well. My cousin had explained that Avenues ran north-south and the east-west boundary was Miami Avenue. Streets ran east-west and the north-south boundary was Flagler Street. Furthermore, I had already been around downtown through the walking tours my cousin gave me during the weekend.

I had with me the letter I was to deliver to Sister Miriam. She received me without any hesitation, despite the fact that I had no appointment or anything like that. She was a petite woman, obviously dressed in her religious habit. She received me at her office and I sat down in front of her across her large wooden desk. She read the letter from Universidad de Villanueva and then asked me if I wanted to go to school or to work. I explained to her in Spanish that I wanted to work so that I could bring my parents over from Cuba. She seemed to agree with that logic. Then she made a phone call right in front of me and, in a matter of one hour, there was someone there who was picking me up to take me to the *Miami News*. Immediately, I thought what a great idea it was for Sister to send me to the newspaper! I had an inclination for journalism since I was in the Marist *bachillerato* and the Catholic Action organization. Furthermore, a classmate of mine who lived in Altahabana, Juan Pella, had planned to write a weekly newsletter for the urbanization using his typewriter and mimeograph stencils which we were to run at the Marist school. I truly thought Sister had a great idea!

A man from the newspaper came to pick me up in a station wagon. We arrived at the *Miami News* building near the Miami River. It was then that I found out that I would be working selling newspapers, rather than in the area of journalism. I tried to convince myself that, despite my opinion that journalists were above such things, they are in business—at least in part—to sell newspapers. The man who was to be my supervisor signaled for me to take off my jacket. He gave me an apron to put change and collect the money from costumers and drove me to the corner of Brickel Avenue at SE 8th Street. There was a brick building at the Northwest corner of that intersection where a radio station was located. I set up my supply of newspapers on that corner.

I do not remember getting any particular instructions. If my supervisor had given me any, I do not think I would have understood them anyway. My English was not that good yet, since I had never been in a position where I had to speak it to make myself understood. But, I had taken the job and it seemed adventurous enough. So, immediately I started trying to sell newspapers crying out, "Paper, paper, *Miami News*!"

This is how I made money: The newspaper boy would earn two cents for every daily paper he sold and five cents for every Sunday paper. At the end of the first day, I had made a dollar and change. In retrospect, this activity may have been illegal, since I did not even have a social security number or an immigrant visa. However, I felt very proud to have been able to make some money in Miami. Therefore, I invited my cousin to eat at the Royal Castle just across and north from *Cielito Lindo*, the Dade County Court House building. At the time, the *Cielito Lindo* was an iconic building in downtown Miami. My cousin was one of the many unemployed in Lola's *Cuban Barracón*. Needless to say, we had a very light dinner—*chili con carne* and two small hamburgers—purchased by most of the money I had earned selling newspapers. Then we walked back to Lola's house.

The next day on the job, I found out that my inefficiency with handling the money could turn out to be in my favor. Some customers from buses signaled to me that they wanted to buy a newspaper. A few times, a customer would hand me a dollar bill, I would hand them the paper, and while I was trying to get the right change to them, the bus would leave as the traffic light changed. In essence, that costumer had paid one dollar for the newspaper. I felt bad for the customer, but thought that it was good for my finances.

While in Miami, I saw—besides my cousin—two of my classmates who had already arrived in the United States. First we met with Manuel Revilla, who was working for the Western Union, delivering telegrams in the downtown area on a bicycle. He looked well and did not speak very much about what kind of living arrangements he had or if he was going to school at all. The other classmate that we saw in Miami was Luis Díaz. He was looking for employment. It was Luis who told us about the rations that were being given to refugees at the Gesu Church. At the time, we each got one large can of tomato soup every day.

After a couple of days, I decided to follow my parent's advice and traveled to Tampa via Greyhound bus, despite the fact that my "career in journalism" would be left behind. I called my uncle and aunt and advised them of my decision. My cousin Ramoncito stayed at Lola's *Cuban Barracón*.

I took an evening bus and arrived in Tampa in the morning. My Aunt Carmen and Uncle Emilio were living in Tampa with Morejón and his wife, Katie. Morejón, as previously mentioned, had been my Uncle Emilio's protégé in Cuba and had left the island in January 1959.

My uncle had plans all along, if the situation in Cuba remained the same, to go up to New York where his son Emilito was already working. Uncle Emilio, Emilito and his wife, María Ofelia, had left in the summer of 1960 for Spain, where Emilito had been accepted to take a post graduate architecture course. Once he completed the course, they had decided to go to New York. However, while Emilito found work in New York, Uncle Emilio came down to Tampa in order to be closer to Havana and to wait for his wife, Carmen, and his daughter Muñeca, who had remained in Havana when he had gone to Spain. Aunt Carmen and Muñeca traveled directly to Tampa from Havana via National Airlines. Muñeca initially had come to Tampa with Aunt Carmen, but had returned to Havana in order to take some exams at Villanueva.

At the time of my arrival in Tampa, the major concern on Uncle Emilio's and Aunt Carmen's minds was the fate of Muñeca, who was still in Havana. When would Muñeca arrive? Consequently, we went daily to the Tampa Airport to see who was coming in on the flight from Havana. Then, for reasons unknown to me then and now, Muñeca phoned to let us know that she would be flying into Miami instead. Therefore, the three of us, Uncle Emilio, Aunt Carmen, and I rode to Miami by car. Emilio had bought a used, green 1955 Chevy in Tampa from someone connected to Morejón. That car served him well. He not only used it to take us from Tampa to Miami, but then he used it to go to New York, and later on, to go from New York to Miami. I think I still saw him driving it in the 1970s in Miami.

Muñeca arrived the day after we arrived in Miami and appeared well. However, she did not do well at the José Martí International Airport in Havana. As it turns out, several relatives had given her jewelry to bring to the United States. Cubans were not allowed to take money or anything of much value off the island. Some children lost their dolls at the airport because the authorities thought that the *peluches* (stuffed animals) had been filled with money or jewels. In Muñeca's case, she did not bring any *peluches*. However, she was wearing a number of bracelets, rings, and necklaces that appeared to be excessive in the eyes of the authorities. I am sure my father was not involved with Muñeca's contraband. My dad would have gone for the suitcase!

She must have looked loaded down with contraband because she was pulled out of the line of passengers departing from the *pescera* and taken to a separate room. There, she was ordered to take her clothes off in front of two *milicianas* and then she was body searched. Obviously, she was very upset by this and because they took all of the jewelry she was wearing. Nevertheless, she was happy to have been able to leave the island. After we picked her up at the Miami International Airport, we took her to a room Uncle Emilio had rented in a rooming house on SW 12th Avenue near SW 7th Street by the Gordon Funeral Home. Obviously, the mortuary was in no way related to the Cuban Gordon family. Our room was in the front of the second floor. It had a basin where you could wash, but the actual toilet and bathroom were in another room that was accessible from the hallway onto which all the rooms opened. The four of us—Uncle Emilio, Aunt Carmen, Muñeca, and I—slept in the one room. Ramoncito was still at Lola's *Cuban Barracón* that night.

While we were there, I was informed that Muñeca and Uncle Emilio had found out about a *beca*, a scholarship, which would be available to us. So, arrangements were made for my cousin Ramoncito to leave Lola's *Cuban Barracón* in NW Miami within a matter of days. I would also definitely leave behind my newspaper business and the rooming house on SW 12th Avenue.

We did not know it then, but we were on our way to officially join the Unaccompanied Cuban Children's Program of the Diocese of Miami. I am sure Father

Walsh would have liked me to clarify this now and I gladly do so. My cousin and I were not officially in Operation Pedro Pan because we left Cuba by our own means and we were not immediately received at the airport and transferred to some sort of facility or picked up by relatives at the airport. The latter process was officially labeled Operation Pedro Pan. It began in December 1960 and ended in October 1962 with the Cuban Missile Crisis.

Before we found out more about our *becas,* another classmate, Juan Pella, wrote this in his first letter:

Havana, January 20, 1961
Dear friend:

I hope that you are well, as much as possible, in the company of your cousin and other relatives. You can't imagine the emotion that it has given me to read your letter that arrived yesterday.
I went to Zenón's house yesterday because "we had no classes." "But Faura, Hector, Juan, and Novoa did."
Zenon's sister asked about you and I told her that you send your regards. She was, as you know, in the Priarist school and they "had no classes either."
Faura read in our classroom the letters he got from you and Luis Díaz.
Imagine, Zenón is learning English! Now he says he will go to Tampa. For him travelling the world has become very easy and in-expensive: He uses his imagination!
Humberto is washing dishes "dishes washer"(sic) as they say over there and earns $14.50 a week. I think when he comes back he is going to be weighing 80 pounds.
Here, we are all good. All of us miss you and truly feel your absence. Yesterday when I went up to Zenón's home, I went up the hill and remembered the many times I went up with you. Many indelible memories went through my mind that I will never forget.
I'm reviewing some English and want to see if I can get a private tutor or professor, but they are somewhat scarce right now.
I imagine your cousin must be "shakespeando" a lot. I am happy for that and hope that soon you will speak perfect English.
Ah, I forgot. Brother Teodoro is more "chitinous" than ever. When

I went to the airport for your departure with Lorenzo and then Zenón, we did not go back to school in the afternoon. He gave us a grade of 50 points. That is "shameless" don't you think?
If you see Revilla over there give him my regards and a hug on my behalf and tell him to write to me with his address.
Well, I've overextended myself, so when you write back feel free to overextend yourself also.
Receive a hug from your friend who will not forget you,

Juan E. Pella

I suppose the emotions mentioned in this letter have to do with the fact that my letter confirmed that I was away. It is evident here also, that the departure of any of us from Havana elicited a feeling of loneliness and absence in those who were close to us and remained behind. There was great deal of emotional pain evident in the ones we had been left behind, not just in those of us who had left due to the emerging civil war environment.

Pella gives testimony about the student strike mentioned earlier. In a way, these letters confirm better than any possible set of press agencies, the existence of an issue, a disorder, a problem in the Cuban society of the time. He even points out in a way that should not alarm any authority censuring the letter that at least four students in my classroom did go to school that day. Faura was already working in the Underground movement, as I noted earlier. Hector and Juan would eventually depart from Cuba.

Zenón's sister was also my friend. She was going to another Catholic school and did abstain from going to classes on account of the student strike. Adherence to the student strike appears to have been widespread.

Humberto is another former classmate, who had left the school to come to the United States with his family in 1960 before we started our fourth year of *bachillerato*. He kept in touch with several of my classmates. It will be noted that Humberto was employed and making $14.50 per week working from 6 A.M. to 6 P.M. washing dishes. That amount of money, even in Cuba in 1960, was not sufficient to cover the usual expenses of room and board.

We are told that Zenón is taking up English classes with an exclamation. Zenón was, in fact, not very fond of learning English for reasons that are not apparent. However, Pella was very studious and, if I may say so, a man of letters. He wanted to take English classes, but he did not have a teacher. Obviously, when he tried to write in English, he translated from the Spanish and came up with "dishes washer" (*lava platos*) for dishwasher.

Why is Brother Teodoro labeled as "chitinous"? Brother Teodoro must have been in his late forties when he became our lead teacher in the fourth year of our *bachillerato*. He was short, blondish, and his facial skin was somewhat red from the effect of the tropical sun in Cuba on his naturally pale complexion. He covered most of the subjects we were taking, including natural history, zoology, and botany. In the course of his lectures, when he first mentioned the word *quitinoso* (chitinous) with his strong Spanish accent, we were all impressed, particularly by the way he pronounced the *T* and the ending–oso. On account of that experience, which was felt independently by many us, we began to call him *quitinoso*. He had explained on more than one occasion that chitin was a natural polymer forming the exoskeleton of some invertebrates including arthropods. We did get to dissect a Cuban lobster in the zoology laboratory. In that session, Brother Teodoro explained that chitin was the main component of the lobster exoskeleton. Then he went on to point out with a probe that the chitin was what made the exoskeleton of the lobster so hard. Since we thought that brother was "so hard" on us, we began calling him, in private—he never knew about this—*quitinoso*.

In fact, Brother Teodoro was very strict about the rules of the school and the classroom. One time, on the birthday of the Brother Director, Brother Eusebio, there was a celebration with all students in the main schoolyard and the choir, directed by Brother Teodoro, performed several pieces. The person who usually served as master of ceremonies for these birthday celebrations was Brother Juan Salvador, who taught us chemistry. On that particular occasion, and for reasons unknown to me, Brother Juan Salvador asked me to serve as the master of ceremonies. I did, but I asked, "Do you have a script?" Indeed, Brother Juan Salvador did. I just read the script that he had prepared and everything went well. That is until we got our weekly grades the next week; I had an overall grade of 60. That is 60 out of 100. That was a grade to which the brother in charge of your classroom arrived at by subtracting your penalties for the week from 100. Everyone started with 100 points Monday morning. As the week went by, you got points deducted for homework not done, absences, and conduct issues. Well, when I asked Brother Teodoro about my grade, he explained that "I had been disrespectful" during the birthday celebration for Brother Eusebio. What he understood as disrespectful was that in one of the choir numbers I introduced the number likes this: "Bajo la experta batuta del director del coro, el Hermano Teodoro Fernández, el coro del colegio va a interpretar…" (Under the expert baton of the Choir Director Brother Theodore Fernandez, the school choir will sing…)

Actually, that was what was written in the script given to me. He took as sarcasm the issue of the "expert baton" and there went my missing 40 points.

In his letter, Pella was reporting that Brother Teodoro punished them for not going to classes when they should have. Indeed, he was tough, like chitin!

At the end, he went back to remembering some of the classmates who were absent. He mentions Manuel Revilla, who had left sometime in the month of October or November. Revilla, as noted earlier, was working for Western Union, delivering telegrams in downtown Miami. It is not difficult to imagine how the news from one person in exile spread rapidly to the community of students with whom each of us interacted. Note that Faura, at one point, was reading letters from Luis Díaz and me in the classroom. Not only were emotions left behind in turmoil, the entire fabric of the class seems to have also been damaged.

At the time, unbeknownst to me, the Cuban Ministry of Education had announced that the school year was—on that, the "Year of Education"—going to be shorter than ever before. The academic year was set to end on April 15, 1961. The first semester, *primer parcial*, exams were to take place at the end of February. The second semester exams, *segundo parcial*, were to take place starting April 3. By April 15 all schools were to end classes. The remainder of the year was to be dedicated to the National Literacy Campaign. The latter had already been started in the summer of 1960 but, in April 1961, it was to take the country by storm.

One member of my class had already joined those efforts in 1960. I did not. I instead assisted my mother, who was a teacher in a public school with the gathering of information for the national student census. We walked our assigned territory in the Lawton section of La Víbora and took demographics, and filled out forms for every household to complete the student census. The forms were legal sized, mimeographed sheets of paper, on which we would fill in the names of the persons who lived in the house, the school age of the residents, and other demographics. The experience of helping my mother conduct the student census of 1960 gave me ample evidence of how other families lived in the neighborhood where I had grown up from birth until I was eleven years old. Some families seemed to have all the amenities of a household in 1960. However, most families were noticeably less well off than we were. I remember that most families were rather timid to provide any information, but did agree to it when they were shown official documentation regarding the student census.

Havana, January 22, 1961
My dear Tony:

I got your loving letter and by it I can tell that you are fine. That makes me very happy.
Here, as always, today we went to Mass at the Marist School and then we went to Altahabana.
I would be very pleased if you found something to work on. Otherwise, if you are doing nothing you will get bored. Try to see if there's anything in Miami, as the weather is very cold in New York and, besides, it is much farther away.
I thought you'd be in a school by now…if you can't find one, have patience. I know that you are well prepared for work also.
Take care of yourself from the cold, and write to us so that we know about all of you. Antonio always comes in here to see if there are letters and he reads them …
Muñeca these days has been taking her exams. I do not know when she will go there. I ask her and she tells me: I already wrote to Papito.
Give my love to everyone, and for you a hug and many kisses from your grandma that you know loves you,

Amparo

So it is with this, my grandmother's first letter that I hear of love, in Spanish *cariño, te quiero,* since my arrival from Cuba. My parents were more worried about my departure than they were probably ready to admit. My grandmother Amparo was at the time seventy-four years old. She gave me the impression that they were doing the same things they did before my departure. Perhaps, they were trying to make believe that nothing had changed. They went to the mass at the Marist School at La Víbora. That had been the school where I began my education in first grade. It had also been the school where my father had gone to school with his brother and cousins years before.

Then after mass, officiated by the school chaplain Father Gerardo Fernández, also known by the student body as Father Pitillo, they went to Altahabana. They spent the afternoon there, had lunch, and then went back to her home on San Francisco Street, Number 320, fifteen blocks away from the Marist School. Emilito used to walk that distance on school days back and forth when he was at that school's *bachillerato* in the early fifties.

Then she turned to my current issues. I am not sure if she wished me to go to school or work. I do get the impression that she expected me to do well in whatever I did, provided I was not bored!

Again, she brought up the issue of the cold weather. Since my father visited her daily, I am sure that she shared the same concerns about my asthma and the cold environment with my father and mother.

As far as Muñeca was concerned, we again note that she is taking exams. She lived in the same matriarchal house with my grandmother where I had grown up. That house on San Francisco Street is where I lived from birth until I was eleven years old when my father and mother purchased a new house and we moved to Altahabana. Abuela Amparo began her letter with love and ended with sharing her love with everyone!

CHAPTER 7

BEYOND THE POLITICS: MY PARENT'S FEAR

"Many parents did become hysterical and in 1960 you had a growing conflict between the Catholic Church and the Cuban Government. So parents that were devout Catholics and felt close to the Church were very concerned and afraid that their children were going to be sent to atheist schools in the Soviet Union and they would lose their children."
-Wayne Smith

When parents send away their adolescent children to a respectable and highly developed neighboring country—but still a foreign country—it is because of some definite risk or real danger. It is easy for outsiders to label our parents hysterical. The fact of the matter is that, in most cases, the parents who did send their children out of Cuba into a safe haven in the United States were placing their children out of harm's way. They were not too concerned about their children being forcefully and involuntarily taken to the Soviet Union. The danger was felt to come from inside Cuba. Furthermore, the danger was aggravated because divisions, tensions, and repercussions from real or perceived transgressions against the revolutionary authorities were in crescendo. By the time I left Havana there had been searches in one of the Marist schools and some students had been detained by the revolutionary police and state security personnel.

After my parents saw me depart from the Havana airport, they must have felt a great, momentary loss, but also great relief that I was going to a safe haven where I would not be harassed or detained on account of my principles, beliefs, religious, or political inclinations. Soon, however, their greatest fear turned to my health; they were concerned because of my history of asthma. Looking back now, and as a physician, the problem was specifically a propensity of my bronchi to overreact and go into spasms while the respiratory mucosal glands over-secreted a sticky stuff, mucus that eventually—if not mobilized—would plug my air tubes. This fear was noted in the first letter I received from them and in most correspondence from then on.

January 18, 1961

My dear son:

The weather here has been fairly cold since yesterday. I can only imagine that over there the cold has been more intense for you...
Well my son...take good care of yourself in order to avoid having "problemas con tu pecho"...
Receive a kiss from your mother and your father's blessing,

María Luisa and Antonio

They were concerned that I might have *problemas con mi pecho,* that is, problems with my chest—asthma. The medical understanding of asthma back then was more primitive than it is today, but their greatest concern was obvious, the climate change. I must have reassured them in my first or second letter to them. This was their response:

January 19, 1961
My dear son:

I got your second letter and by it I can tell that you're okay. Your mother is very worried that you may have had an asthma attack. I do not think that you have had any asthma, otherwise, you would have said something in your letter. I think you've been well. She's worried because since three days ago the cold weather has been pretty strong here.
Tell me how you've been in terms of your chest. Do you tolerate well the cold weather?
Well, until next time...
Your father,

Antonio

Maternal instincts are beyond that which we as humans can understand. My mother had a premonition, a concern that I was going to be bothered by asthma. Indeed, after I arrived in Tampa under the care of my Aunt Carmen and my Uncle Emilio, I began to have increasing bouts of coughing and wheezing—asthma. I did not mention anything to anyone by mail, but my Uncle Emilio, a journalist at heart, denounced me to my own parents. This is how it played out:

January 23, 1961
My dear son:

We are well. Here it is intensely cold since the 21st, so can I imagine that it will be colder up there, especially when I think that the heating may not be adequate.
Tell us immediately how you are doing from your chest! From your uncle's letter it seems that you have had a cold since you got there. Be careful. Sleep with warm shirt on, that is the shirt that you have been wearing. It is necessary to avoid temperature changes when changing clothes from a warm set of clothes to a cold one.
Yesterday we had lunch at the home of Joaquín. You should know. The good food was abundant as always.
When you go to Miami, try to solve your entry into the school for which you were recommended before you left here.
With regards to the jacket you mention in your letter, if it is as warm and good as you say it is, buy it. You should no longer be cold. You can always use it here in the winter because you know well that the neighborhood where we live is rather cold.
Poppy is very well. He already had the last dose of serum. Around the first of February, he will get the vaccine that immunizes him for life and, afterwards, we will give him the anti-rabies vaccine.
Well my son, write us immediately and tell us how your chest is doing. Tell me if you've had asthma. These issues have us very concerned.
Give a hug to Emilio and a kiss to my sister Carmen and for you as always the blessing of your father,

Antonio

The issue of my chest, that is bronchial asthma, was usually mentioned in the beginning of my parents' letters and at the end. It was like a template of their fears transcribed into the written word so that their innermost feelings would be transmitted to me through the mail. My father had served as a military physician in the Cuban Army. It was not surprising that he ordered me to give him "immediately" information on how I was doing with regard to my asthma. Some varieties of asthma are brought on by temperature changes, but most asthmatics do not get worse when there is an ambient temperature change, but when the bronchi are exposed to allergens that trigger an allergic reaction, resulting in the spasm of the circular muscles of the air tubes and the excessive secretion of mucus. When there is a weather change, there is also a need to take clothing out of storage where dust and possibly mites have accumulated. All of these factors may have been conspiring against me in Tampa, but I did not recognize them. What was clear, however, was that I was coughing and sometimes short of breath because of the bronchial tightening and the excessive secretion of mucus produced by my respiratory glands, leading to the plugging of small airways that were supposed to deliver air with its natural content of oxygen to the alveoli, where the gases of respiration were to be exchanged.

A not uncommon trigger of asthma is small animals' dander. My family has always, as far back as I can remember, had dogs. At this time, in the revolution, only one dog remained with us—Poppy. The issue of specific allergens, chemical structures capable of triggering a full allergic response from the asthmatic patient's immunological system, is complex. However, in the months to come, it would be evident that my asthma would recur when challenged by dust and dog dander. The role of the latter in "the issues of my chest" was eventually confirmed in the physiology laboratory in medical school whenever my team had to work with dogs.

CHAPTER 8

THE *BECA*, SPANISH MOSS, AND PROGRESS ON *MI PECHO*

"These brave boys, homesick Cuban boys clung to each other,
developed bonds of mutual dependency, shared their fears, and confronted their
loneliness. They found solace in their common struggle to make sense
of an unfathomable series of complicated political events in their homeland.
There was a sense of security in numbers. Individually, they struggled,
but together they somehow survived. Alone, they cried and brooded. As a group,
they thrived, laughed, teased, and made the best of their situation."
-Thomas J. Aglio

My first formal encounter with what later we learned was called the Unaccompanied Cuban Children Program occurred at the end of January in 1961. The program was the corollary of Operation Pedro Pan, through which care would be provided to children who otherwise would be homeless in the United States after their escape from Havana. Both programs were associated with Father Bryan O. Walsh, who, as mentioned before, was the head of Catholic Charities in the Diocese of Miami. According to Father Walsh himself, he first made the acquaintance of an adolescent Cuban refugee in November 1960, when he was presented with a fifteen-year-old Pedro Menéndez, who had no place to live in Miami after arriving from Cuba.(1) Cubans were arriving in Miami at a rate of 1,000 to 1,500 per week. Even before Operation Pedro Pan began sending, transporting, and receiving unaccompanied children, there were minors in need of help once they arrived in Miami. It is not surprising, then, that Father Walsh and the Diocese of Miami received a request from officials of the Eisenhower Administration, requesting their assistance in providing lodging and schooling for Cuban children in Florida.

Children were flying off the island like mango flowers in the spring not due to atmospheric winds but to perceived and real threats of communist indoctrination, terror and even civil war. The Cuban Communist government had in place a sequence of hurdles for anyone requesting to depart the island. Therefore, the selective migration of children was not entirely a design or a plan of Father Walsh, the office of Catholic Charities, the United States government, or any of its agencies. The fact of the matter was that the Cuban government was the one entity that controlled the exodus through various emigration barriers, which were subject to change arbitrarily at any time, such as the need for affidavits and a *vigencia*.

When approached by the United States government, Father Walsh is said to have been cautious at first, according to an account shared much later by the then Bishop of Miami Monsignor Coleman Carroll. The American government officials were requesting the services of the Diocese of Miami for the care of 200 children.(2) It was stipulated that support in the form of approximately $200 per institutionalized child per month would be provided by the American government to cover the expenses generated by this request.(3) Catholic Charities agreed to the request, and was ready to open its doors to any Cuban minor through both Operation Pedro Pan and the Unaccompanied Cuban Children Program.

This opportunity was opened to me through my Aunt Carmen, Uncle Emilio, and cousin Muñeca. I was not alone. My cousin Ramoncito, three months older than I, also became a candidate for the new program. He had not found gainful employment, had not been in any schooling for months, and obviously did not seem to have much of a future at the time. He also, on the advice of our aunt, uncle, and cousin Muñeca, became interested in the new program. I remember my aunt and cousin Muñeca referring to the program as a *beca*. A scholarship, indeed, seemed just right for us and what we needed to succeed in our new lives.

It was on a sunny afternoon sometime at the end of January 1961, that my cousin and I were taken to the second floor of the program's office. It was located at 395 Northwest First Street, a couple of blocks from the Dade County Court House, at the time one of the tallest buildings in downtown Miami. We entered the offices of Catholic Charities and sat in front of a large wooden desk in the private office of Mrs. Louise Cooper. She appeared to me to have brown-blondish hair, but that may have been a temporary feature of an otherwise middle age American lady. Mrs. Cooper had been working for the Diocese of Miami pretty much since its inception in 1958. She grew up and studied in Akron, Ohio, and did social work in Cleveland. She had been a social worker for more than ten years by then. She addressed us in English. After a brief introduction, the content of which I cannot remember and very likely I did not understand, I remember she asked us plainly, "Where do you want to go? To Oregon or to Jacksonville?"

My cousin, without any discussion, questions, or concern for my opinion, answered, "To Jacksonville."

She accepted his answer and prepared some papers that later remained in her possession. At that time, I became Number CW-RFG 153.(4) I did not know it then, but that was my number in the registry of the Catholic Charities.

Years later, Monsignor Walsh published a timetable of the involvement of his office in the Cuban children's social services. Here is what he wrote for Tuesday, January 31, 1961: "At a closed meeting of the Catholic Relief Service for their diocesan resettlement directors, I [Father Walsh] spoke at length about the need we had for foster family and group care for unaccompanied children. I stressed the need for keeping secret our participation in getting children out of Cuba.

"One of the first dioceses to respond to our appeal was our neighbor and mother diocese, Diocese of St. Augustine, Florida. I met with Father Sager and Father Lenihan to discuss turning their Saint John's Youth Camp at Switzerland, Florida, into a home and school for teenage boys. Seven children came yesterday from Cuba and seven today."(5)

I was one of the children who had gone in on that last day of January and in the second group to arrive a few days later to Saint John's Youth Camp.

We did not know it then, but the word *beca* was widely used in the handling of the Cuban children's migration, at the time to mean anything from a classic scholarship in a recognized and already organized school, a foster home, or simply boarding in an institution with or without some sort of schooling. Some of the locations and institutions where these *becas* were used to care for the Cuban children were makeshift locations. It must be remembered that this was an emergency situation, in which a safe haven was to be provided for the children to remove them from harm's way in Cuba. For example, in Miami, a set of buildings in Kendall formerly used to care for orphans turned into the Kendall House for Cuban teenagers. In Marquette, Michigan, an orphanage, Holy Family Home, which had been built in 1916 and had closed years before 1961, was reopened to house a group of Cuban children in 1962.

Camp Saint John was not a summer youth camp to us, although we all recognized it as a summer camp that had been closed for some time when we first walked through it. It became our home in winter and from it, we were to go to school in Jacksonville. It is clear from other writings by Father Walsh that his great fear in the last days of December 1960 was that all 200 Cuban children would arrive at one time and he did not have anywhere to place them or care for them. Father Walsh was a responsible man. Fortunately, that did not occur and he was able to find places where the refugee children could be cared for.

The fact that the first location to open up for the Cuban refugee children outside of Dade County back then was a location within the Diocese of St. Augustine seemed remarkable, considering the recent history of Catholicism in Florida. When the Diocese of Miami was formed on the orders of the Vatican in October 1958, there was a great deal of confusion and disagreement between the Bishop of St. Augustine, Archbishop John Patrick Hurley, and the bishop of the new diocese of Miami, Monsignor Coleman Carroll. St. Augustine had been the only diocese in Florida since 1870 and Archbishop Hurley had been its ordinary, meaning its local head, since the 1940s. Prior to being assigned to the only Florida diocese, Hurley had been elevated to Archbishop by Pope Pius XII during World War II when he was named Apostolate Delegate to Yugoslavia. After his assignment in the Balkans, Archbishop Hurley managed well the diocese of Florida and the number of the faithful increased under his watch.

A great deal of what later became known as the Hurley-Carroll controversy dealt with the division of funds, lands, and the assignment of seminarians studying in Ireland as a result of the diocesan division that occurred in 1958.(6) The latter division was somewhat unusual in two ways. First, it did not take into account the input or views of the existing Bishop of St. Augustine. The orders came down from the Vatican and surprised everyone in St. Augustine. And secondly, the division seemed to occur before a massive exodus from Cuba was to occur, not after the new refugees had settled, turning into new immigrants, and becoming an important pastoral issue.

The Hurley-Carroll controversy issue on the funds and lands issue centered on the land purchases performed wisely by Archbishop Hurley in the 1950s, through which he acquired lands for more than $4 million to be used by his Diocese of St. Augustine.(7) Those properties had been paid for in cash, after the Bishop of St. Augustine successfully raised the funds from donors throughout the state. Some of those lands were in the sixteen most southern counties of Florida, which were to become the new Diocese of Miami. Bishop Hurley argued that his diocese had made a major investment in those lands and, therefore, he and his now smaller diocese needed some form of financial remuneration for their investment.

The issue regarding the seminarians dealt with the fact that Florida did not generate enough people with vocations for the priesthood to cover all the pastoral needs of the state, or the diocese, for that matter. Therefore, Irish seminarians had

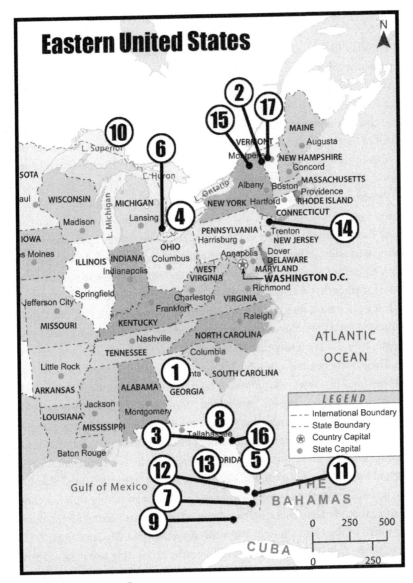

Map Legend

1. Atlanta, GA 2. Burlington, VT 3. Camp St. John 4. Cleveland, OH
5. Daytona Beach, FL 6. Detroit, MI 7. Florida City, FL 8. Jacksonville, FL
9. Key West, FL 10. Marquette, MI 11. Miami, FL 12. Opa-Locka, FL
13. Tampa, FL 14. Ridgefield Park, NJ 15. Saranac Lake, NY
16. St. Augustine, FL 17. Winooski Park, VT

Map of the Eastern United States

been enrolled in a couple of seminaries in Ireland and were being supported, at least partially, while studying to serve the church here in Florida after they became ordained by Archbishop Hurley who during their time in the seminary, had contributed to their education financially. Now with the division of his diocese, there was no clear direction in terms of how the Irish seminarians would be divided to serve all of Florida under the jurisdiction of two dioceses. These and other issues were ongoing at the time. In fact, some of the issues in the Hurley-Carroll controversy were not resolved completely until 1966.

However, we did not know about any such controversy, so going back to that afternoon with Mrs. Cooper, we were shown to a first-floor location in the Cuban Refugee Center, where we were to take a suit and winter clothing that was suitable for our destination. It was *El Ropero*, a clothing depot kind of place at the Emergency Center for Cuban Refugees, where newcomers were able to somehow compensate for what they had left behind in Cuba, but more importantly, to get ready for whatever location they were being sent to by the refugee center. The latter was the official reason the center was there. Cuban refugees had to be relocated to places up north. There was no way that Miami could absorb so many immigrants at the time. There were not enough jobs, housing, or schools. At the time, children or adults leaving Cuba were not allowed to take with them from the island more than five dollars and one suitcase. All jewelry and "non-essentials," according to the communist regime, were confiscated at the airport in Havana. At *El Ropero*, my Aunt Carmen helped us select clothing that might be useful to us in Northern Florida. I picked up a suit, a short coat, a hat, and a couple of shirts after my aunt checked them and found them to fit me and be suitable for my "relocalization." She was always the family expert on getting bargains; I could not go wrong with her choices.

After that, we went to a small cafeteria off Northeast Second Street, maybe a block north of the Gesu Church. We were altogether five. My aunt organized our food selection from the menu and placed an order requesting two meals consisting of Cuban skirt steak, rice and black beans, and fried ripe plantains. When the orders arrived at the counter, she asked for some extra plates and divided the portions so that we all had something to eat. Wasn't she a great bargain hunter?

At the end of that day, we all trusted the Catholic Church. Therefore, we felt more hopeful than a few days before. So, that night we talked about the immediate future, always keeping in mind the thought that we would be out of Cuba for only a short period of time. At least, at that time, we had a plan. I personally thought that a *beca* was something fantastic. I was excited and felt adventurous on the eve of my next experience in the United States.

Early the next morning, we found ourselves at the train station just north of the Dade County Court House. At the time, that was the terminal of the Florida East Coast Railway service. The station no longer exists. It was demolished in November 1963, a few days before President Kennedy's assassination, to make way for the new expressways going through downtown Miami. But on that day in 1961, the Eisenhower administration had been instrumental—through the Catholic Welfare Bureau—in getting seven Cuban youngsters one-way tickets to travel from Miami to St. Augustine. We were obviously in a transition that went beyond what we ourselves knew or understood at the time, but we felt it. I guess it is like a visceral pain from some sort of internal derangement in our own biology that we feel as uncomfortable, but do not know exactly what is going on with the particular tissues undergoing stressors, pressure or injury. The extent and depth of it would only become clear as time went on and we lived our future. No one, I dare say, could imagine these experiences as they related to the original issue—a way out of Cuba.

The train departed on time that morning, at about 9 A.M. or so. We had been met at the station by someone from Mrs. Cooper's office, who entrusted me with the money to pay for lunch on board the train for all the passengers sponsored by the program for unaccompanied Cuban children. Everyone was dressed up, either with whatever they had worn coming out of Cuba or what we had picked up at *El Ropero* at the Cuban Refugee Center. It was a sunny morning, but it was not too hot.

My Aunt Carmen and Muñeca stayed to say good-bye to us. Uncle Emilio was not there. He seemed to either avoid the emotions of this departure or had something more important to do. I have heard of several stories of other children who noted that their father was not in the airport in Havana when they departed. Uncle Emilio was our father figure at that particular point in time.

The sense of adventure was greater than that of reality, for despite the fact that I did not know when I would see my family again, I was looking toward the future with hope. Perhaps looking forwards is a sign of being young like children and looking back is something older folks do. I was young and looking forward to seeing the east coast of Florida. The Florida East Coast Railway was the pride of the state and Henry M. Flagler, one of John. D. Rockefeller's associates and the founder of the Standard Oil Company. The rail line was inaugurated in 1892 when José Martí was organizing the groundwork of the Cuban Revolutionary Party and the war of independence of 1895. It was in Florida where Martí saw from a train the aftermath of a forest fire and noted young, healthy, bright green pine trees emerging from the devastation of the inferno that had seemingly killed all life. It was impossible for us to think of ourselves at the time as young, bright, emerging living trees in a sea

Aunt Carmen, Ramoncito, and the author at the Downtown Miami Train Station in 1961, just before boarding with five other Pedro Pans en route to St. Augustine. Photograph from 8mm frame

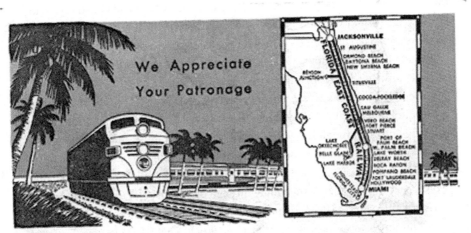

Florida East Coast Railway ticket folder, February 1961

of death for our country had not, yet, been turned into the misery and ruin that it has become at the writing of these pages.

Initially, the Florida East Coast Railway line went down to Key West, but in 1935 a hurricane demolished segments of it in the Florida Keys. The railroad lines were not reconstructed through FDR's New Deal. Instead, an Overseas Highway was constructed. The rails of the demolished railway were used to provide a railing to the bridges of the new highway.

Our trip was entirely uneventful. We did notice that all attendants on the train were black and among the passengers we encountered there were no blacks. I was aware of the racial discrimination in the United States, since I had visited this country in years past for vacations. What none of us knew at the time, however, was that some individuals considered Hispanics to be like blacks or to be black, period. It is fortunate that we did not say much, remained under the radar, and did not encounter any Ku Klux Klansmen.

Somehow, we all knew the arrangement of the passenger train with its dining coach and other facilities. Everyone was comfortably seated and either resting or looking outside through large glass windows. I do not think anyone was engaged in any serious conversation. Besides, in a group of youngsters in which the oldest was sixteen years of age, what perspective or introspection of the situation could you expect with so many issues going through our heads? Not the least of these issues was the nature of the *beca* into which we had suddenly been accepted.

Our lunch was essentially an American lunch. That is, a light meal by Cuban standards of the time. A Cuban lunch would have been a serving of meat—chicken, or beef, or even pork; a soup or pottage with beans and small pieces of pumpkin, potatoes, and Spanish sausage (chorizo); and rice or potatoes. A side of crackers, bread, and butter was usually available. This was followed by a dessert of, perhaps, guava shells with cream cheese or flan. When you compare this fare with a small sandwich accompanied by a celery salad and perhaps a gelatin dessert, you can see and feel the difference without entering into nutritional content. Obviously, not everything in America was leaner than what we had been accustomed to in our homeland. For example, the Cuban breakfast was rather meager compared with the American ham and eggs, bread and butter, pancakes, cereals, fruits and fresh milk. But, in terms of lunch, it was going to be months until we had black beans and rice again!

Somewhere between four and five in the afternoon, we arrived in St. Augustine. We were met by a young man named Ronny and a Spanish priest. They drove us out of the train station in two cars and into our immediate future. We, the newly

FKV   34 L7 $4.85
         60

M. McLoots

Rail Fare $ 1001
Federal Tax $ 100
Pullman $ 1107
Federal Tax $
                 $ 8808
         Total $

Leaving   9:70 am 7/8

Remarks:

41-42-43-44-45-46-47

Father Sager
St Augustine 7/8

CHECK YOUR BAGGAGE EARLY
AVOID THAT LAST MINUTE RUSH

NO. 33 (REV. 2-20-56)

Train tickets for 8 Pedro Pans to travel from Miami to St. Augustine. However, only 7 Pedro Pans traveled that morning.

arrived children, did not know where we were going. It was a rather long drive through winding roads and over small bridges. In all trips the going seems longer than the coming. Then suddenly, the car turned into a wooded estate through an open gate in a fence. A dirt road, again somewhat winding, led us to the front of a two-story stone house, fitted with a large garage on its northern side, and a circular driveway on its entrance facing the east. The house was surrounded by tall trees that were adorned with a strange and gloomy-looking gray stuff that seemed to be growing from the branches. It appeared to me that the trees were crying or had cried and their tears had been condensed by the coldness of the place. We learned later, for at the time it seemed inappropriate to inquire about the names of the plants or the nature of the local flora, that this strange stuff was not a part of the tall trees. It was something out of place–like the way we felt. It turned out that the gloomy threads were part of a separate plant, the Spanish moss, a peculiar plant that lacks roots and grows on branches of trees.

We unloaded the automobiles and entered the house. Upon entering the mansion through its foyer, I immediately smelled old dust. The air was somewhat musty, as if the place had been unoccupied for a long time. Indeed, we learned then that the house had been reopened a few days earlier when the first Cuban children had arrived there in pretty much the same manner in which we had just arrived. We saw one or two of them and immediately took our belongings to the second floor, where each of us occupied a bunk bed of our own choosing. I remember a large room with the bunk beds and a rather large bathroom on the east side of the second floor.

That night, we washed up and then ate in the first floor dining room, at a large table presided over by the Spanish priest. It was a large meal with roast turkey and mashed potatoes. During the meal, we were given instructions on the fact that we were going to be there, in the mansion, only for a short while. In the morning, we would see the actual location where we were to take up temporary residence. We were also oriented to the address of the place we were in. It was a lengthy and cumbersome address that included several towns and at least two counties. In a way, it was as clear as our own futures, but we did not know it then. It read:

St. John's Manor
Box 193
Route 13
Green Cove Springs
Switzerland, Florida

St. John's Manor, La Casa Grande

Soon thereafter everyone was in the bunk beds. At least the group that had just arrived was very tired. The outside was too dark and unknown even for adventurous youngsters to brave just to check it out. The dust in the air of the mansion seemed to be settling. However, I was still very much aware of it.

At about one or two in the morning, I was still awake. I had been pretending to be asleep, but could not sleep on account of a persistent cough. My chest, *pecho*, was getting tighter by the minute. I got up from the bunk bed and went to the bathroom. Sometimes I would expectorate thick, dark yellow phlegm that was clearly noticeable against the white of the wash basin. I turned on the water to wash it out of my sight. The entire bathroom was covered in white tiles with black trimmings. Maybe none of the other twelve or thirteen guys there noticed it, but I did because I spent a considerable amount of time in the bathroom that night. Despite my trying not to disturb their sleep, I certainly made enough noise to bother them. At one time, I remember hearing a loud cry from the bunk beds, *"Quién coló al tuberculoso en el cuarto?"* (Who sneaked the tuberculosis patient into the room?)

I had no medications; the only thing from which I seemed to get some relief was from inhaling warm water vapor. I attempted to breathe with my face near the running warm water. I had turned on and off the faucet to clear my secretions from the basin and noted that the hotter the water the better I breathed. Paradoxically, I was inclining my face into the sink while the warm water was running and noted that my breathing was better when I inhaled the warm vapor. Eventually, however, like a fish fighting a hook on a line, I did get tired enough and rested for a few hours.

In the morning, I went outside the mansion, looked around for the gloomy Spanish moss, and saw a large body of water, the St. John River, just to the west of the mansion. I was able to breathe better outside the mansion than in it. It never occurred to me to sleep outside the mansion, however. The fear of being, not only away from home, but also alone outside the group that formed my current community presented an insurmountable fear to me. Although remaining outside seemed a great option to prevent the pathological reaction of my bronchi, from the mental point of view it proved to be something I did not even consider on account—I think—of fear; fear of the unknown and fear of being alone, although I barely knew my new peers at the camp.

I must have been the talk of the group, but no one actually came to me and called me *tuberculoso* to my face, although they knew well enough, or so I thought, who had been coughing his lungs out the night before. The Spanish moss that had caught my attention when we first rode into the compound was still there. Except that now, in the morning after that spell of persistent cough and asthmatic bronchitis, the scenery seemed more tearful and saddened than when I first saw it.

Vegetation around La Casa Grande

There were two sandy trails coming out of the mansion. One seemed to go toward the east, while the other one, the one through which we had not come in, veered toward the north. I walked each of them and did not get anywhere. Each of the trails was surrounded by thick woods. A very occasional bird seemed to signal that there was life in the forest, but it was not the vibrant sounds of morning birds announcing a bright day ahead.

As I walked, I felt better both in terms of the cough and also in terms of the difficulty breathing that had accompanied me throughout the night. I thought I had had an asthma attack. I had suffered from asthma since my childhood, requiring nebulizer treatments administered both at home and at a hospital clinic. Tubing was attached from a very loud air motor to a chamber form where a medication could be inhaled. The medication was placed in a glass chamber, which was part of the inhaler that my father called in Spanish *la cachimba* (the pipe) that got washed thoroughly after each treatment. The glass device had a narrow port of entry at its bottom, where the hose pumping the air was attached. The air went into a very small glass tube that created a jet and served to nebulize the medication from the glass chamber. The vapors of the nebulized medication came out at the top through a glass tube bent at a right angle, which was much larger than the entry one. My mouth was placed on the opening of this larger glass tube as I breathed in the nebulized medication. That medication would have helped me the night before, but the air pump itself would have weighed much more than what I was allowed to bring out the island with me. Besides, I had not had an asthma attack of such severity since we had moved out of La Víbora about five years before. Who would have thought that asthma would come back now? What could Aunt Carmen and Uncle Emilio say or do if they would have seen me the night before? They were following my father's instructions in not taking me up north on account of my history of asthma. How could this have been foreseen?

When I returned to the mansion, there was an expedition being prepared to travel into the actual place where we would be residing. I joined them and went into one of the automobiles, which rolled down the sandy trail heading northward. The trail, consisting of bends and twisting turns, was filled with vegetation, which made the passage very narrow for the car. Despite the difficulties in negotiating the narrowness of the road, we made it to the camp about 300 feet from the mansion.

The camp was in a clearing where small plants had been removed. Several tall pines and scrub oaks had not been cut and came out of the sandy soil below and got lost in the sky at the top. Judging from their heights, the pines must have been there for a very long time. The camp consisted of three structures, two of them seemed identical. The two identical structures, which were built end to end in the east-west direction, were the dormitories. The largest structure was located in the eastern most segment of the clearing. All these structures were constructed from cement blocks and appeared fairly modern. Actually, we found out sometime later that they were built in 1959.

All the structures were locked. Ronny, the American who received us at the St. Augustine train station, opened one of the identical cabins and we went inside. Immediately, upon entering, I began to cough again. There was a dusty odor that appeared to be even stronger than the ambience I encountered when entering the mansion the night before.

Each of the two identical cabins had two sections and in the center the bathrooms and area for hygiene. There were bunk beds with bare mattresses and pillows in the portions of the cabins designated as dormitories. I think there were a couple of chests of drawers also, but I am not sure. In the bathrooms, there were two rows of open toilets, an open shower, and a large, round basin where residents were expected to wash their faces and hands, and brush their teeth. Water flow was controlled by pressing a round foot pedal that went around the entire basin.

The larger hall to the east of the compound was the dining hall, kitchen, and lounge area. The latter was going to be used as a study area once we moved into the camp and started school at our *beca*. The main seating area of the hall was furnished with rectangular picnic tables of the kind that have seats on both sides attached to the legs of the structure. The southern side of the dining hall was the location of a modern institutional kitchen, including a large, industrial refrigerator and a cafeteria-style washing device with a hanging hose. The ambience in this large hall seemed less violent to me and my air passages than the air in the dormitories. Just north of this larger cabin was a large bell, which was used routinely to call for events.

One of the Cubans who had arrived in the initial group that literally opened the camp, turned on a faucet to demonstrate the odorous properties of the camp water. Something that we, the newcomers, had suspected already because the water in the mansion was of the same nature as that of the camp proper. He said, "*Es agua sulfurosa!*" That is, it is sulfur water. Someone explained that in Cuba there were springs of *agua sulfurosa* and many claimed that the water had medicinal properties. As for us, at the time, it was just water that smelled like rotten eggs. I then remembered the chemistry lessons of Brother Juan Salvador a few months before my departure from Cuba. We took ferrous sulfide and warmed it carefully, if not it exploded, in the presence of hydrochloric acid. The result was visible in the form of

Camp St. John in 1961. Photographs from 8mm movie frames

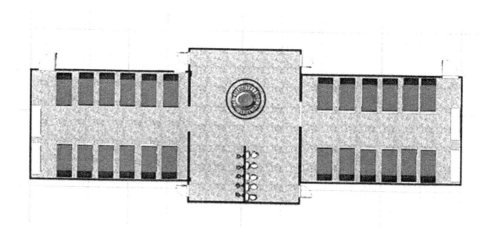

Diagram of our sleeping cabins at Camp St. John

Bell at Camp St. John

a gas emanating from the test tube—hydrogen sulfide. It was not only visible, it was sensed through our noses even far away from the experimental site. It smelled like rotten eggs. I also remembered that hydrogen sulfide gas was supposed to be toxic. I had also experienced sulfur water on family outings in Pinar del Río in western Cuba. My father had never mentioned that sulfur water was toxic. In fact, it was supposed to be medicinal.

As our first encounter with the camp came to an end, we boarded the automobile and headed back, through the tortuous sandy road, to the mansion, *La Casa Grande*. A lunch was awaiting us. The Spanish priest said grace and we sat down to eat.

In the late afternoon, before dinner, while resting in one of the bunk beds on the second floor of the mansion, I began to cough violently again. This time my illness came to the attention of the priest and Ronny. The next thing I remember was being driven by Ronny out of the camp. I was sitting in the front passenger seat and Ronny was driving. Ronny turned north on Route 13, and then turned to the left. After going off the main road for a few minutes, he stopped at a house and we went in. It was a medical doctor's office and house. They took me in immediately. I suspect that the camp must have called before they actually took me there. The doctor checked me just as quickly. I only remember getting an injection in my arm and very soon afterwards, within seconds, I began feeling drastically better. The cough subsided and Ronny took me back to the camp.

Sometime later, I explained to my dad in a letter that I had been ill with asthma and an American doctor gave me an injection that "cured me" suddenly. He explained that the injection was probably adrenaline, epinephrine, which is a drug used to treat severe asthma that had never been given to me before. My father commented in his letter that, in Cuba, it was considered *un arma de dos filos*, a two-edged sword which could help you or hurt you. Scary.

When we got back to the mansion, dinner had already finished. Ronny offered me a sandwich and something to drink. I accepted it, but I was not very hungry. The injection had made me somewhat nervous, but I was not having difficulty breathing. It took a couple of days before we were asked to move ourselves to the two barracks. We got our stuff in some order and literally set up camp at St. John's. Each barrack or cabin had two sections, or halls, divided by a large washing area with a sink, showers, and a toilet area. Each hall had about ten bunk beds. I was assigned to the first barrack in the second hall, the one away from the dining hall. There was little in the way of furniture besides metal bunk beds. Except for an occasional drawer, we were to live literally out of our suitcases stowed away underneath the bunk beds.

The respiratory issues in my *pecho*, the wheezing and coughing, unfortunately, did not get better. In fact, they got worse. One morning, early in the month of March, I was taken to one of the Catholic hospitals in Jacksonville, St. Vincent's Hospital, with persistent fever, wheezing, and a worsening sore throat. The latter had rendered me unable to swallow properly. Because my oral and respiratory secretions got accumulated in my throat, I often gargled when I tried to speak. Luckily, my first nickname at the camp, *tuberculoso*, did not stick. I guess it made me sound into some sort of contagion to be avoided. However, soon thereafter, the respiratory issues did allow the crowd of my peers to name me something else, *gargarita,* which stood for "little gargle" on account of the fact that I gargled often when I tried to speak. This was because my upper airway was so swollen that I had problems swallowing food, drink, or even my own saliva or secretions.

On that occasion, Ronny did not take me to the country doctor again. He went straight for the hospital emergency department. It did not take them much time to find out that I was sick. They admitted me to the hospital. Years later, I requested a copy of my medical records from St. Vincent's Hospital. The remainder of this account about my stay at the hospital is greatly enhanced by details noted in those records.

The face sheet noted that I was Tony Gordon. My father and mother were "unknown" and in Cuba. My address was:

Care of:
Mrs. Louise Cooper
Catholic Charities
Miami, Florida

My residence, as I already noted in the earlier chapters was St. John's Camp, Switzerland, Florida.

I was admitted to Room 534 in the south wing of the hospital under the service of Dr. Adams.

The hospital was located on the north side of the St. Johns River as the latter turned from its southern roots to empty the canals and rivers of Central Florida into the Atlantic Ocean. The last segment of St. Johns River, before emptying into the Atlantic Ocean, runs east to west, but most of the river runs south to north. When we were at the camp, we were told that only two rivers in the world ran south to north, the other one being the Nile River. However, since then, we have found out otherwise. For example two famous rivers in the Americas, the Niagara River in New York and the Magdalena River in Colombia flow south to north, as well.

The hospital was a red brick building. The reader should be aware that the first and last hospital I had visited before this event was the military hospital in Havana, the Carlos J. Finlay Hospital in Marianao, completed in 1945. To me, the Cuban hospital seemed much more modern than St. Vincent's. No wonder, years later I learned that the original St. Vincent's Hospital, the area where I had been admitted, had been built in 1916.

I do remember that I was placed in a hospital room with a window facing the St. Johns River. I occupied the window bed. Several hospital workers came in to check my blood pressure and temperature. I do not remember that anyone spoke Spanish, except for one of the resident doctors. His name was Dr. Iglesias. I must have been exhausted, because soon after I was placed in my hospital bed I went to sleep, although it was not night, yet.

Later that same day, when I woke up, I was surprised to see that the bed by the door had been occupied by an older patient. I became horrified when I saw the older gentleman on that bed turn around and look at me. His face was like that of a monster. He had no nose and a growth of hair like a horn was growing from where the bridge of the nose would have been. He must have figured out from my expression that I was horrified at his facial appearance.

"Hello," he said.

"Hello," I answered.

Then, he began to try to explain his condition and I stopped him.

"Sir, I do not speak much English," I said.

He then spoke slowly. I watched attentively and got the impression that I was following his explanation accompanied by his body language and gestures. I gestured back with my expression that I was able to understand some of what he was attempting to communicate to me. This is what I thought he said. I understood that he had had a growth in his nose, a tumor. The doctors removed the growth and the nose and were presently taking skin from his scalp down to the nose in order to remake part of his face and something that looked like a nose. The explanation satisfied me. I was no longer afraid that he was a monster. I do not think he said anything else for the balance of our acquaintance.

The night was uneventful, but the morning proved to be exciting. When I woke up, the sun was already shining through the window facing the St. Johns River. Actually, I did not wake up on my own accord. A technician woke me by attaching various sets of wires to my arms. At first, I did not move and pretended to be asleep to see what in the world was happening. But then, the technician placed more sets of wires on my legs and was pushing my left shoulder to install more wires on my chest. By that time, I had already followed the wires and seen that they all went into a metal box and that the metal box was connected to the electrical outlet by the head of the bed.

Without moving or speaking, I thought to myself, this must be an electrical treatment. "Could this be an electroshock therapy?" I asked myself silently. I had heard of such treatments for various mental conditions in Cuba. If so, why was it being administered to me? Was it a mistake?

Without seeking an explanation—for none had been given to me as to what was being done—or waiting for an answer to the series of questions going through in my mind, I decided to get out of there, otherwise, I thought her next stop would be to place wires on my head and I was going to be shocked with electricity.

Immediately, I sat up and jerked all the wires from myself, pushed aside the technician, jumped out of bed wearing a hospital gown and underpants and ran through the hall and down the stairs. I do not know how I found my way out of the ward and into the lobby. I do remember coming down the stairs. Did I understand the sign that indicated the exit? In short, I had become the product of ignorance and fear and not guided by any logical reasoning, but by the instinct to escape into a safe place, however unknown that safe place might be.

The next thing I do remember was that I was being literally captured in the main lobby of the hospital, just as I was approaching a large door opening toward the St. Johns River.

Two large men dressed in white caught me by my armpits and upper arms and actually lifted me so that any steps I took were totally in vain in my attempt to escape from them. The next thing I remember is being again in the same room where the incident began, and surrounded by members of the medical staff.

Dr. Iglesias came forward and sat on my bed. He asked me in Spanish what was happening. I explained to him that when I was waking up I saw a person placing electrodes on me. I confided that I thought I was going to be electrocuted. I was afraid.

He explained that I was getting an electrocardiogram, an electrical tracing of the heart's activity. He went on to explain that the doctors thought that I had some sort of complication from the throat infection that was affecting my heart. They were very interested in following the progress of my condition by studying my electrocardiograms. He also explained that my asthma was being treated and was already a little better, but they were concerned about a heart murmur and very inflamed and infected tonsils. The head physician in charge of my case, Dr. Adams, had discussed with Dr. Iglesias and the other residents that the two issues appeared to be related. In short, they were concerned that I had acute rheumatic fever and that is why they were giving me aspirin and antibiotics.

He reassured me that no one was going to harm me, much less electrocute me. I believed him and the remainder of my hospitalization was uneventful from the standpoint of my behavior.

There were no further misunderstandings during my hospital stay. I actually enjoyed the morning rounds and recognized Dr. Adams, a late middle-aged, short man with blondish hair, rounding and advising the house staff as they auscultated, listened to my heart and lungs.

In the mornings, a group of doctors came in and listened to my heart. Dr. Iglesias asked me questions in Spanish about how I felt. The chief doctor, Dr. Adams, did not say very much in front of me, but he did seem to me to be their teacher.

In six days I was discharged back to the camp, after I had been successfully treated for these diagnoses:

Rheumatic Fever
Adenovirus Infection
Asthmatic Bronchitis

Upon arriving at camp, I felt reassured because I was given a warm welcome by the guys. They made me feel like a hero as I approached the cabin that was, for the time being, our common home. Paradoxically, at that time, an environment that had been totally foreign a few weeks before seemed like home, for now.

I was not the only one who became ill while at Camp St. John. However, during my stay there, I was the only one who required hospitalization. In the course of my stay at Camp St. John there was an epidemic of *varicella*, also known as chicken pox. I wrote to my father in Havana about it and he mentioned in his letter to me "that it was better if I had it then because if I were to have it later I might have more serious complications." I had a mild case of it. There was at least one other epidemic in Florida City. Cases of measles were reported in the camp where younger children were housed in small groups in apartments and attended to by Cuban houseparents.

Since all the institutions where Cuban refugee children were cared for were secret, in reality they were semi-clandestine; aspects of the physical and mental health of the children were not and have not been available. To my knowledge, the health authorities of St. John's County, the State of Florida, and the Centers for Disease Control have never reported on any epidemics in camps or communities of Cuban refugee children. But again, since the camps and orphanages were supervised through an agreement between the Catholic Church and the

U.S. government, perhaps, the proper public health issues were addressed but remain classified.

There have been several studies of the emotional and psychological issues of the Pedro Pans done, but long after the time in which we were institutionalized.(8) One issue that seemed important to study for experts in social psychiatry has been the psychological reactions of displaced persons. In general, it has been found that all displaced immigrants tend to be anxious and depressed at some point in time during the climax of their displacement to at least a mild degree.(9) Most individuals have not been totally disabled and have been able to adapt to their new culture and surroundings. Adding to the complexity of our situation in Operation Pedro Pan and the Unaccompanied Cuban Children's Program, both anxiety and depression are difficult to diagnose in adolescents because they can be hidden behind feelings and behavior that are part and parcel of their growth and development. In this regard, my worsening asthma at the time may have been aggravated, not only by the dust and the cold and other environmental factors, but also by undiagnosed anxiety and, perhaps, depression. The former may have been at the root of the intense fear I felt during the electrocardiogram fitting, when I literally lost control and ran away from my hospital room.

Some of the factors that place immigrants at risk of this type of behavior in their new environments are failing communication, insecurity, and anxiety. Failing communication was, indeed, a factor in my sudden emotional decompensation because I was not aware of what the technician was attempting to do. Was it a cardiac test or was it an electrical treatment? The language barrier proved to also be a factor in preventing proper communication between the patient, myself, and the staff. And thirdly, the level of anxiety normal for anyone with an asthma attack and admitted to a foreign hospital without appropriate instructions on what exactly to expect from the hospital admission, all added up to a formidable set of stressors.

I do not know of any formal study that was carried out about these specific emotional and health issues in the unaccompanied Cuban children who were cared for by foster parents or institutions at that time. There were no systematic observations of either our physical or mental health performed while we were there. Considering the number of children and youngsters involved in the Unaccompanied Cuban Children's Program, on the order of more than 8,000 individuals, one could imagine that valuable clinical data on both the physical and the mental issues of the entire process of change could have been gathered. Considering our ages from six to sixteen years old, invaluable sociologic and clinical data on migration and institutionalization could have been obtained. Such data could, in turn, have been used to understand better our own situation and responses. Furthermore, other children, migrations, and issues dealing with people uprooted from their environment into a foreign country may have benefited later. Although the twentieth century has been called "The Century of the Refugees," unfortunately migrations and institutionalizations have already proven to be a major problem of international concern also in the twenty-first century in Europe, Asia, Africa, and in the United States.

But back at Camp St. John, we were not consciously aware of anxiety or depression. Some individuals had difficulties going to sleep, but they found a refuge in the middle section of the cabins where the bathrooms were located. We survived without being counseled, for the most part, or analyzed. At the time, there was a collective feeling that even if any one of us got sick enough to go into the hospital, the camp staff and the Catholic Church were going to accompany each of us through whatever came up. After all, the *beca* was a work in progress, but it seemed just right for us at the time.

CHAPTER 9
BISHOP KENNY HIGH SCHOOL

"We thank the keeper of our years,
For insights won through toil and tears,
For all remembered faces dear,
For sunlit hours and visions clear,
For friends who shared the year's long road,
And bore with us the common load,
For comrades of a single day,
Who sent us stronger on our way,
For hours that levied heavy toll,
But brought us nearer to our goal."
Yearbook Dedication, Crusader 1961

When I came back from the hospital, I noticed an important addition to the camp. A used school bus painted in a faded blue-gray had been made available to the camp to move us around. The bus had a sign on each of its sides: U.S. AIR FORCE. No one explained how it came to be in our possession, but the bus served as our method of group transportation from then until we left the camp.

The U.S. Air Force bus was our school bus to and from Bishop Kenny High School. The trip to Bishop Kenny was not short. The bus took the same road that passed through the front of the camp, Route 13, and headed north. As we were approaching the city of Jacksonville proper, without crossing the St. Johns River, we took Atlantic Boulevard and a few blocks later we were dropped off at Bishop Kenny High School.

The school had just changed into a co-educational institution, with the girls' school located just in front of the boys' school and divided by Kingsman Avenue. The boys' school was the original Central High School located just behind the Assumption Church. Assumption Parish was founded by Bishop William J. Kenny.

U.S. Air Force school bus used for transportation of Cuban children in the Jacksonville area. Photograph copy made from 8mm frame

In 1952, Archbishop Hurley of St. Augustine opened Central High School in Jacksonville to serve as the Catholic academic secondary school for all parishes in the diocese. The following year, the name of the new school was changed to Bishop Kenny High School to honor the first bishop of the diocese who had been born in the United States.(1) Indeed, Father William J. Kenny was born in Delhi, a small community in central Upstate New York. In his youth, he worked at a newspaper in Scranton, Pennsylvania, and while there, saved enough money to pay for his college education. He entered into the seminary from St. Bonaventure College and was later ordained into the priesthood by Bishop John Moore, the second bishop of St. Augustine. Father Kenny was originally assigned to the only Catholic parish in Jacksonville, the Immaculate Conception, in 1879. He did not know it then, but he would become a leader of the community and the church. He made himself known during the 1889 yellow fever epidemic and the 1901 devastating fire, which burnt 466 acres of Jacksonville in a few hours. In 1902, following the death of Bishop Moore, Father Kenny was elevated to the episcopacy. Considering his legacy in Jacksonville, it is not surprising that Bishop Kenny was well respected by the entire northeast Florida community, as can be appreciated from the following quote from a newspaper account in the aftermath of the 1901 devastating fire: "His calm, clear judgment and excellent advice were accepted by the leading businessmen all through the trying days that followed, and through his efforts, the merciful work was greatly simplified, and many who otherwise would have suffered in silence, were brought to the attention of his co-workers and their wants supplied."(2)

Bishop Kenny was also known for having founded the first African-American Catholic parish and school in the state of Florida, St. Benedict the Moor. He also founded seven other parochial schools from 1902 until 1913 when he died from a heart attack.

Returning to our first experiences at Bishop Kenny High School, when we arrived the very first time, classes were already in progress. We had previously been given our schedules of classes depending on our age. My personal class schedule went something like this: First Period, Mathematics; Second Period, Chemistry; Third Period, United States History; Fourth Period, Bookkeeping; Fifth Period (right after lunch), Physical Education; and Sixth Period, Civics and English for Foreign Students.

On my first day on the grounds, I entered the second period class, a chemistry class, and sat in the middle toward the back where there was an empty desk available. The teacher, Sister Francis Joseph, went up to the board and wrote a chemical formula: "$NaHCO_3$"

Bishop Kenny High School 1961 Yearbook

Then she turned around and asked the class, "What is the name of this compound?"

I immediately raised my hand to the astonishment of all present. The teacher signaled for me to speak and I said, "Bicarbonate of sodium."

"He is right," she exclaimed. "This is sodium bicarbonate.

And then she went on to explain something, probably about sodium bicarbonate, but I did not understand the discussion at all.

All other classes were uneventful, except for the bookkeeping class. The teacher was another nun, whose name I do not remember. She was talking about credit and debit and I thought I was following her fairly well. But I could not understand why she kept saying 'shit.' Yes, that is right, I thought she said shit. Except that very soon I found out it was not shit. Whenever she said sheet, I understood that she said shit. In that particular class there were a couple of Americans who seemed to be joking among themselves. For a while I thought that their mannerisms and signs were related to what I perceived as a total disgrace, a nun proclaiming shit in school! But in due time, I got my ears tuned to the subtleties of English pronunciation.

The Civics and English for Foreign Students course was a special class for all eight older Cuban students. I am not even sure what the official title was that they gave the course, but I understood it to be a remedial course to get us up to par with everyone else in the school. It was taught by Jorge Cunill, who was a Cuban counselor at the camp. He used the civics textbook to explain the basics of American government. The organization of the federal government was understandable and similar to what we had learned in Cuba about the branches of government. The entire period was to be taught and carried out in English, but invariably some Spanish was spoken and we were often reminded to speak in English. The English part of the class, however, was indeed a remedial course in which we were using a sixth grade English book as our textbook and workbook. Basic writing and grammar were, in my understanding, the main issues being addressed by the course.

After the last period of the day, we sat down to listen to the announcements made through the loud speakers located in every classroom. This is the way I remember it. At the end of whatever announcement there was—the nature of which was totally foreign to me—there was a brief moment of silence. Then someone else came on and said something like this: "Today, Bishop Kenny High School has opened its doors to Cuban boys escaping Communism in the island of Cuba. Many of you will have them as classmates for the remainder of the school year. The administration and the faculty ask all of you to assist them in getting oriented to our school. These Cuban students have left their homeland in haste and have not been allowed to come with their parents or their belongings. With regards to their uniforms and school supplies, we are asking all of you for donations. We are asking you to bring tomorrow any older or extra uniforms, black pants, red or black ties, white shirts, etc.… so that the Cuban students will have a uniform to wear. We ask all of you for your prayers in these challenging times."

At the end of the day, everyone in the camp was excited about going to Bishop Kenny High School. There was an air of hope in the environment that had not been there before. Furthermore, we got to see girls, even if from far away.

Camp life had been monotonous until then. Now we were really getting into the *beca*, with the addition of the classes at a recognized Catholic high school. Wake up call was a little after 6 A.M. the next morning; the camp bell was rung and one of the Cuban counselors started his way through the cabins turning the lights on and asking everyone to wake up. On school days from then on, we got dressed after our morning hygiene rituals and went out to the larger cabin that housed the dining facilities, where we had our breakfast.

Our breakfast was usually American coffee, toast, a 240-milliliter carton of milk, baptized by us as a *tarro de leche*, and corn flakes. Occasionally, we had scrambled eggs and orange juice on the weekends. After breakfast, we gathered our school gear and went into the U.S. Air Force bus for our ride to Bishop Kenny High School. Most of the time, we talked amongst ourselves, but sometimes we sang songs. What songs did we sing? We used to sing often "*Adios Muchachos Compañeros de Mi Vida*," (Farewell Companions) a 1927 tango which was popularized by Carlos Gardel in Latin America and Louis Armstrong in the United States. Other songs we sang had to do with our previous schools in Havana. A group would sing the alma mater of the Belén School in Havana. Others would sing the La Salle anthem. We, the Marist alumni would sing the Marist anthem in honor of Marcellin Champagnat. If you have the impression that we were filled with nostalgia and felt like we were being pulled in two opposite directions by a very strong past and an uncertain future, you have the right idea.

On our second day of school, the morning ride to Bishop Kenny High School seemed shorter than the day before, since the bus driver already knew the way. The bus dropped us off at the parking lot of the Assumption Catholic Church and Grammar School, which was located right next to our school at the corner of Atlantic Boulevard and Kingman Road. From there, we all walked into Bishop Kenny High.

We got there on time for the first class. To our surprise, a room had been set up for all donations to be dropped off. There was an excess of black pants, white shirts, red ties, black ties, ball point pens, notebooks, etc. We were truly grateful. However, in case no one said it then, thank you, thank you very much! I think I got a couple of white shirts and a couple of pants and ties and headed to my first period class on time. The morning announcements then came up through the speakers: "Please stand. In the name of the Father, the Son, and the Holy Spirit, Amen."

Then the announcer proceeded: "I pledge allegiance to the flag of the United States of America and to the Republic for which it stands, one nation under God, indivisible with liberty and justice for all."

Immediately, the U.S. national anthem was played. As I stood in my place, I felt an immense sense of sadness. I asked myself *Why can I not be in my own school? Why do we have to be the subject of charity? Why can I not hear my own national anthem?* Interestingly, the words of the Pledge of Allegiance did not wake up my emotions in the way that the music of the *Star Spangled Banner* did. I had never heard the Pledge of Allegiance before, while I had heard the American national anthem many times at baseball and basketball games when American teams played in Havana. Furthermore, my dad was an avid listener of the *Voice of America* short-wave transmissions. The American national anthem was not new to me. The experience of being the subject of a massive donation, of being hundreds of miles from home, away from family and friends was indeed new. These latter issues were, in my opinion, what led me to have feelings of anguish and despair, accompanied by a couple of silent tears that ran down my cheeks.

The first period class was the Advanced Mathematics class of Mr. James Durant. He was explaining pre-calculus, the range and domain of functions, sets, etc.... Some of the Cuban students in the class were rather advanced in mathematics and they were just right for Mr. Durant's class. However, I felt I was not. This was, in my opinion, the hardest mathematics class I have ever taken. To make things worse, at one point in time, I got the impression that Mr. Durant thought we knew much more mathematics than we actually understood. We were eight Cubans in his class and maybe a couple were up to understanding pre-calculus.

American History class was fun, but reading the book was very difficult, not because the book was poorly written, but because my English was so primitive. American history class was taught by Mr. John Baldwin. He was covering the Tennessee Valley Authority (TVA) when we joined the class. We had heard about Franklin Delano Roosevelt (FDR) but did not know about the TVA. I never made any connections between the Cuban Agrarian Reform and the TVA! Even to this day, if I see a tractor that is not being dismantled I exclaim, "The revolution has not been through here!"

Bookkeeping was a blast once I realized that the Sister was talking about sheets. This type of course was taught in the *comercio* section of our secondary school in Cuba. Students who were going to join the work force, study business careers, or become public accountants took the four year *comercio* course. The other students who were planning to enter the university to study careers in engineering, the natural or physical sciences, medicine, and law were enrolled in the *bachillerato*.

Lunch was eaten in the school cafeteria. It consisted most of the time of hamburgers or hot dogs. Sometimes we had macaroni and cheese. And, yes, the lunch was also accompanied by a small carton of milk, 240 ml, our *tarro de leche*.

My physical education period was scheduled right after lunch. We students took a shower right after the exercise class. I paid little respect to an old fashioned Cuban tale that claimed that taking a shower after having eaten a meal was unhealthy or would lead to some collapse or fainting spell. I just brushed that aside without any problems, because my father had explained to me that there was no scientific basis for such a belief. Obviously, no one experienced any untoward effects from physical education and showering after lunch, whether they were a Cuban or not.

When school finished, we all went to the spot where the U.S. Air Force bus had been parked next to the school. We got into the bus and rode home the same way we had come in the morning. At the end of the second day, everyone arrived back at camp with some kind of homework. The dining hall was full of guys trying to make sense of what had transpired in school. A Cuban counselor, Mr. Bravo, tried to explain mathematics to the younger ones. I decided to read up on history. I picked up an English/Spanish dictionary and began reading about the TVA. It must have been a couple of hours before I gave up. I had read one paragraph, almost a quarter of a page.

From that point onward, it was bound to get better. But believe me, my English improved very slowly. We all continued to speak mostly in Spanish among ourselves while at the camp. We had been transplanted during a period of major changes in our own biology, adolescence, into a culture and a school curriculum which was somewhat different, to put it mildly, than what we were accustomed to. In another dimension, we were still being pulled by two poles, one in the past in Spanish and the other one beyond ourselves in an uncertain but definite future, in English.

Many, including myself, thought at the time that we would be in exile for a short time. My cousin Muñeca had first left Havana in the fall of 1960 and had returned at the end of the semester to take her examinations at the *Universidad Católica de Villanueva*. Perhaps, that was the way most of us thought of our present

Rolando O'Farrill and other students walking out from the boy's building at
Bishop Kenny High School in the spring of 1961.
Photograph from 8mm movie frame

back then. However, very soon, we were going to find out that what we had thought of as a frivolous and transient adventure, which was to occupy our lives for a short time, would turn into a much longer journey. That long journey, I dare to say, was never in the minds of our parents when they sent us to a safe haven in the United States. At the end of the day, short was another word, which with the advent of the Cuban revolution, had acquired a different meaning. Since then, for us, it became a word with variable and uncertain meaning, depending on your point of view, the resolution of your vision, your point of reference, and whatever else was happening at the time.

CHAPTER 10
REKINDLING RELATIONSHIPS AND DISMANTLING THE CLASS

"Children became the arena in which a larger battle between communism and capitalism or between Christianity and communism was played out."
-María de los Angeles Torres

Havana, February 22, 1961
Dear FRIEND:

You can't imagine the deep joy and sincere gratitude I felt when I carefully read your letter. I've just received it. I have enjoyed reading it and I'm answering it driven by the best feelings of Friendship.
I am well and my parents also, thank God. Once again, I appreciate your intention to clarify what may have happened during those disagreements that may have come between us. No doubt, I had to suffer your unexpected departure, as I expressed it to your mom at the time I spoke with her. I understand now, as I understood when I spoke with María Luisa, that the date for your trip was unplanned. My only joy is that I went together with you on the bus that you, Zenón, and Lorenzo took heading to the movies the day before your departure as we did —in the good times—when we went together to the commercial district of Havana to buy hobby supplies, bats and balls.
The bonds of friendship that unite us cannot be separated. As you remember, you and I were together since we were in kindergarten when Silvia, my aunt, and my mom, Ofelia, gave us our first lessons. We are already taking exams. We all passed the physical education

test... It went very well because we performed all the exercises required of us. The Natural Sciences course (Zoology) test was on Monday. There were five questions at 20 points each and quite easy. The Mathematics test is on the 25th, on March 1st it is the Spanish course test, and Chemistry and Physics are on the 6th and the 10th. Classes will end on April 15 on account of the literacy campaign. Watch this, March 10 is the last exam of the first semester and April 3rd the second semester exams begin. That is, there are some 20-odd days during which we have to mecharnos cantidad.

After that, classes will not start again for us—the older students—until January 1962 ...

Your father called me...and told me you were going to a school in which Spanish was used in the mornings and English in the afternoons. If you're not learning English by now, we are going to hang you from a pole...

I hope you answer me soon and when you do, do not forget to tell me what is going on with your cousin Ramoncito. By the way, tell him not to pull too many people's legs and regarding both of you: Do not get into a lot of mischief.

Your dad told me that they were cleaning the sports grounds of your school. Take advantage and try to play as much ball as you can. The baseball field in our school here has not been used since you left. It is how you left it. Neither Brother Balbino nor anyone else has gone out to play....

Ah! I forgot. At this time, we—all your classmates—are all united because we have abandoned the hostility that had separated us. I know this will make you happy.

Tony, although I'm no good at giving advice, I would like to tell you not to abandon your religious principles and do not waste one iota of time; study, instruct yourself, and advance forward...give all my regards to our friends who are over there, and my best to you from your brotherly friend,

Juan González Pérez

Aside in the margin: *"May God bless us and the Virgin pray for us. Say three Hail Mary's in the evening."*

Juan González in the group of students photographed in 1959 with our
Agrarian Reform tractor.
Marist Yearbook, 1959

Juan can be seen on the left side of the photograph at the Marist School yard with the group that helped the most in the fundraising to purchase the International Harvester tractor donated to the Agrarian Reform in 1959. He also appeared in the photograph of our excursion to Jibacoa with Brother Balbino's third-year of *bachillerato* class in the first half of 1960. Juan was the natural leader in our classroom. He was charismatic, intelligent, and friendly. I do not have a record of my letter to him, but considering his intense and sincere reply, I understand that indeed he had embraced the values, and the understanding of those values, that had for very complex but real reasons, divided us for a short time. Juan, like myself, was a fervent supporter of the revolution in January 1959. While I turned against the revolution in the summer of that same year, Juan appeared to continue to support the revolution even in 1961. I should be fair and emphasize that he "appeared" to support the revolution because he was never known to have done anything against those of us who were openly against the Castro regime. Juan's external behavior may have been influenced by the fact the Revolutionary Minister of Education, Armando Hart Dávalos was very close to his family. Essentially, we were divided by the issues that the revolution brought forth in our lives.

In his memoir about Operation Pedro Pan, *Defining Moments*, my friend José Ignacio Ramírez gives a detailed account of his reunion with Julio, his childhood friend whom he left behind when he left Cuba somewhat "unexpectedly." That is, Ignacio left his friend without saying good bye, as I did. Julio did not know that Ignacio was leaving Cuba in pretty much the same way that Juan did not know of my departure date. Upon Ignacio's return to Cuba in the 1990s, he rekindled the friendship that had been eclipsed for a long time. It was only through sincere discussion, transparent analysis of their experiences, and direct, personal contact between them, that their different ways of looking at our complex reality back in the early 1960s became one vision for both of them. In the case of Julio and Ignacio, they had to make up for years of absence and misunderstandings. They accomplished it by a face-to-face meeting that lasted a whole afternoon without any distractions. They met in the middle of the country near the town of Aguacate in the old Havana province, where they had spent most of their childhood in peace.

Whatever misunderstandings there were between my way of looking at our reality and Juan's were minor compared to those that existed between Ignacio and Julio. Furthermore, the issues between Ignacio and Julio had a forty-year lapse, during which the fermentation process made the entire social and personal chemistry between them much more difficult to repair than Juan's and mine. This letter from Juan in response to whatever I wrote to him served the same purpose as the

The Marist Junior Varsity Baseball team at the school near the Plaza Cívica in 1959. Juan Gonzalez and the author in the right corner

tedious and difficult rekindling of friendship that Julio and Ignacio accomplished during hours of discussion "under the sun and on the railroad tracks."(1)

I bring this issue up because the truncated civil war of the early 1960s in Cuba has not had a closure, yet, even fifty-five plus years after the fact. The one effect of the Cuban revolution on all Cubans from all walks of life has been to divide us. Families and friends have been divided, and in some instances they have continued to be divided because the environment sometimes appears hostile to rekindling friendships. Most of the time this is because the individuals involved are not sure how the other will react to any kind of rapprochement. It does take courage and faith to admit that all parties who have suffered division during the Cuban revolution have been misled and deceived by one or another entity. The testimony shared here through this letter from Juan to me and the experience shared by José I. Ramírez in his memoir are important pieces of the puzzle with which all Cubans and divided communities need to deal in order to find common ground, healing, and closure about those difficult and complex times.

Both encounters, my own with Juan back then through the mail and Ignacio's with Julio many years later, point to the fact that through personal, one-to-one, sincere, transparent encounters, one can hope that understanding and healing can take place in the course of time. This is possible if there is the will to do it and if the forces that have triggered the division have abated or been eclipsed by the passage of time.

As Juan was finishing his letter, he went back to this issue of healing the division. He stated, "...we—all your classmates—are all united because we have abandoned the hostility that had separated us. I know this will make you happy." I felt that he was very kind to me in recognizing that I would be very pleased about the conclusion of the hostilities that separated us. Unfortunately, the conditions from where the hostilities began to emerge are still part and parcel of the Cuban situation and, therefore, more divisions are still pulling people apart than bringing them to an understanding and reconciliation. In short, reconciliation is difficult to accomplish because it requires the need and desire of at least two independent individuals who exist in a social and political environment. Unfortunately, this will not always be possible.

Going back to the text of Juan's letter, it is not clear from his letter if I wrote to my dad that we were going to a bilingual school or that he himself gleaned that information from what I had written. The truth of the matter is that we never went to a bilingual school. In any event, whether I invented this story—which I doubt— or my father shared something I wished for, but did not have—which is probably true—this type of misinformation became part of what parents and children discussed on the island. In fact, this sort of information became another *bola* that was spread regarding the conditions under which the unaccompanied Cuban children lived outside of Cuba. One cannot blame either side for this. It was a generalized misunderstanding that centered on wishes and expectations and not on real facts. How can anyone blame either side for not sharing the facts? After all, it was during a civil war and the facts during a war are always a matter of secrecy or propaganda.

It is necessary to elaborate on the issue of my need to learn English. From Juan's and earlier letters, the reader has noted that my parents, my grandmother, and my peers seem all to be concerned about this issue. They were all very interested in my progress in English. According to Juan, my father claims that he would "hang me from a pole" if I did not learn English. This is not to be taken literally; my father was not an abusive person. When you take an exam in Cuba and you fail it, you are said to have been hung (*colgado*). Neither Juan nor my dad meant to literally hang me from a pole as if I had committed some atrocities in the war!

Having explained the figurative speech as noted above, I must confess that I was never very good in my English courses in the Marist school. At that time, I did not feel I had to learn English. I found it a lot more difficult than chemistry, Spanish, history, or mathematics, perhaps, because somehow I had decided that I did not like the English course. Perhaps, it was a way of rebelling against my family's wishes. I am not sure. The bottom line, however, was clear: I found English difficult.

My father would have told you the following story regarding my interest in learning English. In the summer of 1957, my dad presented me with his plan to have me take private English classes from a tutor during the school break. I had nothing else to do, so twice a week I began taking private classes at home. The teacher was an old and professorial gentleman. He was a very good teacher. He had me dedicate a notebook to my English class, in which I was to write all my questions and homework. Several weeks went by. Then one afternoon, the teacher asked me at what time my dad arrived home. I told him that it varied, but by six in the evening he was usually home. The next week, the teacher came at precisely that time and asked to speak with my father. This is what the teacher said to him: "Dr. Gordon, your son is very nice, but he has no interest whatsoever in learning English. I think you are wasting your money on these lessons."

My father reluctantly accepted the teacher's recommendation to stop the classes. Little did I—or for that matter, my father, or even the good old English teacher—know that a few years later I was to be in a position where English would prevail. It would impose itself on my life, whether I liked it or not. It would not matter anymore if it was easy or difficult. English was the language of my new environment and, while in the past it could be construed that it could have been helpful to learn it, at that time, it was a mandatory requirement, not from a school curriculum or official or even the Cuban revolution, but from the necessities of life in the place where I had found refuge.

It is also evident in this letter, that Juan had not lost his religious beliefs. In fact, it is tempting to argue that Juan and I shared religious beliefs, which we had both acquired while growing up in Catholic families and attending a Catholic school from first grade onward. In Juan's case, he not only encouraged me to not abandon my own religious beliefs, but at the end, he wrote a prayer and proposed a prayer campaign for us to follow in the evenings. Our common religious beliefs served to bridge the serious differences that had distanced us for a short while. However, the same could not be assumed to be the case in most relationships and friendships that had been torn apart between Cubans during the revolution. Obviously, religious beliefs are not going to be a key issue for all individuals who need to heal their differences to re-establish friendships and relations. However, at least one aspect of commonality seems necessary in order to re-establish a broken personal bond. That common bond may very well be the need for both sides to reconcile their friendship.

There is one term that Juan used that needs to be explained. When he was describing the new schedule of examinations and points out that the second semester material would have to be covered in a little over twenty days, he exclaims, "*Tenemos que mecharnos cantidad!*"

Essentially, he exclaims that they would have to study and work very hard. The term *mecharnos* comes from the nouns *mecha* (wick) and the *mechero* (the burner). The most famous of the *mecheros* to us *bachillerato* students was the *mechero de Bunsen* (Bunsen burner). That is, the allegory refers to a wick and a burner. What students meant back then when they said *mecharnos* was that they were going to work hard and constantly like the burner burns constantly as long as there is fuel delivered to the wick and oxygen in the air. Perhaps, an equivalent phrase in the American culture is to state that the student is "burning the midnight oil" when they stay up at night to study hard for an exam.

February 22, 1961
Dear friend:

May God grant that you be well when you receive this letter, we are pretty good.

I went by your house with the bike as your mom asked because they were going to sell it. I took care of it as if it were mine. It does not make any sounds when you ride it. I have greased it and maintained it like new.

Poppy is bigger and fatter and when he sees me he goes wild.

Luz, Rosita and Fermín—father and son—are fine. Also Milagros and her daughters are doing well. Every Sunday I go to visit Gloria and her sisters and they all ask about you.

In our class, we are now 8 pupils...Brother Juan Salvador's Chemistry and "Zero Next."

From what your mom tells me, the school you are in must be pretty. Tell me about the room you have over there. Having any fun?

Well...perhaps we will see each other soon...then I will speak with you more openly...

Goodbye to you from your friend and buddy who always remembers you,

Luis Faura

Faura is also in the same photographs as Juan, noted above. In fact, it was Faura who took a commanding position at the head of the tractor, standing probably on the ledge of the balcony of the first floor of the school. It will also be remembered that Faura was the individual who was left to do whatever I was doing at home, in terms of preparing leaflets and fliers for the anti-communist movement in our school. I had not known that he was also given my bicycle, however. That was reasonable, because he lived at the other end of Altahabana by the National Hospital and he had no bicycle of his own. If he had to go back and forth, the bicycle saved him time. Besides, I had no use for it!

Luz, Fermín, and their two children, and Milagros and her daughters also lived in Altahabana. Luz and Fermín were related to Milagros' family. All of them had been in a brief exile in the late 1950s on account of the Batista dictatorship. Their children had come back to Havana in 1959, very fluent in English and with the latest rock-and-roll records. They all danced rock and roll very well. Milagros' husband was a professional pilot who had been flying weapons and supplies into the Sierra Maestra mountain range from exile during that phase of the civil war. All of them, eventually, were to leave Cuba months after Faura's letter.

The *bola* about the *beca* kept moving around. Faura was inquiring about my room. He did not know that it was a room shared by twenty other kids. But, how would he know if I did not tell him! He was also inquiring about "having fun." It is natural for teenagers to be looking to have fun, but there was little in the way of fun that was programmed into our routine. Later on, as camp life became more organized, there were some fun activities.

Faura confirmed that there were only eight of the original class of twenty-five students in our classroom. The class was being dismantled. His comments about Brother Juan Salvador should be explained. He was our chemistry teacher. When he gave our lesson daily, that is when he quizzed us to check if we had done our homework, and often did it orally. Other times, he did it by posting a question on the blackboard—blackboards were truly black back then—and had us write down the answer on a piece of paper that he collected and graded afterwards. However, when he gave our lesson orally, he was very fast in delivering his judgment and grade. He started at one of the first rows of desks. He called the name of the student. The student would stand, listen to the question, and if he did not answer within five seconds, the brother would say, "*Cero, siguente*" (Zero, next.) The next person behind was to stand up and answer the same question. If the question was too hard, maybe there would be several *Cero, siguente* judgments in a row. If you started to answer but he did not see clearly that you were getting it correctly, he stopped you and again said, "*Cero, siguente.*"

Havana February 23, 1961
My dear son:

Yesterday I received your letter, the third since you're in school. You have not acknowledged or said anything as to whether you have received a letter of mine in that place.
Today your uncle Cesar had his operation and he came out perfectly well. Your mother accompanied him all morning in the hospital.
As I was saying in my second letter, I want to know the name of the Father who is the director or the school principal, as well as the religious congregation to which the school belongs.
Here we are as always, our malanga *is hard and overgrown, so cheer up to be there! Here you would be just as we are, tangled in the* malanga.
Next Sunday I will go to Mass at the Marist School. I suppose

you've written to the Brothers. They're "crossing Niagara Falls on a bicycle" because at any moment they will nationalize private schools....

In the last letter...I asked you to buy me the vaccine (Hepatitis Virus Vac Dystemper and Hepatitis. Pitman Moore) for Poppy. I also asked this from Muñeca because here in Cuba this vaccine cannot be found and Poppy needs it. Listen to me, do not buy it until I tell you again because I want to communicate this to Muñeca and wait for her answer.

She has not gone to New York yet because last night she spoke with Eduardo on the telephone and she was still in Tampa with a feverish cold.

Eduardo leaves Thursday for Spain by the steamship Guadalupe. *It was to leave Friday but the departure was advanced...*

All our neighbors send their gratitude and greetings to you. They are very grateful to you for having sent them postcards.

Something ...I must tell you about Poppy. He has become very sassy. He thinks of nothing more than sneaking into the automobile to go for a ride. When I get ready to leave the house, I have to give him to your mother to hold him. Otherwise, he will get into the car with me. Well son, may God continue to help us to be together soon. Receive the blessing of your father,

Antonio

My father numbered the letters and was concerned that I might not, yet, have received any of his letters at my new location, Camp St. John. Indeed, the address to the camp was long and there were at least two correct ways of writing it. There was only one letter that arrived, later than it had to, with several rubber stamped messages from the postmaster, advising me to inform those who were writing to me not to send letters through Jacksonville. It was a letter from Pella, another one of my peers at the Marist School, in which he added the word Jacksonville below Switzerland to the address. The American postal workers did not like that at all!

Regarding my father's request for the name and address of the director of the camp, I was looking and waiting for someone to give me the address of Father John Joseph Lenihan who was the director of Catholic Charities in the Diocese of St. Augustine at the time. Eventually, I did send my father his name and address and

I do remember that Father Lenihan mentioned having received a letter from my father. In his letters, my father would continue to inquire about Father Lenihan and remind me that he did not get an answer from him. When I inquired about looking up my file in the archives of the Unaccompanied Cuban Children Program and Operation Pedro Pan held at Barry University, Miami, Florida, I thought I would find the letter from my dad to Father Lenihan or perhaps a copy of Father Lenihan's letter to my father. However, I did not.

My uncle Cesar was my mother's youngest brother. He lived all his life on the family farm near Manzanillo in Calicito in the former Oriente Province. His son, who was also named Cesar, joined the Rebel Army in the Sierra Maestra to fight Batista's dictatorship. Cesar junior arrived in Havana with the *barbudos* and served in the motorized traffic police for a few months. For reasons that were not clear then and he never clarified later, he resigned from his assignment in the revolutionary police in Havana and returned to Caliticto to his family and the farm. Although he was recognized there as a *combatiente* (combatant) of the revolution, he led a simple life until his death from a heart attack.

In the meantime, the overall situation in Havana—according to my father—had gotten tougher. That is the gist of what my father was writing when he said that "the *malanga* is hard." *Malanga* is a tuber that is grown in the Cuban countryside. At one point in time, when Fidel Castro was threatening to cut business relations with the United States, he exclaimed, "*Comeremos Malanga*," that is, we will eat *malanga*. However, as the repression increased, farms were confiscated, the land was cultivated, but fruitless, and the public administration became more incompetent and corrupt, it became difficult to even find *malanga* in the food markets or the countryside. My father was pointing out that I was better off outside of Cuba at Camp St. John than trying to deal with the Cuban *malanga* at the time. The *malanga* was also difficult for the clergy. When my father writes that the brothers are *"crossing Niagara Falls on a bicycle"* he is using a Cuban slang. In Cuba, if you are *"crossing Niagara Falls on a bicycle"* you are in trouble and having enourmous problems with whatever you are doing.

The issue about Poppy's vaccinations had already been noted in a previous letter and will continue to be an issue in several letters later on. Poppy may have needed the specific vaccination requested on account of the fact that he was getting ready to depart from Cuba. However, it may have been a vaccine that he would have obtained in the course of simply growing up.

There was something more profound going on with Poppy, however. I am impressed by the fact that Poppy seemed to understand that people were disappearing from his environment. There were only eight left in the classroom at the Marist School. There were a dwindling number of kids in Altahabana. But, there was also my absence from the house and the neighborhood. It was my take, therefore, that Poppy had not turned "sassy." He had always been a very quick and smart dog. Now, he had turned vigilant, so that he would not remain behind, left alone. In my opinion, Poppy knew that, at that time, people were departing from his environment and eventually he himself would have to leave to a place that he did not know under conditions that he could not imagine, otherwise, he would be left alone. Despite the fact that he may not have understood how he would fare in leaving or to where he would go, or the why of the situation, he did not wish to remain behind. He wanted to be part of his community, his human family.

JMJ Havana February 24, 1961
Dear friend:

I have received your kind letter of the 12th and have not had time to write back to you. I do so at this time because as you will realize there is no school today, February 24th.
Pella is a little out of the group. He is no longer joining us in our outings to the library or to Zenón's house.
Brother Teodoro has started the Botany course. Since we have no textbook, he dictates his lectures, including the names of rare plants. When we ask him to repeat something, he exclaims, "Ave María Mochacho." Then we laugh.
Brother Teodoro did not receive a letter you wrote to him but he was very happy when he received the one you sent him with mine. Have you written the school address correctly? Just in case, I am sending you the correct address now: Number 807, Independencia Avenue between Conil and Santa Ana streets.
Your papa and your mama are fine. They have gone several times to attend Mass at the school and we have gotten to talk there. As I have understood it, you are at a La Salle boarding school or something like that.
I hope you're with us soon, I say within a month or two. As you know, classes will end on April 15. We believe we are not going to get to that date without having the school seized. Lately, there is talk that already the Marist School at Camagüey has been confis-

cated. The brothers feel the same as we do.
I have many other things to tell you...
Here you have friends that do not forget you. With nothing else for
now, goodbye to you from your faithful friend and classmate,

Lorenzo
P.S. Give my regards to all out there. It was very beautiful the stamp
you sent me.

Lorenzo seemed concerned about Pella, another one of our peers. He had not been hanging out with the remainder of the group in Havana. Pella will come up again in these letters. Not everyone tolerated the stressors with the same resilience as everyone else.

Lorenzo noted that they have already started the second semester, although some of the exams for the first semester have not been completed. The absence of a textbook may suggest that there was lack of consensus within the leaders of the Ministry of Education. Or, perhaps, there is no textbook, because there were no resources to provide a textbook in the public institutes. More likely than not, however, the lack of textbooks for that shortened semester in the "Year of Education" had to do with the fact that the entire official program of studies for the semester was outlined and mimeographed to be distributed to all professors and schools accredited in the Institute. A textbook would have provided a more extensive and complete coverage of the subject matter. One other reason for not selecting a textbook might be that there could have been material considered anti-communist or pro-Yankee by the revolutionary authorities in some of the books reviewed for selection by the authorities.

Whatever the reason, in that shortened second semester of 1961, there were no textbooks in the private schools or the public Institutes of Secondary Education. The latter were the public secondary schools in Cuba. Secondary private schools were accredited in Cuba through their affiliation with their district Institute of Secondary Education. Students attending private secondary schools were examined by the professors at the Institute of Secondary Education and their own private school teachers. At the conclusion of the *bachillerato*, the student received—provided the work was satisfactorily completed in both—a diploma from the Institute and one from the private school. The Ministry of Education, according to the Constitution of 1940, was responsible for delineating the content of each course of study required for graduation from secondary education. Therefore, the Institutes of Secondary Education served as the accrediting centers for the private schools and if there was no textbook for Botany at the Marist School, there was no textbook assigned anywhere else, including in the Institute of La Víbora where our school was accredited. In the greater Havana area, there were four Institutes of Secondary Education at the time.

The *bola* about the *beca* continued to go around, but every time with a different twist. Lorenzo seemed to think that we were at a boarding school directed by the Christian Brothers of La Salle. I do not think that I ever said or wrote anything to suggest that version of the facts. The Christian Brothers of La Salle were great educators, but I do not know where Lorenzo got the idea that they were directing Bishop Kenny High School.

Rumors were also being spread about the situation in other cities in Cuba. It is not clear if the Marist School at Camagüey had been closed, yet. Officially, the school in Camagüey was closed when all other religious and private schools were closed several months after Lorenzo's letter was written. Lorenzo acknowledged having received a secret message on the envelope underneath the stamp in one of my letters. It is unfortunate that I do not remember what I wrote under the stamps.

As the spring of 1961 made its appearance, there was still a longing manifested by various relatives and friends in their letters. They seemed fairly sure that our exile would be relatively short, on the order of a couple of months. The examinations were in progress, but the prospects for success were not favorable, because the semester was rather short, there was no textbook, and the students were not centering their attention on the subject matters assigned to them. They were still overwhelmed by the worsening socio-political situation. The alphabetization campaign had taken precedence over anything else in the school calendar. The practice of directing the national attention to a specific revolutionary program would be repeated multiple times during the revolution. For example, in the late sixties the campaign for the production of ten million tons of sugar essentially paralyzed all other activities in the country, except for the production of sugar.

School would not start again for the upper classmen until January 1962. Was it necessary to sacrifice the second semester program in order to accomplish the literacy campaign? Who knows? But, who would be able to question the judgment of the only and *máximo líder* (highest leader) of the revolution? Considering the alternatives, if a student was not going to participate, for whatever reason, in the literacy campaign, what was there for him or her to do until January 1962? Depart

Group of Pedro Pans at St. Patrick's Catholic Church in Jacksonville, Florida, in 1961. We were invited to partake of St. Patty's celebration by the pastor, Fr. John J. Lenihan. Photograph from 8mm frame

the island? Who knows? The overall situation was turning, if anything, harsher. There was also a feeling that everyone was leaving or getting ready to depart. My assessment is that this trend had not even escaped the observation of our family dog, Poppy.

CHAPTER 11

UNDERSTANDING THE REVOLUTION:
REPRESSION AND SEPERATION

"There will be a new homeland. And this new homeland in a new world can only be built with new men and women. And that is what Cuba is expecting from you. The Cuba of tomorrow will expect all of you not to make the tragic errors that have led to the present crisis. Let us pray to our Lady of Charity, La Vírgen del Cobre, that she may hear our prayers for world peace. May the dove of peace descend upon our country and around the world."
-Father Salvador de Cistierna

Havana, March 1, 1961
My dear son:

Yesterday I received your letter dated February 24. We were greatly surprised that in it you say how sick you were. I tell you it was a surprise because in your previous letters you were saying that you had been ill only one day, on your arrival. It was wrong not to tell us how you were really doing. In this matter of your health, you owe it to me not to hide anything because we are concerned, as well as you ought to be. If your health is not good, we will go there for you or you will come back over here, and we'll manage in whatever manner we can. So I ask you, please do not hide anything from us and tell us frankly anything with respect to your health as soon as it happens.
You should send me the full name of the director of the school as well as the name and complete address of the medical doctor who treated you. I want to write to both of them.

*Today is the first day that the family of the "Red Corsair" will be
in New York for María Ofelia must already be giving birth to her
first child. I guess they passed by you on the way up north.
Well my son, do not hide anything about your health because we
already have enough in being separated from you. May God protect
you and receive the blessing of your father,*

Antonio

Obviously, I was not thinking of what the evangelist had written, "…all that is secret will be made known to all." (Matt. 10:26). Or like the Spanish proverb reminds us, "You can pick out a liar sooner than you can tell if a man is limping." Whether you take the high road of the Gospel or the proverbial route, I was caught attempting to give misinformation, or better, yet, not giving any information. At that time in the past, the beginning of March, I had not gone into St. Vincent's Hospital, yet. They were referring here to the asthma attack that occurred when I first arrived at the St. John's Manor in Camp St. John.

My Uncle Emilio had left Cuba for Spain in order to accompany his son, who was going on a scholarship, a real *beca*. According to the Cuban authorities and the revolution, he was not supposed to still be off the island nation, much less in the United States. Therefore, when he wrote to the family in Cuba, he used the pseudonym the "Red Corsair." He claimed that a corsair had permission or patent to be somewhere and his permission had been given to him by the communists, that is, the "Reds." Uncle Emilio was known in the family as being one of the most informed and level-headed individuals. At this point in late February 1961, he was writing to my father in Havana to have some bottles of Polar beer in the refrigerator for him. It may be that Uncle Emilio was, indeed, thinking that the conclusion of the civil war was near. On the other hand, he may have been writing to lift my father's spirits. Even in simple family matters, it was difficult to clearly define interpersonal messages in times of war when there is also the fear of the authorities reading your mail.

I declare myself guilty of hiding my true health status, particularly with regard to my illness when I arrived at camp. With regard to my relatives passing through the camp on their way from Tampa to the New York area, that is a different story. In her letters from Tampa, Muñeca had advised me that they were planning to go through Jacksonville and stop over at the camp to see both of us, Ramoncito and me. However, in subsequent letters, we learned, after the fact, that they had postponed their departure date from Tampa on account of a snow storm in the New York area.

In the meantime, the time for the birth of María Ofelia's first daughter was rapidly approaching. By then, Uncle Emilio decided that they had no time to take the scenic route out of Florida. They just drove directly out of the state and into the Northeast.

It was difficult at the time to explain to my parents in Cuba that changes in plans on the part of Uncle Emilio and the delayed nature of the postal services all conspired against the visit so desired by the family to Camp St. John. Obviously, my parents would have liked Uncle Emilio and the Tampa troupe to go through Jacksonville on their way to New York City. They would have seen and reported on how they found us at the camp. However, in any final analysis, I think that all these various forms of misinformation eventually added to the uncertainty of living during the revolution. Eventually and invariably, the truth always surfaced in one way or another.

Havana, March 1, 1961
Highly esteemed Tony:

You probably thought that I had forgotten you, but I was waiting to get your address. Yesterday I was surprised to get a letter from you. You cannot imagine the joy you gave me....
Most Sundays your parents, my parents and I go out to have lunch and spend a beautiful time together. The other day I finally got Rosita and Cañete to go with us, but believe me, it took a tremendous amount of coaching.
Here everything is as good as or better than when you left. The priests and nuns are defending themselves like "cats on their backs." On the 14th we had the feast of St. Valentine and we had a party where everyone had a good time. I imagine a lot...and I imagine that you already know English and you are also pleased with the school you are attending.
I also imagine there are very pretty girls over there. Boys would not be scarce there. Since boys are disappearing from here, make friends with some boys so that you can bring me one as contraband when you come back.
I hope you write as soon as you can and tell me many things from over there, just so that I can dream.
You are appreciated,

Ameli

Families seem to be spending more time together. At that time, Ameli took credit for getting Rosita and Cañete to go on one of their outings. Cañete and his wife lived next door to my father's house. They had no children and were rather reserved. Cañete was a lawyer, who worked for a while at the INRA (*Instituto Nacional de Reforma Agraria*). He was my contact in getting permission to go visit the agrarian cooperative in the area of Caimito near Havana in the fall of 1960.

Young people were also trying to have as good a time as they could. However, aside from the party for St. Valentine's Day, there was a feeling of sadness as Ameli pointed out that there seem to be no boys in the neighborhood anymore. In terms of the children and adolescents who came to the United States and entered the Unaccompanied Cuban Children Program, in April of 1961, 61 percent were boys and 39 percent were girls.(2) Ameli's impression of the exodus of the children from Altahabana may have been not only correct, but also a barometer of what was happening in the Greater Havana area. Before closing her letter, Ameli does let us see that she wants to dream. This is a sign of youth and also of hope. For if she had no hope, her dreams would turn into nightmares.

Havana March 3, 1961
My dear son:

I received another letter from you yesterday and another the day before yesterday and by them can tell that all is going well.
You asked my opinion regarding your purchase of a roll of film. Use the one you think will give you the best results. You also need to look at your wallet. I do not know how you are doing as far as your money.
As for trading the movie camera for a photographic camera, see what you need and if you need to change it for another one do it. Or if you can, buy the photographic camera without trading the movie camera.
I see you had a mathematics examination.... I guess you will have the grade. When you do find out your grade, please tell me the results of the exam.
I also want you to send me the names of some of your peers, and if they have parents in Cuba, their addresses so that I can meet them. I want to see if they have any way of sending money to their children and the manner or way they do, so that I can send you something.

Get me a map of Florida like those that are given away in gas sta-
tions. Send it to me so that I can use it to guide me with respect to
the location where you are and the road to it, etc.... Do not forget
this, you ask at any gas station and they will give it to you.
Well son, receive a kiss from your mother and your father's blessing,

María Luisa and Antonio

Since they wanted to have pictures of me and the school, I had thought of trad-ing my Brownie movie camera for a photographic camera. But by that time, I had bought a set of two 8-mm movie rolls of film at a drugstore. The film was not ex-pensive. The developing was to be the more expensive part of the process. I did not develop the films until much later, and it was not until a couple of years later that we were first able to project the pictures.

Mathematics was my worst subject at Bishop Kenny High School. I have no idea why I mentioned the exam to my parents in my letter. I could have figured out that they would ask me about how I did. The issue of the grade on the first math exam would come up again. I do not think I ever told them just how badly I did.

They were clearly interested in checking out the location where I was in Florida. However, the mention of a map and roads suggested that the thought may have crossed their minds to travel by car to wherever I was. Even if they did not think of this, I thought that, perhaps in the future, they would appear at the camp by car, maybe without any warning. This was not a farfetched idea without a prece-dent. A couple of times when I went into seclusion on a religious retreat, my parents drove up to the gate of the seminary inquiring about "where the children were." Obviously, they were reassured and directed to go back where they had come from! However, getting out of Cuba during this phase of the revolution was not as easy as taking a country road and driving to one of the seminaries on the outskirts of Havana in the mid-fifties. This discussion also suggested that the dreams which Ameli mentioned in her letter were not exclusive to the children and adolescents who had remained on the island. We, who were off the island, were also prone to do our fair share of wishful thinking and dreaming.

For younger readers, I should explain that up to the 1970s, it was common for the gas companies to distribute free printed maps of states and even countries pub-lished by the oil companies. The maps were given away as promotions at most gas stations. Invariably, they had clear, accurate, and updated maps of roads and cities so that a driver unfamiliar with the terrain and traffic could find their way. Obviously, there were no smart phones or internet back then!

> *Havana, March 9, 1961*
> *My dear son Tony:*
>
> *Yesterday I received your letter dated February 27 and by it I can tell that you are well and content over there. I was hoping you'd say something about the mathematics exam ...hope you have done well. As you must know by now, María Ofelia gave birth to a girl weighing eight and a half pounds. So you see, Emilito is already a* papá. *I can only imagine how happy he must be.*
> *My son, you do not know how strong our desire to see you is. May God grant us this wish soon.*
> *Last Sunday I went to church at the Marist School and spoke with Brother Teodoro and Brother Juan Salvador. I offered our house to them, and they were very happy to have that option. They then took me to see the Brother Director, Brother Eusebio. I made him the same offer and told him that I had room at home for three brothers. They assured me that if they have problems they would come to our house.*
> *Tonight we are going to the cinema to see the movie* The Bridge over the River Kwai, *since they are showing it again and I have a great desire to see it. Ameli is going with us.*
> *I'm painting your room in a light green color. It is called "Ice Green." It is coming out very nicely and I am sure you will like it.*
> *I got a tailor to fix my jackets for 3 pesos each. He has fixed them as if they were modern with a narrow lapel.*
> *I have submitted my resignation in the Hospital M. I'm waiting for them to accept my resignation any moment.*
> *Well son, send me your photo, and receive a kiss from your mother and your father's blessing,*
>
> *María Luisa and Antonio.*

I got the impression that they were getting increasingly anxious to be reunited with me. At the end of the letter, they bring up the issue of a good photograph again.

This, combined with the news of the birth of Emilito's daughter in New York, made it more obvious that the folks left behind in Cuba felt very strongly the distance and circumstances that kept us apart. From today's perspective, however, my heart feels tight when I realize the strength of my dad's faith in my quick return. I was expected to be back home in a newly painted room with the color of spring, rebirth, and hope.

Ameli had already brought up the issue that the priests and nuns were under stress due to the circumstances. In fact, if the parents in Cuba had been concerned about the massacres and separations of the Spanish Civil War from 1936 until 1939, the Marist brothers who lost 166 members during that civil war must have also been aware of the danger. The priests and religious orders, brothers and nuns, were subjected to public pressure through speeches from the higher ups in the revolutionary government, including Fidel Castro himself. They were also harassed by the militias and very often their quarters and schools were searched.

My father was a Marist alumnus and during this difficult time he offered an alternative space for up to three brothers in our house in Altahabana, where they could stay and, perhaps, hide if they had to escape the revolutionary offensive. If the brothers were to be removed from the premises of the school in one way or another, they now had another home where they knew they would be welcomed. It should be understood that many of the brothers serving in the two Marist schools in Havana were originally from Spain, but they had been in Cuba long enough to feel like Cubans. This was also true for many priests and religious leaders in other congregations. For example, the director of the Florida City camp for younger boys and girls of Operation Pedro Pan was Father Salvador de Cistierna. He was assisted by lay staff and by the *Religiosas Filipenses*, nuns from the Our Lady of Lourdes School, which was diagonally adjacent to the Marist School in La Víbora. The documentary film *The Lost Apple* was filmed on location at the Florida City camp, with the purported intension of showing how Cuban parents sent their children away to save them from communism. Although Father Cistierna was originally from Spain, you can appreciate his feelings for our homeland, our *Patria*, in the following transcript of a speech he gave in that camp and featured in the film *The Lost Apple*.(1)

"We all here have the mission and grace to be working here to keep you safe.

"We are greatly pleased when we hear these songs, when we hear your laughter, but we know that there is a sadness and loneliness that must be covering your souls.

"I do not want these shows and attempts to entertain you to keep you on the sidelines, on the sidelines of this critical hour and the historic times we live in. I want you to experience the world.

View of Florida City facilities where Fr. Cistierne worked during 1961-1962 in Operation Pedro Pan with the Religious Sisters of Our Lady of Lourdes in Havana. Photo courtesy of University of Miami Cuban Heritage Collection

"Your presence here in Florida City, under the welcoming skies of the United States, far from the country of your birth, torn away from your parents, should be telling you something.

"This is not normal. There's something wrong with the world.

"In this world, I wish you boys and girls to turn into men and women with a great responsibility.

"I want you to look ahead and find out there a new society, a new world waiting in front of you.

"There will be a new homeland and this new home in a new world can only be built with new men and women and that is what Cuba is expecting from you.

"The Cuba of tomorrow will expect all of you not to make the same tragic errors that have led to the present crisis.

"Let us pray to our Lady of Charity, the *Virgin of El Cobre*, that she may hear our prayers for world peace.

"May the dove of peace descend upon our country and around the world."

Notice that at the end of this very clear and powerful prayer he states, "May peace descend on our country." Actually he did not use the word country, he said in Spanish *patria*. He did not say your country because, like the Marist brothers noted above, the religious leaders who had been on the island for some time, he felt as if he was Cuban.

Going back to the letter, my father was always looking for bargains. In that sense, it should not be surprising that he found a tailor shop where he could have his suits and coats altered. In the setting of the times and having expressed a clear desire to see me, this meant, in my opinion, that he was already getting his clothes ready in case he had to come to the United States.

Hospital M is the Military Hospital. My father was reinstated into the medical corps of the Cuban military medical corps in January 1959. He had entered the Cuban Army in 1930 as a medical student. His resignation when he was fifty-one years old appeared on the surface to be premature. However, he did not feel that he could get a permit to leave Cuba if he still belonged to the staff of the Military Hospital.

Havana, March 9, 1961
Jesus is always with us.
Very appreciated Tony:

I got your letter and I am glad to know that you are happy there.
From your father I know you are with the reverend fathers and are

continuing your studies...I ask of the Lord to help you because
you'll find some difficulties with the language...I know that you
always measure up to the circumstances...
Every day I see your father, I ask him if you have written. He told
me today that you have not written since Friday. Write to him
often because your letters gladden him very much.
Some days he stays in the hospital a long time. You know how well
he takes care of the patients. We all appreciate his work and the
service that he performs is great. Pray often to the Lord for him
and your mother, for having such good parents is an immense gift
from heaven.
Here we are, wishing that everything gets better....
And regarding Muñequita, give her our congratulations for being
an aunt. Also congratulate her mother for being such a young
grandmother.
May you receive from me and all of my sisters our best regards and
may you know that before Jesus and Mary you will not be forgotten
through our humble prayers,

Sister Isabel Arana

Sister Isabel's letter was a most appreciated communication with a very clear but humble message and prayers throughout. She was the community director of the Sisters of Charity, who ran the *Hospital Hogar Cristo De Limpias*. The hospital is now the *Hospital de Rehabilitacion Julio Díaz*. Presently, the hospital is part of a network of health care facilities where foreigners are cared for on the island. Back then, when it was the *Hospital Hogar Cristo De Limpias*, it was a chronic rehabilitation center for the *Organización Nacional de Rehabilitación de Inválidos* (ONRI). As such, it served as a rehabilitation center for medical and surgical units of the ONRI for the entire country. At one point in time, Muñeca had worked at the hospital. That is why Sister Isabel sends her Muñequita, a greeting and acknowledges the birth of her niece.

It was good to learn that my dad was spending more time at the rehabilitation hospital. In the past, he used to spend more time at the Military Hospital. I knew that my father had a vocation to serve patients. However, the appreciation expressed in this letter by Sister Isabel for his presence and services there was a boost to me with regard to his morale.

The Spanish nun sent with her letter a postcard with these words, "Revolution is building." Indeed, in its original Latin form the word revolution meant building, presumably something needed and new. When I traveled to Rome in 1999 for the canonization of St. Marcellin Champagnat, the founder of the Marist Order, I saw a sign in front of the hotel which read *Attenti Revolutione*. I knew that Italy was one of the strongholds of communism in Europe, but the sign had nothing to do with ideology or politics. It simply notified the public that they were reconstructing the bus station in front of the hotel. They were building something needed and new. Anyone who sees Havana, and Cuba for that matter, now will wonder what kind of building has been taking place since many of the island's structures appear dilapidated and destroyed as if they were the targets of enemy artillery.

Havana March 11, 1961
My dear son:

Last night we lost electric power in Altahabana after a bomb exploded. We were talking to our neighbors outside when it happened. Your English teacher, Alonso, came here to see me. Also Zenón's father came to see me. He wanted to know how you got the beca *for the school you are in now. I told him that my brother-in-law had solved that problem in Miami. He's going to send Zenón abroad, chances are to Spain.*
Also, this week the son of engineer Reynieri left for Costa Rica. Next week Adita Ponce de León is going to Panamá and her boyfriend will travel to Venezuela. Ameli will soon also be going to a school in that great nation.
Well my son, receive a kiss from your mother and your father's blessing,

María Luisa and Antonio

The situation in Havana was not getting any easier. A bomb had exploded near Altahabana and it resulted in at least the loss of electrical power to that neighborhood. Later on in the letter, we learn that others from the neighborhood were also leaving Cuba. It is worthwhile to note that although the exits out of Cuba took them to various countries, in this case all of them in Latin America, eventually in a matter of days, or perhaps months, all of them arrived in the United States. At least, that was the case with the individuals from our community in Altahabana.

Some couples who were engaged had to part in different directions. That was the case for Adita and her boyfriend Fernando. Fernando was actually Adita's fiancé and they had plans to marry, but at the time, they were not married. They eventually got back together in Chicago, where they married and happily started a new family. It is very likely that those folks from Altahabana who went to countries in Latin America did not have an American visa at that time, since the United States Embassy in Havana had already closed. It should also be noted that couples like Adita and Fernando sustained a great deal of stress in their relationships. However, in the case of Adita and Fernando, the relationship was tested, survived, and served to unite them truly forever.

Ridgefield Park, N. J.
March 21, 1961
My dear Tony:

We have received your letter where you congratulate Emilito and María Ofelia for their baby girl.
In it you write that you have spent a few days in the hospital. I did not know anything. When you can write back to me, tell me what happened and why were you taken there.
Many kisses to both of you from one who loves you and does not forget you in Christ,

Muñeca

My family in Cuba and in the New Jersey area did not find out about my hospitalization until after the fact, since I would have been the only one to report it to them and I was ill in the hospital. Except Ramoncito, who was still at the camp with me and who didn't think to write to them. Besides, who would have thought of writing a letter back then when I was escaping from an electrocution? Then, when I finally wrote to them that I had been in the hospital, they all requested for me to elaborate on the experience and so forth. Obviously, they were concerned and they wanted to know the details of whatever happened. However, by then, in my opinion, they could have waited until I told them personally. This is the way I felt: The emergency, so to speak, had passed and I had to look forward to getting through my courses at school and looking for a new *beca*, and focusing on the past would not help.

Havana March 22, 1961
My dear son Tony:

On the subject of the varicella epidemic in the school, that does not seem important. If you catch it do not worry about it. It is best for you to get it now while you are young than if you get it when you are older... If you catch it do not rub or pull out the scabs. Let them spontaneously fall off so as not leave scars.
On the subject of your mother going there for Holy Week and Easter, it is difficult. There are many problems. As you know, the money situation here is such that we cannot exchange Cuban pesos into American dollars. Let us see if there is a miracle.
Last Sunday we had lunch at Boca de Jaruco *with Fuentes and his family, Rosita and Cañete and of course the great Poppy. Last night we went to the cinema to see* The Unforgettable Song, the Life of Chopin. *We went with Rosita and Cañete who also wanted to see it. As you know this is the third time I've seen it, but it is not boring because the music is so fantastic.*
Well I guess you have received the pictures I sent you. Tell me, did they open the envelope?...
Well my son, receive a kiss from your mother and your father's blessing,

María Luisa and Antonio

Boca de Jaruco is an inlet in the northern coast of Cuba just east of Havana harbor. It was one of the locations where the original "*Old Man and the Sea*" movie was filmed in the 1950s after Ernest Hemingway became the Nobel laureate in literature in 1954. Times had changed in Cuba and at the time this letter was written, there was a suspicion on my father's part about the authorities opening the mail. The pictures he sent arrived and both of my parents were in them, along with some of the family remaining in Havana, in front of the house in Altahabana, posing with Poppy.

There was an uneventful epidemic of varicella (also known as chicken pox) at Camp St. John in the month of March 1961, as I have already noted in a previous chapter. I am sure the epidemic was thought to be a benign process and we would all get better with just rest, fluids, and topical care. What would have been the re-

Some of the Cuban Gordon family gathered in Altahabana. They sent this photograph to my cousin and me. From left to right: Alicia Buznego, cousin-sister of my father; my father with Poppy; my mother; Abuela Amparo, my father's mother; Isabel Gordon, cousin-sister of my father; Aunt Ofelia, sister of my father; and Uncle Ramón, brother of my father. On the bike is Ernesto Rencurrell, son of Aunt Ofelia. In the iron rocking chair is Josefa (Nena) Etchegoyen, the widow of my father's uncle Antonio Gordon. Kneeling in front of Aunt Ofelia is Ramón Rencurrell, the father of Ernest.

sponse if a different type of epidemic, say hepatitis, gastroenteritis, influenza, etc., would have emerged at the camp? Considering the semi-clandestine nature of the Unaccompanied Cuban Children Program and the entire operation of the camp and our presence there, a more serious epidemic requiring intervention by the public health service would have been a challenge. After all, miracles did happen!

> *Havana March 23, 1961*
> *Dear friend:*
>
> *I hope when you receive this letter you find yourself well. Here, we are all fine.*
> *We have not gotten news from you for some time. Have you forgotten us? Here we remember you and the others a lot.*
> *The club is doing well… except that almost every day there is a fellow from the G-2 around us.*
> *I am sending you the last pastoral letter. I hope you receive it.*
> *I can only ask you to write to us more frequently, when you have a chance without sacrificing your studies.*
> *And without further ado, hoping to see you soon among us.*
> *Goodbye from your friend that will never forget you,*
>
> *Enrique Suárez.*
> *Keep for me the postage stamps from the U.S. and Cuba and other countries if you can. I am sending you a very pretty stamp here.*

Lorenzo was writing with a new pseudonym. He had not received news from me in a while. Lorenzo, like my parents, was not aware that I had been admitted to St. Vincent's Hospital. Lack of contact with us in exile was most discouraging to him. I should have understood that they needed to hear from someone off the island to let them know that we were still "well."

Their situation in the Underground, even when they were going to school, was rather unique and dangerous. As he noted, there were often operatives from the G-2 secret police in and around the school, which he referred to as "the club." It is not difficult to imagine the atmosphere of fear that resulted, and the impossibility to concentrate on any kind of studying. The worst experience, in my opinion, must have been the one these circumstances generated for the Marist brothers. As noted above, some of them had known in their own soul and flesh the horrors of the Spanish Civil War when many brothers were killed. Some of those brothers who lost their lives during the Spanish Civil War have now been elevated through the canonization process to beatification because they died defending the Catholic faith.

I note his word usage at the end of the letter. Why did he write "Goodbye"? It was not clear to me then. Was he thinking that he would not write again? Was he, as Pella seemed earlier, entering into depression? The answers were not clear at that time. We will see later. At least, he was still sending a message with the stamps and was requesting that I save stamps for him.

> *Havana, March 25, 1961*
> *My beloved grandson Tony:*
>
> *Days ago I received your letter and by it can tell you're okay... Antonio brought me your letter and I am gladdened for both of you because I know that you're studying...*
> *Try to speak in English because that is the way that you will learn it. On Sunday we went to Mass at the Marist School. It was very crowded as it was Palm Sunday. We got tired of waiting for the Mass, the priest had gone to Lourdes to say mass there.*
> *Emilito sent me the picture of his little girl. She is beautiful.*
> *Ernest...is very chubby and strong but Ofelia does not want to send him to school...*
> *Much love to you all and many kisses from your grandma who loves you so much,*
>
> *Amparo*

My grandmother Amparo was very glad that we were in the school, and as far as she knew, out of trouble. She advised me to speak in English because, in her experience, that is the best way to learn it. I feel also that since my dad visited her every day, she was being coached by him to impress on me the importance of learning English. They had no idea that this time I had no choice but to learn English!

It was noted that Palm Sunday Mass at the Marist School at La Víbora was delayed because the one priest had to celebrate both masses in the two nearby schools. This may have occurred because there was a shortage of priests. Many American priests had already been asked to leave the country in 1960.

Obviously, Grandmother was very happy for Emilito and María Ofelia, but also for herself. She was already a great-grandmother! She obviously longed to be with her first great-granddaughter. Her desires would have to wait. In retrospect, the thought of not ever getting to see her never crossed her mind.

Ernest was the youngest of her grandchildren. He was only four years old at the time. His mother, Ofelia, did not wish to send him to school, yet. Was it because of generalized fear? Was she concerned about having her child indoctrinated or taken away from the family? We would learn more about Ernest in the months to come.

Havana, March 29, 2961
My dear Tony:

What a nice surprise I had when I received your letter. It gave me much pleasure reading it.
I guess what you say may be true, that you do not have time to write, and that is why I appreciate your letters even more.
How good it is to hear that you are so happy and you can graduate in June. You do not know how we should thank God for the luck you've had. God must be with you and help you to move forward, since you have to also deal with a new language.
You probably know that your parents are sad to have you away, but also proud, knowing that you are so dedicated to your studies. All the efforts you make will be few in order to reach the end, it will be hard. And then you will be rewarded.
May God grant that you continue to be so happy and not forget, either of you, because life is not all flowers and when we face the thorns we have to bear them with patience and resignation.
Hugs and kisses for both of you and know that your great aunt loves you,

Nena

Nena was the widow of the late Dr. Antonio María Gordon Bermúdez. We all called her Nena in the family, but her real maiden name was María Josefa Etchegoyen. Her husband was the brother of my grandfather Ramón, the late husband of my grandmother Amparo. Antonio and Ramón were nephews of Anacleto and Esteban Bermúdez, who were both in the first year medical class in Havana in 1871. As mentioned above, the entire class was accused of anti-Spanish activities. Anacleto was sentenced to death by firing squad, *el paredón,* and Esteban to six years of forced labor in *Las Canteras,* the rock quarries. He and all other Cuban medical students condemned to prison terms were pardoned in mid-1872 by the Spanish crown. By then, however, Esteban had full blown tuberculosis from which he died in 1892.

Returning to Nena, she was already in her 90s when she wrote this letter. I find a lot of love and depth in her message and her advice. She was not taking any roundabout way. She clearly stated that my parents were sad. They were also proud that we were doing well, however. I want to write that we were seemingly doing as well as we could. Hence, the importance of keeping up with the mail, the communication, and all possible contacts sharing whatever was going on with some vision of hope for the future. She was, perhaps, reassuring all of us that we would see each other again. However, I never saw Nena again.

Nena never left Cuba again. She died in the hiatus between the October Cuban Missile Crisis in 1962 and the establishment of the Freedom Flights in 1966, a period during which there were no direct flights between the United States and Cuba. She had two daughters; Pilar was the older one and then Isabel. At about the time when my great uncle died in 1921 from heart failure, Isabel contracted pulmonary tuberculosis. After getting all the treatments for that dreadful illness available in Havana, long before there were any specific anti-tuberculosis drugs available, she was advised to go to The Trudeau Sanatorium in Saranac Lake in Upstate New York. Nena took Isabel to the sanatorium and Pilar traveled with them. They spent a few months there while Isabel was undergoing the first set of treatments.

While they were there, Pilar met the son of a Spanish man who had gone to Saranac Lake to be treated for tuberculosis. He had been referred to Dr. Trudeau by a health facility in Puerto Rico where his father had some sort of business and his tuberculosis was diagnosed. Pilar fell in love with the son of the Spaniard, Manuel Benero. Nena and Pilar came back to Cuba, while Isabel remained interred in the sanatorium. The distance between New York and Havana did not make the love between Pilar and Manolo dissipate. Instead, it became stronger. Eventually, before Isabel completed her treatments, including the introduction of pneumothoraxes to collapse the lungs and deprive the tubercle bacillus—responsible for the tuberculosis—of oxygen, she came back to Havana. By then, Pilar and Manolo had married in Saranac Lake in 1925. They grew their family there and traveled to Havana periodically to visit all the family they had there. They lived in Saranac Lake until the late 1960s when Mr. Benero died. Isabel made it out of Cuba in 1968, several years after her mother had died.

Havana, March 29, 1961
My dear son Tony:

We received the photos but they are of poor quality, photographs made in those booths for 25 cents always come out with people disfigured and ugly.
The day before yesterday the parents of your partner at the school Rolando O'Farrill came to our house. We talked a lot about all of you. We will pay them a visit next week.
Regarding your thought of having us visit you, ... María Luisa and Blanquita cannot go because they cannot go without money. What are they going to do if they just fly into Miami without money?
As for what you say about the University of Notre Dame, it seems too grandiose to me. You must take it easy. Also, explain to me how this is possible since we cannot send a penny from here and even if you have a beca *you need money for your personal expenses.*
I also received a letter from your Uncle Emilio and they are well... he wants me to put a few bottles of Polar beer in the fridge because he will soon be in to drink them cold.
Well my son, hoping to see you soon. Receive a kiss from your mother and your father's blessing,

María Luisa and Antonio

I attempted to get a photograph to send them in one of those booths where, indeed, as my father said, you could get a set of poor quality small black and white photos for twenty-five cents. Obviously, despite this, a good quality photograph was still pending. I am sure they did not mean to say that I was ugly and disfigured, but perhaps I was, and they blamed the twenty-five cent photo studio!

Networking in Havana was on the rise between parents who previously did not know each other, but whose children were together in one of the institutions of the Unaccompanied Cuban Children Program. The parents of the exiled children were trying to communicate with each other. Rolando O'Farrill was a very lively young man I met upon arriving at St. John's Camp. He was very fond of a small hat he picked up in *El Ropero* at the refugee center. He used to model it and look at himself in the mirror and exclaim, "Isn't this hat *coqueto* (flirtatious, cute)?" Because of that, and the fact that he did it so repeatedly, people began to call him *Coqueto*.

My cousin Ramoncito was called *Piloto,* and I was called *Gargarita,* but we were not the only ones with a nickname at the camp. In fact, the nicknames were one of the troubling issues Mr. Thomas Aglio found when he arrived at Camp St. John in the summer of 1961 to become the headmaster. This is how he explained it:

"The enclave of Cuban adolescents stared at me dressed in suit and tie. They were silent. I felt that I was being X-rayed by their piercing eyes. I wondered in astonishment, *Who are all these look alikes?* It was the same as meeting twins for the first time, except that there were dozens of them. What sinister man had cloned all these Cuban youths and placed them here? They appeared to be identical with no distinguishing characteristics, no identifying differences...

"Prior to this first encounter, I had been given lists of all the names of the camp"occupants." I studied those names countless times, practicing the pronunciation and memorizing as many of the sixty as I could, but I had no face to put with them. Now I could begin the arduous task. But alas, there was an obstacle in my path. I discovered soon that the majority of the boys had nicknames for one another.

"A few were familiar, like Charlie for Carlos, Pepe for Jose, Tony for Antonio, and Mike for Miguel. Then there were Lorito, Perry, Para, Chico, El Topo, Gallego, and Diente, to name a few. All the rest were an enigma to me... It was like a code, a sign of their in-group familiarity, which served them well in their bonding. Later, I would discover that not all these nicknames were complimentary or flattering."(3)

I thought nothing about this issue of the nicknames at the time. Then later on, I began to think that I had never been anyplace where everyone had a nickname. In fact, at the camp, we knew each other by our nicknames. Curiously, in the mail that was to come in from Havana from my peers at the Marist School, I note now that they were also calling themselves by nicknames at about the same time. It is true that in the past, some individuals were known by a nickname but, in general, it was a nickname related to their own name like Tony or Pepe. The word for nickname in Spanish is *nombrete,* which has a somewhat negative or demeaning connotation to it.

From today's perspective, the issue of the nicknames for all of us under stress, both on and off the island, but in different circumstances, may be significant. In retrospect, this may show that we all, perhaps, felt in need of a new identity. Then I wonder if the whole issue of the nicknames had something to do with the fact that people were using pseudonyms. Was it possible that we did not want anyone to know our real names because someone might report us to the secret police as a counter-revolutionary? Probably not, the nicknames were given to us by our peers. I do not think that anyone suggested himself to be called this or that *nombrete.*

Nicknames have been associated with friendliness, playfulness, good humor, morality, or immorality, success or failure, popularity or unpopularity, and home-sickness.(4) Several of these categories may have applied to the nicknames we gave each other. Which of these was the most relevant or prevalent explanation for our nicknames? We may never know. Some of the nicknames have been forgotten. For example in reunions of the Pedro Pans I have had to introduce myself as "the cousin of *Piloto*" because invariably they did not remember me or Ramoncito as such. However, the fact was that nicknames were permeating our environment for all of us at that time.

In a previous letter, I had shared with my parents the possibility of my mother coming for Holy Week. At that time, we were discussing the possibility of my mother and my aunt Blanquita coming to see us. The latter was Ramoncito's mother. None of these invitations or suggestions got anywhere. For any of these suggestions to have had "traction," we would have needed the means and ways to get them out of Cuba and support them after their arrival. Essentially, they could not come because of multiple issues. An important one was the funding once they arrived in the United States. However, more importantly than that were the series of permits that were required by the Cuban revolutionary government before any Cuban could leave the island legally, and the fact that returning to the island was not easily accomplished at the time. I should say that in those two attempts to get them to leave the island, I was attempting to have them come and be as safe as possible outside Cuba.

By the end of March 1961, all eight of us in the last year of high school at St. John's Camp were faced with our immediate future after graduation from Bishop Kenny High School. What was going to happen to us? At the time, we did not know ourselves of any regulations in terms of ages at the camp. While Operation Pedro Pan did have age regulations, from age six to age sixteen, the camps were perhaps more flexible in the age requirements. Anyhow, we were being advised to find a college or university that would offer us a scholarship upon graduation from high school. Cuban counselors at the camp assisted us in writing letters, in which we explained our situation and the need we had for assistance for continuing our education. I remember sending many handwritten letters to colleges and universities. Maybe one of them went to Notre Dame University, but I have no record of any answer from them. At any rate, my father's comments were rather practical. How is this being arranged? Who is going to pay for your personal expenses? Do you not know that we cannot take money out of Cuba? And I could have added one more question, even if we could take money out of Cuba, do we have enough money to pay for an American college or university? I did not know!

At the conclusion of March 1961, we at St. John's Camp had been through a common health challenge and I had been through my own personal illness requiring hospitalization. There was a benign epidemic of varicella, and I spent several days interned at the St. Vincent's hospital with strep throat, rheumatic fever, and bronchial asthma. School work was progressing. It seemed likely that all eight of us in the twelfth grade were going to graduate. Back home in Havana, there was still harassment of priests, nuns, and Catholic school students. The G-2 secret police were known to be going in and out of the Marist School near the Plaza Civica. There were bombs exploding and loss of power. More and more young people, including two-thirds of the fourth year of *bachillerato* at the Marist School near the Plaza Cívica and most of the male adolescents in Altahabana, had left the island or were planning to do so in the near future. Somehow, the people back home and those in exile, as noted by the testimonies of my relatives in New Jersey—including my level-headed Uncle Emilio, were planning on a rapid resolution of the Cuban situation and the return of all exiles into a new Cuba…a Cuba of tomorrow, like Father Cistierna had said in that speech captured on film in *The Lost Apple*.

CHAPTER 12

THE DOWNTOWN EXPERIENCE:
PRANKS, COMMERCE, AND GIRLS

"LORD, you have probed me, you know me:
You know when I sit and stand;
You understand my thoughts from afar.
You sift through my travels and my rest;
With all my ways you are familiar.
Even before a word is on my tongue,
LORD, you know it all.
Behind and before you encircle me,
And rest your hand upon me.
Such knowledge is too wonderful for me,
Far too lofty for me to reach.
Where can I go from your spirit?
From your presence, where can I flee?"
Book of Psalms 139:1-7

Ever since we had access to the Air Force bus, we were taken on Saturdays to downtown Jacksonville for a 4-to-5 hour outing. Those outings broke the camp monotony when there was no school. It was at that time that we were given our weekly allowance, which amounted to two dollars per week. That is, if we had behaved and we did not have to pay any penalties. I guessed then that the Saturday outings to downtown Jacksonville were supposed to expose us to new aspects of life in the United States with which we had to become familiar in order to adapt to our new environment. In retrospect, it was also a way to have us away from camp for a few hours, a time during which the staff did not have to babysit us. Whichever of these two reasons was mostly true, the Saturday outings provided us a time during which we saw some aspects of ourselves that we would not have known existed otherwise.

Camp Monotony and our demeanor when we had no school or outing.
Photograph from 8mm movie frame

Here are some of the most notorious events that occurred because we got to go downtown on Saturdays.

Near the place where we were usually dropped off at about eleven in the morning or twelve noon, there were a number of surplus stores of the Army and Navy type. At the time, it had been a little over fifteen years since the end of World War II, and surplus military articles like emblems, uniforms, hats, and even some weapons were sold for very little money. Many of us visited those stores and actually bought some emblems and army hats, *boinas, quepis*, military wedge hats. It was in one of those stores that I first realized that some of us had experience stealing. Yes, stealing. Well, it was petty theft, but still stealing. The ones I considered thieves with experience were very quick and before you knew what was going on, they were gone with whatever it was that they wished to steal. To my knowledge, no one was caught stealing. If this whole thing would have been a baseball game and someone had been keeping score of those who tried to steal and were "safe," no one would have been "out." I cannot be sure of that, because if one of us was caught stealing, he might have been reprimanded by the storekeeper and the word may not have gotten around. That would have been unlikely because we were invariably in small groups, never alone.

There is a proverb in Spanish that goes like this: "*Dime con quien andas y te dire quien eres.*" (Tell me who you hang around with and I will tell you who you are.)

The truth is that I found out that if you hang around guys who steal, you end up stealing also. The proverb proved to be true. It is sad to admit, but some of us who had no experience at all with stealing began to experiment and, indeed, tried it, did it successfully, and confessed it later.

The camp kept getting more refugees every so often. They arrived invariably in the late afternoon. They probably took the same train route that my group had taken from Miami, leaving in the morning and arriving at St. Augustine in the late afternoon.

Sometime during the month of April, we began to plan a reception for the newcomers. Something like a *novatada,* a sort of initiation rite. We posted a lookout on the road that led directly from the camp to Route 13 to alert us of the arrival of new refugees. They usually came in a single car. By then, we were dressed up—as best as we could—with our military hats and shirts decorated with emblems from the American armed forces, from the bounty we had collected downtown. A squadron would be set up and marching orders were given by one selected to be the officer. The backdrop for this performance was the U.S. Air Force bus and the sleeping barracks, which were easily visible.

As the car bringing in the new refugees came closer to the barracks, the squadron would begin to mark the steps and shout, "*Uno, dos, tres*," etc....and then march in formation as in a military parade. The marching continued and some other orders such as, "*Flanco derecho,*" (turn to the right) were voiced as the refugees were getting off the car.

Their faces would noticeably show their awe. Some appeared to be pale and in emotional shock. They did not know what to think about what they were seeing! Some of those children had been only a few hours in one of the holding houses or Camp Matecumbe in the Miami area. Others had been at one of the houses or in a camp for several weeks. Then someone from the group pretending to be military personnel would go up to them and tell them that we were getting ready to fight the Castro regime. Some actually sighed in relief because they thought that they were somehow going to be taken back to the island of Cuba. Or, perhaps, some thought they had been kidnapped by a communist insurgency inside the United States. Not one of us on the reception side of this *novatada* ever thought of the many outcomes that could happen when real people were exposed to the prank. A few of the newcomers cried. No one's emotions stayed the same as they had been before. But then, we were all changing rapidly, especially in those moments when we were transferred from one place to another in total ignorance as to where we were going, because we had never been there before and had no control over where we were being sent. After all, we were refugees so what else could we have expected.

Then, as they were getting their bags from the trunk, we would keep marching. As they went in the dining hall cabin, we would disband. Very soon after that, we would break the news that the entire parade was a prank. As the two groups, the newcomers and the older ones got to know each other, we became closer to each other. At the end of the day, somehow, even in spite of our personal reasons for getting involved in the prank, the reality of our times was becoming clearer, and hopefully more bearable to both groups, which would end up as one.

The experience also led some to open up and talk seriously about our situation, what they were feeling, the uncertainty of the present, and the lack of clarity when attempting to plan a future. What could we do to expedite the resolution of the impending civil war in Cuba? It was still a time when most people thought that we would be outside of Cuba for a short time, perhaps, for a few more months, and some of us wanted to be useful to our *Patria*!

Another interesting event was also related to our Saturday outings to Jacksonville. It was the purchase, or near purchase, of a used car. The reader will understand the term "near purchase" as the story unfolds. One of the central figures in this adventure was my cousin Ramoncito. Ever since he arrived in camp, he had been nicknamed *El Piloto*. Since he had been living at Lola's *Cuban Barracón* with exiles that had been pilots or worked for the airlines in Havana, Ramoncito would tell stories about flying and airplanes. Everyone was getting a nickname in the camp; therefore, it is not surprising that his was *El Piloto*, the pilot!

Several of the guys, led by Ramoncito, went up to a downtown used car lot in Jacksonville and apparently fell in love at first sight with a 1950 black, 2-door convertible Studebaker automobile being sold for $50. This was in 1961 when a brand new car could be purchased for anywhere between $2,000 and $3,000. They began making offers to the apparent owner of the lot. According to the story we got later on, they got the price down to $35. Evidently, the car had some defects, so apparently it was not too difficult to negotiate the price downward, considering the condition of the car. They were ready to make the purchase and got all their money together. In total, they came up with $21. The salesman, probably tired from the discussion at the end of a Saturday afternoon, agreed to take a partial payment for the car because the buyers claimed that they would bring more "associates" into the deal. The purchase of the convertible was, as far as the guys were concerned, a done deal.

So it was, that on that particular Saturday, four of the guys who had not shown up to take the bus back to the camp at the designated place and time, nearly purchased a used car. To everyone's surprise, they showed up later in the camp driving a black convertible 1950 Studebaker. Immediately, there was great interest in the camp as to what was going on. Some felt very joyful that there was a convertible in the camp. Perhaps, some thought that they could go to school in it. Or, perhaps, they could take it out on dates in the evenings.

At first, it was not clear how the car had gotten there, but anyone who was interested soon got the full story and was given a ride inside the camp and invited to become an "associate" in the purchase of the vehicle. The car made quite a lot of noise when it was started up. It produced a roaring sound when the accelerator was pressed. If anyone did not hear the initial commotion or its aftermath, they certainly saw and smelled the cloud of black smoke that came out of the tail pipe. It was obvious that the car was not in top shape. Something seemed to be sticking in the transmission when the driver tried to change gears. Others with less automotive savvy were fine with just getting a ride around the clearing in front of the cabins, despite the fact that the car had no seat in the back. But then, Cuban ingenuity was not invented by the revolution. Immediately, someone brought in a piece of a tree trunk of the appropriate length and set it in the back to serve as a seat.

The counselors did not seem to know what to do with this new twist on camp life. During the next day, a couple of the campers who had some experience in mechanics began testing the car between trips, as nearly everyone got to ride in the vehicle on the grounds. But, in general, the car served to get together a few of the guys interested in mechanics, and obviously in business. At least the interest in mechanics seemed to be something positive since the automobile was the instrument by which some guys could learn something new that could be useful to them later on. At the end of the day, however, there were riders and mechanics, but no associates or investors!

Piloto's talent for sales became evident during the impasse generated by the incomplete purchase of the used car. As soon as *Piloto* got his message across, several individuals agreed to participate in the purchase of the vehicle. The next day, on a Sunday, they drove off to the car lot where the car was originally obtained. They took the sum of money they had raised from the new associates, gave it to the dealer who expected to complete the sale of the Studebaker. The Cubans then headed back to camp. This was what we at the camp thought had occurred at that time.

Having partially completed the second stage of the purchase, they got in the car and began their drive back to the camp. While crossing the bridge over the St. John's River on US 1, the car had to stop at a red light as the down slope of the bridge entered the southern bank of the river. There was a traffic light at that intersection of US 1 with Route 13 where anyone on his way to St. John's Camp would turn right and head down south to the Mandarin and Switzerland area. Well, we already know that the car had a faulty transmission and it was missing the back seat. What no one knew up to that time was that the brakes were in bad shape. Yes, as the car came down the slope of the bridge, the driver, *Piloto*, was not able to stop for the red light and the 1950 Studebaker crashed against another car right in front of it, a car that was stopped while the traffic signal was on red.

The details of the crash were only known to those who were riding in the 1950 Studebaker, but the aftermath of it got everyone's attention. Later on, the damaged car was towed into the camp, so the story began to get around that one of the "associates" had crashed the 1950 Studebaker. Obviously, there was a lot of fear on my cousin's part, since the police had given him a traffic ticket. Ramoncito did not have a valid Florida driver's license. There was no automobile insurance either. As the weeks went by, a notification was received about a court appearance.

Meanwhile, the crashed Studebaker was kept in the side yard in front of the cabins. Since the car had already so many defects, the crash only added minor issues to its body. After a few days of work, the group of mechanics had been able to start the motor and the car was seen to move several feet forward and several feet backwards. However, it never again, at least to my knowledge, served as a means of useful transportation.

Time went by relatively quickly after that. The driver had been one of the eight of us who were to leave camp sometime in June to another site of the program for Unaccompanied Cuban Children, where we were to polish our English. Before our departure, Father Lenihan came in and sat down with Ramoncito. The latter explained to the priest that things did not go as planned after he got the group to follow him in the purchase of the car. Then the priest let him know that there would be no court hearing and that the court, after knowing the details as explained to them by Father Lenihan, had dismissed the case. *Piloto* and the car investors were able to breathe better!

Nevertheless, several months later, one of the "associates," Coqueto, wrote to me at my new home:

> *Switzerland, Florida*
> *July 19, 1961*
> *My dearest friend Tony:*
>
> *First of all I'm going to ask you to forgive me for having delayed so many days my reply to your letter although it was not my intention, I could not write to you. For several days I was in Miami.*
> *Well Tony, I am happy because you're having fun and you're happy over there.*
> *In Miami I met a lady who claims to be a close friend of your family. She asked me about you and Piloto, Ramoncito.*
> *And apropos of Ramoncito … Tell him that I received a letter from the dealer where we bought the car, in which they tell me that I have a week to pay the remaining twelve dollars we owe. The truth is this: Where the hell am I going to get that money since the priest says he cannot give me a cent? What a guy that Piloto is!*
> *The camp is now, I think, in its best shape. Since all of us are behaving well (even me). And the cars are not getting lost anymore, etc… Our teachers are also behaving well with us. They hardly ever deduct anything from our allowance and also give us permission every time we ask for a leave. I even asked and got my permission to go to Miami for a few days without having to write to Mrs.*

Cooper.

From here I will tell you that Migiro (Pepito) got involved with a jeva *the other day at a party and he made out with her. Hey, I think he got a triple.*

Another one who surprised us was Manunga, who batted a good line drive. And, Migiro was caught trying to steal home.

Gárgara ... Well, say hello to everyone over there including Piloto and tell the others that I do not forget them, although they may not believe it.

Get a hug from your brother or cousin,
Rolando O'Farrill.

Tell me if you have a jeva. *I think my folks will go to your home again.*

Aside from the fascinating nicknames disclosed in Coqueto's letter—some of which have no translation into English—there are two issues in this letter that need to be explained. First, we will address the issue about the *jevas* (Cuban slang meaning girls). Secondly, we will take the issue of the letter from the lot dealer where the 1950 Studebaker was "nearly purchased."

Considering the *jevas*, one aspect of our growth and development that has not been evident from the letters of my relatives, or peers from the Marist school, was how our developing sexuality was dealt with during this time. In his letter, Coqueto clearly brings up the subject. He reports on an outing that occurred to the beach in the summer. My group had already left the camp at that point. I can confirm *Coqueto's* impressions about the beach outing because I also received a letter from *Migiro*, attesting to the fact that they had gone to the beach and were having fun with girls there. *Migiro* is not as explicit as *Coqueto* in his description of what happened with the girls. However, *Coqueto* writes of the sexual advances he observed through the traditional baseball metaphor. For example, I guess that *Migiro* was "caught stealing home plate" means that he was actually going to have sex with a girl but he was stopped just before intercourse. Hopefully, *Migiro* was stopped by the girl herself and not by her boyfriend or a guard at the beach. It is not clear at all to me what exactly *Coqueto* meant when he claimed that *Manunga* "batted a line drive."

Another event worth noting regarding *jevas* happened during one of our weekly trips to downtown Jacksonville and involved three of us. We missed the bus. I do not think that we stayed behind on purpose. We just missed the bus. Realizing our situation, we began to hitchhike. We began to ask for a *botella,* Cuban slang for a ride. We got down to San Jose Boulevard, but not as far as the Mandarin area. As it was already getting dark, we decided to call the camp. We knocked on the door of a house on the east side of the highway and, sure enough, someone opened the door. I told them that we were Cuban refugees and we lived in a camp down the road and we had been left behind by our bus. I asked if I could call the camp. The lady told us to come in and offered us some water, perhaps refreshments. After I had told the people back at Camp St. John that we were on our way, the family offered to take us to the camp.

I do not remember when it was that I realized that the daughter of the house was a sweet, blond girl of about the same age as we were. They had asked us about our religion and we said we were Roman Catholics. They explained that they were Methodists. I told them that there were a number of Methodist churches in Cuba. Sometime during the refreshments or during the trip down to the camp, I asked Ann, the girl, if she would want to go to the Bishop Kenny Prom with me. To my surprise, she said yes! And, she had a friend who would love to go to the prom with my cousin Ramoncito. So it was in this convoluted manner that we got dates for the school prom.

We were fortunate to have the Unaccompanied Cuban Children Program cover the costs of renting tuxedos for all eight of us for the senior class dance. Ann's parents provided my cousin and me with transportation to the dance, which was held in the school cafeteria. Our pictures were taken by a professional photographer and the cost of the picture was also covered by the Unaccompanied Cuban Children Program. No one else from the camp, except for us eight seniors, went to that particular dance. In terms of the allegorical manner in which *Coqueto* wrote about relations between boys and girls, I only got to first base. That is to say, I only got to kiss the girl!

For me that was more than I had expected, since a couple of weeks prior to the prom I had no date or hope of speaking to a girl to even ask her to the dance. I was very surprised when Ann asked me during the Bishop Kenny Prom if I would go with her to her prom at Landon High School. I said yes, of course. She made the arrangements; her parents paid for my tuxedo rental and, again, provided the transportation from the camp to the dance. Unfortunately, I never heard from her or her family again. Ann was a very sweet and pretty girl and her family was generous to the point of making me feel at home in a very foreign place. The most likely reason I never heard from them is because I did not write to them or thank them enough. I am very sorry that I never wrote to thank them for their help during those rites of passage of American culture. There were too many things happening and our future was very uncertain at the time.

Ann and Tony at the Bishop Kenny High Prom on Friday evening, May 5, 1961

Finally, let us get back to the conclusion of the story of the 1950 Studebaker. From *Coqueto's* letter, the reader can appreciate that in July the dealer from whom the Studebaker was "nearly purchased" wrote to one of the "associates" who still resided in the camp, requesting full payment in the amount of $12. Up to the time that I received *Coqueto's* letter, we all had been made to believe that the 1950 Studebaker had been paid in full. The car, however, was never paid in full. Apparently, *Coqueto* tried to get financial help from Father Lenihan in the camp, but to no avail. Nobody knows what happened to the car that remained abandoned on the grounds of Camp St. John in June 1961 when the group of seniors left the camp. I would not be surprised if the car was towed back to the lot where it was "nearly purchased."

Coqueto mentioned in his letter another interesting car story from camp life. I am referring to his comment, "Cars are not missing anymore here." One day, in the late afternoon, sometime in the month of May, *Coqueto* and Angel Castro got into the car of Ronny, the head counselor, and I joined them on the spur of the moment. I found that Ronny had left his keys in the car and drove off in the 1958 Chevy, which had been parked in front of the dining hall cabin. I took off through the sandy roads going by La Casa Grande and then up the road to Route 13. When we got to the point where we could see the entrance to the camp, we saw a group of guys and the Spanish priest, who were entering the camp from the road. They were getting back after taking a walk to the small country store and gas station we visited in the evenings. The store was located about two or three tenths of a mile south of the gate to the camp.

We were caught! Immediately, I stopped the car and the three of us jumped out in two directions. They jumped to the right of the car and tried to hide in the bushes to the right of the sandy road. They were found fairly soon. I jumped out the driver's side of the car and got into the woods on the left side of the road. I walked through the snake-infested woods until I reached the back side of the cabins. I managed to get to the second cabin without getting injured, took off my clothes, and got into a shower. Just as I turned the water on, a couple of counselors came through taking attendance. I was saved by the skin of my teeth! *Coqueto* and Angel Castro never told anyone who was the third person in the car. It was me.

Where were we going? We were going to Miami! What were we going to do in Miami? I do not know. Maybe call family members in the United States. What would they do? I do not know. How much money did we have? I had none! The entire attempt to escape from St. John's Camp was absurd and something that occurred on the spur of the moment. Perhaps, the best possible explanation of it was that it was a prank we pulled on Ronny. Perhaps it was just the inmaturity of adolescent children who when they are growing up –lacking experience and foresight—

they do not consider the consequences of whatever they do on the spur of the moment.Whatever the reason for it, this behavior suggests the presence of deranged emotions and unexpressed desires in many of us that were not being addressed by those running the camp; for example, it was not appreciated that we needed more social exposure than what was possible under the circumstances. Despite all these unthinkable stories, "the camp was in the summer of 1961 in its best shape."

Most outings to downtown Jacksonville were not as notorious as these. My group would usually have lunch at a small Italian restaurant near the location where we were dropped off. The usual lunch consisted of spaghetti and a glass of milk. There were no *tarros de leche* at that small restaurant. Then we would walk around and sightsee downtown, particularly the stores. On one occasion, we were approached by three women who became interested in the jewelry being worn by one of us. I do not remember who he was, but he was wearing a golden chain around his neck with a large religious medallion. Initially we were glad to know that some women were interested in us. However, very quickly we saw red flags in their behavior since a couple of them were getting very close to us and had their eyes fixed on the jewelry. One of them went immediately for the necklace and medal one of my peers was wearing. We ran away as fast as we could. We decided that those three women were prostitutes and they were after the jewelry.

In the final analysis, our experiences in downtown Jacksonville served as a way for us to examine the American culture. We found that there could be danger in the environment, but mostly only when related to certain people who did not seem to be wholesome. Most of the people we encountered seemed honest. The owner of the used car lot where the 1950 Studebaker was "nearly purchased" was probably somewhat naïve. However, Ann's entire household proved to be exceedingly understanding and excellent people. I am sure that Americans also were examining us. I am afraid that we fell short of the ideals we had learned in our Catholic schools and homes in Havana. In fact, if it would not have been for the political influence exercised by Father Lenihan and probably the Unaccompanied Cuban Children Program, some of us may have had to face the judicial system. At the end of this chapter where some of our mischievousness has been recalled, we do well in reciting the conclusion of Psalm 139:

> *"Where can I go from your spirit? From your presence, where can I flee?*
> *I ascend to the heavens, You are there; if I lie down in Sheol, there you are.*
> *If I take the wings of dawns and dwell beyond the sea,*
> *Even there, your hand guides me your right hand holds me fast."*

CHAPTER 13
A LONG DISTANCE TWIST, A ROMANCE, OR ANOTHER *BOLA*?

When you're young love is the purest feeling you can feel.
Do not look for a grand future for which we do not know if it will come or what
we'll find in it, whether roses or thorns. So do not miss this opportunity for an un-
known future. Live in the present ... and have faith in the future."
-Amelí

Something happened at St. John's Camp that I must share here. I do not know who started this project, but I know that I got into it. This was not a *bola* for us who were taking part in it, although one may argue that for the individuals on the other end, it could have been considered—at least initially—a *bola,* as you will appreciate soon. Essentially, since there was time set aside for writing letters in the evenings, someone suggested that we open up a contest in the camp. It must be remembered that we were about eighty lonely adolescent boys, who were adapting to a new school, a new country, and a new language in a new world. The contest had to do with something that was fairly prevalent in the camp, the unmet needs for social interchange with girls. Although Bishop Kenny High was co-educational, most classes back then were not co-educational. The girls had their own school across the street from where the boys' school was located. In some classes, the girls did come over to the boys' side, but not in all classes. Obviously, there were absolutely no girls in the camp, except for the lady who served as our cook. Ah, there was another lady, the wife of a Cuban teacher, who was also a teacher herself at the girls' school at Kenny High. The couple lived in "La Casa Verde" which was located somewhere between "La Casa Grande," the Manor, and the camp cabins.

Some of the boys at Camp St. John had been talking about making friends with girls at school, but those relationships, if any at that time, were long distance. However, at least one of the seniors, Gus, seemed to have a growing relationship with a girl named Bernadette. I venture to claim that most conversations between the boys at Camp St. John and the Kenny High girls were on the telephone, by mail, or from some distance away, such as from one side of the street to the opposite one.

The contest had to do with getting answers and establishing a pen pal relationship with a girl in Cuba. I, therefore, wrote two letters to two girls that I had known in Havana and I thought there was a possibility that they might answer me. In the course of several months, I did establish a long distance relationship with only one of the girls. I think the best way to appreciate how the relationship developed is to go over her letters. Unfortunately, my letters to her are not available.

> *Havana, March 1, 1961*
> *Highly esteemed Tony:*
>
> *You probably thought that I had forgotten you but I was waiting to get your address. Yesterday I... was surprised to get a letter from you. You cannot imagine the joy it gave me...*
> *I also imagine there are very pretty girls over there. Boys would not be scarce there. Since boys are disappearing from here, make friends with some boys so that you can bring me one as contraband when you come back.*
> *I hope you write as soon as you can and tell me many things from over there just so that I can dream.*
> *You are appreciated,*
>
> *Amelí*

As the reader may recall, I had received this letter from Amelí. What I didn't discuss in Chapter 10 is that this letter was in response to the letter writing campaign we had begun. I knew this girl from the neighborhood where we lived. Her father was also a physician and knew my father. In short, I knew her and her family. I already knew from my parents' mail that they were sharing an occasional Sunday with her family. Obviously, she became a good candidate with whom to try to establish a pen pal relationship.

In terms of this, her first letter, it is necessary for the purposes of establishing a baseline for this relationship at the onset of the letter writing process to note not only the content in the body of the letter, but also the greeting and the closing. Her salutation is rather cold. In Spanish it read *Muy estimado*, Tony. The closing is also reserved. In Spanish it read *Te aprecia*, Amelí. Since this was the first letter, these parameters are the baseline of the relationship. Let us see how these changed—if at all—in the fullness of time.

> *Havana, March 29, 1961*
> *My dear Tony:*
>
> *Here we remember you and all out there...very much. I think I have not told you that we have formed a youth association here of which I am the secretary. We also have published a newspaper that, God willing, I will send you the two first issues of because they are very good ... You and the group who are out there have been appointed honorary members because you are outside the country! ... But we all have hope that very soon everybody will be able to return, since the courses you are taking will be completed soon and all of you will be coming home for the summer holidays.*
> *I tell you, I am sometimes very sad ... I see that as time passes, gradually we are being left alone and most of the people we loved are no longer here. But what can you do?*
> *You say that you have a girlfriend. If so congratulations. If not, look for one so you do not feel so alone. Sometimes I think of you and all who are outside this country and feel as if something presses against my chest, as if my heart is squeezed. Then I think how it must feel to be away, alone without any family or even friends. But sometimes I think that you all will find new friends and forget for a moment that both you and we are hurting.*
> *I went to Dr. Alejandro's visit and he recommended me to take a little trip to help my nerves. But as Aunt Martha is so badly ill with cancer that has invaded her completely, we are expecting at any moment the final outcome. Since I really like her, I have always loved her very much, she has asked me not to go away from her side. Naturally, I am here like everyone else waiting to see what happens.*
> *Well Tony, write soon because you cannot imagine the happiness you are giving me through your letters.*
> *I remember you always,*
>
> *Amelí*

I could not help but appreciate, at that time, that I was coming up in the scale of adjectives in Amelí's penmanship and probably in her heart. Notice that this time she is addressing me as *"Mi querido Tony."* From her comments, I am sure she knew that I did not have any girlfriend at the time!

First, she tells me about general things, like they had organized a youth association in Altahabana. They had made all of us outside the country "honorary members." Then she got into a series of statements that reflected the insecurity of the times. She thought of how lonesome we are outside the country, but she noted that she was also lonesome. I feel that we were all feeling the loneliness and the stress of those times on both sides of the Florida Straits. Both groups, on and off the island, thought that the hostilities would end soon, however. That is why she was relating that we were going to go home for our summer vacations.

The issue about Dr. Alejandro and Aunt Martha had to do with the situation in Cuba. It was not clear who Dr. Alejandro was, but it probably referred to Fidel Alejandro Castro himself. However, Aunt Martha is code for Cuba. The country had been invaded by a malignant cancer, communism. Amelí and others were waiting for the end of the battle, thinking it would be soon. Obviously, they were optimistic on the outcome, because pretty much everyone they knew was against the communists.

The closing is definitely more promising than the former " *Te aprecio."* At this pointin time I am led to belief that she will remember me always.

Havana, April 13, 1961
My dear Tony:

You do not know how much joy I get from your letters. The second one you sent me dated April 5 came in two days later than the one you had previously sent me. Therefore, I did not even have time to answer you.

I imagine you must be very well and excited to spend the holiday with us…

With regard to the projector, I spoke to your father the same day I received your letter and he said literally: "I cannot believe he asked for it." You know that your Aunt Martha was ill and bedridden. I have several rolls of films, movies, with which I am entertaining her. That is why we cannot send you the projector. But if she dies, it's safe to say that you will be here because your course is about to

end as well as the life of poor Aunt Martha. So either way, you will
have the projector.
About the newspaper, I'm hoping the third issue will be out so you
can see the major improvements in it...
Well Tony, hopefully soon you will end your classes so that you can
be with us forever more and not to be separated again,

Amelí

I am keeping score with the salutation which is steady at *"Mi querdio Tomy",*
but what about the closing? The closing is getting more interesting. Note that she
actually stated that "you can be with us forever more and not to be separated again."
This sounded like a major confession on her part. But no, not so fast. She was writing about the "classes that will end soon." The context of the declaration is a
metaphor, a fantasy.

She was noted to be rather clever and intelligent. She spun the issue of the
movie projector, which I mentioned in case there was a way to have my movie projector shipped to me so that I could see some of the movies I was making. Except
that she answered in the Martha code noting that "she needed the projector as long
as Aunt Martha was ill, etc."

I may have been writing too many letters to her. She did not even have time to
answer them. Then, it came to pass that the Bay of Pigs Invasion occurred. And
then, her next letter would be from several weeks after the invasion. This was a
good sign. She did not stop writing despite the signs of war. This was a good sign
in my progress toward a long distance relationship!

Havana May 12, 1961
My dear Tony:

You cannot imagine the joy I felt when I received your letter. But
then, I received another one the day after with even greater joy.
Here for now there is not much to tell you, but I guess you know
enough of what has happened.
You remember how large and diverse our group was. For several
months, only we three remain from our group here. There is also
another group, you know. But we do not interact with the other
group.

*Soon I'll make a picture worthy to be sent to you...for you to put
in a small frame in your room.*

*As far as the newspaper, the truth is that it came out badly. It seems
that there is not enough enthusiasm now to do it as we had when
we first started.*

*Well Tony...do not stop writing to me. You do not know how much
good your letters do me. Your letters are always so loving as the
true friend you are. Before concluding let me congratulate you on
your graduation.... For now I leave you because I want to send the
letters right now.*

See you soon, love you,

Amelí

She referred to "another group" in the neighborhood. When the last member of each of the families who left Altahabana left Cuba, the house would be turned over to the revolutionary government. A revolutionary government official would come in and complete an inventory of everything in and around the house. In a matter of a few days to a few weeks, that property would be occupied by a revolutionary family. At the time, houses and properties in Altahabana were being assigned to revolutionary physicians. I did not get to know any of those families, but Amelí did refer to them when she pointed out that "there is another group" in the neighborhood. Paradoxically, in future phases of the revolution, some of those families also sought asylum, if not in the United States, then in other countries such as Algeria or Ethiopia. The houses would then be turned over again to another revolutionary family. It is not certain if the revolutionary government kept up the practice of assigning houses in Altahabana exclusively to medical doctors. But who knows how many generations of "revolutionary," divided families have passed through the houses of Altahabana by now.

She had been writing about sending a photograph of herself. Sending a photograph to me in the mail under those circumstances gained me another point in the contest of showing how "advanced" my pen pal relationship was in standing.

She is still reminding me "how much good my letters" are for her. I am still loved in the closing. She wrote that she "will see me." This may mean that she is already seriously planning to depart from Cuba or that she is hoping for a change in the political situation through which exiles would get to return to the island.

Havana, May 25, 1961
My dear Tony:

Since you have not yet answered my previous letter, I decided to write to you to see what is going on with you.

A few days ago, as I announced in my previous letter, I went to eat at your uncle's house with mom and dad and family, naturally. We had a ball but then what a horrible shame! This is what happened. I started taking in aperitifs and then they served a meal with an excellent wine and as a result of taking in all these mixtures I got sick. After dinner we sat on their balcony and there was a fresh breeze at which time I fell asleep. I felt like I was on a cloud floating. You cannot imagine how we remembered you and Ramoncito. Imagine!

I saw the pictures you sent. You are looking well and we all concluded that you are being treated to the royal table. I also saw Ramoncito, whom I did not recognize. He seems not to be eating from the same table as you! He looked hungry.

Tell me about your love. Did you decide to tell her? Remember that there is nothing better than to feel loved by someone, this is truer when you are away from family. When you're young love is the purest feeling you can feel.

Do not look for a grand future which we do not know if it will come or what we'll find in it, whether roses or thorns. So do not miss this opportunity for an unknown future. Live in the present...and have faith in the future.

Love,

Amelí

She reported that she may have eaten and or drunk too much at my Uncle Ramon's apartment when her family and mine had a get-together. She is obviously being honest about what, indeed, happened to her. Then she went on to inquire about a topic I had been writing about. She does not know it, but she was the subject of my love at the time. Then she ended with a memorable set of lines that I chose to share at the head of this chapter: "Do not look for a grand future, which we do not know if it will come or what we'll find in it, whether roses or thorns. So, do not miss this opportunity for an unknown future. Live in the present...and have faith in the future."

> *Havana, July 3, 1961*
> *My dear Tony:*
>
> *Do not think for a moment that I have forgotten you, on the contrary I have thought of you because I knew that since you have not received letters from us you would be concerned. But the truth is that it was not our fault. I hope this letter finds you rather well in the College.*
> *With regards to your parents' departure, I think everything is in order, the only thing missing is that God also has to have the same opinion. I have been presented with the opportunity to possibly go to Spain but I need, so that you know, to try to get a school in New York or as close as possible to New York since I have family there, although I cannot stay in their home permanently because they are too many and are in the same situation as me.*
> *Also I have a letter from a school which recommends me based on my morality and all of that series of things...I have full confidence in you, and in your previous letter you spoke of one or two schools in Indiana and one in Virginia... I hope that you take great interest in this and give me a prompt response. If I get it, all will be well soon and God willing I'll be there.*
> *Now changing the subject since the last issue is driving me crazy I'll tell you something of my life.*
> *I feel so alone and what happens is that I am alone. Here everyone has taken off following different paths. But what are we going to do? Just wait and have faith that everything will be resolved. Do you believe that?*
> *Another of the reasons why I had not written you is because I wanted to take a good photograph and I was waiting for it but they are not ready yet.*
> *If you knew what I'm going through with this mess? Yet I have the full assurance that if it is in your hands to be able to resolve this issue you will do it.*
> *Tony, this letter is loaded with requests that I hope you regard with*

the greatest interest possible. I won't hassle you anymore and in my
upcoming letters I will cover more interesting things than today.
Please Tony, find out for me, as soon as possible.
Love you always,

Amelí
Write me soon.

She wrote about an issue that became the most popular of the topics in the letters I received from my peers at school and my friends elsewhere. She was writing about the fact that she feels she needs help in getting to the United States be it in the form of a visa waiver—which she did not ask for in the letter—or with regard to places where she may find a *beca*, which would include somewhere where she could live and go to school for a while. At that time in the revolution and the truncated civil war, it was still a temporary fix that most of us were looking for.

The fact that she confided in me to assist her with those resettlement issues was ample proof that the relationship had advanced. Although it was reassuring that she had placed her trust in me and my abilities to find her a place for resettlement, it sounded scary from today's perspective that someone would place their hope in a 16-year-old boy, who was trying to adapt to a new country himself and, in the process, tried to escape from a hospital where he was getting treatments, and almost succeeded in stealing the car of the head counselor at his encampment. At any rate, at that point in time, I did have a few months more experience than she did on the issues of *becas*. Her last sentence: "Please, Tony, find out for me, as soon as possible" has to do with the issue of finding her a school, an institution, a *beca* in Virginia or New York or somewhere nearby to her relatives.

Havana July 6, 1961
Dear Tony:

I just received your letter and I am answering it so you do not complain that I do not write to you. Actually, what happened is that recently a series of things have distracted my attention. But I hope that the same things that have kept me from writing to you soon will result in us being, if not together, at least very close.
The little postcard you sent me is very pretty and the one you sent your father is also pretty. Wish I could be there.

A few days ago I sent you a letter full of despair...I explained to you in it as best I could that I may depart to Spain.... Your dad told me that you would talk about this with your uncle Emilio to see if I can get what I asked for.

Here we are pretty good but somewhat bored. It is only Sundays...when I go to lunch with your uncles, your parents and mine that I am not bored. I'm the youngest of the group.

On Tuesday we went to eat chicken at Pio Lindo; your parents, mine, another couple, my sister and I....

...There is nobody here, Fermincito and Rosita are gone and others have gone to Prague and Moscow Ernesto P, L Carlos F. Do you think I like being alone? So write often because I love to receive letters from all over the world and of course yours, too.

The other day at your house I met a girl named Gladys who told me that some time ago she received a letter from you that had surprised her very much because she did not expect anything like that from you. She did not tell me what you wrote but I can imagine you know how quick I am. I think the girl that you have been writing to me about in your letters is her! I think your letter to her was a true statement or declaration of love.

Now, this is my advice. You should know that she is a bit older than you and she does not think of boys like you as boys. I tell you, "Te lo digo no por la idea de que pierdas las esperanzas, pues a lo mejor triunfas, el diablo son las cosas." *(I tell you this not so that you lose hope, because possibly you will triumph, you never know.) Oh, and forgive me for being so nosy.*

Now here it is 12:25 P.M. Let me see if I call Buznego and I can get my photograph so I can send it to you...

Well Tony, I think I am running out of literary material, so hopefully in your next letter give me the answer your Uncle Emilio has with respect of finding a school for me.

Now I am going to write to Elenin who is Miami and she sends me Chiclets in her letters. So far she has not failed me.

I hope you make some international friends...I would love to meet them. Why not take a picture with a group of them? Ah, you owe me a photo. Well Tony ... You'll see soon as you meet girls how your boredom will dissipate among your international friends.

See you soon, love you,

Amelí

I came through as someone rather demanding, according to her perception in her first line. Apparently, I had complained that she was either not answering my letters or writing less than I anticipated. Either way, my attitude was probably inappropriate for the circumstances and definitely not in parallel with the concept of tolerance and love that I wanted to convey.

I guess she had been busy with issues regarding the documentation needed in order to depart from Cuba. She felt that she might end up nearby to wherever I would be. However, in the next few lines she reports that she may have to leave for Spain. Obviously, a sign of a wide range of possibilities all united through the perceived need to have to depart from Cuba.

The expertise and connections of my uncle Emilio are again made manifest. I do not think that she ever met my uncle Emilio anywhere, but I could be wrong. Either way, she is counting on uncle Emilio as if he were her own uncle. For the purposes of the contest, that is something favorable for me!

Next topic in line is the fact she is lonesome. The crew from Altahabana left Cuba to various places, not just the United States. I can think of those who went to Colombia, some went to Panama. Others, as she is pointed out, went behind the Iron Curtain.

She had written about it before, people were taking their own paths, different paths.

Not everyone who left Altahabana did it because they were seeking refuge from communism. Two of the individuals who are mentioned in this letter, Ernesto and L Carlos F, left Cuba for countries in the Soviet Bloc. They were Cubans, but their parents had arrived in Cuba in the aftermath of the Spanish Civil War and may have been leaning, at that time, toward the communist regime of Fidel Castro. One of these individuals, Ernesto, went to school in the Soviet Union and years later escaped through Czechoslovakia. In summary, it appears that most of the children from Altahabana who left the island, eventually sought freedom, not serfdom.

Then she comes to the climax of this letter. In the beginning, I wrote to two girls. One was Amelí and the other was, yes you guessed it, Gladys. I do not remember what I wrote to Gladys and she has never mentioned it to me, despite the fact that she did leave Cuba several years later with her father and mother and I have seen her with her family on a couple of occasions. I feel that whatever it was that I wrote to her must have been very inappropriate and embarrassing; otherwise, she would have mentioned it to me. What I never thought could happen, did occur, however. The two girls with whom I had selected to establish a pen pal relationship met in the most unlikely of places, my parents' home. I do say the most unlikely of places because I do not think that Gladys ever set foot in that house while I was living there!

Amelí had good advice for me. "Gladys is too old for you!" And, indeed, she was by a couple of years!

Then she wrote in Spanish that she wished I not lose hope and, perhaps, I will triumph, but then she invoked some sort of "devilish luck" using a Spanish slang meaning by chance.

Amelí did not know it, but I had triumphed with her because we had exchanged many letters in the course of a few months. There was something greater than anything personal in the substance of our letters. It had to do with the very same thing that caused the exodus from the island. At the end, she got back to the real important issue at the time, the connections to get her out of Cuba and to find her a place to stay in or near New York, where she must have had relatives.

Havana, August 17, 1961
Dear Tony:

Today we received ... (your mom's) letter from Antonio and soon he will be with you and bring you a picture of me....
I do not have a visa waiver...but Antonio has all the data required to see if you can move my case... because it seems to me that you have connections out there....

Love,
Amelí

Finally, in August of 1961, she confided that she does not have a visa waiver. In my own experience, everyone in Havana with whom I was exchanging letters at that time, mentioned and requested that I help them obtain a visa waiver. Amelí was no exception. She finally left Cuba in November 1961. She first came into Miami and, from there, she wrote that she might go to Michigan. I lost track of her and saw her many years later in Puerto Rico, where she eventually migrated with her parents, married happily, and raised her own family.

What began as an exercise to establish a pen pal relationship with two girls nearly backfired because the two girls met in my father's home in Havana. The relationship with one of the girls did seem to develop into something positive, but all letters were busy with the issues that were most serious at the time: The loneliness in Havana, the fear of repression, and the need for help in getting out of the country in view of the increasing violence and repression. Letters had to be written in some kind of code to protect those individuals in Cuba from reprisals from the government, who systematically censored the mail.

What had begun as some sort of contest to determine who was better at establishing a romantic relationship long distance began to crumble a few weeks after it began. The uncertainty of our own futures and the turns that the opposition against the Castro regime took pushed the so-called contest way back in terms of our priorities. Perhaps, a few of the guys boasted as to how they were expressing themselves in their letters, but I did not. No one ever passed around or read aloud the letters we received. Therefore, the accounting of points to determine a winner never took place.

In terms of my own feelings, I must admit that what began as just an exercise in long distance communication evolved in evoking romantic feelings on my part, which were not seconded on the other side. True love is somehow similar to the strand of life, the double stranded deoxyribonucleic acid (DNA). If the nature of the one strand is not complemented by the other, the pairing cannot stand together, much less reproduce.

One further observation seems appropriate now. The path of most of the adolescents in exile followed their families, even distant relatives. Once Amelí was outside of Havana, there was no further need or time to spare for writing to me. The most important reasons for the letters she wrote was to make me feel better and to have me write back to her. My letters seemed to make her feel less lonely, as well as helping her get some idea of what this place was like. But when the burden of living under communism was lifted, life went on for most people.

CHAPTER 14

THE BAY OF PIGS INVASION: *CONSUMMATUM EST*

*"And so, my fellow Americans: ask not what your country can do for you–
ask what you can do for your country. My fellow citizens of the world: ask not what
America will do for you, but what together we can do for the freedom of man."*
-John F. Kennedy, 1961

The schoolwork at Bishop Kenny was manageable, although I still had serious questions about my progress in Mr. Durant's Advanced Mathematics class. Our outings on Saturdays to downtown Jacksonville were providing a much needed space where we felt we had little in the way of supervision for at least a few hours. Mail kept coming in and most of us received an ample number of letters almost on a daily basis. On many occasions, Father Lenihan himself delivered the mail to us. By April 1961, St. John's Camp could have been thought of as running on automatic, except for the day when the old Air Force school bus did not make it to school. Jorge, one of the Cuban counselors usually drove the bus and the other counselor, Arce, served as the conductor, so to speak. That is, he took attendance and if things got too noisy, he tried to calm us down.

On that particular day, however, Arce and, perhaps, up to one-third of the students were absent for reasons that I do not remember. The bus got on its way heading north on Route 13. Jorge began taking attendance. Some people were responding for some of those who were absent. Jorge noticed it immediately and began to turn his head away from the road to look back into the cabin and actually see who was there and who was not.

Just north of the camp, Route 13 curves to the left. After the bus took that curve Jorge was turning his neck and torso to his right to look back into the cabin and ascertain who was there doing what. The bus then veered to the left. Jorge turned his attention back to the control of the vehicle immediately. When he went to correct the course, he overdid it and we almost went off the road on the right side. Then Jorge turned the stirring wheel to the left, the bus went off the road and turned sideways into a ditch.

I was sitting in the right rear of the bus and saw the whole thing develop in front of my eyes. I held onto the horizontal bar of the seat in front of me and I tried to remain sitting in my place no matter what. As the bus landed, I had rotated 90 degrees to my left, but I was still holding to the front seat bar and my feet were still on the floor of the bus.

Immediately, after a few loud expressions of fear, everyone calmed down. A few of the passengers sustained minor injuries. We all began climbing out of the bus through the emergency exit on the right side. The left side was face down in the grassy ditch. As I was getting out, I saw several police cars and a van from a local television station. Some of the passengers were being interviewed by both the authorities and the journalists.

A couple of hours after we had left the camp, we were all, somewhat safely, back in it. We missed school that day. No one dared blame Jorge for the accident. After all, it had been some of the students on the bus who had begun responding for those who were not there who started the chain of events that resulted in the accident. We thanked God for the fact that we had survived and our bus did not flip a couple of blocks down the road, where we would have gone down off the road into a creek of the St. John's River. That would have been a catastrophe.

After we arrived back at the camp and settled down, we planned to watch the news on television because we were sure that the news of the day in that corner of the world would cover our accident. Everyone in the camp, including the counselors, was glued to the television set in the large dining hall, expecting to see the report on the bus accident. At the end of the news hour, we were all somewhat disappointed that the story never aired. At that time, we ourselves did not know that not only the entire Operation Pedro Pan was somewhat semi-clandestine, but that the Unaccompanied Cuban Children Program was also not supposed to be in the news. Nothing else was said about the accident then or in the days after. The bus had some dents and scratches, but since it was so old and its paint was already in bad shape, most people did not even notice that the bus had survived a potentially serious accident with more than thirty children on board.

On April 14 my father wrote:

> *I see that the food is good over there, although there is no rice, beans or stew. That is the reason behind the fact that Ramoncito*

is not gaining weight. He always ate here in Cuba two or three
plates full of rice and stew, especially if it was black beans.
I hardly see the boys in Altahabana anymore...
Yesterday, El Encanto store completely burned down, nothing was
left standing. I really feel sorry for this because you know it was
the major department store in Cuba. Well, circumstances so require
it. May God soon bring peace to this island of cork.
Receive the blessing of your father,

Antonio

The loss of El Encanto, located on the corner of Galiano and San Rafael Streets in the commercial district of Havana, was probably the result of sabotage by the Underground. It was a time during which the revolution was turning into a civil war, and anyone who was suspected of being against the revolutionary government faced going to jail, being tortured, and, perhaps, even submitted to a mock trial or shot at the *paredón*.(1) All anti-Castro activities were, therefore, clandestine. My father refers to Cuba as *la isla de corcho*. This is an allegory that has been used to describe the ups and downs of the Cuban republic in the first half of the twentieth century. The social and political situation on the island was thought to behave in a manner similar to a cork on the ocean. With increasing repression, political pressure, and financial distress, it could sink. However, if allowed to be free and prosperous, it could resurface again and float.

Then, the invasion occurred. On April 17, 1961, we were informed that an invasion force had landed on Cuba's southern coast. The initial reports available to us through the camp counselors and the radio and television newscasts were rather favorable for us, since the invaders were reported to be advancing. School work ceased for us. Everyone in the camp was trying to contact family in and outside of Cuba.

Despite the radio and television reports noted above, a careful review of the *New York Times* from April 17 until April 20 yielded a more somber reality. If we would have read it then, we could have learned, even since the very beginning of the coverage, from the clear discourse of President Kennedy that: "The United States intends no military intervention in Cuba."(2) On the other hand, Soviet Premier Khrushchev was also clear in his statement at the time: "As to the Soviet Union, there should be no misunderstanding of our position: We shall render the Cuban people and their government all necessary assistance in beating back the armed attack on Cuba."(3) Both leaders of the two world powers during the Cold

War agreed that a quarrel over Cuba could escalate to involve the entire world. Obviously, the facts spoke much louder than the rhetoric, and an agreement must have been reached between the world powers.

Back at Camp St. John, one of the Cuban counselors immediately told everyone that he had been promised by his friends that he was going to be notified about the invasion so that he could join the anti-Castro forces. He felt that his friends had somehow betrayed him. The invaders, I thought, must be the ones who had been recruited by Colonel Martín Elena. It seemed that the invasion was to be the trigger that would make everyone's wishes for a short exile a reality. There were high hopes in the camp that the civil war that had been brewing had finally gotten to its final stage. Perhaps, as everyone had expected, we would be back home by summer.

The first written news I got from my family in those difficult days came in from my cousin Muñeca, writing for the entire family who resided up in northern New Jersey at the time.

> She wrote:
> *Ridgefield Park, N. J.*
> *April 19, 1961*
> *My dear cousins:*
>
> *First, I wish that you are doing well in school.*
> *We are also perfectly well and we are very happy with the news from Cuba. According to the information aired by the American TV today, Che Guevara has been seriously injured.*
> *The main purpose of this letter is to let you know that whatever happens in Cuba, both of you should remain right there. Call us if there is anything going on and you have to leave the school because we will go and get you. At least my father and I will go...*
> *Remember to be calm no matter what.*
> *Cuba's mail is interrupted. I will send a letter to grandmother Amparo through Spain via Eduardo... Do not worry about not receiving news from Havana. It is logical. You already know that we have to have confidence in God and pray for those who are there.*
> *I imagine that the priests and nuns in Cuba must be going through Hell...I trust they will have left the schools and convents already. You can imagine how Mima is with all of this... Sometimes she gets desperate and very anxious...*

The weather here is horrible... Be happy that you did not have to come up here...
Well, my dear cousins, remember that you must behave well and be calm. Please answer me and tell me what is going on over there...
Many kisses...

Muñeca

Although we now know that the invasion was doomed by April 19, and crushed by April 20, on account of the fact that the invaders were running out of ammunition, had no air cover, and Castro's air force had not been totally annihilated, the news media in the United States was broadcasting misinformation even on April 19. The misinformation about Che Guevara being wounded may have surfaced from the fact that Guevara was said to have joined Fidel Castro in the area of the Australia sugar mill near the landing site of Brigade 2506 in order to direct the counterattack against the invading force.(4)

Since the invasion "was thought to be going so well" for our cause, my family in the United States was obviously concerned that if, indeed, the invasion succeeded in toppling the Castro regime, our *becas* might be immediately terminated. Hence, she reassured us that "they would come and get us" if there was a need for that. To my cousin and me, this was reassuring, but what about the situation for most of the guys at the St. John's Camp who had no relatives in the United States? What did they think in terms of having to deal with the sudden closing of the camp? In the setting of the invasion and the hope for the liberation of Cuba, there was also the uncertainty of our situation.

Back in the camp, even on the day of the landing of the invasion, several guys tried to make phone calls to their families in Havana, but they quickly found out that there were no phone lines available to Havana. Some did get through to speak with relatives in other parts of the United States, however. They invariably confirmed the news about the invasion and the generalized feeling that an early victory was in sight.

In those days, I received a letter from Juan Pella from Havana, dated April 16, 1961. Pella wrote about the departure of Zenón the week before and did not give any sign in his letter that anything was happening in Havana. However, in our home in Altahabana, there had been signs of something happening. My mother was awakened by the sounds of bombs on April 15. Indeed, the airfield in Columbia had been bombarded along with the one in San Antonio de los Baños, south of the city of Havana. The Columbia airfield is about 15 kilometers from Altahabana. My father was asleep and my mother tried to wake him up.

"Antonio, I hear bombs," she said.

"María, do not worry. It must be thunder. All has been postponed," he answered.

"Antonio, I think they are bombing something," she repeated.

Obviously, I did not know this at the time, but learned it much later. Indeed, in my opinion, what seemed to have happened was that the vast network of people in the Underground had been misled and misinformed that the invasion was going to be delayed. In reality, the bombing was supposed to completely take out of commission the revolutionary Air Force. It did not. Furthermore, the Underground was supposed to pour into the streets and make passage of Castro's forces out of the cities and their encampments difficult by blocking streets. The militia never had any problems in getting to the Bay of Pigs area, because the Underground had been misinformed. In reality, members of the Underground were captured in their own homes and neighborhoods.

The immediate balance of the invasion by the Brigade 2506, the major battle in our truncated civil war, was as follows:

Castro's Forces: 176 killed and thousands wounded.(5)
Brigade 2506: 118 killed, 360 wounded, and 1,202 captured.(5)

More importantly, the Underground was dismantled when more than 100,000 people in Havana alone were arrested and held in jails, theaters, stadiums, sports fields, schools, clubs, or anywhere else a detention area could be improvised.(6) Some escaped, others were killed, but all their connections were broken and their trust in their leaders vanished. Those who were not imprisoned had lost faith in their superiors in the Underground. The entire anti-Castro and anti-communist movement had been mortally injured.

Juan Pella went to the movies on that Sunday. Maybe if he had not gone to the theater, he would have had the real feeling of war described by Carlos Eire(7) as the bombings of the airfield in Marianao occurred very near his home. But Pella, who lived about 15 kilometers from the bombed airfield, did not report any news. Unfortunately, the Underground was also in the wrong place, at the wrong time, and misinformed about its battle station— the streets—to engage in the fight.

Ridgefield Park, N.J.
April 22, 1961
My dear cousins:

The main reason for this letter is to let you know that we just received a Western Union cable from grandmother Amparo in which she tells us: "WE ARE ALL WELL."
I tell you to not worry... Remember that difficult days will come for everyone because what has occurred in Cuba has been serious...
I think you should not call to Cuba on the telephone because we could bring more calamities on them because the situation is so delicate over there. Here I have heard that the people who have been called from the United States have been arrested and subjected to an interrogation at the police station...
Do not forget...we have to be strong and offer all the setbacks...to our Lord. We are Christians and Christ calls us to truly learn how to bear the cross. Offer Him the cross of the sacrifices of these days and you will see that He will promptly reward you.
Hopefully we can see you soon and be reunited again in Cuba.

Muñeca

Despite the assurances of my cousin Muñeca about placing our trust in God, I had many worries. God can assist anyone who believes by providing a perspective, a hope at the beginning of the battle, the necessary courage to fight during the battle, and satisfaction that all has been done—Consummatum est (John 19:30)—at the conclusion of the battle. At some point thereafter, we had to arrive at the realization that despite our hope in God's will, the confrontation did not go according to our desires, our will. God cannot be a cop-out. God is the infinite being. How are we to expect that He is going to provide outcomes according to our timetable? Or, for that matter, according to our own limited perspective and desires? Impossible!

God did provide, however. He did provide the strength to make it through those difficult, uncertain, and misinformed times. I feel that He did provide for me. He provided the tolerance and the understanding that allowed us to go on and not become completely rebellious against the status quo in and outside the exile circles. It was not difficult to blame one political party or the other for the fiasco of the invasion. But after all, we Christian human beings cannot think of God as something abstract and distant. We must think of God having a relationship not only with us, but also with all other brothers and sisters. Hence, our relationship with those around us, in particular those who are part of our families, is also part of our beliefs and our highest values. So what sense does it make to think of God and forget about my father and mother? None.

I knew that my father was active in the Underground movement against the communist government. As of April 17, he was still, to my knowledge at the time, part of the Rebel Army and working as a physician at the Military Hospital in Camp Columbia. By the April 19, we had already heard through guys at the camp who communicated with relatives in the Miami area that there had been massive arrests in Havana. Indeed, the Underground was dismembered at that time, with most of its members jailed. Therefore, I felt very uneasy about what might have happened to my parents, specifically, my dad. At the time, I felt that he had been arrested. If that had been the case, where was my mother and how was she doing?

My family went on to write:

> *Ridgefield Park, N.J.*
> *April 22, 1961*
> *My dear Tony:*
>
> *I just got off the phone with you and I set out to write to you immediately...*
> *I think you should not call Havana because you know that today anyone can get into troubles with those beasts over there!*
> *Unfortunately, there is nothing we can do for our loved ones except to pray more.*
> *Have great faith in God, my cousin! I'm sure that he will protect us all and especially Uncle Antonio. For your peace of mind, I tell you that every day I pray for him and I'm pretty sure nothing will happen to him.*
> *I found you very anxious when I talked with you today. What's wrong? Are you sick?*
> *Today or tomorrow, Pilar will talk to Nena and Isabel and she will ask them about our folks back home. If we find out anything, we will let you know...*
> *I give you my word that whatever we find out I'll tell you right away.*

But why, on what, do you base your suspicion that something has happened to Uncle Antonio? When you write back to me, use as sender the name: Zoila Diaz, Miami, Fla. That way we avoid your Aunt Carmen reading the letter and getting more anxious than she is now...

Do not be discouraged by this small setback that we have suffered from the invasion. It is true that in some form it was a fiasco...

Take care of yourself and you know that I love you,

Muñeca

How long has it been since you've gotten a letter from Cuba?

Pilar was our cousin who had lived in Saranac Lake, New York, since the 1920s where she founded a new family when she married Manuel Benero. Pilar's sister, Isabel, was in Havana where she taught English and French and took care of her very elderly mother, Nena. That call to Havana from Saranac Lake did occur. The report from Nena and Isabel was that they were all well.

Muñeca suggested in her letter that I use the name of one of her friends, Zoila Diaz, as the sender in my letters. She apparently did not want my Aunt Carmen to open and read my letters because she was already somewhat distressed emotionally on account of all these issues, not the least of which was my father's fate after the invasion.

Still, there was no direct confirmation of any news from my father or mother. During this time, I would take long walks alone along the sandy trails of St. John's Camp. The Spanish moss continued to remind me of the sadness in my heart. It seemed then that the physical distance between North Florida and Havana was much longer that it actually was. I guess, using Mr. Durant's terminology: It approached infinity. In reality, the physical distance was not that immense. However, to cross that physical distance one would have to cross a series of political and financial obstacles that were, in reality, impassable for me. So, while thinking of the fate of my parents, my usual walk involved walking through the road that led from the camp proper and the clearing in front of the cabins directly to Route 13. I found out that from that particular trail I could see more clearly the skies. I was able to overcome the cover of the tall trees and Spanish moss and tried to look beyond my own reality in order to find hope to go on living.

Since then, that particular sandy road has been obliterated by overgrown vegetation and the second gate to the camp where it reached Route 13 has been closed.

Since it was in that particular part of the camp where I experienced such a great solitude and I felt the worst, including the fear that I would never see my parents again, I was glad to see when I revisited the camp fifty years later that no one could walk through that "passage" again because that trail is no longer a way out.

It was not until May 10, 1961, that I received a letter from my parents again. Since then, however, I had learned that my father had been spared another imprisonment. My family in New Jersey had communicated directly with my Aunt Ofelia and grandmother Amparo and they reassured them that my father was well. This is what my father wrote after the invasion:

Havana, May 10, 1961
My dear son Tony:

Yesterday I received a letter from you and I see that everything is getting ready for graduation...
As you'll know by the press of that country all private schools in Cuba have been confiscated and nationalized. The brothers are not in the school anymore... they all are going to other countries.
I wrote to Father Lenihan and I guess he has not received my letter because I have not received an answer. I hope to know the answer to the issue I discussed in the letter regarding what will happen to you after you graduate.
We would like to come see you. Let's see if God...helps us.
I'm not in the hospital anymore because on April 29 they let me go. So at present I am only working at the Cristo de Limpias Hospital. Within a few days, a friend of mine who lives in Puerto Rico will send you 70 dollars. I believe that within the next 15 days you will receive it. I guess it will be a money order or check. Anyway, Father Lenihan will facilitate the method of payment, save that money, because if you go to New York with Carmen and Emilio that money will cover the trip by bus, which is cheaper.
Hopefully God can help us and you will keep studying. In case you do not get a scholarship, you will go with your uncle and aunt to New York and there we'll see what you can do.
Always try to speak in English with your fellow Cubans so that you can practice and also correct yourselves.
We thank God for our good health and are waiting to see when we

can be together again. Yesterday Amelí also received a letter from you and I see that you are happy with your graduation. She was vaccinated yesterday. It is possible that she will depart for Spain in the near future. Poppy is very good and strong.

Well my son, may God help us all and you receive a kiss from your father,

Antonio

It was good to know that even Poppy was doing well after the attack. My mother wrote a separate letter this time:

May 10, 1961
Dearest son:

I hope you find yourself well, as well as Ramoncito. We are fine as are the others in the family who remember you fondly.

I am very pleased to know how good a student you are and the big interest that you have in graduating.

Hopefully you can achieve this desire.

I spend my days thinking of you. Do you remember all those nonsense issues that I raised Hell about? I think they distracted me so much, that I miss them now. May God grant that we will soon be together to enjoy those times as well as the good times between the fights.

Well son, see my letter says nothing of importance but at least you see my point. I am really anxious to see you in person together with us. Receive a million kisses from your mother who loves you so much,

María Luisa

In terms of the immediate future, by May we were already getting ready for the graduation. The Unaccompanied Cuban Children Program had already announced to us in the senior class that there were plans to send us to take a summer English course. Details were lacking, but my father did know through my correspondence about that possibility, because in a previous letter in early April, he mentioned that I should be able to travel to Saranac Lake, New York, and visit our cousin Pilar from Vermont. My mother's letter was filled with her emotions and her obvious distress at knowing that I am far away. I am sure that she felt that, perhaps, she might not see me again. She appeared to be somewhat depressed. It is not difficult to explain her comments about those times when she had punished me and appreciate that she was searching through her life and concentrated on issues that were not the most joyous.

My father continued to insist that I should not become a financial burden to anyone. He had made an arrangement so that I could have some money. The arrangement consisted of my father giving an amount of money to a person in Havana, who was a relative of someone who was in Puerto Rico. Then, the individual in Puerto Rico would send me a money order for the amount agreed upon. I think I got a little over one hundred dollars altogether from March until August. It was a creative scheme that allowed my father to evade Castro's regulations. Through this convoluted manner, he managed to get some money to me while I was in St. John's Camp.

This was the only letter, the one he wrote right after the Bay of Pigs fiasco, where he did not write down a sender on the envelope. Some of the letters that made it through censorship at that time did have a stamp with the word: *CENSURADO*.

By the time this letter arrived, I had already spoken with them on the telephone. The following letter from Muñeca gives us an idea of my impressions at that time:

Ridgefield Park, N. J.
May 6, 1961
Dear Tony:

First of all...I tell you I do not think that Uncle Antonio has been in jail because, if that would have been the case, I think it would be very unlikely that they would have released him. I do not understand why you insist on this? Is it because you know something you are not telling me?
We received today a letter from grandmother and another one from Uncle Ramón. In it we are told that they are all well. The letter is dated May 3rd.
In that letter, Aunt Blanquita...tells me that she became worried on account of what happened on the bus. What exactly happened on the bus?
I am glad that you got to talk on the phone with your father... and,

despite what you tell me about his mood being sad, I think that he may be saddened because of the unfavorable developments in our country.

Since your father lost his job, you should not think that your father and your mother are going to go hungry... You have no reason to think that. Although it is true that in Cuba there are shortages of food and many foods are scarce, do not think your parents are going to be hungry. Do you think that while some in our family have a penny your father will go hungry? As long as someone in our family has a penny your parents will never go hungry.

If Uncle Antonio has left the Military Hospital and stayed with the work at the Cristo de Limpias Hospital, it is because he considered that to be the best for him and he knows his stuff. Also, I think what is happening is that he is sad—like all of us—on account of the fiasco of the invasion.

Do not forget that every day we have to have more faith in our Lord because at the end He is going to give us the solution to the Cuban crisis. You can be sure of that.

On the question you have right now regarding returning to Cuba, I'll give my opinion. First of all, as I said above, the problem of Cuba will not be eternal and with God's favor we will have the solution soon.

I do not think you should go back to Cuba in any way. I think that far from being an economical solution for your parents, you will be a problem. Remember that the diploma you will have is from the United States. In today's Cuba that just makes it useless.

Other than that, in Cuba there is only work for the communists and everyone knows that you are not one of them.

Do you remember the hospital where I used to work? Everyone who did not join the militia was dismissed, left out. Are you going to surrender to them so that you can be accepted?

No, Tony, we need to have more confidence in God. We never give up and we know that God will protect us because we pray with faith.

Remember that right now, the only peace that your parents have is in knowing that you are away from Cuba and out of reach of international communism.

Do not think more about going to join your parents because you will regret it for a lifetime. Going back to Cuba would be a terrible mistake.

Now we just need to think about trying to get a beca *to continue your studies...*

Today I talked by phone with Father Kelly, who was rector of Villanueva in Cuba. He said that today or tomorrow the priests from Cuba will arrive. When they come, I'll go to greet them and I'll tell you what is going on over there.

Many kisses ... who loves you in Christ,

Muñeca

The distance from home and my heartfelt solitude were responsible, in my opinion, for my consideration to return to Havana to join my parents. I did not want to be without them. Indeed, the Bay of Pigs Invasion had turned into a major event for me and for many others. It was a catastrophe. After the Bay of Pigs, the number of children arriving in the United States without their parents increased appreciably. By the end of the Operation Pedro Pan and the Unaccompanied Cuban Children Program, approximately 80 percent of the children arrived after the Bay of Pigs Invasion fiasco.(8)

My uncle Emilio could not stay out of this discussion about my immediate future and my thoughts of going back to Cuba. He wrote:

Ridgefield Park, N.J.
May 10, 1961
Dear nephew:

A few days ago I wrote to you and I've yet to receive a reply. But as I am persistent, I am writing to you again...

First I want to wish you that you continue to enjoy good health. The first thing to do is not to die. After that you need to have all your affairs in order in that school. Third, you have to keep me informed of the present and immediate future without leaving things until the last minute.

Remember that nothing ventured, nothing gained, and you have to make the most of the chances that come your way as the occasion presents itself...let's grab that chance and run with it...

I see you've asked for...a college scholarship. My advice is...you seek the advice of the directors and officers of the school...

So I want you in the first place to investigate the issue well. Then to make sure who should arrange for you to continue to study in this country, for any kind of return to Cuba cannot be thought of as long as the ruling Communists are there, and you well know that your parents have intentions of leaving the island.

It is not a matter of despair or to think about working prematurely. You have to prepare to get ready for as long as we live in these indecisive circumstances. If we find ourselves that we can be...back to Cuba, there will be enough time to make new plans, but for the moment for you two, the right path is to study, this is the path that will give you the most benefit in this country to be able to work afterwards. Have no doubt that whatever you study will serve you so that your parents can be free from those concerns. Don't you think?

I know you are a serious thinker. So I write to you as if you were a grown man. I know that you are a man all right, but you're not done growing yet. Do you understand me?

With affection and hugs...I wait for your answer.

Love,
Emilio

My concern regarding my parents' situation had to do with the fact that I felt that my father's main livelihood was now gone. He was no longer working at the Military Hospital. I was glad to be reassured that "as long as anyone in the family back in Cuba had anything," my father and mother would not be lacking funds for their basic needs. However, the question still lingered as to what it was really like in Havana at the time. How truthful were my parents in reporting on their own situation. Or for that matter, how true was the reporting of Isabel or Abuela Amparo from Havana? I knew that my own reporting, in terms of being so glad for the graduation, etc., was not entirely true. My main concern was with the fact that right after the fiasco of the invasion, I did not know if I would ever see my parents again and I did not know how they really were. I just read in between the lines and saw my mother's emotional appeal, feeling sorry for minor issues of discipline that may have occurred years ago. The tone of my father's voice when we spoke on the telephone had been rather somber. Reconciling all of these stimuli with the events in our most recent history, including my departure from Cuba, proved to be a most difficult task to accomplish.

The invasion of Cuba was not a surprise. What proved to be a surprise was the actual Bay of Pigs Invasion. It had been labeled by the CIA, Operation Zapata. Why was an invasion not a surprise? The news media had been given ample evidence that an invasion of the island was being organized. In 1960, there were multiple reports discussing the recruitment, training, and planning of an invasion of the island to fight the Communist forces.(9) In fact, in March 1960, the Eisenhower administration reported publically that an invasion force made up of Cuban exiles was being planned to topple the revolutionary and dictatorial government of Fidel Castro.(10) Therefore, an invasion was not a surprise. What was a surprise was the Bay of Pigs Invasion, because it was ill-executed in terms of coordinating the uprising of the Underground, providing supplies to the invasion force, and air cover once it landed.

The tempo of both the Underground and Castro's forces had been in crescendo on the island just prior to the invasion. We already learned about the sabotage that resulted in the destruction of El Encanto. That was the work of the Underground. Since then, I also learned that my father, as medical director of the Cristo De Limpias Hospital located just outside Fontanar near the Havana José Martí Airport in Rancho Boyeros, had ordered that two large red crosses be painted on white backgrounds on the roof of the hospital. Indeed, two red crosses were painted on two sections of the roof. My father had argued that the hospital was a healthcare facility, not a fortified garrison. Therefore, he did not want to have his hospital bombed.

One morning in April before the actual invasion occurred, my father arrived at the hospital and saw a group of *milicianos* putting up sand bags on the roof. He inquired and they told him that they had been ordered to set up an anti-aircraft battery on the roof of the hospital. Subsequent to that, he climbed on the roof and ordered the *milicianos* to dismantle what they were doing because the hospital could not be used to place an anti-aircraft battery. He pointed out to them the two red crosses on white backgrounds that had just been painted a couple of days before.

The next day, when my father arrived at the hospital, he noticed that the *milicianos* had paid little attention to his orders. The sand bags were in place and an anti-aircraft battery had already been installed on the roof of the hospital. My father went into the hospital and discussed the situation at hand and what he planned to do with the nursing and administrative director, Sister Isabel Arana, a religious sister of charity. He went up to the roof with some of the maintenance staff of the hospital. He asked the *milicianos* to dismantle the anti-aircraft battery and the battle stations and get off the premises. With the help of some of the men on the maintenance staff, he then proceeded to dump from the roof to the ground the sand bags that bordered the battle station. As far as I know, the hospital was not fortified during the invasion.

Although I did not know while I was at Camp St. John about these events at the Cristo de Limpias Hospital, I did know enough about my father's anti-communist activities to be concerned about his fate during the failed invasion and its aftermath. I do consider it a miracle. Perhaps, it can be attributed to my cousin Muñeca's prayers, that my father was not arrested, killed, or in any way harassed—aside from being fired from the Rebel Army and the Military Hospital. After all, he had already requested to resign from his post there. He had dedicated all his professional life up to that time to working at that medical center.

In short, the Bay of Pigs Invasion served to demonstrate to all concerned that a civil war was in fact being fought. However, it was a shortchanged and rather asymmetric confrontation. The exile forces had placed their total allegiance—mostly blindly—in the United States, and the United States had other priorities in their defense and foreign policy agenda at the time. The Soviet Union had also taken a position that was clear from Premier Khrushchev's statement that they would not allow Castro's forces to fail. Therefore, the invaders had, of necessity, to fail. For if they would have won, then the Soviet Union would have gone into Cuba to push back the invaders. And then, according to John F. Kennedy's words: "In the event of any military intervention by outside forces, we will immediately honor our obligations under the Inter-American system to protect this hemisphere against external aggression."(11) The Bay Pigs may have saved the world a major conflagration. However, for the cause of an independent and democratic Cuba, it dismantled the Underground in such a way that it never again was able to reorganize and fight against communism on the island. The invasion fiasco also provided one more step toward the consolidation of a totalitarian communist regime in Cuba. All Catholic and private schools were confiscated. The only way to be educated in Cuba from that time onward was to partake of the educational programs offered by the communist government. Children and youth, in general, who did not fit that particular way of thinking, were on their way out of Cuba through the massive use of safe conducts or "visa waivers." The parents of those children, who now had no independent educational programs or schools under communism, would also be candidates for "visa waivers" and safe conducts until October 1962, the next crisis in the Cuban dilemma.

Marist School near the Plaza Cívica
The school was also known as the Marists at El Cerro and the school at the Centro Cívico.

CHAPTER 15
OUR MARIST SCHOOL: *DE DIOS Y DEL MUNDO GLORIA, DE LA JUVENTUD GUIÓN*
(Glory of God and the world and guiding light of our youth.)

"The nationwide victory celebrations in Cuba were punctuated by the rifle execution squads, search raids on Roman Catholic Churches, a continuing wave of arrests and denunciation of Yankee criminals."
-Tad Szulc

In the aftermath of the Bay of Pigs Invasion, all Marist schools were nationalized, that is confiscated. I had entered the Marist School at La Víbora in 1952 when we lived in my grandmother's house in the Lawton neighborhood at San Francisco Street, Number 320. My father attended that school and graduated in 1928. My older cousin Emilito also attended that school and graduated from it in 1954. My Uncle Ramón, my cousin Ramoncito, and my second cousin Manolo Buznego also attended the Marist School at La Víbora. On my mother's side of the family, my second cousin Evelio also attended the Marist School in Havana.

In 1956, my parents purchased a new house in Altahabana. At that time, I transferred to the new Marist school near the Plaza Cívica. The latter school opened in 1955 and replaced a smaller Marist school originally opened in 1931, and located in a large house in La Calzada del Cerro serving the Cerro neighborhood. By the time we moved to Altahabana, there were two Marist schools in Havana and the brothers had divided the Havana metropolitan area into two sections—one to be served by the school at La Víbora and the other by the new school near the Plaza Cívica.

Curiously, the second *parcial*, semester, classes, and examinations ended the same day the bombings began prior to the actual invasion. The temporal coincidence of the ending of the school year and the onset of the bombings just prior to the invasion of Brigade 2506 raises questions. Could it be that there was some sort of secret agreement between the parties and this was no coincidence? For example, what would have occurred if the bombings and invasion would have happened with the schools and universities in session? Would the students involved in the Underground at the secondary level and university students have become involved in the struggle to topple the communist dictatorship? Since, according to Underground sources—among them my father—they received orders that the invasion was being delayed several times, could the invasion have been planned to occur just after the academic year had ended? We may never know. At any rate, the academic year that had begun in September 1960 had by then come to an end. Juan's letter summarizes the situation of my peer group in Havana at that time after the failed invasion:

AMDG Havana, May 11, 1961

Dear friend:

May God grant that you be well when you receive this letter. I assume that you'll be studying hard so that you can graduate as you said in your last letter. You must forgive me for not answering your March letter, in those days I was busy. Despite my desire to answer you, I could not distract myself for a moment. I am sorry to tell you that the postcards you said you were sending to each professor were not in the envelope. Perhaps they were lost.

On Monday the 8th I received your last letter and the next day I went to your house to see your parents. I just talked to your mom and she was fine. I did not see your father but your mom says he is okay. I did not remember at first impression who Poppy was but then I remembered when I saw him. He is great, so friendly and "silent" as ever but I found him a little sad, maybe because of your absence. He looked most distressed lying on your parent's bed.

All private schools, including ours, were nationalized... On the occasion of the literacy campaign, the second semester was quite rushed, which cost all of us to fail in several subjects, even myself, which can give you an idea of the matter...

I write to you on the day of the Ascension of the Lord, a sad day for the apostles but also necessary in order to have the Holy Spirit, the consoler and fortifier, sent to them and us.

Remember the Virgin Mary in this month of May. For the first time, we have not been able to celebrate her month in school together.

My mom and dad send their best regards to you. I think that every time I am more appreciative of your sincerity. May God want us to be as you say friends forever, I appreciate you,

Juan

Juan could not have taken time off his school work during March and the beginning of April, because he was attempting to complete the work for the second semester and do well on the final examinations. Juan was the only one in the class who passed the mathematics course with the lowest passing grade, *aprobado.* He was correct in that I was studying hard. However, our examinations were not as difficult as those prepared by the Institute of Secondary Education at La Víbora for the Catholic and private schools. Aside from the fact that the semester had been appreciably shortened, the examinations seemed to have been more difficult than what was expected. Pella wrote independently from Juan in this manner:

Havana, April 16, 1961
Dear friend:

These are my best wishes that upon your receipt of this letter you find yourself as well as possible considering you are away from your homeland... I feel that although you may be having a great time over there—it's still somewhat painful being away...
We finished the exams for the second semester. In mathematics and physics by the Institute, we were all hung, all except Juan who did get 65. Quite a horror! The exams were very difficult...
Goodbye to you from your friend,

Pella

The observation by Juan that Poppy was saddened was made when he observed our pet dog on his visit to my mother. The issue of Poppy will come up again later. At this time, however, I think it is appropriate to note that there was a lot of networking between the folks that remained behind in Havana and that was not necessarily easy. Juan probably had to take two buses to go from his house on San Lázaro Street near the Malecón to Altahabana. His concern and need to be present, near, and helpful were very much appreciated. However, in the course of those

Out of the Marist students in this photograph taken a year earlier in 1960, only two would remain on the island by the end of 1961. Jaruco Excursion, Marist School Yearbook, 1960

times, perhaps not enough gratitude was expressed and demonstrated to Juan and all the others whose friendship was proven beyond a shadow of a doubt.

There were two Marist schools where the intervention by the revolutionary government got somewhat nasty. Brother Pedro explained it in a letter written after he had been exiled in Miami in this manner, in which he also summarized memories of his two years of teaching at El Cerro, the Plaza Cívica school:

JMJ, July 2, 1961
Centro Hispano Católico
Miami, Florida

Most remembered friend:

I am pleased to write these lines from these cozy and free beaches of our America. It was time.
From the first of May we were suffering in Cuba because Fidel ordered our forced exile. However, we were not given ways out but instead new obstacles were erected every day. You can imagine! All schools had to be searched and submitted to a full inventory by the militia forces and there were no areas or parts of the properties in which they did not get into before we were able to get out.
In Santa Clara we were lucky. The officers that intervened in our school were very humane with us. Not so in Camagüey or in El Cerro, where we were handled as prisoners. Finally we were able to rid ourselves of this human hyena at the service of communism. From the day we arrived in Miami on June 15 we felt free. There are only four brothers left in Cuba that are to come later.

Before leaving Havana, your father, mother, uncle, and aunt came to see us. All are fine. Your father is tall and skinny as ever. Your young mom is quiet as she is accustomed to be. They are very proud of your studies. I was told you had finished high school and already wished to study medicine. Go ahead, do not defraud their hopes. As you know your parents have had to suffer in this life for the unpropitious circumstances that Cuba has had for years. I remember when you were leaving class with your mother on certain days to visit your dad who was imprisoned. Always remember that

you received the basic religious principles in the Marist school...
Receive a cordial embrace from someone who does not forget you
in his prayers,

Brother Pedro

The schools were nationalized, intervened in, confiscated, or perhaps turned into prisons, where the religious faculty was kept under house arrest and harassed. The psychological trauma from that experience has never been fully discussed. The brothers would not openly confess to what they went through because they were, in my opinion, humble and did not wish to appear as victims of the issues of this world—the world of the flesh—of deceit, of communism, of falsehood, and betrayal. Theirs is the kingdom of God, of understanding, of brotherhood, love, and peace. This trauma must have brought into their minds, however, the collective experience of the Marist Order during the Spanish Civil War. At least one of the brothers at El Cerro had a memory of when Marist seminarians were detained by Spanish Republican forces during that conflict and they were all going to be taken away as prisoners. At that time, Brother Juan Salvador, a native of Cuba, was separated from the group that was being taken away by the communists. Why was he spared prison and possibly death at that time? The United States consul intervened and pointed out that since Brother Juan Salvador had been born in Cuba, he took responsibility for him. This memory was confided to me by Brother Juan Salvador. I bring it up in this context for two reasons. First, to note the impact of the intervention and imprisonment in their own schools on all Marist brothers and other religious orders on the island vis-à-vis the Spanish Civil War, a most unfortunate memory. And secondly, to note that even a few years after the Platt Amendment had been derogated, some officials in the Foreign Service of the United States considered Cuba as a state somewhat linked to the United States.

The impressions of imprisonment noted by Brother Pedro were shared by other brothers. Later on in August, Brother Teodoro, our fourth year of the Cuban *bachillerato* teacher, wrote from his exile:

Guatemala, 18 August 1961

Remembered alumnus:
I was not kidnapped as the other brothers from the Marist School
at El Cerro at the Plaza Cívica were. I was incognito in Guanabo

Brother Pedro with his second year of bachillerato class at the
Marist School near the Plaza Cívica.
Marist Yearbook, 1958

Beach from the same day the invasion landed until the middle of
May. We experienced...weeks of much unrest and we were man-
aged by the militia at the Villa Marista.

Brother Teodoro Fernández

However, not all Marist brothers were imprisoned. One of the brothers at our Marist School at El Cerro left religious life at the time of the intervention in the school. It was former Brother Francisco, who was originally from Guatemala and taught at the time the fourth grade class. Whether he was planted to be a religious person and spy by some international communist plot or turned away from his religious and Marist vows at the time, we may never know. However, in a letter from Zenón, also from May, he noted that the former Brother Francisco had seen him accompanied by Lorenzo around Villa Marista and had pretended that he did not recognize them. Zenón thought that Francisco gave them a break because if he would have made an issue about the fact that two Marist students were trying to get into the Villa Marista to check on the brothers, they—that is Zenón and Lorenzo—would have been detained for questioning. Paradoxically, the place where there had been a Marist Seminary and a sports field for the school at La Víbora had turned at this point in time into the headquarters of the Cuban State Security apparatus and a detention, interrogation, and torture center. The first prisoners in Villa Marista were the Marist Brothers who were working in the schools in Cuba in 1961.

The brothers had officially been told by Fidel Castro himself in his speech at the Plaza Cívica that the schools were nationalized and they had to leave the country. It was a forced exile. But what about the students at the Marist School, my peers? How were they doing? Their situation is summarized here in this letter from Lorenzo:

JMJ Havana, May 24, 1961
Dear friend:

I hope that when you receive this you find yourself well.
I have been delayed to write this for various reasons that I cannot
explain now. Over here, we are all fine. I understand that Luis
Faura is in the Oriente. Wong...had to keep working at the school,
and aside from work on our own, has to go do guard duty from 6

PM to 6 AM at Baldor. Otherwise, he is fine.
Grades are in. I only passed 4 of five subjects.
I do not know if Zenón told you that I am planning to leave Cuba.
I need to know if everything will be well with me there, since right
now I have no way to make any arrangements.
Remember the stamps... Without another thing to say, goodbye to
you, your friend who remembers you and appreciates you,

[The signature was illegible]

Lorenzo had sent a message written on the envelope and covered it with the stamps required for postage. This message was written in block letters in pencil. This is what he wrote: "Wong prisoner twice. They are looking for me on several charges. I'm hiding and can never get out."

He has used an allegory in the body of the letter to explain that Wong had been detained and in jail for counter-revolutionary activities. Brother Juan Salvador also acknowledged the despair in the student body at that time:

Miami, July 30, 1961
Very dear Tony:

I have received your letter. Many thanks for remembering me...
Wong has been jailed. Collazo has been condemned to 15 years of
forced labor. He was tortured.
It is believed that they have shot at the paredón *Raúl de la Cruz,*
the student from La Víbora who used to imitate Fidel.
Jorge Sánchez is in danger of death.
Pray very much for our Patria.
Viva Cristo Rey! (Long live Christ the King)
Receive a strong hug,

Brother Juan Salvador

The letter from Brother Juan Salvador in short sentences came through as a very strong testimony of despair that was felt throughout the community of my teachers and peers at this time. Our feelings off the island were not very different, as it is noted in the letters exchanged after the Bay of Pigs between my relatives in

REMITE, L.L.
RETURN TO
CALLE MORRO #60
HABANA. CUBA.

VIA AIR MAIL
CORREO AEREO
PAR AVION

SR.: TONY G. PALOMINO
BOX 193 SWITZERLAND
ORANGE DALE ROOTE.
GREEN COVE SPRINGS.
FLA. U.S.A.

Lorenzo's letter is written in block letters to avoid being discovered by State Security censors on account of his handwriting. The message beneath the postage stamps clearly conveys the sense of urgency and frustration that permeated Cuban youth.

New Jersey and myself when I seriously considered returning to Havana in view of the lack of news from my parents for almost three weeks. The dwindling community of my peers had apparently been disbanded. Faura went away to Las Tunas in the former Oriente province, where he had been born and he had relatives. He stayed with them while the revolutionary programs tried to capture all willing Cubans into their ranks.

Collazo graduated from our school in June 1960. I knew him because he had been president at our school of the *Juventud Estudiantil Católica*, during that year. It was under his leadership that we participated in the *Congreso Católico Nacional* in the fall of 1959. At that time, in the closure of the *Congreso* there was a major demonstration of faith at the Plaza Cívica with the attendance of Catholics from all over Cuba. I participated in the security commission for the event and carried one of the torches that illuminated the processions that came together at the plaza

Crowd of Cubans attending Holy Mass at the Plaza Cívica José Martí in 1959,
during the National Catholic Congress; notice the use of head veils
by women before the II Vatican Council.
Marist School Yearbook, 1960

in front of the monument to José Martí with the Cuban patroness, the Virgin of Charity, also honored after her statue was brought from her sanctuary in El Cobre in the province of Oriente. Many of the Marist students from schools outside Havana in Santa Clara, Cienfuegos, Ciego de Avila, Camagüey, and Holguín stayed at our school near the Plaza Cívica during the *Congreso*.

Returning to Collazo, he was also the leader who organized the successful fund raising campaign through which the student body of our school donated a tractor to the Agrarian Reform. Collazo can be seen in one of the photographs published in the school yearbook for 1959-1960 standing on the tractor. Unfortunately, Collazo was not the only one who placed his faith in the revolution and learned later that he had been misguided.

By the end of May, the Marist School near the Plaza Cívica, like the hopes and destiny of my peers and the Marist brothers themselves, had changed radically. My father gives us a glimpse of his observations at that time:

> *Havana, May 24, 1961*
> *My dear son:*
>
> *I received two letters from you yesterday, one from the 15th and the other from the 17th. By them I see that you are bored. Be calm, everything has to come to a solution. Did you receive the money from my friend in Puerto Rico?*
> *I have not received an answer yet from Father Lenihan. The 26th of May, the day after tomorrow will be three weeks since I wrote him. Ask him if he has received my letter. It was in English, my cousin Isabel helped me write it.*
> *There are no brothers in the Marist school. It hurts when you pass by the school and see that it is all full of banners with communist slogans, ñángaras. The place is full of militiamen, malicianos. Is it possible that God can leave behind the school under such conditions?*
> *Yesterday, Zamora came...to greet...me. Zamora had come to Havana to see Pablin, who was part of the invasion forces and is now a prisoner.*
> *A kiss from your father,*
>
> *Antonio*

Enrique Collazo. Marist School Yearbook, 1959

Enrique Collazo can be seen standing on our Agrarian Reform tractor a couple of months be-fore his graduation from the Marist School in 1959. Marist School Yearbook, 1959.

With the Cuban revolution, new words came to be part of our vernacular. For example, the word *ñángara* meant communist and it presumably was the shorter version of another new word, *comuñanga*. Also, with the Cuban revolution, new names populated the birth certificates of the newborns. The most famous of these are those that begin with the letter 'Y' like Yamisleidy, Yosvani, etc. The latter practice had been made known internationally through the famous blog, *Generación Y* by Yoani Sánchez, who wrote it from Havana. Curiously, Victor Hugo pointed out in *Les Misérables* that new names began to appear in France after the French Revolution. What deeper significance this may have is not clear to me now. Except, of course, that we were witnesses and participants in the Cuban revolution and our involvement with the French revolution was only an intellectual, historical, and literary experience.

There has been another linguistic phenomenon during the Cuban Revolution that has not received much attention. Words have been used interchangeably that had not and should not be used interchangeably because each of them has their own different meanings. The individual who defined this confusing trend in the communications of Cubans was Monsignor Pedro Maurice, Archbishop of Santiago de Cuba. In 1998 while introducing Pope John Paul II to the Cubans, he also introduced the Cubans to the Pope, noting that in Cuba the words *nación, revolución, partido* (for the communist party), and *patria* (fatherland) have all been used interchangeably since the revolution. Obviously, this malignant practice had been and continued to be a major cause of concern, causing not only confusion to anyone who listened, but disgrace, rejection, and even death to the unfortunate Cubans who may not even be aware of the inappropriate use of these terms and others interchangeably.

Our Marist School appeared to be a communist bastion by the end of May. At the beginning of the school year that had just been completed, there were anti-aircraft guns in front of the school. At that point, anyone passing by the school could easily see that the battle, "one of the many struggles" of the Cuban Civil War, had been won by the communist revolution. In the process, the Marist School, its teachers, the students (my peers), and our values had been defeated. In short, the school had become communist territory. Anyone going through the Avenue of Independencia or the Rancho Boyeros Highway from that time on would never know what the place had been before or how we dreamed of another Cuba inside those premises. Soon thereafter, the building was turned into a Ministry of Education facility named after a guerrilla fighter who died before Batista's departure, *Instituto Politécnico de Telecomunicaciones Osvaldo Herrera*. Like my father wrote to me, "Be calm, everything has to come to a solution...." But this was not the solution for which we were either fighting or praying.

Furthermore, in terms of the larger cause, the Cuban Civil War, that enclave stands today as "genuinely" built by the revolution. Wouldn't it be something if anyone who passes by the Calzada de Rancho Boyeros and looks at that building heard a voice from afar telling them that in the block of classrooms and fields in between the Santa Ana and Cunil Streets, there was a class of Cuban boys who dreamed and fought for a democratic and free Cuba where all Cubans, regardless of creed, political ideology, or socio-economic status, were to be to respected and listened to. Maybe a voice is something too dramatic and illusive. Perhaps, someday there will be a historical sign outside or inside the premises of the Marist School near the Plaza Cívica with a succinct and truthful story, telling all visitors how it was that the school turned into what it is now; or, perhaps not. Because there would have to be so many signs on the island of Cuba that there would be no funds or space to erect such remembrances and acknowledgements of what could have been and is not.

Before the month of June, my father wrote in this manner, after he had gone on an outing to Western Cuba:

My dear son:

Last weekend we spent 2 days in La Palma on the little farm of Dr. Fuentes. We spent two days very calmly and relaxed, away from the war of nerves that is going on here in Havana. The place is very nice...near San Vicente that you should remember, and very tranquil. I repeat, because you cannot even hear a radio since there is no electric current.
We ate some very good prawns fished out of the river that passes through the little farm.
We plan to spend several days over there next time we have a chance to go fishing. There is also good hunting, but this cannot be done because you are not allowed to have a rifle or a shotgun. When I go again I will take a few pictures to send them to you.
Well my son, hoping to receive news from you soon, receive a kiss from your father who is very proud of you.

Antonio

Yes, it is true that there was a psychological war going on, a war of nerves. However, there was also in the process, the truncated civil war. Or wasn't Wong in jail? Were the Marist Brothers not sent on a forced exile after being detained in their own schools? Was Raúl de la Cruz not assassinated at the *paredón*? Was Collazo not tortured? Despite their best hopes, my parents, and for that matter, Dr. Fuentes and his family, probably never returned to *la finquita*, the little farm. Those prawns were to be remembered forever since they were not to partake of them there ever again.

CHAPTER 16
GRADUATION: SEARCH FOR ANOTHER *BECA*

"Education is not to train to make a living,
But to temper the soul to the difficulties of life."
-Pythagoras

Since the month of April, we in the group of seniors at St. John's Camp had been advised to begin writing letters requesting a *beca,* so that we could go on with our studies after graduation from Bishop Kenny High School. Some of us took that suggestion more seriously than others. I was then, and most of my close associates from Cuba will also tell you even now, an optimist. Therefore, I took on the additional duty of writing letters in English whereby I tried to explain my situation, my departure from Cuba, and my desire to continue to a college education. I was hoping that through my letters, anyone who received one of my petitions would feel almost obligated to offer me some sort of assistance.

The first issue had to do with to whom and where to address the letters. We were advised to inquire in the school library at Bishop Kenny for Catholic colleges. So I got myself a list of places that I thought sounded friendly and began sending letters. I had our Cuban counselor, who taught us the sixth period English class, review the letters and make the necessary corrections in order to send a clear message.

In a matter of days, I began receiving answers to my letters. All of them were rather short and to the point. I was being notified that the deadline for requesting scholarships and admissions had already passed. Obviously, an applicant would have to be admitted to the college before any consideration for scholarship assistance was to be discussed. It was also common to read in the answers I was getting that "all our scholarship funds have already been awarded."

In view of such negative feedback, I expressed my concerns to my relatives up in New Jersey. This issue of looking for ways to continue my education after graduation was occurring at the same time that I had declared I was thinking of returning to Havana after the Bay of Pigs fiasco. This is what my uncle Emilio wrote:

Ridgefield Park, N.J.
May 10, 1961
Dear nephew:

I see you've asked ... for a college scholarship. My advice is...you seek the advice of the directors and officers of the school you are attending now...

So I want you in the first place to investigate the issue well. Your goal is to be sure who should or could arrange for you to continue to study in this country...for any kind of return to Cuba cannot be thought of as long as the ruling Communists are there...
I wait for your answer.
Love,

Emilio

Therefore, I inquired about the issue further and found out that the most authoritative answer was to be obtained from the National Catholic Welfare Conference. I wrote to them and I got the following answer:

National Catholic Welfare Conference
Department of Education
Ref: Catholic College Scholarships Available to Cuban Students
Dear Mr. Gordon:

Herewith are the names of colleges offering scholarships. We would suggest you write directly to them.
Very sincerely yours,

Rt. Rev. Msgr. F.G. Hochwalt
Director

Immaculata Heart College, Los Angeles, CA
Mount St. Mary's College, Los Angeles, CA
Marymount College, Palos Verdes Estates, CA

Loretto Heights College, Loretto, CO
Fairfield University, Fairfield, CT
Dunbarton College of Holy Cross, Washington, DC
Immaculata Junior College, Washington, DC
Mundelein College, Chicago, IL
Rosary College, River Forest, IL
Marian College, Indianapolis, IN
St. Mary-of-the-Woods College, St. Mary-of-the-Woods, IN
Mount St. Scholastica College, Atchison, KS
St. Mary's Dominican College, New Orleans, LA
St. Joseph's College, North Windham, ME
Boston College, Boston, MA
University of Detroit, Detroit, MI
Madonna College, Livonia, MI
College of St. Teresa, Winona, MN
Webster College, St. Louis, MO
Mount St. Mary College, Hookset, NH
College of St. Elizabeth, Convent Station, NJ
Seton Hall University, South Orange, NJ

Some of these schools were not available and others were only girl's schools. I wrote to more than half of these colleges and got the same types of answers I had received before. Some of the schools had no dormitories. None of them, at the time of my writing, which was obviously late in the admissions process, was open to newcomers.

Our prospects to obtain a scholarship or even admission at a college or university appeared dismal. The counselors who were assisting us in reviewing the letters we were getting back were overwhelmed, because they were consulted by each of us eight seniors seeking help. They advised us that, if we did not get some sort of forms to fill out or something to send back to the schools, we were not being considered for anything serious like a formal application and admission process, etc. So it was that the following letter got lost in the shuffle and I only noted it months later when I was reading again my letters and putting them away in order.

Loyola College
Baltimore, Maryland
Office of the Dean

May 26, 1961

Mr. Antonio M. Gordon
Camp St. John
Box 193
Switzerland, Green Cove Springs, FL

Dear Mr. Gordon:

Thank you for your letter which I received today, in which you inquire as to the possibility of receiving scholarship assistance in connection with your attendance at Loyola College.
Loyola College is a school for day students only, and does not provide any boarding facilities on campus for students, although arrangements for board can be made in approved homes in the nearby area. The College at present is helping several South Americans, African, and Asian students, and as much as it would like to be of assistance to you, it appears that such aid for you next year would be unlikely. Surely the most we could do for you—if we could even do that—is to give you a tuition-free scholarship, but you would have to look out for your room and board expenses. I do not mean to close the door altogether to you, but the present circumstances here indicate that it is unlikely that we could grant you even scholarship aid.
I will be happy to keep your letter on file, and in the event that you wish to pursue the matter further at a later date, please do not hesitate to do so.

Sincerely,
Rev. Aloysius C. Galvin, S.J.

Imagine! "Surely the most we could do for you is to give you a tuition-free scholarship…" I did not follow up on this but, as an optimist, I think that this would have been a unique opportunity to go on studying in this country. However, by the time I realized what I had on hand, other developments had come up in my life, which will be made clear later in this book. In retrospect, this offer—although fantastic—was lost because I did not realize I had it, my counselors did not pay attention to it, and in the final analysis, I had to do something else in order to assist my family. Curiously, Loyola College of Baltimore was not on the list of colleges and universities available to Cuban students.

Our final examinations, as I already noted, were nothing compared to the ones my peers who remained in Havana had to endure. In American History we got a special final examination covering both the first and second semesters. I remember it had several open-ended questions. The nature of the questions inquired about the discovery of America, the Hispanic-American War, and some other issues that I cannot remember. Obviously, in my opinion, Mr. Baldwin wanted to give us Cubans a chance to go on with our education. He and Bishop Kenny did not do what the Cuban communists had done to my peers who remained behind—write a very difficult test through which all or most would be flunked. They cut us some slack and we took the opportunity and ran with it. This is another instance in which our gratitude was not expressed then and needs to be expressed now and in the future.

At the end of the day, both of my grandmothers had faith that I would graduate from the school. This is what my paternal grandmother wrote:

Havana
May 26, 1961

My dear grandson Tony:

I got your cute postcard and letter. You do not know the joy it gives me to see that you remember your poor grandmother. You are always in my thoughts. You do not know how I wish that I could be there for the graduation of both of you. I ask that God be with you always and bring you both good luck.

If at graduation you have pictures taken, please send them to me. I think you will be rather handsome. I would give anything to be there for that graduation so that I could see you.

I have days when I feel good, but others when I feel anxious. I would like to see all of you here. You know what is weird; sometimes I think I will not see you again.

... When you graduate, even though you may not know where you will be going, always write to me so that I know about you. Always take care of yourselves so that you do not get sick...

May the time fly so that we can see you soon, because I always miss you a lot. I realize that it has been good that you have been there learning and making other friends. Receive many kisses from your grandmother who loves you very much. Do not forget to write to your grandmother. Your letters cheer me up.

Amparo

Sometime during the summer, my mother traveled to see her family in the Oriente Province in eastern Cuba. She must have reminded by maternal grandmother to write to me. This is what she wrote:

Calicito
August 29, 1961
My dearest grandson:

These are my best wishes, that when you receive this letter you are well. Here, we are all well thank God.
Tony, I'm very sorry that I had not been able to answer your letter. I see that you're doing well and I am happy to learn that you have finished your studies.
I always remember you with love and wish to see you in the future. Your cousins remember you as well as the others also.
I'm also grateful for the card you sent me.
Well, I send my love to you...your grandmother who loves you and wants to see you,

Clotilde

We took our class graduation picture right in front of the school, all dressed in the traditional white gowns. Since a few weeks before the prom, we had been issued our graduation rings. So it was on June 2nd, 1961 that we went up to a church in Jacksonville and graduated from high school. I remember going to the graduation with Mr. Bravo in an old car he owned. There were no pictures of us taken on that particular day. We had no relatives in attendance! We took our seats, all dressed in the white gowns, in the church. We boys were sitting on the left side, the benches to the right as you looked from the altar. The girls were on the other side. I do not remember what music was played by the organist. I was too nervous.

Bishop Kenny High School 1961 graduates. The Pedro Pans in the class were: a) Carlos Sánchez, b) Gustavo Sánchez, c) Jesús Suárez, d) José Antonio Rodríguez de los Reyes, e) Jorge Carballeira, f) Antonio Gordon, g) Jorge Martínez, and h) Ramón Gordon.

Then someone started to call the names and we stood up and walked up to just in front of the altar where Archbishop Hurley was handing out the diplomas. My name was called as follows: "Antonio Palomino Gordon."

When I got back to my seat, I carefully opened the case of the diploma and noted that it read: Antonio Gordon.

Through the courtesy of the Alumni Relations Office at Bishop Kenny, I have a copy of the official list of the graduates who marched in the graduation in 1961. Some of the names of the Cuban students were written incorrectly. This is how they appeared:

Alvarez, Jorge Carballeira was written for Jorge Carballeira, who after going up to the summer English course at St. Michael's College, did some sort of engineering work on the West Coast. Why was Jorge's name written incorrectly? In Spanish, the complete name of an individual is written with the given name, the surname, and the second surname. The surname in Spanish is the father's last name or surname. The second surname is the mother's surname. Some of these names at our graduation were written as if we were Portuguese! In Portugal and Brazil, the complete name of an individual is written with the given name, the surname and the second surname also. However, the surname in Portuguese is the mother's last name or surname. The second surname is the father's surname. Since Carballeira does sound as if it had roots in Portugal, the error may have been explained by the confusing rules governing Hispanic nomenclature.

Martinez, Jorge Luis was written correctly.

Palomino, Antonio Gordon was my entry. I left the Unaccompanied Cuban Children Program after the summer course at St. Michael's.

Rodriguez, Jose Antonio was written correctly. Tony Rodriguez went on to college and became a medical doctor with a specialty in radiology.

Sanchez, Carlos Martin was written correctly. Carlos worked for the Unaccompanied Cuban Children Program as a counselor in Northern Michigan after he completed the course at St. Michael's for Foreign Students.

Sanchez, Gustavo Juan was written correctly. Gus went to Indiana University after completing the course at St. Michael's.

Suarez, Jesus Manuel was written correctly. Jesus came out of the program after St. Michael's and was looking, in his last letter to me, to enter the University of Miami.

Suarez, Ramon Gordon was written incorrectly. His diploma read Ramon Gordon. He presently writes his name as it was originally inscribed in the Cuban registry of births and it appears in his passport as Ramon de Gordon. This is my cousin Ramoncito. He also worked with Carlos Sanchez in the Unaccompanied Cuban

Jorge Martínez and Santiago Aguilar
In 1961, eight Cubans graduated from Bishop Kenny High School. In 1962 and 1963, Santiago Aguilar, Alberto Araoz, Modesto Burgos, Angel Chávez, Raúl A. Hernández, Octavio Mestre, Emilio Morán, and José I. Ramírez also graduated. In all, 16 Pedro Pans graduated from more than 140 Pedro Pans, who went through Camp St. John.
Photograph from 8mm frame

Tony Rodríguez looking out the window on our way to Burlington, Vermont, in 1961. Photograph from 8mm movie frame

Carlos Sánchez and Jesús Suárez outside the Eastern Terminal in New York in 1961 en route to Burlington, Vermont. Photograph from 8mm movie frame

Gustavo Sánchez at Camp St. John in 1961. Note that the tractor behind Gus was not donated to Castro's Agrarian Reform by the Diocese of St. Augustine. Photograph from 8mm movie frame

Children Program and later on became a very successful salesman of anesthetic and dental equipment, supplies, and medicines.

Curiously, there were eight Cubans graduating from high school at Bishop Kenny High School in Jacksonville. These were my new peers. Back in Havana, there were eight of my peers who, for the most part, did not pass the grade fully because they failed any number of subjects. Even the brightest and most studious of the class had failed some subjects. One world was obviously closing, but another one was, indeed, opening.

I do not remember who gave the valedictorian address, any other speech, or any details of the graduation. But, if I had to select a speaker for the event, I would certainly recommend my Uncle Ramón. In fact, if I would have had more inspiration and imagination back then, I would have nicknamed my Uncle Ramón, Pythagoras. Here is why:

Havana June 9, 1961
My dearest nephew:

You do not know how much I liked the Bishop Kenny sticker I received from you as a souvenir for my car. Well, for me the merit it has is that it was sent by you. That means that you remembered your uncle and aunt, and I, for one, think it is invaluable so that I will place it in a privileged location. It should be clarified that I had a Bishop Kenny sticker that my son sent me, but this one that you have sent me is as big in my heart as the one my dearest son sent me was to me.

A few days ago, we talked with Brother Teodoro. I assure you he is a very nice person… He sends his greetings to you both and wishes that God bless you and grant you success in your studies.

We also talked with Brother Pedro who was your professor in the first and second year of bachillerato. Naturally, he confirmed that you are a good student… You need to understand that studying is not just to complete a career but a journey to warm the soul, to live. I hope that both you and my son recognize these truths and enter into serious studies so that you will be able to live well and prosper in the future.

I send you from here the sincere affection of your uncle and godfather and may God bless you both,

Ramón

He did not quote Pythagoras when he wrote: "You need to understand that studying is not just to complete a career, but a journey to warm the soul, to live." But, the essence of this sentence is a well-known aphorism attributed to the famous Greek philosopher and mathematician. Uncle Ramón could not have said it better. The administration and faculty at Bishop Kenny did know that we had already been warmed almost to the point of being burned by the Cuban revolution, its aftermath, and the shortchanged civil war that was being waged in the setting of the Cold War. Archbishop Hurley, despite his *diferendo*, or dispute, at the time with Bishop Coleman Carroll of Miami, did know that we had been through a lot. Archbishop Hurley knew war and devastation as he was Apostolic Delegate to Yugoslavia after World War II. It was there that he acquired the title of Archbishop. At the time, he was an Archbishop who was directing the Diocese, not the Archdiocese of St. Augustine. There was no need for us to undertake any more tests. We were ready to be launched into the world to sink or swim. And in the final analysis, this group of eight, I am glad to report, swam!

Curiously, the 1961 yearbook, of which we Cubans who arrived in February at the school had no knowledge of or its content at that time, was dedicated in this manner:

> "To those whose foresight, zeal and sacrifice have brought
> Bishop Kenny High School into being,
> Whose care and catholic concern
> Have placed us here as students,
> Whose inspiration and example
> Are the foundation and model
> Of our Catholic Education....
> Our Parents,
> This book of memories is gratefully and affectionately dedicated."

Who could have thought that eight Cuban adolescents sent, expelled, exiled from their homeland on the strong recommendation and sometimes orders from their parents would be graduating from high school in Florida at that time? Not even the most optimistic! But then, who would have the vision to dedicate the yearbook of that difficult year to our parents. Indeed, it was dedicated to our Cuban parents for theirs was the foresight, theirs was the zeal, and theirs was also—beyond a doubt—the great sacrifice without which none of us eight Cubans would have been there.

Besides our parents, we must also be grateful to Bishop Kenny High School. Our gratitude also had to be expressed to the Unaccompanied Cuban Children Program and the generous funding provided not only initially by the Catholic Church, but also—in great measure—by the United States government. In 1961, the tuition for Bishop Kenny High School was $250 per year. The arrangement negotiated by Father Walsh with Mr. Abraham A. Ribicoff, Secretary of Health, Educations and Welfare in the Kennedy Administration, provided $6.50 per child or youngster per day(1) to the institutions where the children were assigned. I presume that those funds went through Father Walsh and Catholic Charities to Archbishop Hurley and Father Lenihan, for the administration of funds to cover all of St. John's Camp's expenses, including our tuition, books, and fees at Bishop Kenny High School. Our gratitude has to be extended to all these parties who provided for us at a time when, otherwise, we would have been homeless.

CHAPTER 17
ONWARD TO ST. MICHAEL'S ENGLISH
PROGRAM FOR FOREIGN STUDENTS

"My purpose today is to discuss some features of America's position, both at home and in her relations with others. First, I point out that for us annual self-examination is made a definite necessity by the fact that we now live in a divided world of uneasy equilibrium, with our side committed to its own protection and against aggression by the other. With both sides of this divided world in possession of unbelievably destructive weapons, mankind approaches a state where mutual annihilation becomes a possibility. No other fact in today's world equals this in importance – it colors everything we say, plan and do. There is demanded of us vigilance, determination, and the dedication of whatever portion of our resources that will provide adequate security, especially a real deterrent to aggression."
Dwight D. Eisenhower, Annual Message to Congress on the State of the Union,
January 7, 1960.

It was the summer of 1961, and as the graduating seniors were getting ready to depart from St. John's Camp, the idea of adding some sports to our camp routine came up. There was obviously more time to spend on the premises since eight of us had already graduated from high school. The rest of the guys at the camp were also finished with whatever grade they were enrolled in. We were all on summer vacation! The idea of being able to play some baseball on the premises was appealing to us all. We had played several semi-official softball games against the team "Crusaders" at Bishop Kenny High. Our softball pitcher was Modesto, who threw a very fast underarm pitch with which most American batters were overwhelmed. I guess we did not play baseball against the American team at school because we just did not have a good enough baseball pitcher. We just had an excellent softball pitcher. After all, we had not been selected for this *beca* on our merits or talents for baseball, softball, or any sport.

Adding some sports to the daily monotony also appealed to the camp administration. They must have figured that activities were very important if we were to maintain some sort of discipline during that summer. In a short time, arrangements were made for the swimming pool to be cleaned and properly chemically treated so that it could be used. It was a Junior Olympic-sized swimming pool. In a matter of a couple of weeks or so, the pool was ready and by the time we left the camp, the guys were already enjoying it. A set of safety rules was written down and disseminated to avoid accidents in and around the pool.

Baseball is, and has been for some time, the national sport of Cuba. We wanted to play baseball, but there was no field where we could in the camp. There were tall trees and woods all over the camp that prevented having a space where baseball could be played. Someone proposed to clear a part of the woods so that we could have a space to set up a field. The administration agreed and we were supplied with hatchets and picks to cut down the small trees just to the south of the dining hall. Every day, a crew of campers got the tools and got to work cutting down enough *maleza* to clear enough area of the thicket. By the time we left the camp, we had only gotten as far as clearing a space where we could have placed home plate and the batters' boxes. The space for a baseball field was never completely cleared. Years later, when I visited the camp, the clearing where home plate was to be located was still there. The size of the clearing is presently barely twice what had been cleared before we left in mid-June 1961.

Our departure date was not known to us until a couple of days before it actually occurred. It was not clear to any of us why mystery surrounded the date. Obviously, some of us had feelings of déjà vu, since our exit from Cuba had been a secret from anyone but our closest relatives. Before we left the camp, Father Lenihan spoke one-on-one with each of us who had graduated. Some of us who had done something shameful were not too eager to have a talk with the priest managing our lives at that time.

However, I do not think that anyone got reprimanded or punished. Father Lenihan must have been a forgiving person in his heart. He took the opportunity to give each of us a small prayer book, *Jesus My Life,* copyrighted in 1958. I still have mine. He dedicated my prayer book with these words:

> "Tony,
>
> Keep up your prayers and Holy Masses every Sunday. Cuba is Communist because of all the Masses and prayers missed.
> God bless you,
>
> Fr. John J. Lenihan"

Dedication written by Fr. John J. Lenihan on the devotional he gave us when we left to our next assignment in the Unaccompanied Cuban Children Program.
Photograph by Manuel Buznego

It was not Father Lenihan's intention, I am sure, to remind us that Cuba was quickly, and definitively, going into the Soviet Bloc orbit. But he did. Some of us still thought, at that time, even after the fiasco of the Bay of Pigs Invasion, that it would be possible to spare Cuba from the chains that were quickly linking its future to that of the Soviet Union sphere of influence.

It was not his intention, I thought, to blame the entire revolutionary process and its aftermath on me for not attending Holy Mass on Sundays, or dedicating myself to prayer more constantly and fervently. But, I felt he was suggesting just that. Perhaps he meant to imply that many individual Catholics in Cuba did not attend Sunday Masses or pray fervently. Perhaps.

It had been estimated that, although up to 90 percent of Cubans were nominally Catholics, perhaps, only 20 percent of them were practicing Catholics. But even if we were only 20 percent practicing Catholics, the God of Abraham had promised to spare the destruction of the sinful even if 10 people were righteous.

In the Book of Genesis, we read in Chapter 18:20-33:

> [20] *So the LORD said: "The outcry against Sodom and Gomorrah is so great, and their sin so grave,* * [21] *that I must go down to see whether or not their actions are as bad as the cry against them that comes to me. I mean to find out."* [22] *As the men turned and walked on toward Sodom, Abraham remained standing before the LORD.* [23] *Then Abraham drew near and said: "Will you really sweep away the righteous with the wicked?* [24] *Suppose there were fifty righteous people in the city; would you really sweep away and not spare the place for the sake of the fifty righteous people within it?* [25] *Far be it from you to do such a thing, to kill the righteous with the wicked, so that the righteous and the wicked are treated alike! Far be it from you! Should not the judge of all the world do what is just?"* [26] *The LORD replied: "If I find fifty righteous people in the city of Sodom, I will spare the whole place for their sake."* [27] *Abraham spoke up again: "See how I am presuming to speak to my Lord, though I am only dust and ashes!* [28] *What if there are five less than fifty righteous people? Will you destroy the whole city because of those five?" "I will not destroy it," he answered, "if I find forty-five there."* [29] *But Abraham persisted, saying, "What if only forty are found there?" He replied: "I will refrain from doing it for the sake of the forty."* [30] *Then he said, "Do not let my Lord be angry if I go on. What if only thirty are found there?" He replied: "I will refrain*

from doing it if I can find thirty there."³¹ Abraham went on, "Since I have thus presumed to speak to my Lord, what if there are no more than twenty?" "I will not destroy it, he answered, for the sake of the twenty."³² But he persisted: "Please, do not let my Lord be angry if I speak up this last time. What if ten are found there?" "For the sake of the ten," he replied, "I will not destroy it."³³ The LORD departed as soon as he had finished speaking with Abraham, and Abraham returned home.

This is a passage from Sacred Scriptures in which the nature of God the Father is clearly revealed, along with the power of prayer. Ours is a forgiving God. A God who will respect the community because there are ten righteous persons in it. If Cubans were as sinful or neglectful of going to Sunday masses and prayer to cause the anger of God, were not in the entire Cuban nation at least ten righteous Cubans?

But going back to Father Lenihan's dedication, could it be that his idea of a prayer was a call, a communication, a desire, or a wish for which there cannot be a negative response? Was a negative response to any prayer from a living human being a sign of a fault or sin in the person praying the prayer or could it be a sign that God himself had a greater, perhaps more encompassing, plan in mind? Wasn't the prayer of Christ at Gethsemane a prayer of a wish that did not come to spare him from precisely what was to occur because there was so much more at stake at that time than just the immediate pain and suffering of the one individual praying, even though that one individual was the Son of God himself? Could it be that our pain and suffering has not been simply our fault for lack of prayers, but rather our privilege through which we have learned more about our humanity, our neighbors' nature, and God's plans for us, than what otherwise had been apparent to us and everyone around us?

Could it be that our work in terms of prayer as it regards to Cuba is not yet completed? Is it possible that we, the Cubans in exile, could serve as the leaven that will grow the spiritual life of all Cubans and assist in the healing of the historical issues that have prevented our people with Cuban ancestry from thriving in our own homeland?

But wait a moment! What am I thinking? Certainly by then, the beginning of the summer of 1961, Father Lenihan knew me. Certainly, after supervising our camp for more than four months, he must have arrived at the conclusion that I was not aspiring to be a saint at that time. Well, maybe I could become a saint if I went through some sort of transformation *a la* St. Francis of Assisi or St. Augustine, perhaps. Then, perhaps, I could aspire to be a saint.

But then, I do not think that he meant to write a dedication that would last a lifetime. A dedication that still today causes me to reflect and ask: Could it be that individuals in and outside the Church did not actually understand the complexity and the process through which Cuba moved into the communist orbit and we ended up in the United States as unaccompanied children? Is it possible that the entire Cuban revolution and its aftermath could be understood as avoidable through prayer?

And yet, throughout these years since June 1961, the more I think about Father Lenihan's dedication, I have realized that learned people, even individuals who had been in contact with the Cuban refugees but, perhaps, did not understand our language, our history, or the Cuban revolution and its aftermath may think that indeed we were personally responsible for not only letting Cuba be pulled into the Soviet orbit, but keeping it there for more than fifty years.

To a certain extent, this latter statement is true. We were all responsible. Yes! But what has not been widely recognized or accepted is that when I write *we*, I mean exactly that, we. Both Cubans and Americans are responsible because the Cuban revolution has turned into the Cuban phenomenon—a process that is still ongoing, despite the fact that the civil war has been over since the 1970s when the United States opened an interests section in Havana and Castro opened his interest section in Washington.

The Cold War has already been declared *de facto*, finished since the Soviet Union was dismantled. Is it possible then, that not only we the Cubans, but also the Americans, have been conspiring—sometimes, perhaps, without knowing it—to maintain the status quo in Havana? Could it be that no prayer could have saved Cuba from the Soviet Bloc because all parties, including the Soviet Union, the United States, and even the Catholic Church and Spain, were somehow parties of an arrangement or an agreement that was never in any way, shape, or form presented to or consulted with the Cuban people, or for that matter the American people?

Who knows? I certainly do not know. But I do know that what up to now has appeared evident should be questioned, re-examined, analyzed transparently so that there is no question as to what prayers, if any, were not answered and why.

Returning to our departure from Jacksonville, we had arrived in the Jacksonville area by train, but were to leave by plane. Our tickets, however, were of the stand-by type. That is, we had tickets for our final destination to travel to Burlington, Vermont, where St. Michael's College was, with Eastern Airlines. On June 15, we went up to the Imeson Municipal Airport North of Jacksonville. We had already an idea of what it looked like and its location because when we went up to St. Patrick's Catholic Church—the church where Father Lenihan was parish priest at the time—for the feast of St. Patrick's in March, we took a walk to the airport. We

A group of Pedro Pans at the Jacksonville Municipal Airport in 1961.
We visited the airport on St. Patrick's Day when we walked from Fr. Lenihan's parish to the
airport. Photograph from 8mm movie frame

discovered the airport because airplanes were flying right over the church and appeared to land nearby. The airport, it turned out, was rather near the church. We, the refugee children, had a great deal of interest in airplanes, perhaps, because we had left our home country in an airplane and we were far from home.

Since we had stand-by tickets, we waited to get on the airplane, but we did not get on a flight that particular night. We went again on June 16 and were not able to get seats. In the process of trying to get onto the airplane, we checked our luggage each time. On June 16, we ended up being handed an extra suitcase that did not belong to us. I took the bag and examined it. The bag contained some personal hygiene items and underwear. When we returned to the airport the next day, I did not return it. I took the bag! That is, I stole it. Somehow it seemed adventurous and, perhaps, we felt that we had our future stolen from us.

The incident of the stolen bag is a very shameful memory. I feel compelled to tell the story because it did occur and also because waves of refugees from Cuba who arrived after the 1960s have not infrequently been publicized to do as I did then and have been labeled as misfits and antisocial. I feel that at that particular time, I was as misfit and antisocial as any one of my compatriots.

That does not make the robbery and incident right or better, but I feel that by making it public it is now real for the entire community to know. Therefore, we can all be judged as misfits in one degree or another and we can feel better because at least on this account we are not divided; we are Cubans exiled from a homeland that continues to be a large farm or prison from which individuals still have to escape in order to feel themselves free.

Finally, on that night, on June 17, we flew out of Jacksonville on a four-engine propeller airplane. Father Lenihan had been right in guessing that I was not a righteous person!

Upon entering the airplane I was very surprised when each of us—like all other passengers—was handed a small box with three cigarettes. Apparently, it was a promotion, as we later found out was not unusual at the time. When the plane was already in flight, a signal was given through the lights above each seat that the cigarettes could be lit. Immediately, many of the passengers did light up. No one who saw that entire routine questioned the propriety of passing out cigarettes for all to smoke in the closed cabin of an airplane. No one raised any questions about the fact that teenagers were being given free cigarettes through which they might become addicted to tobacco. And, no one in their right mind on that plane would have thought that by 1964 the Surgeon General of the United States would declare that "cigarette smoking was harmful to your health." Who would have thought that by 1988 smoking on an airplane would be entirely prohibited because if anyone smoked, all passengers would be exposed to the toxic fumes of burnt tobacco and its additives? At the time, only two or three of the eight Cubans in route through the Unaccompanied Cuban Children Program were smokers. However, in the course of the next few years, most of us acquired the habit before we tried to distance ourselves from tobacco later on.

The flight was a *lechero* flight. What is a *lechero* flight? It is a flight that has frequent stops like the milk man, the *lechero*, who stops at every house in order to deliver a bottle of milk to each family. Our flight was to stop in Washington and then at New York's Idlewild International Airport. The latter was renamed a few years later the John F. Kennedy International Airport.

We got to New York in the morning. My family was waiting for us there. Uncle Emilio, Aunt Carmen, Muñeca, and Emilito all went up to the airport from New Jersey and spent a couple of hours with us before we boarded a smaller Eastern Airlines plane to Burlington, Vermont. They were happy to see us and I am sure they gave us all kinds of advice, but I do not remember exactly what they said.

On the way to Burlington, Vermont, we changed planes at Idlewild International Airport in New York City. Our family in the New York and New Jersey area came out to see us. In the picture, there are two women, Muñeca and Aunt Carmen. Photograph from 8mm movie frame

Upon entering the Eastern Airlines Terminal, we immediately found out that there were other Cuban refugees there. We inquired and learned from them that they were waiting to board a plane to Vermont also. There were nineteen boys and one girl, who had come in by Eastern Airlines, also from several of the houses and camps in the Miami area for unaccompanied Cuban children. The plane that took us to Vermont was a two-engine propeller plane. It was also a *lechero* flight, which was to stop in two or three cities before reaching our final destination.

When we arrived in Burlington, Vermont, we were picked up at the airport by someone from St. Michael's College and taken to our dormitory in a couple of vans. We must have taken some sort of back road(1) because, fairly soon and without going through anything that looked like a city, we were already in front of the college and headed toward our dorm.

St Michael's had been approved to offer a course in English for foreign students since 1954. We did not know it then, but each of us had been issued a student visa in order to attend St. Michael's. The individual visas were issued by the U.S. Immigration and Naturalization Service in St. Albans, Vermont. This is what my student visa for "Non Immigrant 'F' Student Status" stipulated:

English Program for Foreign Students

"This is a program to meet the needs of foreign students who need a better knowledge of English conversation, reading, writing, and understanding than they possess to continue their studies in the United States or for business or professional reasons. The full program is sixteen weeks in length, occupies the student full time during this period, and is open to men during the academic year and to men and women during the summer session. This U.S. I-20 is issued with this condition that the student does not request permission to accept employment during this concentrated program."

This new immigration status and documentation were completely unbeknown to me or any of us. However, it does appear from the records reviewed by me at Catholic Charities of the Archdiocese of Miami fifty years later that such a visa was a requirement for anyone attending the program at St. Michaels's. Who knows, if we did not have that type of visa, we might have placed the college in some sort of jeopardy.

Upon our arrival at St. Michael's, we were presented with our letter of admission to the program. Since none of us had filled out any application materials to the college, the paperwork must have been done entirely by the office of Mrs. Cooper. At the time, St. Michael's College must have had in the order of 3,000 students. There must have been about 50 students, out of which 28 were Cuban refugee Pedro Pans, in the English Program for Foreign Students that summer. The English Program for Foreign Students had offices and classrooms in a set of wooden halls located toward the west side of the campus in the general area where the Kline Center and the McCarthy Arts Center are presently located. The type of construction of the wooden halls and the proximity of an Army base, the Ethan Allen Camp, suggested that those wooden installations dated from World War II when the college served in one capacity or another during the war effort. Years later, I remember looking at press reports and television images where the Mariel refugees had been housed in Fort Chafee in Arkansas and Indiantown Gap in Pennsylvania and noted that the wooden barracks where the Mariel refugees were housed were—if not identical—very similar to those we occupied at St. Michael's in the program for foreign students.

Our first order of business in Vermont was to get a room in the dorm. I was housed on the second floor in the southwest corner of the building. There were two of us in each room. There was one shower and bathroom facility on each floor. The rooms were rather austere, with two small beds, a chest of drawers, and a simple desk. Soon thereafter, we were gathered in the wooden building where the English Department for Foreign Students offices and administration were located. We filled out some paperwork there and were handed meal tickets with which we could have all our meals in the college cafeteria.

The next day, we were all given placement tests and, immediately, based on our performance in them assigned to one of four groups: Basic, Intermediate, Advanced, and High Advanced. I got into the Advanced group. My teacher's name was Mr. O'Brian. He was a very nice, easygoing, tall, red-haired graduate student. There were nine students in my group distributed as follows in terms of their nationalities: Two were from Costa Rica; one from China; one from El Salvador; one from Colombia; one from Quebec, Canada; and we three Cubans.

Classes were conducted every day from Monday through Friday. We also had time dedicated to spend in the language laboratory, where we listened and interacted with materials on tape. Our weeks' activities were rounded out by evening music sessions in which a musician with a guitar came into an auditorium in one of the main buildings of the college and taught us songs like "Oh My Darling, Clementine" and other classics of American folklore. One of the Pedro Pans who arrived from the Miami area, Emilio Cueto, also added to our entertainment playing Cuban music on the piano. He also played the piano when a visiting Cuban priest celebrated mass in St. Michael's.

Wooden buildings at St. Michael's College where the program in English for foreign students was housed. Photograph from 8mm movie frame

ST. MICHAEL'S COLLEGE
Winooski, Vermont, U.S.A.
DEPARTMENT OF ENGLISH FOR FOREIGN STUDENTS

Academic record of:	Parent or Guardian:
Gordon, Antonio Ramon c/o Mrs. Louise Cooper Catholic Welfare Bureau, Inc. 395 N.W. 1st. Rm. 207 Miami, Fla.	Mrs. Louise Cooper (same address)

COURSES:	DATES and NUMBER OF WEEKS	GRADE*
ELEMENTARY		
INTERMEDIATE		
ADVANCED	26 June to 18 Aug., 1961 (8)	80
HIGH-ADVANCED		
ENGLISH FS 102		
TEACHER TRAINING COURSE & WORKSHOP		

RECOMMENDED IN BASIC ENGLISH FOR COLLEGE

ENGLISH PROFILE TESTS RECORD*

	1	2	3	4	5	6
	INITIAL	Aug 17				Level Required for College* Recommendation
DATES: JUNE 27	1961	1961				
						88
STRUCTURE	90	92				
						60
READING	56	78				
						88
AURAL COMPREHENSION	78	98				
						70
ABILITY TO WRITE	57	93				
						70
ABILITY TO SPEAK	71	85				

Total Number Weeks .... 8 .... Total Number Hours of English 150

Remarks: ....

Not Valid As An Official Transcript Unless Signed and Sealed

ERNEST A. BOULAY, *Chairman*
Department of English for Foreign Students

* — For Interpretation See Other Side

My level of performance in English in the summer of 1961

Once a week, we attended the theater at the college. The theater group from the Catholic University in Washington, DC practiced at St. Michaels's in the summer. Therefore, we got to watch the whole repertoire of plays that were later shown at the Catholic University in Washington in the fall of 1961. We were able to see several plays including *Death of a Salesman*. After the theater sessions, we were privileged to mingle in the theater with the actors, drama and theater students, enjoying some non-alcoholic refreshments and practicing our English, as we asked questions and got some answers from the actors and drama students.

Aside from being able to buy and eat our food in the college cafeteria with more variety and flavors than what could have been possible at Camp St. John, we began getting an allowance of $5 on a weekly basis. This was more than twice our allowance at Camp St. John. Mail was received on a daily basis. Muñeca wrote:

> *Ridgefield Park, N.J.*
> *July 3, 1961*
> *Dear Tony:*
>
>
> *Yesterday I received your letter, and I am really happy for you because I see that, thank God, you are happy in the new college. In a letter I received from your father, I think he says that he is coming between the 1st and 15th of this month. What is the situation with your mother? I do not know if she is coming. If she is staying behind in Havana, it is in order to prevent having to surrender the house to the authorities.*
> *Congratulations on the allowance you get all the weekends...*
> *...Answer me right away but not in English please. Congratulations for your letter in English and congratulate me because I was able to understand you. It is a miracle! Many kisses for you and Ramoncito.*
>
> *Love,*
> *Muñeca*

I was already attempting to write in English to some of my nearest relatives! Aside from the college routine, my cousin Ramoncito and I immediately got in touch with our cousin Pilar in Saranac Lake, New York, as I had been instructed by my father. This is what Pilar wrote:

View from my room in the wooden barracks at St. Michael's College in 1961. Photograph from 8mm movie frame

July 3, 1961
Dear Tony:

I've been calling on the phone without being able to get you and I write in case I am not able to talk with you on the phone. Manolo tomorrow will have the itinerary of the ferry boats leaving and arriving from Burlington to Port Kent, State of New York. If you go by bus to Burlington—like you told me—then you can catch the ferry and we will wait for you at Port Kent...
Your dad and uncle called here thinking that you were here. They will call again on Saturday. Call me collect to agree on a plan.
We'll pay for the ferry. By phone, tell me if you have cash. Your father said that this week he sent you money...
The ferry is 85 cents and I will pay you for it when you arrive here because you are invited. The trip is very nice. Notice when you cross it that Lake Champlain is very large.

A Kiss,
Pilar

Dear Tony:

If this letter reaches you before Saturday call us on Friday night around 7, so that the call does not cost you anything tell the operator this: I want to call Saranac Lake 1186 and reverse the charges. That way we can agree on how we are going to meet you in Port Kent.

Hugs,
Manolo

We took the bus to downtown Burlington and walked to the wharf of the Lake Champlain ferries. We were the only passengers who were traveling at that time without an automobile. In about one hour we were docking at Port Kent in the State of New York. We immediately saw Pilar and Manolo. They greeted us and showed us to their car, a red 1960 4-door Chevrolet Impala. Manolo drove us to their home in Saranac Lake. It was a historical house in more than one respect. The Beneros had lived in that particular two-story brick house since 1938. My father, Aunt Carmen, and Uncle Emilio had visited Pilar and stayed in that house back in 1939 when they had gone to visit the World Fair in New York and took a trip to Upstate New York to see their relatives.

Pilar and Manolo could not have made us feel more at home than they did. Pilar cooked Cuban food and we ate so much that I got some indigestion the first night I was there. What kind of Cuban cuisine? White rice, black beans, and roast pork were some of the things she cooked for us all the way up in northern New York State near the Canadian border. Once at St. John's Camp, a Cuban couple cooked a Cuban meal for the entire group of Cuban refugees and brought it to us on a Sunday; since then we had not had any Cuban food.

We returned to Pilar and Manolo's place several times during our stay at St. Michael's. Every time it was a treat. We could not have thanked them enough for having provided an oasis to our internment in institutions. They showed us around the town of Saranac Lake, took us to see nearby Lake Placid where the winter Olympics had been held in the past, and for a while, we felt like we were on a real vacation. Curiously, our experience in Upstate New York in the Adirondack Mountains and various lakes that abound in the region was similar to my parents' impressions at the *finquita* of Dr. Fuentes near Viñales in western Cuba. It was a respite in the middle of a psychological war. My parents' war was against communism. My cousin's and mine was a war against ignorance, attempting to conquer a foreign language. When I began writing to Pilar in English she returned to me the corrected letters with her reply. Pilar did not know it but she had become an adjuct faculty to the program for Cuban refugees at St. Michael's! In the final analysis, we were turning into immigrants like the Hungarians had in 1957.

CHAPTER 18
THE "VISA WAIVERS": ALL CUBANS ABOARD

"No, it wasn't false because there was no validity to the whole thing. It was simply a notification that the visa waiver had been waived and it had been waived for all children up to 16 years of age. So it didn't have to be an original signature, the photocopy worked just as well."
-Father Bryan Walsh

My time at St. Michael's was not all school work in Vermont and vacation time in Saranac Lake. In part, because of the immersion course in English and also because of the deteriorating situation in Havana, I was asked to help in obtaining "visa waivers" for several individuals. This is what I wrote to Mrs. Cooper in Miami verbatim:

August 8, 1961
Mrs. L. Cooper
Miami, Fla

Dear Mrs. Cooper:

This is in order to ask you about one visa to:
Name: Juan Edelberto Pella López
Birth Date: 19 August 1944
Address: Ave. San Francisco # 142, Reparto Altahabana, Havana, Cuba
He want (sic) to leave Cuba. I ask you for the visa waiver if you can and take him out of Cuba....
Well, Mrs. Cooper, I think that I don't have more to ask you today.
I am waiting for your answer.
I remain very truly yours,
Antonio Gordon

In examining this letter written by me originally in English, I get the impression that I had read a number of formal letters of rejection from the various colleges I had addressed requesting a scholarship. Otherwise, the closing of this letter I wrote in English seven months after I had arrived in the United States would not have been so formal. Furthermore, there are hardly any errors in grammar or punctuation in the closing of the letter in comparison with the greeting and the body of the document.

There are two things that appear obvious. The first is that, like most Spanish-speaking English learners, I was translating from the Spanish and writing in English. Hence, "Creo que no tengo nada mas por hoy," sounds fairly well in Spanish but, "...think that I don't have more to ask you today," would earn a number of red marks from my English teacher including, word usage, rewrite, and what not. The second thing that comes through in the letter is a sense of urgency. Notice that I ask Mrs. Cooper regarding my peer Pella to "...take him out of Cuba." I was not going to take all responsibility for these requests. I passed mine to Mrs. Cooper or anyone who would read my letters! The visa waiver for Pella was granted and, according to records I reviewed in my file at the Catholic Charities of the Archdiocese of Miami, a letter had been sent to Pella and a notification to Pan American Airways in Havana that Pella had a visa waiver.

I also requested a visa waiver for my cousin Ernest, who at the time had just turned five years old.

I obtained the following letter in Spanish from the office of Mrs. Cooper:

July 14, 1961
Mr. Antonio Gordon
St. Michael's College
Winooski Park, Vermont.

Dear Antonio:

By this means I have the pleasure to inform you that the "Visa Waiver" for your cousin Ernesto has been granted.
Inform your family in Havana of this and let them know that they should go to the Pan American Airways office.

Sincerely,
Mrs. Louise Cooper
Supervisor

For reasons that were not clear then and are not well understood today, the visa waiver had been granted for my cousin Ernest, but it did not get to the office of Pan American Airways in Havana. When his mother, my Aunt Ofelia, and his father Ramón Rencurrell went to get the visa waiver, it was not there. The Pan American office in Havana just did not have the information. In view of that, my family in the New Jersey area dispatched another cousin to Washington, DC to inquire at the Department of State about the visa waiver for Ernest. The following letter from Emilito's wife gives us an idea of what was going on then:

> *Ridgefield Park, N.J.*
> *August 15, 1961*
>
> *This is because my brother went to Washington yesterday and asked for a duplicate of the visa waiver of Ernesto Rencurrell Gordon and they told him that he had been denied the visa waiver. But I think that you may have given them another name.*
> *Data needed:*
> *a) Full name of the child. What name did you use?*
> *Ernesto Gordon Rencurrell*
> *Ernesto R. Gordon*
> *Ernesto Rencurrell Gordon*
> *Ernesto Rencurrell de Gordon*
>
> *b) Address of the Association who claims him:*
> *Miami or New York.*
> *c) Phone for Mrs. Cooper*
>
> *We need the duplicate urgently because without it the departure from Cuba of Ernest cannot occur...*
> *For all of these issues... write to your Mrs. Cooper for her to go negotiate another visa waiver if we cannot get a duplicate.*
> *Well Tony, take care of this right away... and you receive the love of your cousin,*
>
> *María Ofelia*

I immediately wrote to Mrs. Cooper and to one of her assistants, Miss Sandra Carbonell, in Spanish in the strongest terms. I explained that I had already written to clarify the whereabouts of the visa waiver for "my little cousin." On account of the issue of Ernest's visa waiver I was to act "right away." His mother, my Aunt Ofelia and Abuela Amparo in Havana were getting into a panic on account of the fact that everything was ready for Ernest's departure except for his visa waiver— which had already been said to have been issued, but had not appeared in Havana's Pan American Airways offices. The pressure worked. In a matter of a couple of days, Mrs. Cooper wrote back that the visa waiver for Ernest was not only issued, but was in Havana.

By mid-August, Ernest was able to fly out of Havana accompanied by Emilito's sister–in–law. In a matter of a day or two, both of them were in New Jersey through the social services of the Cuban Refugee Emergency Center. They did not know it, but by mid-August, another *Cuban Barracón* was forming quickly at Emilito's apartment in suburban northern New Jersey. Eventually, in that two-bedroom apartment, we were eleven Cuban refugees and only two individuals were gainfully employed.

At around that time, when I was still at St. Michael's, Muñeca confided that she was also in need of help. This is what she wrote:

> *Hear this Tony, I need you to do me a favor, if you think you can… Elena is in Jamaica and cannot come over here because she does not have a cent and has no family. As you can imagine, she needs to get into a boarding school in this country as quickly as possible. I told her that you are trying to find something for her but nothing has come up. I wish for you to write to Fr. Lenihan and request his help in finding Elena a place to stay in this country. I think he has connections and maybe can find something for her…*
>
> *I also want to tell you about me…I want to study English and finish my career in one year. Explain to Fr. Lenihan what I am telling you and we will see if he gets interested in our situation. We need to learn English… do not forget to give him the details of our desperate situation, that's very important.*
>
> *Muñeca*

Indeed, I followed my dear cousin's request and wrote not to Father Lenihan, for I did not think that he could do very much about this issue of finding a boarding school for two young women aged twenty or twenty-one, but to the office of Catholic Charities in Miami. I wrote instead to Mrs. Cooper. However, Mrs. Cooper did not take the issue. She never addressed any of Muñeca's or Elena's "desperate situations" in her letters to me. Elena, I should have explained, was our neighbor in the Lawton neighborhood in Havana. She was my cousin Muñeca's best friend and classmate at the Lourdes School and obviously had gotten out of Cuba to Jamaica, but had no way to get into the United States at the time.

Three of my peers at the Marist School near the Plaza Cívica wrote to me at about this time or shortly thereafter, requesting assistance with their visa waivers. I wrote to Mrs. Cooper, requesting that a safe-conduct be issued to them. All of them eventually got their visa waivers, but they were also requesting them through others and I do not have written confirmation about the granting of their documents. Therefore, I do not think that my requests were the ones that resulted in the granting of their travel permits.

The visa waiver proved to be an emergency safe-conduct document. Without it, the passenger could not depart from Cuba to the United States or enter the United States. It is evident that it was not only acceptable to the government of the United States that a Catholic priest was allowed to issue a permit to enter the United States; it was also acceptable to the Cuban revolutionary government. Otherwise, no one would have been able to obtain an American visa to leave Cuba after January 3, 1961, when diplomatic relations broke between the two countries.

Cuban children first, and then later on adults, were allowed to enter the United States after the American Embassy in Havana closed in January 1961. Without this emergency measure, Operation Pedro Pan would have ceased before the majority of children and youngsters who benefited from it ever, literally, got off the ground. I believe the granting of powers to issue visa waivers to a local social work agency, Catholic Charities under the direction of Father Walsh, was a unique and unprecedented measure. Cubans were the first to have this privilege that enabled them to enter the United States.

For example, the concept of the visa waiver was never evoked or granted when the passengers of the St. Louis who were Jews escaping Nazi Germany in 1937 were not allowed to disembark either in Havana or in Miami, despite the fact that the Jews on board had relatives in both cities at the time. There were more than sixty children on the St. Louis who ended up in refugee homes in France and other countries when the St. Louis went back to Europe and disembarked in Antwerp.(1)

Many of those children subsequently died as the advancing Nazi offensive occupied Holland, Belgium, and France.

Visa waivers became formalized into the State Department repertoire of visas in 1968 through an act of the United States Congress, thus, facilitating tourism and short-term visits to the United States. Officially, the first country generally recognized today for having had the privilege of being granted visa waivers was the United Kingdom in 1988, not Cuba in 1961. Presently, the visa waiver program allows citizens from thirty-eight specific countries to travel to the United States for tourism, business, or while in transit for up to ninety days without having to obtain a visa. All countries selected to be in the visa waiver program are high-income economies. The new visa waivers are similar to the "visa waivers" for Cubans only in name, for ours were not offered for tourism, business, and definitely not for ninety days!

While waiting for a way out of Cuba through the visa waivers, Lorenzo and Pella wrote about having gone to the movies earlier in the year. They went to see the Soviet film, *La Llamada del Cosmos* or *The Heavens Call*. It was the first science fiction film produced entirely in the Soviet Union. Lorenzo and Pella did not appreciate the historical position of this work, *The Heavens Call*, in the history of the Soviet film industry. They did not know it, but science fiction had been, up until then, an entirely American phenomenon.(2) How could my peers have appreciated the Soviet story? They reviewed it in their letter as a *paquete*. The translation of this term is not straightforward. The Spanish dictionary accepts several meanings for the word *paquete* but none of those words means what Lorenzo and Pella wanted to express. This is what they meant: a story that was not believable. When you say to someone in Cuba, *"Me metieron un paquete,"* that means you were told or given a false story.

Obviously, the Soviet film *The Heavens Call* could not be by definition a professional *paquete* because it was fiction, science fiction. However, one of the characteristics of science fiction is that it should be believable. However, the two Cuban amateur film critics did not find it to be; in the setting of being harassed and persecuted in Cuba by a revolutionary government that was protected by the Soviets, they did not see the qualities of the film that other critics applauded. In order to make the most of the film, one would have to dissociate the politics of the times from it. That was not possible for anyone who felt oppressed by communism.

The Heavens Call cannot not be understood outside the Soviet and American worlds at the end of the 1950s. It should be recalled that in 1957, the first man-made satellite "Sputnik" was launched. Along with increasing Soviet propaganda,

CATHOLIC WELFARE BUREAU
DIOCESE OF MIAMI

REV. FATHER BRYAN O. WALSH, S.T.L.
EXECUTIVE DIRECTOR

REGIONAL OFFICES
MIAMI   FORT LAUDERDALE

395 N. W. FIRST STREET — SUITE 207
MIAMI 36, FLORIDA
FRANKLIN 9-2503

A QUIEN PUEDA INTERESAR:

Se hace constar que a _____
_____ le ha sido concedida la "Visa Waiver" por
el Departamento de Estado a peticion del Catholic Welfare
Bureau, Inc.

Pan American y K. L. M. han sido notificadas. El solicitante debera dirigirse a dichas oficinas para hacer la reservacion y comprar su pasaje.

Si Pan American y K. L. M. en la Habana no hubiesen recibido la confirmacion de la "Visa Waiver", el solicitante debera de esperar unos dias y tratar de nuevo.

Bryan O Walsh

(Rev. Fr.) Bryan O. Walsh
Director

MEMBER OF THE UNITED FUND OF DADE COUNTY

The visa waivers issued for Cuban children were essentially letters signed by Fr. Bryan Walsh accepted at the time in lieu of any standard visa. In general, if the child was from 6 to 16 years old, the blanks could be filled out and the visa waiver on its way through the appropriate governmental offices and Pan American Airways in Havana.

a new era, the Space Age, had been launched. According to Soviet thinking, it was an era of the cosmos in which communism was to overtake capitalism. It is difficult to blame Lorenzo and Pella for not clearly seeing the benefits of a communist victory. After all, they had associated communism with the fact that they were out of their school, they felt that they were flunked by communist professors from the *Instituto de Segunda Enseñanza de La Víbora*, and their families were being subjected to the scarcities and irregularities that followed the institution of the Agrarian Reform, mostly because of the communists.

The plot of *The Heavens Call* was about an orbital station, built to help equip a spaceship journeying to the planet Mars. However, the leaders of the American astronauts were eager, by hook or by crook, to overtake the Russians in the space race. As a result of their haste, the American spaceship fell into a swarm of meteorites on its way to Mars. At the end, the Soviet cosmonauts rescued the Americans, who would have otherwise died.

The assessment of this fictional Soviet film by Lorenzo and Pella serves to illustrate the general attitude of Cubans at the time, with regard to the communist versus capitalist struggle. Cubans, at least the Cubans closest to me, were not communists. In fact, all peers and friends with whom I exchanged mail during these months of 1961 finally requested from me a visa waiver. It seemed that everyone who knew about the possibility of a way out was willing to take it. Without knowing it, I had turned into a visa waiver broker!

However, in general, Cubans had not, at that time, understood that the fiasco of the Bay of Pigs Invasion was a major defeat, a turning point. It was a symbolic fiasco of greater proportions than just a battle lost for the records of the CIA. From that point on, the cause of freedom and democracy-loving Cubans on the island who were anti-communists, and the Cubans in exile who had sought asylum in order to organize and participate in the fight against the Castro forces, were to be sidetracked or abandoned by the complex priorities of the United States. The formalities of such abandonment would be made clear after the October missile crisis in 1962. For the time being, the only way out was through a special safe conduct known as the visa waiver.

Both Pella and Lorenzo got their visa waivers. Lorenzo was able to leave from Cuba before the end of 1961. He spent a few weeks at Camp Matecumbe in South West Dade County, Florida, and from there was transferred to Camp St. John. He attended Bishop Kenny High School, but did not graduate there. He was transferred to a foster home in the care of a retired military family in Sarasota, Florida. Pella would not depart Cuba until 1962, through Operation Pedro Pan. For reasons that are not clear, he went back to Havana after being housed at Camp Matecumbe.

Years later, I visited him and we spoke over a meal for a couple of hours, but he did not elaborate on the circumstances at Camp Matecumbe. He just said that he did not feel well with the others in Camp Matecumbe. By the time he was there, his friends from Havana, Lorenzo and Zenón, had long been assigned to other camps and foster homes. Pella was a sensitive person and used to stutter. I can imagine that he felt ridiculed and felt that he was better at home with his parents than away. I wonder what his nickname was. Whatever it was, I think it must have been a derogatory one. His father was rather old at the time, older than my father. He died in the 1960s and Pella stayed at home with his mother. He worked as a teacher on the island and sought refuge again with his mother in the 1990s. He settled in West New York, a town in New Jersey, where I saw him. He died there from cancer a few years after arriving in the United States.

CHAPTER 19
BEYOND ST. MICHAEL'S DESPAIR AND REALITY

"No tuve primavera, me la robó un tirano
Entré súbitamente en un afanoso verano
Abracé un puñado de recuerdos para cubrir la desnudez
De un niño que se quedó sin niñez."
("My spring was gone, stolen by a tyrant.
All at once into an eager summer I entered,
Clutching a handful of memories, that would clothe the nakedness of a boy,
Left without his childhood.")
-Jose Azel[7]

My father eventually departed from Cuba. Aside from the set of documents that were required from all Cubans who were attempting to leave the island at the time, he was required to have special permission from the Ministry of Public Health, through which he was allowed to be absent from his post as a physician at the Cristo De Limpias Hospital. Officially, he had a valid reason to leave Havana. He wanted to come to the United States to see me. Obviously, he was concerned about leaving his wife and dog behind. Furthermore, he had always expressed a great deal of respect for the United States as he noted in a letter regarding some menus I sent him after being discharged from St. Vincent's Hospital in Jacksonville. This is what he wrote:

My dear son:

"What an ingenious way to provide patients their meals. I see that everyone can choose among the possibilities that are printed on the

---

[7] José Azel, Ph.D. arrived in the United States through Operation Pedro Pan and works presently at the Institute for Cuban and Cuban American Studies of the University of Miami, Coral Gables, Florida. He published in 2014 a volume of poems from where this quote has been translated.

form. In truth, Americans are at the forefront of everything...
For the time being, your mother will stay here and I'll explain to
you when I am there what we are going to do eventually.
I would like to get a seat for departure on or about the 24th of July.
We will see if this can be achieved. When I arrive in New York I'll
call you on the phone."

Antonio

He did not get a seat for departure until August 3. He did not know it, but by that time in the concourse of the Cold War, the Berlin Wall was being planned and by mid-August it was going to divide the city and the world. Was it forever? No one knew. However, when my father arrived in Miami via Pan American Airways with a tourist visa, not a "visa waiver," he was immediately detained at the airport. As it turned out, he was informed that, at that time, all men who were traveling alone coming from Cuba were being detained and interrogated because the American authorities were concerned that Cuban spies were being infiltrated into the United States. The latter explanation for his detention at the Opa-Locka Center, in the same buildings and location where later there would be a camp for unaccompanied children, was not known to us at the time, and much less to my mother who had remained in Havana. Only my father knew and he explained what had occurred after he was released when I saw him later on.

The term Opa-Locka is short for Opatishawockalocka, a word that means "wooded hammock in a swamp" in the Seminole language. Curiously, the first influx of people from Cuba into this area of Florida occurred when Americans settled on the Isle of Pines, now known as the Island of Youth, migrated to Florida during the dictatorial regime of Gerardo Machado in the late 1920s and early thirties. At that time, and soon thereafter, with the derogation of the Platt Amendment and the signing of a new agreement between the Cuban leaders of 1934 and the administration of Franklin Delano Roosevelt, the Isle of Pines became Cuban territory.(1) Up to that time, after the defeat of Spain in the Hispanic-Cuban-American War, the Isle of Pines had been United States territory. During the Second World War, the airport at Opa-Locka and surrounding areas were used for military purposes. Interestingly, in the 1950s, the CIA conducted covert operations from the second floor of the enlisted men's barracks, Building 67, one of the military wooden buildings near the Opa-Locka Airport.(2) The CIA operation succeeded in overthrowing the leftist government of Jacobo Arbenz in Guatemala in 1954.

My dad did not know this, but he was detained in the same general area from where the recruits for the Bay of Pigs Invasion were sent to training camps in Guatemala in blacked-out airplanes. The operation launched in March 1960 by the Eisenhower administration with the purported objective of downing the communist threat and revolutionary government in Cuba, and was much larger than the successful operation set up against the Arbenz government.

Furthermore, in April 1961, the exiled leader Jose Miró Cardona and his closest associates were flown and gathered into Opa-Locka, because it was from there that they were supposed to be flown to the beachhead conquered by the invaders in Cuba. From that beachhead, they were to be recognized as the legitimate government of Cuba and their request for military support was to be honored. Instead, after waiting in Opa-Locka for hours and days for the signal to go into Cuba, Miró Cardona and his associates were flown to Washington where they met with President John F. Kennedy. The exiled leaders were reassured by Kennedy, that despite the failed invasion, the United States would assist with the liberation of Cuba.(2)

However, in August 1961, the wooden buildings near the Opa-Locka Airport were being used to detain and interrogate Cubans seeking political asylum in the United States. My father spent four days in detention. Aside from the fact that he told me the story, his Cuban passport was stamped in Havana with his departure on August 3, 1961, but his official entry into the United States was stamped by the U.S. Immigration and Naturalization Service on August 7, 1961.

During his detention, he was persistently interrogated about his "stay in Panama." This was very hard on him because he had never been to Panama or knew anything about Panama. He repeated his answers and apparently became rather distressed. This was not only because the entire detention and interrogation were unexpected, but because while he was going through the interrogations he was aware that on August 6 the Cuban government announced that Cuban currency was going to be changed(3) and he was helpless to do anything about it. All banknotes from the Republic of Cuba were to be demonetized and exchanged one for one for new revolutionary banknotes. What worried my father the most about the entire issue was the fact that he had left my mother with what he thought was enough money, but she would only be able to exchange 200 pesos. The revolutionary government accomplished the preparations for the currency change entirely in secret. They argued that a lot of Cuban currency was outside the country; they had to take control of the currency, and ordered all points of entry into the island closed for three days until the exchange was completed. Whatever Cuban currency was being held by the exiles abroad or even by the U.S. Naval Base at Guantanamo became worthless. No one was to get into or out of Cuban territory during those three days of currency exchange. In reality, there were not millions of dollars in Cuban currency being held by exiles outside of the island.

Up to that time, the Cuban currency was printed in the United States by the American Bank Note Company and in Great Britain by the Thomas LaRue Company. From that moment onward, the Cuban currency was printed in Czechoslovakia, a recognized member state of the Soviet Bloc. During the period of currency exchange, most stores and places of business in Cuba were closed, except for those providing the most essential services. Nearly 3,000 exchange posts were set up throughout the island. The one exchange post serving Altahabana was set up in the bank at the shopping center located on A Street at 6th Street, where one of Faura's brothers used to work. Each family was allowed to exchange up to 200 old pesos for 200 new pesos. Any amount greater than 200 pesos was to be brought all at once and deposited in special accounts from which nothing could be withdrawn for at least one week. With the help of Faura's brother and some relatives, my mother was able to exchange more than 200 pesos during the crisis. My father did not know that, and his concerns were real because my mother was no longer working at the time. Her time was essentially spent getting the paperwork ready for her and Poppy to depart from the island.

Back in Opa-Locka, once the interrogators were satisfied, my father was taken to a hotel in downtown Miami where he spent about one week while he got in touch with the Cuban Refugee Center. The refugee center had arranged through social service agencies to provide temporary quarters for Cubans who were to be relocated to other areas of the United States soon after their arrival. Since my father had relatives in northern New Jersey, he was being relocated to New York. Eventually, he got to New York on August 18 by train; the same date that I arrived in the Big Apple from Burlington, Vermont, after completing the English Course for Foreign Students at St. Michael's.

Emilito and his father picked up my dad at the Port Authority Train Station first and then came for us at the Idlewild International Airport. My cousin Ramoncito had asked for permission to spend some time with his family in the New York area and his request had been granted. Therefore, we both became separated from the group of Cubans who had been at St. Michael's College and were en route back to Miami.

My first impression when I saw my dad was that he appeared much older than the way I remembered the last time I had seen him seven months before. He seemed sad and when we got to talking in private, he told me about being unexpectedly detained in Miami and held in Opa-Locka. He was particularly worried about the testimony that he had given, since he had been asked to sign some documents, the nature of which he did not remember. He appeared worried. He also had reservations about what might have been on a taped interrogation, because he did not remember exactly what he had said. A couple of days after settling in New Jersey, a letter arrived at Emilito's apartment addressed to my dad. It confirmed that "they," the CIA, were aware of his whereabouts and he was advised to go to an office in the New York area to seek help regarding employment. We did go to the office in Manhattan, where he was told that he could go to a location in New Mexico where he could work. My dad took the information, but he was not in any condition mentally to embark on a move to New Mexico alone. There were too many things on his plate at the time, not the least of which was the issue of the currency change in Havana and the immediate future of my mother.

I could not remain idle without attempting to help. I wrote to St. Michael's College regarding our situation in the *Cuban Barracón* in New Jersey and got this answer from Mr. Boulay:

St. Michael's College
Winooski Park, Vermont
United States of America
25 August 1961

Mr. Antonio Gordon
15 Lincoln Street
Ridgefield Park
New Jersey

Dear Antonio:

Thank you for your good letter recently received in this office.
I am very much interested in your father's problem, but am not certain what can be done from here to help. Believe me, however, I am certainly most willing to do anything and everything that I possibly can.
Would you please write me just as soon as possible giving me some details about—age, experience, previous positions, etc, etc. This will give me what I need to start whatever action I may be able to.

As soon as I have this information from you, I shall write him
with—I hope—some kind of reassuring news.
Please send me these details right away.

Sincerely,
Ernest A. Boulay, Chairman
Department of English for Foreign Students

I do not think I ever thanked Mr. Boulay for his encouragement. I need to do that now, at least posthumously since Mr. Boulay has since passed away. I also need to thank him for grading my letter to him as "good." However, that probably only meant that he could understand what I was trying to express. The letter was very much poor in terms of giving him the appropriate information with which to tackle the enormous task I was requesting of him in assisting my dad in his resettlement. Someone else, upon receipt of such an incomplete letter from a student no longer enrolled in his program would have discarded it.

I should report further details on how the *Cuban Barrancón* in Emilito's was "organized." We were eleven in all, counting Emilito, his wife, baby, and sister-in-law, who occupied the master bedroom; Uncle Emilio, Aunt Carmen, Muñeca, and Ernest occupied the second bedroom. The rest of us—my dad, Ramoncito, Emilito's brother-in-law, and I—shared the small living-dining room and the floor of the small kitchen. In accordance with the unwritten "requirements" for a *Cuban Barrancón,* only two of the eleven were gainfully employed at the time.

I was not the only one trying to get help. It turns out that another set of relatives found out that my father and I were in Emilito's *Cuban Barracón.* In the early 1950s, the son of a cousin of my mother, who lived in the small town of Céspedes, located in between the town of Florida and the City of Camagüey in Cuba, had immigrated to the United States because he was looking for advancement in life. That was not common, but it was also not unusual. He had gone into Havana looking for work and business opportunities and found none to his liking. The next thing to do back then was to look for a future in New York in the United States. Noel settled in New York at first and then northern New Jersey. He had turned out to be a wizard at electronics and was the manager of a local electronics company in Passaic, New Jersey. His brother Joe lived nearby; he had also looked for a better future in the United States after seeing the success of his brother and before the arrival of communism in Cuba. Both of them were married with children and provided considerable help to my father and me.

It turned out that Noel was able to get me work at the company where he worked in Passaic. By the end of the month, my father and I had moved to Noel's attic and I was gainfully employed as an office boy and shipping and receiving assistant clerk. I could not believe it, but I still had serious difficulties with English when I started work in the electronics company. I had trouble understanding spoken English, despite a set of respectable documents attesting that I was: "Recommended in Basic English for College." I went to work with Noel in the morning and returned in the afternoon. I had my lunch at work from a sandwich shop run from a nearby home by some Eastern European refugees. In the evening, we had an abundant evening meal every night at Joe's place. His friendly wife, Isabelita, always cooked a hot meal for us and her family.

Noel and Joe had connections in Passaic. We visited their family doctor, who had treated their late brother Juan for a congenital coagulation disorder. He was most gracious and took my father to the Beth Israel Hospital, where he recommended him to work as a house physician. However, my father's state of mind was not optimistic as he felt very much homesick, dispirited, and far away from his wife. He felt, in the context of his departure and the currency change in Cuba that he had abandoned her. He did not take the job. Instead, he found out from some of his friends in the Miami area that a course in English and Medicine was being organized by the University of Miami School of Medicine through which Cuban doctors in exile would be able to get ready to pass the required examination of the Educational Council for Foreign Medical Graduates (ECFMG). That course was also sponsored by the American government, in an effort to assist Cuban medical doctors and their families in resettling in this country. With a certification from the ECFMG, he would be able to work in a hospital, train for a second time—this time in the United States of America—and eventually obtain a license to practice medicine in one of the fifty states.

By the beginning of October, he was back in Miami. By that time, Uncle Emilio and Aunt Carmen had moved down to Miami with Ernest and Muñeca. Muñeca—and her friend Elena also—had gotten a job with the Unaccompanied Cuban Children Program in Florida City. My father lived in a second-floor, two-bedroom apartment just across from the north side of the Corpus Christie Catholic Church in North West Miami with his sister and brother-in-law. My dad spent his days walking to the airport every day to check who was arriving from Cuba, visiting friends, and getting ready for the upcoming course. Our roles had suddenly turned around. I was up north and working for a living, and he was down south and looking to get into a school. Things were better on more than one account, however. I could send him money directly, he was getting a refugee allowance amounting to about $60 a month from the U.S. government sponsored Cuban Refugee Emergency Center, and I did not have to send him money through Puerto Rico. Secondly, my dad was a good man. He did not steal luggage with underwear or take cars for a ride that did not belong to him.

CHAPTER 20
WHO WILL BE ABLE TO SEPERATE US FROM CHRIST?

"The Communist regime that oppresses Cuba would take many things from us but there is something that it has not been able to detach from us: Christ."
-Brother Maximiliano

My mother survived the departure of my father and the unexpected, truly secretive, and clandestine currency exchange that got the picture of the arrival of Fidel Castro into Havana on January 8, 1959, and the effigy of Camilo Cienfuegos onto the new Cuban bills. After my father's departure on August 3, she had a surprise waiting for her when she returned home to Altahabana. A letter from Dr. José Ramón Machado Ventura, until recently Vice President of the Castro regime, who at the time was the minister of the Ministry of Public Health, was waiting for her. My father had left Cuba with a permit that allowed him to depart the island. He was also supposed to go to the ministry and report some details about the trip before he was to have been allowed to depart. Obviously, he had left without going to that meeting. In one of my mother's first letters to my dad in August, she communicated the content of the letter from the minister to my father, but aside from generating some anxiety, nothing else was done about it. Several weeks later, she received more correspondence from the ministry, stating that if my father did not return in thirty days, he would have to submit a certified letter requesting an extension of his leave. He never did write this either.

My mother wrote to me her first letter after my dad's departure in this manner:

Havana
August 11, 1961
Dearest son:

It is my greatest wish that you find yourself well in union with your cousin and your daddy. I'm fine thanks to God. Your grandmother and other family here are also well.

Today I received your letter dated August 4. Prior to that, I received another one with a few photos. It gave me great joy when I saw how well you look. May God also provide your daddy with such fortune. I am very happy to know that he is there, because you know that the weather in Spain is very unfavorable for him, particularly now that the winter is harsh.

I have a lot of desire to see you and be with you but I am calm because I know that everything happens in its due time.

Well son this is a midnight letter because it is night here and I still have some things I must do. That is why I wrote your letter first so that you may have news from your mother... Tell your daddy many loving things. I am waiting for your letters. I say goodbye for now with hugs and kisses for both of you from someone who does not forget you for a single moment, your mother,

María

    This was the first letter my mother wrote after my father left Cuba. By that time, the crisis of the currency change had already been managed. She was lonesome, but already engaged in getting as many of our personal belongings as possible out of the house since, eventually, the house with all its contents would be submitted to an inventory and confiscated by the revolutionary government at the time of my mother's departure. Months later, she would explain how she moved just about everything from our house to the houses of relatives and friends. Some of the latter were folks who had been patients of my father and felt very near our family, despite the fact they lived some distance away in the Bejucal area outside metropolitan Havana.

    This way of trying to safeguard our belongings that mother undertook was followed by many Cuban families. It is interesting to point out that the fate all of those belongings was going to be governed by circumstances that included the fact that Cubans would continue to seek asylum out of Cuba in waves. The "wave" during which I left Cuba was followed by several others in which most of the people who were safeguarding the belongings of previous exiles also left the island. Eventually, most of the belongings of any Cuban who sought asylum off the island were confiscated. There were rare exceptions. Some items were salvaged through friendly embassies, which channeled them out of the country in their diplomatic mail or service. In that manner, some of my family's belongings—including university diplomas and some pieces of jewelry—were taken out of Havana through my Uncle Emilio's connections in the Spanish Embassy in Havana.

My mother appeared to be happy that my dad was out of Cuba, because by then she also knew that he was involved in the Underground. It was obvious that it was only a matter of time before he would have been detained and put in prison. We know this because of the climate metaphor she uses, "I am very happy to know that he is there, because you know that the weather in Spain is very unfavorable for him, particularly now that the winter is harsh." My father never had any documentation or intentions of going to Spain at that time. My mother had quickly adapted to the literature of the times by disguising information so that the Cuban censors would not get the gist of what was passing before their eyes. After all, since my mother was writing in summer, why should she be so concerned about the cold climate "now" in Spain?

Although she did not mention Poppy in this particular letter, she kept me notified of Poppy's situation through the mail. On one occasion, a little later after the date of this letter, she reported on the following scene. There was a possibility of expediting the exit from Cuba of my mother and Abuela Amparo with Aunt Ofelia and her husband Ramón Rencurrell. The latter visited my mother in Altahabana and they sat in some of the remaining chairs in the house. Poppy was on the floor, also sitting down. Rencurrell advised my mother that they had found a person, a connection, who would facilitate their documentation to leave Cuba, even before the end of 1961, but Poppy could not go with them. My mother later on explained that Poppy was very attentive and quiet while this conversation was going on in front of him. The issue revolved around the fact that "the connection" that Rencurrell had found would facilitate the trip via KLM Airlines and that company's policy did not allow for dogs to travel with them. Up to that time, my mother had been planning to depart via Pan American Airways, whose policies did allow dogs to travel, provided they had their papers and vaccinations in order. My mother did not even consider Rencurrell's offer. She decided that if she had to stay in Cuba because of Poppy, she would do so. Rencurrell left the house somewhat dispirited because my mother would not change her mind. This issue of being firm on the decision to take Poppy with her out of the country at the time of her departure came through clearly in a letter of November 10:

... "I will tell you about Poppy that he is doing well, strong, playful and very mischievous...you will see him soon..."

My peers in Havana's situation had turned even more difficult from the perspective of documentation. Pella wrote in September that new regulations had been announced through which any visa, *vigencia,* or affidavits that were dated more than six months prior were going to be declared invalid and the bearer would have to procure new ones all over again. It is not difficult to arrive at the conclusion that, in some ways, my peers were not wanted in Cuba, but other regulations and requirements were set up to harass them if they wished to travel off the island. For example, look at what Lorenzo wrote:

> *Havana*
> *October 3, 1961*
>
> *I also want to tell you that I got my visa waiver through a friend of ours who is in Miami. Now I have to wait, because all my papers including the affidavit, the airline ticket, vaccination certificates, and everything else are at the police station ... I have to wait for them to notify me when I am cleared to depart. When I am notified it will be a telegram that will advise me to go to the Pan American Airways offices, there I will be told the day that I will depart, which should be within 7 days. If I do not depart within that week I lose all rights. I hope that my God will get me out of this communist paradise.*
>
> *Lorenzo*

We must remember that the revolutionary authorities were actively searching for Lorenzo in the aftermath of the Bay of Pigs Invasion "on several charges." Although he was never imprisoned, at that time, his documentation for leaving Cuba was being reviewed at "the police station." Therefore, it is logical to conclude that if Lorenzo was really wanted by the authorities to question him or send him to prison, they were just delaying his departure, kind of torturing him psychologically, but not doing anything concrete and definite to capture him. Were the revolutionary authorities signaling to my peers to stay on the island or in some fashion telling them that they were not welcome? I favor the view that the authorities were letting Lorenzo abandon the island! It is my opinion, that in most cases, we left from Cuba with the knowledge of both the Cuban revolutionary government, and obviously the United States government. Otherwise, we would not have been able to enter this country and benefit from Operation Pedro Pan, the Unaccompanied Cuban Children Program, and then partake of federal loans in order to continue our education later.

Thankfully, by the month of November, both Lorenzo and Juan González were out of Cuba and in Miami in Camp Matecumbe. This is what Juan wrote back then:

Miami
November 13, 1961

My dear friend Tony:

I'm sure that you cannot imagine the joy that I felt upon receiving your letter; I almost cried. I'm not in the Kendall House but at Camp Matecumbe, about five miles from Kendall. The boys who are here are 14 years old and older. Lorenzo is here with me and he has also written to you. In this camp we can only take leave on the weekends...

The Catholic Welfare Bureau is supporting us here. We are getting high school classes with the Marist Brothers who are here: Maximiliano, Luis, Mauro, and Alberto. But since the classes are in Spanish we are not learning English, which is so necessary.

Our stay here is provisional because we are expected to be placed elsewhere in the United States. Lately some of us are being sent to Montana near Canada. Imagine the cold weather!
Tony, my plans are the plans that the Catholic Welfare has for me. Sometimes they place us in good places and other times in not so good places, depending on luck. Tony, you know more about this country than I do, therefore you can give me some advice on what to do. Should I wait for my placement or leave the institution and study and work on my own, as I think you are doing. I wait for

Entrance to Camp Matecumbe.
Photo courtesy of University of Miami Cuban Heritage Collection

your response.

My parents thankfully are doing well as far as can be expected. I
talked on the phone with them last week. Rest assured that I will
visit your father and I will give him the encouragement that you
desire. If you have time tell me more of your life.
...a warm hug your friend,

Juan
And may God have mercy on all Cubans.

Before I wrote to Juan, I had received a letter from my father notifying me that Juan was in Miami at the Kendall House, hence my confusion which was clarified by Juan himself. The routine at Matecumbe Camp involved having classes on the grounds. That was truly a place of transition. The newcomers were handed a set of regulations when they first arrived, which appeared somewhat cold and detached from the actual human drama that was being distilled in the camp. To my knowledge, we never had anything like that at Camp St. John, but then ours was not a "temporary" residence. Obviously, Juan was appropriately concerned about the fact that the classes were being offered in Spanish, not in English.

He was not entirely alone because some of our peers from the Marist School near the Plaza Cívica were also there, including Lorenzo and Fernando Subirats. The latter was photographed in the picture with the tractor donated to the Agrarian Reform that appeared in the 1959-1960 yearbook. Juan asked me for advice about whether it would be wise of him to leave the services of the Catholic Welfare Bureau and join me in New Jersey. At the time, I was helping my dad so that he could study for the examination that would eventually allow him to work and begin some sort of post-graduate training in this country. That was a most important first step for him. In 1961, some states like Texas only required a passing grade on the examination administered by the Educational Council for Foreign Medical Graduates in order to apply for a license and then to take and pass a state test to practice medicine in the state. Considering the fact that I was not living anymore in the attic of my relative's home, but in a rooming house where I rented an eight-by-eight foot room, I advised Juan to stay in the Unaccompanied Cuban Children Program. I was working two jobs, my electronics company full-time job and a part time in the evenings as a stock clerk at the Good Deal Supermarket on Main Street.

In many ways, 1961 had been an exceptional year. However, Thanksgiving came on the fourth Thursday of November in 1961. María Ofelia and her sister Silvia agreed to cook the traditional turkey dinner for the Thanksgiving holiday. Since I did not know how to cook, except for a couple of things that came in a box and you mixed them with water or milk and put them in the oven, I agreed to buy the turkey and take it to Emilito's apartment. That was my first Thanksgiving. It was a new holiday for us Cubans. I had read about it in our English class textbook in the third year of the Cuban *bachillerato,* so we had an idea of what was being celebrated and commemorated. It was a time for sharing and giving thanks for having survived a difficult year the year before. However, despite the feeling of closeness and warmth provided by Emilito's family and the well-cooked and abundant food served, it was a sad Thanksgiving for me. It was sad because I was away from my father and my mother. What could I share with them? Only our hopes and prayers. My father was in Miami, he was not at the table where I sat. My mother kept encountering obstacles for her departure and the uncertainty of ever reuniting with them became evident that Thursday afternoon. After all, it was too early for a real Thanksgiving because the years of peril were not over, yet, for us. In fact, at that point, we still did not consider ourselves to be new immigrants. We were still thinking of a brief and victorious exile. Eventually, however, in a matter of a few months, the Thanksgiving holiday was to seem a happier one, and one that we have adopted as our own.

Several months prior, Abuela Amparo had noted in one of her letters that she had gone to Manolo's house in Altahabana for the birthday of his son Manolito. At the end of October 1961, my dad reported in a letter to me in New Jersey that Manolito and Ondinita, both of Manolo's children, were in Miami. They came out of Cuba under the Operation Pedro Pan like more than 14,000 other children had, but did not go into the Unaccompanied Cuban Children Program like more than 8,000 of us did. Manolito and Ondinita went to stay with some very close friends of Manolo and his wife, Ondina.

At that point, all of the youth in my immediate parental family had flown off the island. Manolo's children had a hard time adjusting. Manolito felt very homesick and Ondinita, his older sister, played the role of the tough one when people were looking. However, at night, she was unable to sleep easily, and quietly placed her head underneath the pillow and cried herself to sleep. At one point, Aunt Carmen offered to take them both for the weekend so that they did not feel bored or lonesome. Later on, Manolito developed daily high fevers and was diagnosed with a serious throat infection. He was probably sicker than I had been when I was admitted to St. Vincent's Hospital. However, Manolito did not have an asthma attack. My father wrote to me, to let me know that he had been in to see Manolito on account of this illness. Whatever was prescribed for him did not abate the throat infection. In a matter of days, Manolo back in Havana had arranged for his children to return to Cuba. Ondinita remembers the trip back home. It was the two of them and maybe two other people on the entire commercial airplane. In fact, because there were not many travelers going back into Havana at that time, there was talk in the press about cancelling altogether commercial flights from Miami to Havana. However, thankfully, that did not occur at the time.

Manolito was only five years old at the time and does remember arriving in the United States and going to his parent's friends place to live near the Miami International Airport. He was impressed with the "very large" military airplanes that flew just over the house where they lived. Shortly after he was returned to Havana, he was treated by Dr. Sergio Fuentes, an ear, nose, and throat specialist close to our family, who took his tonsils out successfully.

With the advent of Christmas, there were mixed feelings about the situation in Cuba and the prospects for the downfall of what had already been termed Castroism. My father had enlisted in an organization formed by former military people that presumably was getting ready to invade the island again. He confided in his letters to me that he did not see anything concrete that made him feel optimistic, however. At that time, there was also a campaign in the United States to recruit young Cubans into the American armed forces, mostly the Navy, the Marine Corps, and the Army. Most of these Cubans thought that they were joining the American military in order to prepare and execute an invasion that would topple Castro and communism in Cuba. In due time, most of those recruits who did not have a military vocation would be discharged from the armed forces sometime during the next year.

Juan wrote for Christmas from Camp Matecumbe. It was a somber holiday, but the message that Brother Maximiliano gave all children and youngsters there was, in my opinion, historical. This is what he wrote:

Christmas Message to all friends at Kendall and Matecumbe:

When approaching the significant days of Christmas, I do not want any of you to be without receiving from this house a cordial greeting wishing you the best blessings for the New Year.

The fact we find ourselves in exile, away from our families and de-

Brother Maximiliano, FMS, nearly two years earlier at the time when the Marist School at La Víbora donated a tractor to the Agrarian Reform. Marist School Yearbook, 1959

prived of so many things should be no reason not to have a truly Christian Christmas. Moreover, these can be the most Christian of all.

In the cave of Bethlehem where the first and authentic Christmas took place many things were lacking, even the most essential, but the main thing was there: Christ was there.

The Communist regime that oppresses Cuba could take many things from us but there is something that it has not been able to separate from us: Christ. With St. Paul we can also say: "Who will be able to separate me from the love of Christ?" (Romans 5:35) Thus, united in Christ who is the center of Christmas, with Mary and Joseph who were the first to celebrate them we can enjoy a Christian Christmas with joy in our soul even though tears will threaten to pour from our eyes because of memories of people and things we left behind.

However, we should be confident that as that child and that family were guided by the Divine Providence, we ourselves will be led to that which will be best for us. As the child in the arms of Mary, let us allow ourselves to be guided by his loving Providence.

Do not forget to give the Christmas gift of our prayers to our brothers who will only be able to have Christmas in the intimate corner of their souls this Christmas behind bars for the sake of our God and our Cuba.

The Midnight Mass, God willing, we will have in our chapel of Kendall...and we will offer it for all those who in the not too distant past have been through these buildings, fields and classrooms who are the men and women of tomorrow who will have in their hands the destiny of a Christian Cuba."

Brother Maximiliano may not have known it, but sometime in December 1961, Christmas was abolished from the Cuban calendar. It was not a religious holiday, a national holiday, or any kind of special day anymore. It was sacrificed for another

Temporary chapel at Camp Matecumbe in 1961. Photograph courtesy of
Brother Rafael Martin, FMS

revolutionary government campaign, the campaign to produce more sugar during the Cuban *zafra*, the sugar harvest.

Despite the prayers, the rhetoric, and the best wishes of all the exiles, including all the children and youngsters supported by the Unaccompanied Cuban Children Program, it was an expectant Christmas. It was, in my opinion, as if we were living in our own lives such a historical moment that we were still in Advent preparing to receive Christmas with its spirit of freedom and love. However, it was difficult to translate the spiritual feelings to the human level on which we lived. The uncertainty, separation, and loneliness that had become part of our lives all conspired to make us feel less than joyful. Most of us did find in prayer and in the Holy Mass, which was still celebrated in Latin, something in common with our own experience and customs. In fact, the Holy Mass was the only thing that had not changed: A reminder of the love of Christ.

CHAPTER 21
MY GUARDIAN ANGELS

*"Veo lo que piensas sobre tí pero en el exilio no es tu edad es que uno sin darse
cuenta se va haciendo hombre y deja de ser muchacho."*
Tu Padre Antonio
(I see what you think about yourself but it is not your age.
Exile inadvertently turns you into a man who is no longer a boy.)

The Christmas prayers from all exiles expressed, in one way or another, their feelings of separation and their hopes for reunification, a return to Cuba, and an end
to the strife from which the entire nation was suffering. On December 23, 1961,
my father wrote from Miami:

" *Ya tu ves la situación, mi pequeño hogar compuesto solamente de 3 personas
andamos dispersados; tu ahí en New Jersey, mi pobre María Luisa sola en Cuba y yo
aquí en Miami viviendo de la caridad. Tu comprendes que asi no puede haber felici-
dad para mí...*" (Now you can see my situation; my small home, made up of only
3 persons, all of them dispersed: you up there in New Jersey, my poor María Luisa
alone in Cuba and me, here in Miami living on charity. You understand that because
of this, there can be no happiness for me...")

Then he went on to relate how the day before he wrote this letter to me, Dr.
Díaz Rousellot, one of the physicians employed in the Cuban Refugee Center, who
had been in the contingent of Brigade 2506, but had not gotten to land on Cuban
soil, told my farther that "*...de un momento a otro van a llamar a servicio y el em-
barcamiento va a ser en Cayo Hueso.*" That is, "...any moment now there will be a
call to arms and the embarkation point will be in Key West."

Obviously, my dad was obsessed with the idea of liberating Cuba. Notice what
he wrote just before December:

Miami
November 30, 1961

My dear son:

....thank God I can tell you that I feel well because I am with my friends. Colonel Martín Elena and Major Leon are awaiting a call into service. We are expecting the arrival of Dr. Teobaldo Cuervo any moment, but he is still being held in an embassy in Havana without safe conduct off of the island....

Antonio

The future did appear to be ambivalent, despite his most sincere feelings about a return to his homeland. And, despite already being enrolled in the medical review course for Cuban refugee doctors at the University of Miami School of Medicine, his extracurricular activities may have been considered to an outside observer as distracting. In fact, they were maintaining his spirits high with hopes of physically conquering the homeland. At the end, although he did not appreciate it then, his dreams and those of the vast majority of exiles were quickly slipping out of probability in the complex scenario of the Cold War.

The story of how Dr. Teobaldo Cuervo and his family faired during the revolution is worthwhile remembering. In the immediate aftermath of the failed Bay of Pigs Invasion, Dr. Teobaldo Cuervo was notified to report to the Military Hospital. Cuervo had studied medicine in Havana and also in Paris, where he sought refuge during the 1933 revolution that brought down the Machado dictatorship. The University of Havana School of Medicine was closed because of that social and political turmoil. Some families sent their children to continue studying medicine abroad. Dr. Cuervo had friends and was very well respected at the Military Hospital. He was advised to stay away from the hospital because the State Security wanted to apprehend him. He took off from their family home in Altahabana with his two older children in a bus to Guanabo, a beach town to the East of Havana. Herminio, the younger of the two sons of Dr. Cuervo, told me the story of how they disguised themselves as *campesinos* with straw hats and made the trip to Guanabo in a crowded bus. Interestingly, it was also in Guanabo that Brother Teodoro, our fourth year of *bachillerato* lead teacher, sought refuge when the Marist School near the Plaza Cívica was occupied by the revolutionary militia.

The Cuervos could not make any arrangements in Guanabo to leave the island by sea. They decided to come back to the capital and try to get political asylum in an embassy. The older Cuervo was fortunate that he had a physician friend who personally treated the Italian ambassador in Havana. Therefore, the connection was made and Dr. Cuervo entered the Italian Embassy to seek political asylum. There was a problem, however; the Italian government did not recognize political asylum seekers. Therefore, Dr. Cuervo spent a few days hiding in the Italian Embassy and then in the West German Embassy through the courtesy of the German ambassador who knew his Italian counterpart. Eventually, they decided that they could get Dr. Cuervo into the Panamanian Embassy, where political asylum seekers were welcome. Since the Cuban revolutionaries would not give Cuervo safe conduct off the island, Cuervo sent a message to a Mexican friend he had met while studying in Paris more than twenty years before. It was eventually through that fortunate friendship that Dr. Cuervo got his safe conduct out of Cuba through the Mexican Embassy. From Mexico City he went to Panama, where he had received asylum. On January 28, 1962 he arrived in Miami.

Meanwhile, Teobaldo, the older son of Dr. Cuervo, who at that time was in the *guardia marina* studying seamanship at the Cuban Naval Academy in Mariel, got on a fishing boat with a friend of their family and sailed away from La Coloma on the southwestern coast of Cuba. They were escaping communism by sea to come to the United States. They entered the Yucatan Straits and went into the Gulf of Mexico, arriving at the post of Mobile, Alabama. They were able to refresh themselves there and replenish their supplies before sailing down near the Florida Peninsula's west coast to Key West, where they asked for and obtained political asylum.

Hemrinio managed to get a visa waiver and was placed on a Pan American flight to Miami after paying the $25 ticket price with a money order. He arrived in July 1961.

Back in Havana, Mrs. Cuervo was detained by the G-2 State Security for interrogation about the affairs of her "missing" husband, but then released. She managed to find someone to assist her in her desperation to leave the island. She did it in the most unlikely manner.

It will be remembered that Dr. Cuervo was apprehended in 1957 in the aftermath of the September 5 revolt, through which a military and civilian opposition group was attempting to down the Batista regime. While in prison in Circular 4 at the Presidio Modelo on the Isle of Pines, presently Isle of Youth, Dr. Cuervo befriended José Ramón Fernández, who had been imprisoned with the Barquín conspiracy in April 1956. Fernández became a fervent revolutionary and communist after January 1959. He occupied a number of leadership positions in the revolutionary government and was later vice president of the regime. It was through him that Mrs. Cuervo and her younger daughter were able to leave Cuba for the United States in December 1961.

My dad was certainly not alone in thinking about the prompt liberation of Cuba. On December 12, 1961, Lorenzo wrote from Camp Matecumbe:

JMJ Miami
December 7, 1961

Dear friend:

I think...you are right in thinking that the problem of Cuba must be solved by both the OAS and the Foreign Legion. I do not know if you knew that the Foreign Legion is ready to ship in less than two months up to 100,000 men between Cubans, Americans and Latin Americans that are already registered in the liberation army. So that I think this issue will be solved even if there is a delay.

Lorenzo

The so-called Liberation Army was not some sort of delusion of Lorenzo's. My father had already written to me that he had registered with it in Miami.

The Organization of American States (OAS) was officially formed in 1948 when the Ninth International Conference of American States was held in Bogota, Colombia. The conference was led by the American Secretary of State George Marshall, who was well known on account of the "The Marshall Plan," through which post-World War II Europe was revived from the devastation of Nazi expansionism. The original twenty-one OAS member states, among which was the Republic of Cuba, pledged to fight communism in the Western Hemisphere. The OAS did not get to work, however, until 1951 in defending the principles agreed upon in Bogota, including the American Declaration of the Rights and Duties of Man.

Fast forward to the situation in Cuba responsible for the clandestine exodus of more than 14,000 children. The OAS had called a meeting for January 1962 of all the foreign ministers of the Western Hemisphere republics to discuss the issue of communist infiltration in the region. When the ministers met in Punta del Este, Uruguay, on January 31, 1962, they voted to expel Cuba out of the OAS on account of these points:

1. That adherence by any member of the Organization of American States to Marxism-Leninism is incompatible with the inter-American system and the alignment of such a government with the communist bloc breaks the unity and solidarity of the continents.

2. That the present Government of Cuba, which has officially identified itself as a Marxist-Leninist government, was incompatible with the principles and objectives of the inter-American system.

3. That this incompatibility excluded the present Government of Cuba from participation in the inter-American system.(1)

The prayer of Cubans, in general, was not that Castro's regime should be alienated from the inter-American system. We felt that Castro's regime had to be completely blockaded or physically overthrown. Essentially, although our Cuban exile leaders did not see it that way back then, the OAS agreement provided room for Castro's regime to operate in Cuba and legitimately oppress and repress Cubans for an undetermined length of time.

The OAS meeting in South America was not the only assembly gathered at the time with regard to the Cuban situation. This is what Juan wrote at the end of January:

Miami
January 29, 1962

Dear Tony:

At last I saw your father in a fantastic Pontifical Mass offered at the Miami Stadium with the attendance of thousands of Cubans, with hundreds of them taking communion. Monsignor Boza Masvidal was there and he spoke well as he always does ...

Juan

The Pontifical Mass was organized by Bishop Coleman Carroll. A formal invitation was published in the newspapers, whereby all Latin Americans were invited. There was a tendency at that time to minimize the obvious, that Cubans were arriving by the thousands and were the vast majority of Latin-Americans in the city.

The published invitation also noted that the sermon would be given by Monsignor Eduardo Boza Masvidal under the title of Auxiliary Bishop of Havana. The local authorities and newspapers of the time agreed that more than 30,000 Cubans gathered for the religious event. A statue of the Virgin of Charity, patroness of Cuba, smuggled out of Guanabo in September 1961, was also on display. Bishop Boza reminded all present that the Cuban Virgin, the *Vírgen del Cobre,* accompanied Cubans in their struggles for independence in 1868 and 1895. She was still there to accompany all of them! Four processions were organized, in which torches were carried. If you looked at the stadium from above, you would see that the lights from the torches came from all four cardinal points and united in the center where the Holy Pontifical Mass was celebrated by the Bishop of Miami. The symbolism was clear, as Monsignor Boza explained in his sermon. All the Americas were to be imbued with the light, symbol of the Holy Spirit, and march themselves into the center of history, Christ. Bishop Boza called for unity in action for all Cubans, but also from all the Americas in the fight against communism. At one point in time in his sermon, this is what he said:

> "In our own country we know how costly it has been and how many sacrifices have been made through the centuries to keep freedom. All of us know that our elders shed their blood in the struggle for freedom and their corpses were wrapped with our national flag many times. This idea of freedom, which is deeply rooted in the Americas, must unite us now in its defense. Today Cuba fights in defense of freedom. All her liberties have been taken away but she will now fight to redeem freedom from those who have stolen it from her…The triple ideal of faith, freedom and social justice should not burn as 21 flames in the western hemisphere, but as a single flame uniting all the Americas."

But then he pointed out:

> "We must forget hatred and personal interests and have one common ideal, disregarding the fact that each one of us may go into great sacrifice. Forgetting small resentments, petty interests and putting aside our comfort, our earthly possessions, if required, for the common benefit and welfare of our fellow men. For the good of all, we must forget small details, being generous as Christ Himself was generous for all men, for peace, and for the common ideal. Fire is the symbol of love and the love of Christ must unite all of us."(2)

The prayer of the Bishop of Havana, the man who, after being incarcerated by the communist revolutionary authorities, when he reached the veranda of the steamship *Covadonga* at the time when he was being forcefully exiled from Havana, turned around to the Cuban State Security personnel and militia who had outraged him and he blessed them in the name of the Father, the Son, and the Holy Spirit, was not enough for the ministers of the American States to take action. Monsignor Boza Masvidal died in exile. His life, perhaps, reassuring all that the message of Christ would prevail: "My Kingdom is not of this world." (John 18:36) Monsignor Boza Masvidal was one of the Cuban bishops who attended the Second Vatican Council with Monsignor Evelio Díaz Cía and Monsignor Alfredo Llaguno Canals. At the time of his death on March 16, 2003, he was still considered a righteous Cuban worthy of being elevated to sainthood by the Catholic Church.

By January 1962, my father was counting the days since the moment my mother had presented her "papers" at the local police station serving Altahabana. He reminded me in his letter: "Today it has been 57 days since your mother presented her papers..." By day 70, according to popular wisdom, the revolutionary officials usually allowed for the petitioner to leave the country.

I had begun on my own to attend the daily mass at a Franciscan parish in Passaic, New Jersey, where I was the only man there aside from the priest among a small group of older Italian women who prayed in Italian. At that point, unexpectedly, in a letter from my cousin Evelio, who at the time did not have serious intentions of leaving Cuba, I learned an ancient story about a boy who was about to be born, and one day said to God: "They tell me that you are sending me to Earth tomorrow. But I am so small and helpless as I am, how can I live?"

"Among all the angels I chose one for you that is intended to look after you," God answered him.

"But tell me, here in heaven I sing and smile and that's our joy," the boy said.

"Your angel will sing to you and you will smile all day and you will feel her love and you will be happy," God answered.

"But how am I to understand when people talk to me if I do not know the language that men speak?" the boy asked.

"Your angel will tell you the sweetest and most tender words you can hear and with love and patience will teach you to speak," God answered.

"What am I to do when I want to talk to you?" the boy asked.

"Your angel will place your hands together and will teach you to pray," God answered.

"I've heard that on earth there are bad people, who will defend me?" the boy asked God.

"Your angel will defend you even at the cost of its own life," God answered. "Your angel will always talk about me and will teach you the way to come back to my presence, but I'll always be by your side," God added.

"My God, it's my time to go, tell me the name of my angel, how should I call my angel?" the boy pleaded.

To which God replied, "The name does not matter, you just call for 'Mama.'"

Then the call came, like the answers to all of our prayers. On February 10, 1962, my mother arrived at the Miami International Airport with Poppy. My father was there to receive them. All I know is their description of the encounter—tight embraces, kisses, all three of them united in one very tight union. Sometime during the prolonged embrace, sprinkled with tears of joy and licks (*lenguazos*) from Poppy, either Mom or Dad exclaimed, *"Al fin!"*...finally! Then, as they began to walk out of the terminal, my dad noticed that Poppy had torn his shirt when he clung to his chest. Poppy had literally ripped his shirt in the excitement of the moment.

My father was living in the same apartment just on the side of Corpus Christie Church where Uncle Emilio and Aunt Carmen had settled temporarily. The owner of the property did not allow pets. Well, at least he allowed Cubans. In some areas of Miami at the time, there were signs stating: NO PETS, DOGS, OR CUBANS. Therefore, Poppy became separated temporarily from my mother and father and was sent to Florida City where the Unaccompanied Cuban Children Program had set up camp in an abandoned apartment complex. Poppy may have been the only Cuban dog to have shared with more than 8,000 Cuban children the experience of being away from home. The place in Florida City was, at least in part, run by the *Religiosas Filipenses*, the nuns who used to direct the *Colegio Nuestra Señora de Lourdes* (Our Lady of Lourdes) in La Víbora. Muñeca had recommended Uncle Ramón and his wife, Blanquita, as house parents in that facility. Therefore, Poppy was taken to Florida City and lived with a small foster family of girls, among who was Clarita, the younger daughter of our friend Joaquin from Fontanar in Havana. Poppy was loved and cherished at the refugee community in Florida City and many of the girls who lived there during that time still remember him.

Back at Camp St. John, they were getting ready to implement the dispersion of all "occupants." In fact, as Tom Aglio described in his memoir distributed on the 50th Anniversary of the Operation Pedro Pan, he had been entrusted with this goal since he first arrived at the camp in the summer of 1961. I think it is better if I just quote Tom Aglio, because this was a very sensitive time and process. This is how he described that difficult time:

Apartments where house parents took care of unaccompanied Cuban refugee children at Florida City. Poppy lived there for approximately four months with refugee girls. Photograph courtesy of the University of Miami Cuban Heritage Collection

"The clock ticked. Time passed. The process had begun. The boys knew little of what was in store for them. And I knew way too much. I had to prepare them for an event that I could not yet share with them. It was as though I was working undercover. It was all for the best, but the period of transition would be difficult, full of unanticipated developments, and fraught with obstacles to easy fulfillment. Much would happen when they would bid each other farewell and depart these premises. It was clear to me that I would not be a spectator in the bleachers watching them play the drama of their life. I would be on the field with them, shoulder to shoulder pushing to victory... There were countless mischievous incidents and events during those months. I imagine that these boys, now grown adults take delight in describing them. They can report on 'stealing the kitchen,' contraband cigarettes, pranks with snakes, mysterious disappearances of deodorants, 'escapes' from the grounds, late for the bus, homework chicanery, pool infractions, and much more. Mostly, I appeared to ignore these issues..."(3)

However, Brother Pedro wrote from Miami:

Miami
January 1, 1962

For several days I got to see and talk to the colony of El Cerro at Matecumbre: Lorenzo, Wong, Juan and also Fernando Subirats. The camp is a little better than before. They have 6 class periods with the Brothers including Brother Maximiliano, director of the High School in La Víbora. Anyway, that does not work as well as might be desired, since they only allow us to organize the issue of the classes. Everything else is done by the employees of Catholic Welfare. Now you know that there are all kinds of people there. There are some from the best schools in Cuba but others are not, and such mixtures are not always good for everyone. Imagine, that from Jacksonville where you were...they have returned seven accompanied by the police because it seems that they did some serious

Marist Brother conducting class in a camp in the Miami area. Photo-graph courtesy of the University of Miami Cuban Heritage Collection

Since the camps were semi-clandestine, there were no reports in the press or anywhere else, including in the short memoire provided by Aglio of camp life in those days that, in fact, some of the "occupants" in Camp St. John had been expelled from the premises and sent escorted by police to Miami.

Going back to Aglio's testimony, he wrote:

"The dreaded day arrived. It was time for me to inform the boys that they would be leaving each other soon to go to foster families throughout Central Florida. Their bond would be broken. There would no longer be safety in numbers. Their interdependence was over. Their crush for survival was destroyed. It was like a radio or TV announcer saying: 'We interrupt this program to bring you a special news bulletin.' I prayed that my efforts for preparation for this day had worked and that they would trust me to do what was good for them. The silence in the room gave way to murmurings and then to animated conversation. Questions abounded. I answered in English and they understood. The language barrier was diminishing. Immediately, another of my responses in Latin, as the altar server, popped into my head: *'Spera in Depo, quoniam adhuc confitebor illi, salutare vultus mei, et Deus meu.'* (Trust in God, I will still give praise to him, my savior and my God.) My performance at this point was crucial. It was essential to do this properly, with my heart and with my head. I had to do it right for their sakes."(4)

Many of the Cuban youngsters in the camp at that time felt that the plan to go on to foster homes as proposed was the best for them. Others did not. At the end, Juan's impression was the one that prevailed, not only in Matecumbe, but also in Camp St. John. "My plans are the plans that the Catholic Charities have for me," Juan said.

In a matter of days, the up-to-that-point secretive plan to close Camp St. John became widely known throughout the Diocese of St. Augustine. The Florida Catholic newspaper and all parishes published announcements asking for families

Last formal photograph of the Pedro Pans at Camp St. John in 1962.
Standing to the right of the photo is Mr. Thomas J. Aglio and to the left is Fr. Lara.
Photograph courtesy of Lorenzo Lorenzo

who would be willing to accept as foster children one or two of the sixty or so Cuban adolescents who were at the time in Camp St. John. School at Bishop Kenny ended and arrangements were made to send each Cuban refugee to his foster home. Aglio described them as "noticeably quiet…. The mood in the camp was somber." Then the night before their departure from the camp, Aglio rang the bell for the last time to assemble them in the hall. He did not feel like a stranger anymore among them. He felt like one of them. This is some of what he said: "I love you. I thank you for what you have taught me. I wish you well in the future. *Te amo, Vaya con Dios.*"

The Cuban boys began to clap their hands, two claps followed by four in rapid succession while they shouted, "ALYO, ALYO…"

And, this is what Aglio felt and observed:

"I cried and some of the boys cried. The catharsis was remarkable. We had completed our journey together. Again, I pondered: What will become of them?"(5)

Back in Miami, my father went on with his schooling at the University of Miami School of Medicine, took the ECMG examination on March 28, 1962, and in late May, received his passing grade and diploma. He tried to get a job in the Miami area, but there was intense competition and his English was still not very fluent for taking medical histories.

Meanwhile, I had come down from New Jersey on a Greyhound bus to join my parents in late May 1961. My Mom kept telling me that I had changed. She literally did not leave me alone for days; she embraced me all the time. Even at night, she would come to my cot and lie down with and embrace me as if I were going to disappear again.

A few days after arriving in Miami, and back at the *Cuban Barracón* just north of the Corpus Christie Church, I began going around to various offices in northwest Miami, applying for a job. I had prepared a short resume with the kind of work I had done at the electronics company in New Jersey. I went from office to office and nothing was available. Then, a secretary at one of the places where I had applied suggested that I apply at the Sabal Palm Drugstore a couple of blocks away, because she thought they needed help. I immediately went up to the drugstore, met the manager and he gave me a job. I had no time to dream of being a pharmacy tech or anything too glorious. I knew that they were looking for a dishwasher. I took off my coat and started work immediately.

Later on that night, I walked back to the *Cuban Barracón*. Everyone was very impressed that I had a job. The issue came up with all the family gathered there that since Ramon Rencurrell had a wife and child, he should be the one to get that job. Obviously, he had more responsibility! So the next day, I showed up with Ramón Rencurrell at the Sabal Palm Drugstore and explained to the manager that my uncle could do the job and he needed it more than I did. The manager, an older American man did not care who did the job as long as the job was done. So, I walked back home to the *Cuban Barracón* and Ramón Rencurrell stayed at work washing dishes. It was an afternoon shift that ended around 10:00 in the evening. Sometime at about 7:00 we got a call from Sabal Palm Drugstore. It was Ramón Rencurrell, who was calling because he had gotten nauseated and became ill, so he was asking to be picked up by Uncle Emilio, who had a car. We went up to the drugstore, picked up Ramón Rencurrell who looked pale and sad. The next day, we decided that since Ramón Rencurrell could not do the job, perhaps, my cousin Ramoncito could. So we walked over there, all three of us—Ramón Rencurrell, Ramoncito, and I. I immediately approached the American manager and explained that my uncle got sick and that since he needed someone to do the job, I had brought my cousin to take the position. The manager did not accept my proposal. He got a little angry and exclaimed in so many words something like this: "No. Do you think this is a baseball game where you change the pitcher every night? No. Get out of here!"

Eventually, my father got a contract to work at the Euclid Glenville Hospital, presently the Euclid General Hospital part of the Cleveland Clinic Health System in Euclid, Ohio. We departed to Ohio in the beginning of July. We four—my father, mother, Poppy and I—all traveled together through the Cuban Refugee Center resettlement program. In fact, we flew out of Miami on the same Eastern Airlines flight that stopped at Tampa, Jacksonville, and Washington, DC on its way to New York. We got off in Washington and took another *lechero* flight to Cleveland on Northwest Airlines.

Since February 1962, I had received two formal admissions letters from two colleges to enter in September 1962—La Salle College in Philadelphia and the Norfolk College of William and Mary. The first one was a miracle through my persistence and I was so impressed that I had even paid from New Jersey the $50 deposit for my tuition. The second I received through the strong recommendation of my cousin Manuel A. Benero Jr., whom we and his parents called Pucho, and one of the children of Manolo and Pilar from Saranac Lake, New York. Pucho was an officer in the U.S. Navy and, at the time, was stationed in Norfolk. Therefore, I had two choices for college, very likely an above average situation for a 17 year old in the United States at that time.

However, in view of the fact that my father's "small home" had been dispersed for so long, I stayed in the Cleveland area. How did I get to stay in the Cleveland area? This is how it happened. Shortly after arriving in Cleveland, I had gotten a job at the hospital where my dad worked. I worked in the maintenance department. In a matter of weeks, I had become very important because I knew how to fix the old wheelchairs that had backs and seats made out of wicker. How come I knew how to do that? Since my grandmother Amparo had several wicker furnishings, a man used to come to the house on San Francisco Street, Number 320, and fix them periodically. I learned how to fix them the Chinese way. Yes, legend has it that the Chinese method of teaching medicine many years ago was for the apprentices to just observe what their teachers were doing for a prolonged period of time. Then, after such attentive observation, they were supposed to perform examinations on patients and surgeries. Well, that must have been the way I learned how to fix the broken and torn wicker. In short, my wicker "experience" became most useful in my first job in Cleveland.

The story went around the hospital that I was leaving for college. The maintenance department consisted of three people—an older man who was our head and another young man who was not going to college. At the time, the other fellow was drafted and sent to Vietnam. I had my two college admission letters, but to attend college, I had to leave my family and the hospital behind. My dad must have taken this up with the chief of staff, and before I knew it, Dr. Vincent La Maida, the chief of staff at the time, was taking me and my documentation to meet Father Joseph A. Meunzer, SJ at John Carroll University. Dr. La Maida had graduated from John Carroll years before. I had already taken the SAT and gotten below average in verbal and mathematics, but an outstanding score of 790 in the Spanish Achievement test.

Father Meunzer listened to the story, which I am sure had been explained to him beforehand; otherwise, he would not have agreed to meet me. He immediately looked favorably on my entrance to the school. In a matter of one week, I received an admission's letter to John Carroll University. I qualified to receive the Cuban loan, which paid for my tuition, fees, and books. The Cuban loan was another corollary of American policy at the time to assist Cuban students who were seeking asylum in the United States. It provided financial assistance to study in any accredited college or university, covering up to $2,000 yearly in tuition and books for undergraduate studies and up to $5,000 yearly for graduate and professional schools.

In the summer of 1963, we came down to Miami to visit Abuela Amparo, who had finally gotten out of Cuba, and the family had moved because the owner of the apartment where they lived "could not allow another *Cuban Barracón*." Times were indeed changing. It was then that I got back in touch with Lorenzo, who had been in a foster home in Sarasota and offered him to come with me to Cleveland. When he got to Cleveland, I took him with his documentation to see Father Meunzer. He received us and also looked at Lorenzo's entrance into John Carroll with favorable eyes. Lorenzo and I attended John Carroll University together.

Months later, Lorenzo arranged with the D.R.E. headquarters in Miami to allow us to have a delegation in the Cleveland area where we could raise funds for their anti-Castro activities. We continued trying to unite young Cubans into supporting the fight against communism and preparing themselves to serve a free and democratic Cuba in the future. The year after, Lorenzo transferred to Cleveland State University and eventually became a radiology technologist. I did not hear from him again after he left John Carroll.

CHAPTER 22

IN CONCLUSION: CUBA, THE UNITED STATES, AND OURSELVES

"Freedom is never more than one generation away from extinction. We didn't pass it to our children in the bloodstream. It must be fought for, protected, and handed on to them to do the same, or one day we will spend our sunset years telling our children and our children's children what it was once like in the United States where men were free."
-Ronald Reagan

Havana in 1960 was a place of hope, but it was already clear that the country was moving quickly into the Soviet Bloc. Most Cubans, even some of the intellectuals like Raul Roa, who were known historical communists, were aware and had expressed opposition to the Soviet Union intervening and massacring the Hungarian youth in their search for freedom in 1956. The vast majority of Cubans were not communists. There were still many unmet promises from the revolution against the Batista regime, not the least of which was respect for human rights and the re-institution of the Constitution of 1940 with the rule of law and the betterment of living conditions and economic opportunities of the most backward rural communities on the island. The struggle that led to Operation Pedro Pan began to evolve in 1959, soon after the exit of Batista, who had been abandoned by the United States during the last months of his dictatorship.

There was danger in Havana. The fear of being arrested or having your children be arrested and interrogated by the G-2, the state security apparatus of the Castro regime organized and operated in the fashion of the East German Stasi, was real and constant.

Catholicism was equated, or at least officially promulgated, to be aligned with Yankee Imperialism because it was anti-communist. The horrific stories of the downfall of Machado and its aftermath and the Spanish Civil War, which had occurred only twenty years before were remembered by many of the adults who eventually sent their children out of Cuba through Operation Pedro Pan and, obviously, the Catholic clergy.

The Nature of the Operation:

Although it was a secret when it began, more than fifty years later, Operation Pedro Pan is widely known in and outside of Cuba. At this point in time, in order to simplify the discussion, allow me to use the term Operation Pedro Pan as equivalent to both the exit of the children from Cuba and the Unaccompanied Cuban Children Program since the latter was the corollary and continuation of the former, in most cases.

To the average individual, Operation Pedro Pan was a way to get out of Cuba and safeguard certain children from communist indoctrination and serfdom. The politically correct version of this history is that Operation Pedro Pan was a Catholic Church led migration supported by the United States government. But, to others, Operation Pedro Pan was a selective migration of some children and adolescents carried out by the Catholic Church with the blessings of both the United States government and the Cuban revolutionary government of Fidel Castro. These are three different views of Operation Pedro Pan. However, it should be clear that Operation Pedro Pan was not a monstrous crime carried out without concern for the wishes of the parents and the welfare and future of the children and adolescents. If this last evil centered explanation would have been the predominant reason for the Operation, it would not have been expected that some children would have been able to return to their parents in Cuba. Although the circumstances were not always ideal, the care provided for the Pedro Pans in the United States in private homes, foster homes, or institutions was the best that could have been provided, given the unusual features of this migration.

These different views of Operation Pedro Pan are correct to a certain extent, but there was much more to it than what has, up to now, been widely discussed. There is ample evidence that the operation began at the request, or at least at the insistence or inquiry, of the CIA or CIA operatives in Havana. It is well known that Mr. David Phillip Atlee specifically asked James Baker, the headmaster of the Ruston Academy in Havana, for help in getting the children of the CIA operatives and the Underground out of Cuba. It may have been assumed that since the Ruston Academy was a bilingual school they could be instrumental in providing a similar educational experience in the Miami area.

Operation Pedro Pan was both a humanitarian and a political manipulation program. It was humanitarian because it did feed, safeguard, house, and educate most of the more than 14,000 children and adolescents who came out of Cuba through its efforts and assistance. Although not all details of all institutions are known, it is felt that the Catholic Church did whatever it could to assist the Cuban children during their exodus. In fact, in the case of Camp St. John located in the Diocese of St. Augustine Operation Pedro Pan may have served to bridge in some way the differences that had separated the Bishop of Miami from the Archbishop of St. Augustine. Furthermore, Operation Pedro Pan was very well received by the American people, in general, and American Catholics in particular. If not, we would not have received more than enough donations in uniforms and schools supplies at Bishop Kenny High School and Tom Aglio would not have been extraordinarily successful in finding foster homes for more than sixty Cuban adolescents in 1962 when Camp St. John was finally closed.

Going back to the situation in Havana, there is ample evidence that the Cuban Underground was in open communication and communion with the Americans in Cuba because the struggle, as seen then, was the fight against International Communism and there were only two poles in the world of the Cold War, the American and the Soviet Communist poles. If we Cubans felt that we were being pushed into a communist way of life and we wished to object to that, we, by necessity, had to work with the Americans. There was no other alternative.

The plan to get out of harm's way children and adolescents who were related to the anti-communist forces or were themselves involved in anti-Castro activities began in secrecy and it continued to be a clandestine operation until March 1962, when the *Plain Dealer* newspaper in Cleveland, Ohio, broke the news. However, by then, the story was already circulating in Central Florida when the Florida Catholic announced that they were in need of families who would take about sixty Cuban adolescents from Camp St. John near Jacksonville. In Cuba, the story spread by word of mouth that there was a way to save the children from experiencing the struggle, although the name Operation Pedro Pan was not known. It was not known by these code words, but the *Centro Hispano Católico* story was aired on the *Voice of America* in 1961; Operation Pedro Pan was a secret in terms of the press and the media. It never appeared in any programming from the *Voice of America "Cita con Cuba"* program or transmissions from *Radio Swann* by the CIA. It spread from word of mouth and person to person, even in the increasingly controlled social order imposed by the revolution. It spread despite the fact that no one knew who would denounce who and prove to be a *chivato,* (an informer) and land you in jail.

The involvement of the Catholic Church in Operation Pedro Pan:

The Catholic Church was involved in what later became known as Operation Pedro Pan as early as November 1960, and it's operational role in this migration was sealed when Mr. Baker visited Father Bryan Walsh in Miami early in December of the same year. The operation required that there be some schooling, lodging, and a social service agency. The Catholic Church agreed to assist with all of these requirements. By that time, the public and parochial school systems in Dade County were already overwhelmed with Cuban refugee children. The Eisenhower Administration first and the Kennedy Administration a little later, provided generous funding, considering the standards of the time, for the room, board, and education of the Cuban children seeking refuge in the United States.

The official position of the Cuban revolutionary government has always been to deny any kind of agreement with the United States with regard to Operation Pedro Pan. However, it is clear from the testimonies in the letters I received during the interval from 1961-1962 and the events that occurred during that period of time that there must have been some sort of a secret understanding or agreement between Cuba and the United States even back then. Otherwise, it is rather difficult to reconcile all the testimonies—some of which have been discussed here and the published data available from this time interval related to the issue of Operation Pedro Pan. There was never a public agreement on this issue, however.

An agreement between the Castro government and the United States at the time Operation Pedro Pan occured is supported by the fact that the very cumbersome and problematic series of obstacles erected by the Castro government for any Cuban who wished to leave the island was minimized and essentially waived for children and adolescents. For example, children were more likely to obtain a *vigencia* than an adult, particularly if the adult was someone in the professions. Some of the older children, like Lorenzo, who had been harassed by the police, were still allowed to leave the island with a visa waiver.

The role of the visa waivers for Cuban children and adolescents soon after the United States closed its embassy in Havana on January 3, 1961, is another fact that supports strongly the presence of some sort of agreement between the Castro government and the United States back then. The provision of having a priest, Father Walsh, grant a visa waiver was also unprecedented in the history of the United States. There were no visa waivers for the Jewish children fleeing Nazi Germany and bogged down in France under the auspices of the OSE.(1) There were no visa waivers from the approximately sixty children who were aboard the St. Louis, the ship that spent nearly a week in Havana harbor and several more days in view of the coast of Florida at the level of Miami attempting to seek refuge for the Jewish passengers who had escaped Nazi persecution. None of those got anything similar to the visa waiver the Cuban children got.

Furthermore, the visa waiver for Cuban children and adolescents was essentially a letter signed by a Catholic priest, attesting that a certain person of Cuban nationality was granted the visa waiver. This special letter, according to Father Walsh's own words, could be copied and the copies were as valid as the originals.(2) Although the information about who did or did not have a visa waiver was also communicated to the Pan American Airlines offices in Havana; the Cuban government did not have to accept such an unusual documentation, particularly if indeed it was attempting to make it difficult for the children to leave the island.

This is how Monsignor Walsh discussed the issue of the validity of the visa waivers later in his life: "So you could take a visa waiver and you could blank out the name and birthdate and write down a new name and birthdate and so on...."

"Was it false?" asked the narrator.

"No, it wasn't false because there was no validity to the whole thing. It was simply a notification that the visa had been waived and it had been waived for all children up to 16 years of age. So it didn't have to be an original signature, the photocopy worked just as well."(2)

It is also noteworthy, that under these circumstances, the Cuban government had to be well aware that there was a systematic movement of children and adolescents out of Cuba. The movement was selectively aiding the departure from the island of individuals who were either anti-Castro activists or would become contra revolutionary activists in due time, if they remained in the island. All students from Catholic and private schools who were not inclined to participate actively in the Literacy Campaign of the revolutionary government were obviously candidates to leave the island.

In this last regard, the secrecy of the Operation, it is important to note that even our dear pet dog Poppy was aware that something was going on, through which people were leaving their homes in Havana. If not, why would Poppy be on the look out to see if the car was leaving and trying to get into the car so that he would not be left behind? Why would there be a saddened expression on his face when there was a question about leaving him behind if my mother departed through KLM and not the Pan American Airways? Furthermore, my friends from the neighborhood where I lived in Altahabana were noticing the obvious, most of the boys and some of the girls were leaving the country.

Therefore, our experience in the process, the documentation contained in the letters I received from my parents, relatives, friends, and teachers, and the published records on this subject matter all suggest that Operation Pedro Pan was coordinated with the knowledge of both the Cuban revolutionary government and the United States government. In this context, the Catholic Church did provide humanitarian support for this massive migration of children. Catholic Charities of the Diocese of Miami was run at the time by a 30-year-old man, Father Bryan Walsh. His operation before Operation Pedro Pan had a $20,000 annual budget. After the operation began, it managed millions of dollars. He was a hard worker, a believer in the social doctrine of the Church, and probably naïve about the Cold War and international relations.

A Clandestine to Semi-Clandestine Operation:

The fact that Operation Pedro Pan was a secret, clandestine operation seemed more important in terms of preventing the population at large in Cuba from finding out about it, than preventing the communist revolutionaries from knowing about it. Our experience was that the operation, although not known by its code name, Operation Pedro Pan, was well known among certain circles in Havana. In short, Operation Pedro Pan was not a true secret. However, if it would have not been a secret, perhaps millions of young Cubans would have flocked to leave Cuba through its assistance. The secrecy seemed to be, in my opinion, not directed toward keeping the communists from knowing about it, but keeping it from being general knowledge to the entire population of Cuba.

I venture to suggest that Operation Pedro Pan was only a small part of the first wave of exiles. Then, there were the waves from Camarioca and the Freedom Flights, the Mariel boatlift, and the Guantanamo rafters. Presently, there is a major migration of Cubans out of Cuba through the jungles and beaches of South and Central America the fate of which has yet to play out. The names given to these migrations are not teams with catchy nicknames fighting for a championship. These are waves of similar people, some battered more than others by the totalitarian regime that had enthroned itself as the status quo on the island, who risked everything to move toward freedom beyond their own horizon of misery, discrimination vis-à-vis foreigners, and oppression under the Castro regime.

On this side of the Straits of Florida, the fact that the Unaccompanied Cuban Children Program was semi-clandestine prevented news coverage of the camps, orphanages, and institutions where the Cuban children and adolescents were living in refuge. Furthermore, this practice of secrecy, probably recommended and enforced not by the Catholic Church, but by the American government, made it impossible to talk about the operation in public or campaign to raise funds for the various institutions where the children and adolescents were getting the help they needed.

The secrecy issue also made it, at a time of war, very difficult to be able to confirm information about the entire program and the situation in the camps. Therefore, there were always a number of *bolas* and misinformation on both sides of the Straits of Florida that, in my opinion, added to the anxiety and insecurity that we felt as participants of the program.

Psychological Issues:

The prevailing wisdom in social work and welfare circles in the United States at the time of Operation Pedro Pan was that it was preferable to place adolescent children in selected foster homes than in institutions. The preferred manner to handle adolescent children in Europe was to place them in group homes and institutions, where their cultural issues would be preserved and the children would not be acculturated to their new environment.(3) Consequently, the United States Catholic Welfare tended to place us in foster homes. Camp Matecumbe and other centers in South Florida were soon dedicated to serve as temporary facilities from where the "occupants" would be placed in foster homes or orphanages.

Some foster homes were excellent and others were not good. Some of the individuals who are recognized in the Cuban American community as products of Operation Pedro Pan were placed in excellent homes. Others did not have the same luck. For example, José Ignacio Ramírez was there when Camp St. John opened its doors in February 1961. He was also there when Tom Aglio closed the camp. José Ignacio remained in the Jacksonville area and continued to attend Bishop Kenny High School. However, he went through three foster homes in a year, and two of them were not good.

At least during my stay at Camp St. John, there was little effort shown with regards to making the place appear to be a home for us. For example, I do not recall that birthdays were recognized or celebrated in our camp. Furthermoe, there was very little, if any, in my experience, professional counseling provided to the children. There were no systematic observations or studies on the behavior or relations of young refugees at that time. It would have been important to determine how we were doing psychologically as individuals and as a group in order to better our situation in the institutions with a view to providing a better chance of success when we were placed in the community.

Anyone can tell you that for all of us it was a stressful, lonesome, and uncertain time. One aspect of the operation about which not much has been made public is the fact that a number of children and adolescents who came out of Cuba through Operation Pedro Pan did not do well in the homes and camps where they were being taken care of. Among my relatives and friends, there were three people who returned to Cuba within a few weeks of having arrived in the United States. Two were in a private home and one was in Camp Matecumbe. The reasons for the return of these three individuals are varied, but essentially they could not adapt here or became ill to the point where either they or their parents in Cuba requested for them to be returned to their home in Havana. How many others from the more than 14,000 children who participated in the operation returned under these circumstances? Was it hundreds? Was it thousands? We do not know. In the case of these three individuals that I know about, all three eventually left Cuba. Two of them departed to Spain in the late 1960s with their entire family, and one departed Cuba directly to the United States in the 1990s, also with his family. What happened to all others who returned because of being homesick, ill, or feeling out of place here? We do not know. It is still a secret.

In 2001, there was a get-together of the individuals who were on the roster of "occupants" who passed through Camp St. John. Altogether, we were 142 adolescents in the camp registry. There were, at the time, 9 individuals who had already died. Details are not available for the causes of death or whether the deaths occurred soon after the camp closed or much later. However, the number of dead in this set of Cuban adolescents appears to be somewhat high. One of our counselors, Jorge Cunill, also died prematurely. Death rates for Cubans involved in Operation Pedro Pan and the Unaccompanied Cuban Children Program have not been studied. It would be interesting to compare the mortality of those of us who left Cuba with the corresponding parameter of those who stayed on the island. Is the mortality rate different for each of these groups? Or, is it similar on account that both groups were forced to undergo serious stressors at a very vulnerable age? Without having the data, but aware of the lives of many of my peers, I believe that both groups may have had a higher mortality rate than expected.

The expected mortality rate for males in the age range from 10 to 50 years of age is reported to be from 0.5 to 5 per 1,000. Therefore, our apparent mortality rate in the set of individuals who passed through Camp St. John was on the order of 14 times higher than what may have been expected from data on the general population of both the United States and Cuba. This type of information needs to be further studied systematically and compared with other centers where the Operation Pedro Pan children and adolescents passed through. One would not expect such a large variation, even though the number of occupants who went through Camp St.

John is a relatively small sample in terms of public health populations. I feel that further data and work in this regard is necessary.

Spirituality and Religious Issues:

Monsignor Walsh was rather proud that out of the more than 14,000 children and adolescents who went through his program, there were 35 with vocations to serve the church and the people of God in the capacity of priests and religious leaders. This was remarkable! However, aside from the influence that Operation Pedro Pan may have had on those vocations, one has to also consider the general background, the situation in Havana, the example of Monsignor Boza Masvidal, the continuation of his efforts in South Florida by Auxiliary Bishop Agustín Román and many others who nourished the faith of not only the Pedro Pans, but all those who came in contact with them.

The infrastructure for the liturgy varied enormously. For example, at Camp St. John we had a large room dedicated to be the chapel of the camp. In fact, a photograph taken by Mr. Thomas J. Aglio was published in the documents distributed during the 50th Anniversary of Operation Pedro Pan in Miami Beach in 2011. In contrast with the ornate and elegant chapel at St. John's Manor, was the chapel at Matecumbe Camp. Brother Rafael Martín, FMS provided me with a photograph of the tent where the chapel was located. That structure seemed reminiscent of the dwellings of the nomad people Abraham led through faith in the very beginning of our Judeo-Christian faith. Perhaps, it was appropriate for us to understand back then that we were truly beginning one more time.

Some of the vocations that developed during Operation Pedro Pan and its aftermath occurred in the most unlikely of places. Take for example the case of Octavio Cisneros. I have learned of his story through my friend Juan Gonzalez, who met Octavio at Camp Matecumbe in October 1961. Both of them were in the first group of Cuban adolescents who went to reopen the Holy Family Orphanage Home in Marquette, Michigan. The orphanage had been closed for years, but it became a hub of humanitarian activity with the influx of displaced Cuban children.

Octavio was born in Central Cuba and was sent out with the "mango flowers" through Operation Pedro Pan. His parents Roberto and Olga were people of faith and they did not wish Octavio to be devoured by the evil of the twentieth century, Communism. He attended two high schools—one with the Priarist Fathers, *Escuelas Pías* in Cuba, and then St. Paul High School in Negaunee, Michigan. His vocation grew as he went on to St. Lawrence Minor Seminary in Mount Calvary, Wisconsin. He completed his theological studies at the Immaculate Conception

This statue of the Virgin of Charity, Patroness of Cuba, is presently at the Peter Pan Archive of Barry University in Miami, Florida. This same statue was originally at St. Raphael Home, a place in the then Diocese of Miami that saw many Pedro Pans pass through that facility during their first few days of exile.

Seminary, Huntington, Long Island, and was ordained to the priesthood by Bishop Francis J. Mugavero on May 29, 1971.

He has served the Catholic Church and the people of God in various capacities since then including: parochial vicar at St. Michael's Church, Sunset Park; diocesan coordinator of the Hispanic Apostolate, pastor of Our Lady of Sorrows Church in Corona; Episcopal Vicar in the Brooklyn East Vicariate; and as rector of Cathedral Seminary Residence in Douglaston. He was named a Prelate of Honor by Pope St. John Paul II in 1988. He serves presently as vice-postulator of the Cause for Canonization of the Servant of God Felix Varela (1788-1853), a Cuban priest who preceded Jose Marti in time and is always remembered among Cubans as "the one who taught us to think."

Father Varela became a Cuban exile after he was elected to represent the Cuban colony in the Spanish Cortes. There, Father Varela spoke openly of liberty, the rights of man, the prevalent corruption in the Spanish colonies, the ill effects of adventurism, and the totally unacceptable practice of slavery. The Spanish failed to see through his words and actions, the need for fundamental reforms in the way the island of Cuba and the Spanish Empire were governed. After becoming a political exile, Varela continued to serve the people of God in New York for almost thirty years, mostly ministering to the recently arrived Irish immigrants in the early part of the nineteenth century. Bishop Cisneros was a founding member and president of the Felix Varela Foundation.

Presently, the Most Reverend Felipe J. Estévez is the Bishop of St. Augustine. He has occupied the Episcopal chair in St. Augustine since 2011. Bishop Estévez also served the people of God in Honduras and in various capacities in the Archdiocese of Miami where he was Auxiliary Bishop from 2003 until 2010. He arrived in the United States through Operation Pedro Pan and attends regularly the Pedro Pan reunions in northeast Florida. Obviously, the impact of the humanitarian involvement of the Catholic Church in the effort to save some Cuban children from being enslaved by communist doctrine very likely served to awaken and nourish vocations to the priesthood.

Two individuals who were not in my class but I knew from the Catholic youth organization at our Marist school, the *Juventud Estudiantil Católica*, JEC. They got out of Cuba via Operation Pedro Pan and entered the priesthood. They were Juan Sosa who has worked for years in the Archdiocese of Miami and has served as pastor in at least two parishes St. Catherine of Siena in Kendall and presently in St. Joseph in Miami Beach. The other is Antonio Martí who became the president of the JEC at our Marist school in 1960 when Enrique Collazo graduated. I saw Tony Martí briefly after he came out of Cuba at the Corpus Christie Church in Miami in the summer of 1961. He was then resettled in Montana through the Unaccompnied Cuban Children Program where he completed a college course in business administration. He married and had one daughter. However, his wife became a victim of breast cancer. Several years after Tony became a widow, his daughter already grown, he entered the Franciscan's seminary and became a friar first and then a priest. Tony presently serves the faithful in California. At the time of the flight of the mango flowers, vocations to the priesthood from Cuban youth were not unique to the Pedro Pans. Troadio Hernández was one of my classmates who remained behind in Cuba and subsequent to the closing of our Marist school entered the seminary in Havana. He became a Catholic priest and still serves the faithful in the island.

On a personal level, during my stay at Camp St. John, I can say that there was not a lot of spirituality or religion there. The Spanish priest who was there when the camp was opened to Cuban refugees did not give us the impression that he understood what was going on within ourselves or in Cuba. Perhaps, he thought we were the bourgeoisie of Havana, the children of war criminals or *latifundistas,* large landowners who exploited farmers, being saved by the Catholic Church. A Spaniard from back then may have had a view of a church that was most powerful in the Spanish society of Generalisimo Francisco Franco. In fact, I do not feel that the Cuban church at the time was socially or politically similar to the Spanish church of that bygone era. He was later on replaced by Father Lara, who was also Spanish and taught at Bishop Kenny High School. I do not think that he was seen as a spiritual leader by my peers who remained in the camp until its closure.

However, I had a great revival after I left the Unaccompanied Cuban Children Program and have maintained my close ties with the Marist Brothers and the Catholic Church since then. It was a feeling that, perhaps, the Spirit was obscured and shadowed—perhaps, by something innocuous like the tall trees with the Spanish moss. After passing through the camp, however, I felt a thirst for the Holy Spirit, a longing to become closer to God. Others have not, perhaps, reported on this sequence of experiences. I have known of many who have found refuge and meaningful spiritual lives in other denominations of Christianity. At this point in time in my life, I find myself more tolerant and understanding than when I was sixteen years old.

There is no question that the Cuban exodus, including Operation Pedro Pan, has been recognized as a major factor in the growth of Catholicism in South Florida. In fact, the territory of the one Diocese of Miami born before the dawn of the Cuban exodus is now under the jurisdiction of four thriving dioceses. This first wave of Cuban refugees, which ended with the Cuban Missile Crisis in October

1962, also almost dismembered the laity and the clergy of the Catholic Church in Cuba. In 1962, Fidel Castro was excommunicated, expelled from the Church, by John XXIII for affiliating and preaching communism and supporting a communist government. Appropriately, the basis of the excommunication was the 1949 Decree against Communism of Pope Pius XII.

A new Church began to form and grow in the midst of the communist repression and terror. It initially had less than fifty priests. By the 1970s, the new Catholic Church in Cuba was officially recognized to have an all Cuban hierarchy. Today, the Cuban Church is the oldest and best organized of the elements of the civil society in the island.

Cuba, under atheist Fidel Castro, succeeded in reducing the Church's ability to work by closing and confiscating all its educational centers, deporting the bishop and 150 Spanish priests, discriminating against Catholics in public life and education, and refusing to accept them as members of the Communist Party. The subsequent flight of 300,000 people from the island also helped to diminish the Church there.

Economic Issues:

The costs of Operation Pedro Pan and the Unaccompanied Cuban Children Program were estimated by Professor Massoud-Piloto at $28.5 million.(4) This was an enormous amount of money, at the time. It is, in fact, more than twice what was budgeted and assigned for Operation Zapata, another clandestine operation.(5) The latter was the code name for the Bay of Pigs Invasion. Essentially, for the United States, in terms of how much money was assigned for the task, Operation Pedro Pan was more important than the Bay of Pigs. Obviously, in general, Operation Pedro Pan was a greater success than the Bay of Pigs. However, these expenditures raise questions about the priorities of the United States at the time and the perceived degrees of commitment felt for the Cuban exiles, the Underground on the island, and the American people, in general.

The amount of money paid by the United States government during Operation Pedro Pan to institutions and individual foster parents appears to be excessive when compared to the prevailing rates in social work during this type of emergency. The United States government paid $6.50 per day, per person to any institution serving a Cuban child or adolescent. The amount paid for foster care was $5.50 per day, per person. Therefore, it is logical to assume that the Diocese of St. Augustine was getting nearly $200 per adolescent for our total care while at Camp St. John. Perhaps, some administrative fee was kept in the office of the Catholic Charities in Miami. These data have never, to my knowledge, been disclosed. However, if you compare these rates with those paid per child for refugee children cared for in England during the Spanish Civil War, and Jewish children escaping Nazi Germany during World War II, you will find that the rates used to support Operation Pedro Pan children and adolescents were much higher.

For example, in terms of the financial burden caused by wars and similar conflicts, the children from the Basque Country, who were exiled in England during the Spanish Civil War, were allotted 10 shillings per week, per child. In 1960 currency this would have been about the equivalent of 2 pounds sterling per week, per child (approximately U.S. $ 6).(6) During a different time but in France, it is noted that the amount of funding required to take care of Jewish children escaping Nazi Germany was on the order of 5 Francs per week, per child (less than U.S. $ 1).(7) In contrast with these data, the institutions caring for Pedro Pans were allotted $45.50 per week, per child or adolescent. Obviously, the Pedro Pans were in a different location and at a different time in history. Therefore, comparisons made without considerations for important variables such as the state of the economy or the market are bound to be deceiving but on the surface it seems that the allowance for caring for the Pedro Pans was more generous than that offered a decade or two earlier for the care of other exiled children. A thorough review of the financial data of Operation Pedro Pan is obviously still pending.

The Program for Unaccompanied Cuban Children was instrumental in providing work opportunities for many Cubans. Recently arrived refugees like Muñeca, her closest friend Elena, Uncle Ramón, and Aunt Blanquita all worked in one capacity or another for this United States sponsored program. My cousin "*El Piloto*" also served the program for a time in the capacity of a counselor at the Holy Family Home in Marquette, Michigan. Aside from the fact that all of them provided a service to the less fortunate refugees who had recently arrived in the United States, they also kept the economy going as Cuban families became resettled in this country.

Socio-Political Issues:

Castro's regime became strengthened as Operation Pedro Pan and the Unaccompanied Cuban Children Program aided and resettled out of Cuba more than 14,000 individuals, who would have been difficult to assimilate in the totalitarian, Marxist-Leninist society emerging on the island. The "Pedro Sin Pans," the children who had to stay on the island who did not fit into the communist agenda, were very often systematically vilified, harassed, called names like *gusanos, latifundistas,* and *imperialistas,* worms—large land owners who exploited farmers and imperialists—meaning lackeys of the United States, the Yankee Empire.

Many of their parents were in jail and were systematically discriminated against on account of their political ideology and religious beliefs. It was not infrequent in Communist Cuba to be prevented from entering the university or specific careers on account of being a *gusano* or a religious person.

On the other hand, all Cubans who have survived the Cuban revolution have been stressed and must feel, deep inside, that they have been proven with fire. While we were interned in exile in a dusty summer camp in the winter of 1961, many other Cubans went through difficult times when they were sent away from their homes and families to the *escuela al campo,* a Cuban revolutionary educational experience in which children spent time on farms. Although the *escuela al campo* was not always a negative experience, it did prove to be a stressor for both families and children. In the final analysis, Cuban children during the 1960s were not spared separation and stressors that changed their natural growth and development whether on the island or in exile.

In the final analysis, all Cubans have been subject to dramatic changes in their lives during the revolution. There is no family that has not been divided and no person that has not been stressed, challenged, deceived, or misled. No one family has been protected. No one individual has spent a bored or tranquil youth. Not one!

The Mango Flowers:

At the time of the Cuban revolution there was a need for change, a revolution in Cuba, but not the kind of change that took the entire country to a uni-personal, prolonged beyond all expectations, and totalitarian, communist regime. The children of Operation Pedro Pan and the Unaccompanied Cuban Children Program were part of the Cubans who were, at that time, aligned with the United States because our fight was against communism. In the balance of priorities of the Cold War, our Cuban priorities did not survive or become as important as the survival of Western civilization and the free world. The cause of a free and democratic Cuba was sacrificed in order to achieve a political balance, a strategic compromise, and peace in the world. Since then, the cause of democracy and freedom in Cuba has been essentially abandoned. The tyranny that was enthroned in Cuba, at that time, the totalitarian dictatorship of the Castros, has been increasingly recognized by all parties, including the Latin American nations, Spain, and the United States. Although the Cuban people have been periodically allowed to escape from the island in various waves, their aspirations for respect of human rights, the rule of law, and the pursuit of happiness in their own homeland has not been effectively addressed. In fact, an argument could be raised that the democratic aspirations of Cubans on the island have been manipulated through periodic crises in which the Castro regime has emerged triumphant each time. Essentially, the American and global status quo has abandoned the Cuban people, despite the fact that the average Cuban, *el cubano de a pie*, exists in miserable conditions under an oppressive uni-personal and uni-partisan regime.

Metaphorically, the Pedro Pans can be thought of as some of the mango flowers who flew out of Cuba between 1960 and 1962, propelled by the forces of the "prevailing winds" at the time. Many others have flown since then. Ours was just the first, clandestine, secret migration out of Cuba, orchestrated for our safety but incidentally also useful to defuse the internal situation and eventually stabilize the Castro regime.

Some of the mango flowers have been fertilized, and despite the very prolonged exile, continue to believe that a new Cuba is still possible. Some of those flowers have turned themselves into trees. These are not the young pines of which Jose Marti wrote and spoke about, *Los Pinos Nuevos*. These are now older mango trees which, at this time, have deep roots in various parts of the world because, although we seem concentrated in South Florida, we have actually been spread throughout the planet. We also have the experience we have gathered on our voyages around the world over the years. I feel we need to heed the call of history, the call from our consciousness to turn our attention to the final liberation and reconstruction of Cuba. The work to be done is not work that can be done with cannons, artillery, or military invasions. The work to be done has to be done with understanding, persistence, love, and in peace. Why does it have to be done? Because the forces of hatred and evil have already failed to provide peace, tranquility, and an acceptable living standard for the Cuban people. They have not provided for the basic needs and aspirations of the Cuban people, whose lives have been a miserable dependency on an incompetent one-party state apparatus. The Cuban people, *los cubanos de a pie*, have been condemned to survive on simulation, evasion of unjust laws imposed by a uni-personal dictatorship, and trickery. If the forces of hatred and evil would have triumphed, as continuously proclaimed in the official propaganda of the Castro regime, please answer these questions:

- Why is the exodus of Cubans off the island still continuing after more than fifty years of communist rule under the Castro brothers?
- Why do Cubans on the island need to receive more than $3 billion annually in remittances from their relatives and friends outside the island?
- Why is the country so hermetically closed and controlled that not even

Google and the World Wide Web are freely accessible to the people of the island in 2015?

- Why are peaceful demonstrators such as the Ladies in White (*Damas de Blanco*, wives and daughters of political prisoners of conscience) attacked and imprisoned weekly even in 2015?

A lot of attention has been paid in the media and international organizations to the United States embargo against the Cuban communist government. Particularly after the statement by President Barack Obama on December 17, 2014, that the United States had been secretly arranging for eighteen months to openly establish diplomatic relations, it has been argued that the so-called embargo has not been effective in democratizing Cuba. What pundits and experts have not stressed enough is that with or without a semblance of blockade called embargo, the recurrent allowance and sometimes encouragement of providing a way out for the young and dissatisfied has essentially kept Castroism afloat in Cuba.

If there would have been a true blockade, the Castros would have been out of Cuba or six feet underground—without CIA support—a long time ago. Just before the war with Spain, the United States imposed a true blockade on the island of Cuba and the surroundings keys. The Spanish lasted less than three months in Cuba. As long as Coca Cola and Benetton can be purchased in Cuba and as long as Italians, Canadians, and some Americans stroll through the safety and beauty of old Havana, reconstructed with funds from the United Nation's UNESCO, there is no reason to invoke any blockade.

In December of 2014, the United States signaled that it was willing to remove the embargo and open fresh relations with the Cuban people through its negotiations with the government of Raúl Castro. When that occurs, there will be only one embargo on the Cuban people, the one imposed by the communist dictatorship on Cuban citizens. However, the risk is that through deceit and blackmail, the Castros will reinforce their hold on power and will continue to enslave the Cuban people well into the twenty-first century, long after the Cold War facilitated their enthronement in Cuban politics.

Division is the one issue that has touched every Cuban family during the revolution. Some of those divisions have been overcome. Others may need attention. Perhaps, not all can be healed, but it is worth looking into because our Cuban nationality has survived a very serious derangement in our development. We have been divided and many of our hearts have been broken. Furthermore, there is something else that has touched Cuba, every person, every adolescent, and every child during the revolution besides the separation and divisions have all been deceived and misled. Our parents were misled if they sent us out of Cuba thinking that we were going to a bilingual school. I misled my parents in my letters making them think that I was "content" most of the time. We were misled in thinking that we had a *beca,* when in reality we were participants, "occupants" of a government program carried out by the Church. The people of Cuba have been deceived because they thought they were enjoying a revolution to establish the perfect socialist state and they have arrived at a corrupt, miserable, and crumbling society where the state is the property of one closed Communist Party. Yes, in third grade textbooks in Cuba the Communist Party is above the State. The exiles have been deceived by the United States, because neither party has done anything definitive to offend or upset the Castro government of Cuba, even after the Cold War had ended. For example, why was Fidel Castro allowed to intervene in American immigration policy in 1994 by ordering Cuban masses to get on rafts and invade the United States? Why was the response to the assassination of four Brothers to the Rescue on February 24, 1996 only a strengthening of the embargo which had been in place since the 1960s? Or, why is it that an American official has not looked at Castro in the eye—like others looked at Machado in 1933 and Batista in 1958—-and told him, "Enough! Stop it, get out!"

At the end, a free and democratic Cuba has been sacrificed like the celebration of Christmas was sacrificed in Cuba by the Communists, because of some sort of political agenda; except that Christmas celebrations are again legal in Cuba after the visit of St. John Paul II to the island in 1998. While Cuba remains sacrificed, Cubans outside the island continue to be of service to the societies where they have been transplanted. The service of Cubans to the world has been, for the most part, a very positive one. Consider that the Cuban *mambises,* the Cuban guerillas who fought the Spanish in the Cuban War of Independence (1895-1898), were the boots on the ground that served to receive and guide the "Rough Riders" and all other American troops in 1898 in order to facilitate a rapid United States victory in the war against Spain. It was back then, and on account of the war in Cuba, that the *Stars and Stripes Forever* march was composed by John Phillip Sousa. The United States then turned into a world power with global territorial extensions, acquired in great measure through the war in Cuba, extending from Puerto Rico to the Philippines Islands.

Probably almost everyone remembers the words of John Kennedy at his presidential inauguration on January 20, 1961, when he said, "And so, my fellow Americans: ask not what your country can do for you–ask what you can do for your country." However, probably no one remembers the next sentence in that memorable speech: "My fellow citizens of the world: ask not what America will do for you, but what together we can do for the freedom of man." Interestingly, in the twentieth century, Cuba was sacrificed for world peace to avoid a nuclear conflagration. Meanwhile, in our exile, we have been instrumental in turning Miami into a growing metropolis, a mosaic of cultures, and as our Mayor of Miami, a Pedro Pan himself, Tomás Regalado has defined: the Latin American city "closest" to the United States.

And what about those trees from whose branches the "mango flowers" were blown off? Those trees are now defunct. They must feel that did the right thing when they let their "mango flowers" fly away for those flowers were not their own. They belonged to nature, to God's creation. Perhpas it is best to think that those now defunct trees are joyous to have contributed their flowers to enrich the entire planet and fulfill whatever it is that all the "mango flowers" were supposed to have accomplished.

Therefore, it is time that freedom loving Cubans, not the Castro regime, be recognized as having historical, American and political capital. This is a time to reconsider our options, to look into ourselves and among ourselves, to honor the legacy given to us by our parents and to move forward toward a new Cuba with all and for the good of all men, women, and children of good will.

EPILOGUE

"Woe to the shepherds who mislead and scatter the flock of my pasture...
You have scattered my sheep and driven them away.
You have not cared for them, but I will take care to punish your evil deeds.
I myself will gather the remnant of my flock from all the lands to which I have
driven them
and bring them back to their meadow; there they shall increase and multiply.
I will appoint shepherds for them who will shepherd them
so that they need no longer fear and tremble;
and none shall be missing, says the LORD."
Jer. 23:1-6

We never heard anything else from Manuel Revilla. Luis Díaz went on to become a medical technologist and then successfully pursued a career in medicine, completing his M.D. degree in the Dominican Republic and then training in internal medicine in Pennsylvania. He has practiced medicine in the Miami area for more than thirty years. Neither of these peers of mine, who came out of Cuba before I did, left the island through Operation Pedro Pan. Someone else who is mentioned in the "deliberations" of our fourth year of the Cuban *bachillerato* class was Roberto González. He also studied medicine and I saw him in the practice of his profession in the 1970s, but I have not seen or heard of him since the early 1980s.

Zenón Arribálzaga came out of Cuba through Operation Pedro Pan and was housed at the Matecumbe Camp for a few months. He was placed in a foster home in Indiana and completed high school in Fort Wayne. He had variable experiences in the two foster homes where he lived. He then went on to Indiana University in Bloomington, where he majored in economics. His parents arrived in 1966 from Cuba through the Freedom Flights Program, which began in 1965 through an opening agreed upon by Castro and President L. Johnson. Freedom Flights (known in Spanish as *Los vuelos de la libertad*), transported Cubans to Miami twice daily, five times a week from 1965 to 1973. Its budget was about $12 million and it brought an estimated 300,000 refugees, making it the "largest airborne refugee

*Manuel Revilla, Marist School
Yearbook, 1960*

*Luis Díaz, Marist School Yearbook,
1960*

Roberto González, Marist School Yearbook, 1960

operation in American history." Zenón and his parents were able to attend Lorenzo's wedding in Cleveland, Ohio, in the late sixties. He moved from Indiana and lived in Wisconsin, Pennsylvania, and Brooklyn, New York. He has been a social worker and is currently working as such in the Bronx in New York City. He is looking forward to retiring in the next year or so with his wife. He has been married once and has several children and grandchildren. I last spoke with him in August 2014.

Zenon's sister left Cuba to Madrid, Spain, where she was in a school for a few years before coming to the United States and rejoining Zenón and her parents. We knew her as "Tati," but her real name was Caridad because she had been born on September 8, the feast of the Virgin of El Cobre, La Caridad. She was fun to be around, friendly, and was always there when we visited Zenon's home, which was located only a few blocks away from the Marist School near the Plaza Cívica. She died in Carolina, Puerto Rico, in 2011 from a very aggressive breast cancer.

Luis E. Faura left Cuba in 1962 without his parents. He never saw his father again. He did not seek to go on studying, but began looking for opportunities to work and become an entrepeneur. He looked for opportunities, but did not find any in Miami and went up to New York where he did find some work. He then returned to Miami when his brothers and mother had arrived from Cuba through the Freedom Flights. He went with them to California where they were "re-localized" through the Cuban Refugee Center. He settled there into a jewelry business where he worked for years. He married twice and had three children. In 1991, one year before Hurricane Andrew struck South Florida, he moved with his second wife, Cristina, to Miami. He did not pursue the jewelry business there, but tried his luck at various retail types of enterprises. When that decade was finishing, however, he felt numbness in the right upper extremity and sought attention from an orthopedic surgeon who, after examining him and getting some imaging studies, advised him to go to the hospital because it was serious. He was diagnosed with a primary brain tumor and submitted to a neurosurgical procedure in one of the best medical centers in the southeastern United States. They could not save his life. He did not do well—soon after surgery he could not speak, then he could not walk, and within six months, he died on November 17, 2000.

Lorenzo arrived in the United States in the fall of 1961 through Operation Pedro Pan and spent some time at Camp Matecumbe, before being assigned to go into Camp St. John. He attended Bishop Kenny High School and was in the group described in the 50th Anniversary pamphlet of Tom Aglio, who closed the camp in the summer of 1962. He was placed in the home of a retired military family in Sarasota, Florida. He graduated there from Cardinal Mooney High School, and in the

Zenón Arribálzaga, Marist School Yearbook, 1960

Luis Faura, Marist School Yearbook, 1960

Lorenzo Lorenzo, Marist School Yearbook, 1960

fall of 1963, came up to Cleveland in a greyhound bus to join me. He entered John Carroll University and began a pre-engineering course of studies. He co-founded with me the fund raising delegation of the *Directorio Revolucionario Estudiantil* (DRE), the Cuban Student Directorate in Cleveland. The DRE was a very active anti-Castro organization. It will be recalled that Carlos Bringuier, who was the delegate of the DRE in New Orleans, Louisiana, debated Lee Harvey Oswald on the radio weeks before the assassination of President John. F. Kennedy in Dallas. Both Lorenzo and I were widely interviewed on radio talks shows in the Cleveland area on the Cuban revolution, the role of the United States in the struggle against Communism on the island, and living conditions in Cuba before the revolution.

Lorenzo entered John Carroll University in Cleveland after I introduced him to Father Meunzer at the Admissions Office. The priest also admitted Lorenzo through some sort of humanitarian criteria not disclosed in the admission requirements of the renowned Jesuit school. However, Lorenzo transferred out to Cleveland State University in 1964, where he completed a radiology technology course. He worked as an x-ray technician for years. He married an American girl in Cleveland and had children, but I lost touch with him after he left John Carroll. I did find out that he later lived in Miami and died in 2006.

Juan E. Pella arrived in the United States in 1962 with a visa waiver through Operation Pedro Pan and went into Camp Matecumbe. He did not stay there to be assigned to another camp, an orphanage, a reformatory, or a good or mediocre foster home. Juan returned to Havana. He became a teacher and served the Cuban school system in various locations, including in the *escuela al campo.* He never married and did not have children. His father died in the 1960s from a heart attack during which Pella himself took him into the Hospital Nacional in the outskirts of Altahabana, where he lived. Years later, he immigrated to the United States with his mother after the collapse of the Soviet Union and during the economic and political upheaval it caused, known as the *periódo especial* in Cuba. He lived in West New York in Northern New Jersey, where his sister had settled years earlier. He worked for a while in Victor's Café in New York City. He had no vices when I left him in Havana in January 1961, but life had taken a toll on him, and by the time I saw him again in 1995 in New Jersey, he was a heavy smoker and appeared crestfallen. He died of cancer in 1998.

Francisco R. Wong arrived in the United States with a visa waiver though Operation Pedro Pan. He was placed in the Holy Family Orphanage with Monsignor Wilbur Gibbs and attended high school at Bishop Baraga. He studied at Northern Michigan College, where he earned a bachelor's degree in 1965. He was the first of

Juan Pella, Marist School Yearbook, 1960

Francisco Wong, Marist School Yearbook, 1960

Juan González, Marist School Yearbook, 1960

my peers at the Marist School to earn a college degree in the United States. He went on to the University of Detroit, a Jesuit school, and completed there a Master's degree, and then to the University of Michigan at Ann Arbor, where he earned his Doctor of Philosophy degree in political science in 1974. From then on, he taught at various colleges and universities and eventually entered law school at the University of California at Berkeley, where he received his J.D. degree in 1976. Since then, he has been active both in the legal profession and in academia as a teacher and consultant on political and international affairs.

He feels rather accomplished and is listed at the University of Miami Cuban Heritage Collection as one of the "successful Pedro Pans." He has been married several times, but has had only one son and two grandchildren. When I last spoke with him in late August 2014, he was already looking forward to retiring, but still working as a consultant and writing.

Juan F. González left Havana through Operation Pedro Pan and arrived at Matecumbe in October of 1961. He brought with him his transcript from the Marist School. Juan had written to me while at Matecumbe, regarding the possibility of leaving the Unaccompanied Cuban Children Program and joining me in New Jersey. At the time, I was living in a rooming house and working two jobs. I had been living in my relatives' attic, but moved into a rooming house to an eight-by-eight-foot room. I had to leave my relatives' attic because it looked like I might have to stay with them forever and they needed their privacy. I was also partially supporting my dad, who was in Miami, studying for the medical exam he was to take in March 1962. Therefore, I did not invite Juan to leave the program and join me. He was at Matecumbe until February 1962, when he was sent to the Holy Family Orphanage in Marquette, Michigan, with a handful of Cubans, including our peer at the Marist School Francisco Wong, to reopen an institution founded in 1915 to care for orphans in Northern Michigan.

Other Pedro Pans were to follow Juan to northern Michigan. On March 18, 1962, *The Milwaukee Journal* published the news that fourteen Cubans had arrived in Marquette in the Upper Peninsula of the state of Michigan. Eventually, there were approximately thirty Cubans in that orphanage. They went to two high schools and the Northern Michigan State College, which is now a university. Juan attended Bishop Baraga High School, which is no longer standing. He had enough credits to graduate from high school from his Cuban transcript, but was lacking American History and English courses. He was enrolled in these courses and also in Speech. While he was attending Bishop Baraga High School, he began working at St. Mary's Hospital in Marquette as an orderly. He was asked to do what orderlies did back then—insert Foley catheters in the bladders of men through their penises, prepare the dead patients for the morgue, and what not. Dealing with death and the corpses of the dead is traumatic for everyone but it can be a major stressor for a developing adolescent. For those who have never done it or seen it, placing a Foley catheter through the penis of a man is always uncomfortable. However, in the elderly, since they have invariably multiple pathologies from strictures of the urethra to obstructions at the level of their enlarged or cancerous prostates, the procedure is invariably very painful. Obviously, Juan found the job stressful, but did it to the best of his ability. He went on working as an orderly when he graduated from high school. However, the stressors began to take a toll on his mental status and he began to feel depressed; he was found hiding in closets at the orphanage and eventually he was hospitalized in a Michigan mental asylum, the Newberry State Mental Hospital. Juan described the place as "exactly the same as the setting of the movie *One Flew over the Cuckoo's Nest*." He spent a couple of months there and came out when he was already eighteen years old. He was given a ticket to go to New Rochelle, New York, where his aunt had been sent by the Cuban Refugee Center through one of the churches' social services agencies.

He worked in New Rochelle as a butcher and a grocer while he lived with his relatives. However, he decided to part ways from there on account of the fact that he had gotten ill with peptic ulcer disease and he did not feel appreciated there. He decided to toss a coin and choose where he was to go by luck. If it landed heads up, he would go back to Michigan and if it landed tails up, he would head to California. He felt that he could do well in Michigan or California because there was work in both of those locations. The coin toss sent him to Michigan. He took a Greyhound bus to Detroit, which was a bustling city at the time. When he arrived in Detroit, he remembered some advice that Monsignor Gibbs had given him, "If you find yourself anywhere in this country and need a place to sleep, go to the YMCA, and then go to any Catholic parish and ask for the Catholic Youth Organization (CYO)." He did it. He stayed at the YMCA and got involved in the CYO of St. Clements's Parish. As it turned out, that parish was the one where most Cubans met and shared their lives in exile.

His mother and father arrived from Cuba in 1966 through the Freedom Flights. Juan settled down when his parents arrived and his mother recommended that he return to college. He applied and got into Wayne State University, where he earned his Bachelor's degree. In the meantime, he met his wife, who had come out of Cuba also through Operation Pedro Pan and had lived for a while in Florida City, where the *Lost Apple* film was made to "show the world what was happening to Cuba's children on account of the communist takeover of the island." They married and have had four children and five grandchildren, all boys! Juan and his wife, Yolanda, spend some time every summer at Sanibel Island with their children, their families, and their grandchildren.

Juan worked for the Social Security Administration for many years, first in Detroit and then in Miami. I caught up with him sometime in 1976 when his uncle was taken to the Emergency Department at Jackson Memorial Hospital in Miami. His uncle suffered from severe peripheral vascular disease and chronic bronchitis. I happened to be on duty that evening when his uncle arrived there and I recognized Juan immediately. We have been in touch ever since to the point that he and his wife were the godparents at the baptism of my youngest child, who was born in 1977.

In 1982 Juan followed his wife's advice and went to law school at the University of Miami. He is presently semi-retired, but still working as a lawyer after serving the community in the capacity of a magistrate in the Miami-Dade Country courts for many years. Juan has also been active in the Pedro Pan Foundation and served it as its chairman during several years. In all, Juan has been a great guy and my best friend. He has allowed me to share aspects of his life that were obviously difficult, so that all may appreciate that not everything was rosy with the Peter Pan children.

My cousin, the famous *"El Piloto"* wondered during a couple of years and finally settled down, completed a college degree, and went into sales. He has been happily married and lives in the outskirts of Wilmington, Delaware. He is retired and spends his time caring for a growing number of grandchildren who have come to enrich his family.

My father completed his review medical course at the University of Miami School of Medicine in the spring of 1962 and passed the examination given by the Educational Council for Foreign Medical Graduates (ECFMG) in March 1962. He got the passing grade in the mail in late May. By then, we had moved to a one bedroom bungalow on NW 53rd street. I accompanied him to a couple of interviews to hospitals in the Miami area, but he finally signed a contract with a hospital that sent a delegation to Miami with the mission of filling its house staff positions. Mr. Jay Collins headed the delegation from Euclid Glenville Hospital in Cleveland, Ohio. Eight other Cubans who had passed the ECFMG test were hired. There he completed two years of post-graduate training in general practice and then obtained a contract for a family medicine residency at the Halifax District Hospital in Daytona Beach, Florida. He enjoyed his time in Daytona Beach because he traveled often to Miami to see his mother and other relatives along with many of his friends including those who had signed up for the Bay of Pigs Invasion of Cuba.

Ramón de Gordon, Piloto.
Photograph from 8mm movie frame

He sat for the Florida Medical Board in 1969 and obtained his medical license to practice in the state. He worked in private practice and in various emergency departments until the late 1970s, when he had a minor heart attack and retired. He died in 1991 from another heart attack and heart failure.

My mother was the single most efficient and loving support of my dad and our small family. She left all her closest blood relatives back on the island in 1962. Her father, Gabino, had died in December 1956, when the revolutionary process was beginning in the Sierra Maestra Mountain Range. Her mother died in 1968 and she was not able to go back home for the funeral because of the abyss that existed then between the U.S. and Cuba. The separation between members of her family were aggravated by the fact that some of her most dear nephews had joined the *Fuerzas Armadas Revolucionarias* (the Revolutionary Armed Forces). The most singular of them, as far as we knew, was Julio Palomino, who had become an officer in the Cuban Revolutionary Navy. My mother helped raise Julio in his first years of life, even to the age of ten years, because his biological mother was not available and Julio's father, my mother's oldest brother Aristónico, was working on the family farm in Calicito in eastern Cuba. Soon after the news from Cuba confirming the death of my grandmother Clotilde, Poppy became ill with intractable vomiting, was taken to a veterinary clinic, and was diagnosed with a terminal canine cancer and euthanized. My paternal grandmother, Abuela Amparo, died in the summer of 1971 from pancreatic cancer in Miami. I should mention that my paternal grandfather had died in Havana in 1944 before I was born.

Finally, I share my own aftermath of the "flight of the mango flowers." I entered John Carroll University College of Arts and Sciences in September 1962, despite my low scores on the SAT verbal and math tests. I had taken the tests in New Jersey more than nine months before entering John Carroll. I managed to graduate in the

Antonio Gordon, Marist School Yearbook, 1960

124th place among 223 graduates in the class of 1966. I had come up from way below average in the SATs to the middle third of a college graduating class with a Bachelor of Science degree, a major in chemistry and a minor in biology and mathematics. I consider it a miracle that I actually graduated from John Carroll University in such a different world and educational system, not to mention in a strange language, which I had openly disliked. I thanked God for helping me get through, for the odds were that I should have flunked out. I entered the school with the idea of becoming a physician and enrolled in all the pre-medical courses. However, with my 2.452 average on a scale of 0 to 4, I should not have been surprised to have been rejected from all medical schools in the United States to which I had applied.

I went to teach chemistry with the Society of Mary at Chaminade High School in Hollywood, Florida, and two years later, got into the graduate school of the University of Miami's chemistry department. I completed a Master of Science degree in chemistry with a 3.2 point average. My major professor was denied tenure at that time and left for a university in his home state of Kentucky, where the highest degrees awarded were Master's degrees. Therefore, he recommended me to Florida State University (FSU), where I entered in August of 1969. Unbeknown to my major professor and me, there was a Program in Medical Sciences (PIMS) starting at Florida State at about that time. A few years later, that program was to become the College of Medicine at FSU.

It was a difficult time because of the course loads and the fact that I was married with three children. There was a lot of uncertainty in my group at FSU about being able to move on to a medical school. I remember one night in the nutrition laboratory thinking about my options and saying this prayer: "Lord, I feel I can serve you as a physician, but I will follow the path you open for me." I was in the first group of four students in the PIMS to finish all requirements for moving on to an accredited medical school and was recommended—along with a group of three others—to Emory University in Atlanta, Georgia, where I began my medical career. I was able to complete the Ph.D. degree I had started at FSU from Emory, traveling back and forth to Tallahassee, and obtained it in biochemical nutrition with a thesis on iron absorption.

Upon graduating from Emory with an M.D. degree, I entered a residency in Internal Medicine at Jackson Memorial Hospital and the University of Miami. I completed the residency in 1978 and since then, I have been practicing medicine in South Florida. I also became involved in teaching and taught in the capacity of an instructor in medicine at Jackson Memorial Hospital until 1984. In 1990, an undergraduate program in medical education was begun at Palmetto General Hospi-

In 1963 there were five Cuban refugees attending John Carroll University in Cleveland, Ohio.
They were Hugo Galetti, Antonio Gordon, Lorenzo Lorenzo,
Reinaldo Gómez, and Andrés Jiménez.

tal, where I had established my medical practice since 1978. The hospital became affiliated with Nova Southeastern University. The next year, the graduate medical education program opened a rotating internship. Since then, fully accredited programs in Family Medicine, Internal Medicine, Cardiology, Infectious Diseases, and Critical Care Medicine have enriched the hospital community and the city of Hialeah and North West Miami-Dade County. I have been with the medical education program out of Palmetto General Hospital and Nova Southeastern University since it began in 1990. At one point in time, I was also co-director of Medical Education at the Westchester Hospital program in Family Medicine. I attained the title of Clinical Professor of Medicine at Nova Southeastern University in 1996.

My medical practice has centered on the care of Hispanics in the Hialeah area. I have also been active in medical research, particularly in the areas of physical diagnosis, thermography, medical education, and matters of public health important to Cubans. I have published several works on the nutritional status of Cubans and Cuban refugees, nutritional support, and the HIV-AIDS epidemic in Cuba. My work on HIV-AIDS was presented at the IX International AIDS Conference in San Francisco in 1990 and the American College of Clinical Nutrition Conference in San Diego in 1992. I also conducted a study where we determined the etiology of the epidemic of "optic neuritis" that plagued Cuba during the *período especial* after the dissolution of the Soviet Union.

I married soon after finishing college at John Carroll University and had four children. One child died; my oldest daughter Zoilita, from anaphylaxis and status asthmaticus in 1982. The family I had founded in 1966 had its ups and downs since the beginning, but a few years after the death of my oldest daughter at the age of 13, the family unit began to crumble. Despite all efforts by our friends, the clergy, and several counselors, a decree of divorce became inevitable. Although we all suffered, I feel that our three living children were the ones who suffered the most from my marital crisis. Presently, I have two grandchildren who are growing fast and looking at their future with hope.

I feel that considering all the details that have been revealed in this book, I can consider myself most fortunate to be alive and to have accomplished everything that I have. Life has taught me more than I could have ever imagined and, in so doing, I have become more tolerant and humane while attending the needs of the sick who seek my attention. After all, there is only one who is good and that is our Father in heaven.

We, the mango flowers, flew out of Cuba and were spared the balance of the Cold War on the island and the horrific violence that followed the Cuban Missile

Crisis. By 1963, it was common for revolutionary armed men to come into a house, based solely on their suspicions or unconfirmed hearsay of a neighbor, take someone to a prison, a collective farm for "antisocials" or to the firing squad. By 1965, internal resistance was essentially wiped out and the communist order based on terror had already been instituted.

At the end of the day, the mango flowers did not fly out of Cuba looking for a better education, or in search of a new family. We left our homes and families behind. Certainly we were not looking for another family who would attend our needs and love us more than the family where we had grown. We were flown out from the toxic environment and the struggle of war through a flight that was perhaps dangerous but facilitated. Although some of the Pedro Pans have voiced opinions to the contrary, I feel that the vast majority of us believe that our parents acted wisely, with sound judgment and sacrifice. They had very few options for our future in Havana in 1960. Our houses were being watched, our schools searched and militarized, and our church persecuted and ignored. While it is true that many Pedro Pans have done well in exile, many others did not. It is time, I hope, that the stories of the Pellas, the Lorenzos, the *Coquetos* and many others be told and placed in the balance of the price we Cubans have paid so that the world may be at peace from a nuclear war. And furthermore, the story of Luis de la Cruz, Cosme del Peso and many other Cuban youths, who remained in the island and were also deceived by the revolution need to be also made known and appreciated. At the end, I feel we are all one people.

When we arrived in the United States, some of us—the older ones—wanted to continue the fight against Communism. The efforts had variable results, but at the end we could not, from our forced exile, turn the tide of history. Cuba had become part of the Soviet Bloc. Since then, the Cold War turned peaceful through various agreements and the policy of détente.

As it is well known, the Soviet Union disintegrated in 1989. Despite the collapse of its communist allies, Cuba has remained a dictatorial, totalitarian state under the rule of the Castro brothers. The price for this peace has been expensive: Freedom, democracy, respect for human rights, and prosperity for Cubans on the island have been sacrificed. With the winds of political will changing since 2014 when the United States declared that it was ready to resume diplomatic relations with the Cuban people, the time has come for the United States and the great powers to stop pretending that the Castro brothers are truly the leaders of the Cuban people. Two pieces of information should suffice to convince all that the Castro brothers do not represent the majority of the Cubans. First, in a survey conducted in the spring of

2015, President Obama was found to be the most popular and favored leader in the island of Cuba, not the Castro brothers.(1) Secondly, the number of Cubans escaping the island in search of better living conditions and freedom has increased steadily in the past few years. The last major Cuban crisis occurred in 1994 when more than 50,000 Cubans took to the sea in any kind of floating vessel in search of freedom and a better future.

The numbers have been building up for the current crisis through which Cubans escapees are flooding Ecuador, Colombia, Panama, and Costa Rica on their desired journey to freedom in the United States. Some have argued politically that this latest massive wave of Cubans escaping the island is favored by the PL89-872, the Cuban Adjustment Act. The latter was passed during the Cold War to faciliatetd the legal admission into the United States of Cubans escaping Cuba's communist dictatorship. All Cuban children who arrived and stayed in the United States through Operaiton Pedro Pan were provided legal immigrant status through this law in 1966. However, the current Cuban exodus is not a political problem but a humanitarian one. As such, all should recognize that the miserable living conditions, overt discrimination in their own homeland and exploitation of the Cuban workers and professionals in the island are the fundamental reasons that have led an increasing number of persons in the island to sell everything they have and escape in whatever manner they can. The only way to stop these recurrent crises is to allow Cubans to have a say in their own affairs and to govern themselves on the island of Cuba through a truly representative government renewed periodically through fair and open elections. As long as Cubans are oppressed and discriminated against in their own country, political opposition is ignored and subjected to isolation, abuse, and repression, and families continue to be arbitrarily divided by the abusive and arbitrary policies of the Castro regime, there will be unrest and masses of people willing to risk everything to look for a better future and be reunited with their own families outside the island of Cuba.

At the end, negotiators, politicians, religious leaders, and business men and women will need to understand that there can be a future market in Cuba and peace in the region when Cuba is again allowed to be free from agreements and bondages whose time has already passed. It will be shameful that the current living conditions, human, and spiritual misery, prevalent in Cuba, the product of more than fifty years of communist rule, deceit, and terror will be allowed to prevail in perpetuity. Anyone who has not experienced or is in doubt about the realities of Cuban life under the Castro regime will do well to review the work of Valladares(2) and Moses.(3) May the future of Cubans not be dictated by biased information, ignorance, or the policies and agreements of yesterday. May it be one of openness and tolerance, and may it be one of peace, prosperity, freedom, and democracy.

Notes and References

Introduction

1. Eire, Carlos. *Waiting for Snow in Havana: Confessions of a Cuban Boy.* Free Press a division of Simon and Schuster, New York. 2003.

2. Ramírez, José Ignacio. *Defining Moments: A Cuban Exile's Story about Discovery and the Search for a Better Future.* CreateSpace Independent Publishing Platform, North Charleston, South Carolina. 2013.

3. Torres, María de los Angeles. *The Lost Apple: Operation Pedro Pan, Cuban Children in the U.S., and the Promise of a Better Future.* Beacon Press, Boston. 2003.

4. *The Lost Apple.* A Documentary about the Pedro Pan children in Florida City camp. Presented on YouTube in two parts, I and II by Eloisa Echezabal at https://www.youtube.com/results?search_query=the+lost+apple. Last Accessed July 4, 2014.

5. García, María Cristina. *Havana USA: Cuban Exiles and Cuban Americans in South Florida 1959-1994.* University of California Press, Los Angeles. 1996.

6. Masud-Piloto, Felix. *From Welcomed Exiles to Illegal Immigrants to the U.S., 1959-1995.* Rowman & Littlefield Publishers, Inc., New York. 1996.

7. Conde, Yvonne M. *Operation Pedro Pan: The Untold Exodus of 14,048 Cuban Children.* Routledge, New York. 1999.

8. Conde, Yvonne M. *Operación Pedro Pan: La Historia Inédita del Exodo de 14,048 Niños Cubanos.* Random House Español, New York. 2001.

9. Torreira Crespo, Ramón, and José Boajasán Marrawi. *Operación Pedro Pan: Un Caso de Guerra Psicológica Contra Cuba.* Editora Política, Ciudad de La Habana. 2000.

10. Gordon, A.M. "Caribbean Basin Refugees: The Impact of Cubans and Haitians on the Health of South Florida." *Journal of the Florida Medical Association.* 1982, pp. 522-7.

Chapter 1

1.   The number of tourist visitors to Cuba has increased steadily. In the 1980s there was already some health tourism. Since the collapse of the Soviet Union, tourism has reached nearly 3 million visitors per year. The tourist industry is wholly owned by the Cuban communist government. Approximately 10,000 Americans visit the island tourist facilities yearly. The last famous Americans who visited Cuba were Beyoncé and Jay-Z. See for example, Cave, D. "Trip to Cuba by Beyoncé and Jay-Z Investigated." *New York Times,* April 9, 2013.

2.   In the summer of 1961, my cousin and I walked up the downtown branch of the Howard National Bank and Trust Company. We were inquiring about opening a checking account. The bank officer who answered our questions noted that we were foreigners and inquired about our native land. We told him that we were from Cuba. To our amazement, the officer thought Cuba was somewhere in Africa. He asked, "Is Cuba on the east or the west coast of Africa?"

3.   Hart Phillips, Ruby. "Cuba Inaugurates President Batista: New Chief Executive Calls for the Economic Application of Continental Solidarity." *New York Times,* October 11, 1940. P. 6, col. 4. Regarding the 1930s revolution, see also by the same author *Cuba: Island of Paradox.* McDowell, Obolensky, New York. 1956.

4.   Hart Phillips, Ruby. "Prio Is Installed as Cuban Leader: One of President's First Acts Is to Cut Retail Costs 10%—Woman Put in Cabinet." *New York Times,* October 11, 1948. P. 4, col.1.

5.   Marrero, Levi. *Cuba: Economía y Sociedad. Azúcar Ilustración y Conciencia.* Vol. 12. Editorial Playor S.A., Madrid. 1983. P. 285.

6.   Delgado García, Gregorio. "Dr. Antonio de Gordon y Acosta, profesor de conocimientos enciclopédicos." *Revista Cubana de Educación Médica Superior.* 2001. Vol. 15, Number 1, Pp. 56-63.

7.   Thomas, Hugh. *Cuba: The Pursuit of Freedom.* Da Capo Press, New York. 1998. Pp. 245-263.

8.   "Execution of Eight Medical Students in Havana." *New York Times.* Nov. 29, 1871. P. 1, col. 2. Front page coverage of the situation in Havana in these terms: "Execution of Eight Medical Students in Havana. Monitors ordered to Havana to protect American interests—Our relations with Spain. Washington, Nov. 28. Very important intelligence from Havana was received here last evening to the effect that a further outbreak of the

volunteers was momentarily expected, and that the Spanish government was powerless. As the safety and interests of Americans would in this case be jeopardized, orders were immediately sent to Key West to dispatch the Monitor *Terror* to Havana."

9. Fountain, William A. *27 de Noviembre de 1871: Fusilamiento de Ocho Estudiantes de Medicina. Ediciones* Universal, Miami, Florida. 2000.

10. "The Maine Blown Up." *New York Times,* Feb. 16, 1898. P. 1, col. 7. P. 2, col. 1. "The Maine blown up. Terrible explosion onboard United States battleship in Havana Harbor. Many persons killed and wounded. All the boats of the Spanish cruiser *Alfonso XII.* Assisting in the work of relief. None of the wounded men able to give any explanation of the cause of the disaster."

11. The policy of *reconcentración* of the rural Cubans into the cities was ordered by Weyler to deprive the insurgents headed by Antonio Maceo and Máximo Gómez of supplies and support. Instead, it caused a great humanitarian disaster in the cities, particularly in Havana where more than 300,000 *campesinos* were attempting to find refuge. My great-grandfather, Dr. Antonio de Gordon Acosta, helped organize and fund during that time a number of medical centers with the Bishop of Havana, Manuel Santander y Frutos, Marta Abreu de Estevez, and Drs. Manuel Delfín, Domingo Mádan, and Rafael Tristá. The centers were known as the *Dispensarios Para Niños Pobres.* There were at least two in Havana, one in Matanzas, and another in Santa Clara. Years later, my grandfather, Ramón de Gordon Bermúdez, who at the time when Weyler was Governor General of Cuba was twenty-five years old, saw Weyler in a Spanish celebration and parade in the 1920s when he was visiting relatives in northern Spain with his family. My father used to tell this story vividly.

12. My grandfather shouted, "Assassin!" His relatives tried to calm him down, but he ran after the Spanish General and continued to shout his feelings to condemn Weyler's legacy in Cuba. The story of my great-grandfather is reviewed in this reference: Tro, R. Del Pasado Médico: Antonio de Gordon y de Acosta (1848-1917). *Boletín del Colegio Médico de La Habana.* Vol. XII. Enero, 1961. Pp. 9-17.

13. Senn, Dr. Nicholas. "Medico-Surgical Aspects of the Spanish American War." *American Medical Association Press,* Chicago. 1900. P. 9.

14. "Cuban Problems Serious." *New York Times.* May 31, 1901. P. 1, col. 4. "The President and his advisers must determine whether the Platt amendment has been 'substantially' adopted by the convention."

15. Lopez-Fresquet, Rufo. *My 14 Months with Castro.* The World Publishing Company, New York. 1966. P. 19.

16. *Enciclopedia Universal Ilustrada, Europea-Americana.* Vol. 16. Espasa-Galpe, S.A. Madrid. 1913. P. 841.

17. Black, J.K., and H.I. Blutstein, J.D. Edwards, K.T. Johnston, and D.S. Mc-Morris. *Area Handbook for Cuba. Second Ed.* American University, Washington. 1976. P. 42.

18. Lopez-Fresquet, Rufo. *Op. cit.* Pp. 3-5.

19. Hart Phillips, Ruby. *Cuba Island of Paradox: The Turbulent Growth of a Country.* McDowell, Obolensky, New York. 1956.

20. Lopez-Fresquet, Rufo. *Op. cit.* P. 4.

21. Hart Phillips, Ruby. *Op. cit.* Pp. 3-20.

22. Carrillo, Justo. *Cuba 1933: Students, Yankees and Soldiers.* University of Miami North/South Center Press, Miami, Florida. 1994.

23. Thomas, Hugh. *Cuba: The Pursuit of Freedom. Op. cit.* Pp. 606-607.

24. *Ibid.* Pp. 607-614.

25. *Ibid.* Pp. 658-665.

26. Lopez-Fresquet. Rufo. *Op. cit.* 76-77.

27. Hart Phillips, R. "Batista in Power after Cuban Coup by the Military." *New York Times,* March 11, 1952. P. 1, col. 1.

28. Thomas, Hugh. *Op. cit.* Pp. 789-802.

29. Laviero, A. "Senate Beats 3 Efforts to Kill or Tone Down Contempt Charges." *New York Times,* Dec. 2, 1954. P. 1, col. 7.

30. Unclassified documents from the American Embassy in Havana available at: http://www.latinamericanstudies.org/embassy-1950-54.htm. Last Accessed July 4, 2014.

31. Torres, María de los Angeles. *Op. cit.* Pp. 46-64.

32. My father knew Colonel Martin Elena. He mentions him in some of his letters during 1961 and 1962. Martin Elena had confided in my father the sequence of developments as described in the text.

33. Lopez-Fresquet. Rufo. *Op. cit.* Pp. 9-11.

34. Marquez-Sterling, Manuel. *Cuba 1952-1959: The True Story of Castro's Rise to Power.* Kleiopatria Press. 2009

35. Thomas, Hugh. *Op. cit.* Pp. 824-844.

36. Marquez-Sterling, Manuel. *Op. cit.* Pp. 59-63.

37. The historical intervention of Matthews appears in three news articles and a book. These are the sources:

38. Matthews, Herbert L. "Cuban Rebel Is Visited in Hideout." *New York Times,* Feb. 24, 1957. P. 1, col. 5.

39. Matthews, Herbert L. "Rebel Strength Gaining in Cuba, But Batista Has the Upper Hand." *New York Times,* Feb 25, 1957. P. 1, col. 8.

40. Matthews, Herbert L. "Old Order in Cuba Threatened by Forces of an Internal Revolt." *New York Times,* Feb. 26, 1957. P. 13, col. 1.

41. De Palma, Anthony. *The Man Who Invented Fidel.* Public Affairs, a member of Perseus Book Group, Cambridge, MA. 2006.

42. Thomas, Hugh. *Op. cit.* Pp. 925-933.

43. Barquín, Ramon M. *Las Luchas Guerrilleras en Cuba: De la colonia a la Sierra Maestra.* Playor, S.A., Madrid. 1975.

44. Thomas, Hugh. *Op. cit.* Pp. 961-973.

45. Marquez-Sterling, Manuel. *Op. cit.* Pp. 151-155.

46. Thomas, Hugh. *Op. cit.* Pp. 974-987.

47. Baker, Russel. "Batista is in Peril, U.S. Aide Says." *New York Times,* Jan. 1, 1959. P. 1, col. 2.

48. Hart Phillips, Ruby. *The Cuban Dilemma.* Ivan Obolesky, Inc. New York. Pp. 1-8.

49. At one point in time in February 1959, my cousin Emilito worked for the new Ministry for the Recuperation of Stolen Goods under its Minister Faustino Perez. My cousin's first assignment was to make an assessment of Batista's personal country home known as Kukine. My cousin found Batista's clothes still in perfect order in his closets. There were no signs that he had any plans to leave the island, because it did not appear that he had taken any of his personal belongings.

50. Various reports verify that individuals in Batista's party arrived in various places including New Orleans, Jacksonville, Florida, and Santo Domingo in the Dominican Republic. See for example: "91 Aboard Plane Seized in Escape: 400 Supporters of Regime Reach Havens in U.S. and Dominican Republic." *New York Times,* Jan. 2, 1959. P. 7, col. 1.

51. Thomas, Hugh. *Op. cit.* Pp. 1020-1034.

52. Lopez-Fresquet, Rufo. *Op. cit.* 41-44.

53. "Cuba Executes 3 as Regime's Foes. 4 Receive Prison Sentences-46 on trial now." *New York Times,* Jan. 18, 1961. P. 9, col. 2-5.

Chapter 2

1. Hart Phillips, Ruby. *The Cuban Dilemma.* Ivan Obolesky, Inc. New York. Pp. 153.
2. *Ibid.* P. 153-154.
3. Hart Phillips, Ruby. "75 Die in Havana as Munitions Ship Explodes." *New York Times,* March 5, 1960. P. 1, col. 7.
4. Best, A., and J.M. Hanhimaki, J. A. Maiolo, K.E. Schulze. *International History of the Twentieth Century.* Routledge. 2004. P. 339.
5. Hart Phillips, Ruby. *Op. cit.* Pp. 206-228.
6. Hart Phillips, Ruby. "Castro Decrees Seizure of Rest of U.S. Property; Cites Cut in Sugar Quota." *New York Times,* Aug. 7, 1960. P. 1, col. 7.
7. Strauss, Ben. "In Havana: Remembering a Minor League Championship." *New York Times,* March 23, 2013. P. 7.
8. Personal communication with Dan Morejón. During 2006 to 2008, the Finlay Medical Society organized a softball tournament at Tropical Park in Miami. Two teams composed of medical staff, pharmaceutical reps, and patients played softball at Tropical Park. Our coach was Choly Naranjo, who knew Morejón with whom he had played professional baseball in and outside of Cuba. Dan Morejón confirmed this data regarding the ambience at the Havana stadium back then.
9. Thomas, Hugh. *Op. cit.* Pp. 1215-1233.
10. *Ibid.* Pp.845-862.
11. Nelson, Lowry. *Rural Cuba.* The University of Minnesota Press, Minneapolis. 1950.
12. Szulc, Tad. "Plan a Military Attack. Kennedy Speech Heartens Rebels. Crushing of Beachhead with Arrest and Raids on Churches." *New York Times,* April 21, 1961.
13. Robertson, Nan. "Hunter College Denies Any Ties with Plans for Visits to Cuba." *New York Times,* Aug. 8, 1960. P. 2, col. 3.
14. "President Spurns Top Cleric." *Miami News,* Aug 10, 1960. P.1, col. 7.
15. During this time, the Revolution took a position against Catholics and Catholic institutions, including the schools. See, for example, these two references:
16. "Troops Move on 4 Seminaries, Jail 5 Priests." *The Voice,* Jan. 13, 1961. P. 1, col.1
17. "Castro Seizes Churches, Schools." *The Voice,* Jan. 13, 1961. P. 1, col. 2.
18. Lagarreta, Dorothy. *The Guernica Generation: Basque Refugee Children of*

the *Spanish Civil War.* University of Nevada Press, Reno. 1984. Pp. 1-50.

19. "Roman Catholics Fear Castro Will Drop Church, Schools." *Miami Herald,* Dec. 1, 1960. P. 21, col. 1-5.

20. Milks, Harold K. "Teach Communism Cuban Teachers Told." *Miami Herald,* Nov. 28, 1960. P. 2B, col. 1-7.

21. "Russian Pledge." *Miami Herald,* Dec. 1, 1960. P. 3, col. 1.

Chapter 3

1. Hart Phillips, Ruby. *Cuba Island of Paradox: The Turbulent Growth of a Country. Op. cit.* Pp. 28-29, 56-57.

2. Personal communication with my father and with Mr. José (Pepe) Sanz. The latter served in the Cuban Republican Army in the 1950s and also knew my father. He presently lives in Miami. Sanz served under Irenaldo's father, Colonel Pilar Garcia, in Matanzas. The latter was also said to have been a cruel man, according to Sanz, who witnessed on numerous occasions soldiers placed in difficult positions—sometimes they "disappeared" — because of gossip or innuendo instead of hard facts or confirmed intelligence.

3. Around Miami. "Arsonists Hit Café of Cuban." *Miami Herald,* Nov. 29, 1960. P. 2B, col. 4.

4. Lopez-Fresquet, Rufo. *Op.cit.* P. 13.

5. "Cuban Refugees Are a Challenge to America's Spirit." *Miami Herald,* Dec. 26, 1960. P. 7A, col. 1-7.

6. Greene, Juanita. "26 Cubans in One Barrack." *Miami Herald,* Nov. 29, 1960. P.1, col. 3-4.

7. The *Miami Herald* published under the rubric of Juanita Greene, three articles on the situation of the Cuban refugees in the Miami area "as if the refugees had written them themselves." These are the three references:

8. "Cuban Refugees Cover Story. Worry with a Smile. Refugees Hide Their Worries." *Miami Herald,* Nov 28, 1960. P. 1, col. 1-7.

9. "26 Cubans in one Barrack but Only 3 Have Jobs." *Miami Herald,* Nov. 29, 1960. P. 1, col. 6-7.

10. "Refugees Trading Jewelry for Food." *Miami Herald,* Nov. 30, 1960. P. 1, col. 6-7.

11. Green, Juanita. "Worry with a Smile." *Miami Herald,* Nov. 28, 1960. P. 1, col. 1-7.

12. Garnet, Betty. "There Will Be a Record 163,000 Students." *Miami News,* Sept. 3, 1961. P. 3B.

13. In September 1960, there were 18 Cuban pupils per 1,000 students in the public schools of Dade County. In the parochial schools, there were 139 Cuban pupils per 1,000 students.

14. The projection in the fall of 1960 that there would be 100,000 Cubans in the City of Miami yielded an uneasy set of statistics: Those Cubans were approximately 1.5% of Cuba's population, but would amount to 40% of the population of the City of Miami back then.

15. McNally, Michael J. *Catholicism in South Florida 1868-1968.* University of Florida Press, Gainesville. 1884. Pp. 99-116.

16. "Latin Women Organize Relief Work." *Miami News,* Nov. 19, 1960. P. 6A, col. 5.

17. "Spanish Center Nun Named Dade 'Outstanding Woman.'" *The Voice,* Jan. 6, 1961. P. 1, col. 4-5.

Chapter 4

1. Torres, María de los Angeles. *Op. cit.* Pp. 47-50.
2. *Ibid.* Pp. 51-55.
3. *Ibid.* Pp. 63-64.
4. *Ibid.* Pp. 56-61.
5. Papanek, Ernst, and E. Linn. *Out of the Fire.* William Morrow & Company, Inc. New York. 1975. Pp. 217-228.
6. Walsh, Bryan. "Cuban Refugee Children." *Journal of Interamerican Studies and World Affairs.* Vol. XIII. P. 389.
7. *Ibid.* P. 390.
8. *Ibid.* P. 391.
9. "High School at Centro for Teenage Exiles." *The Voice.* Jan. 20, 1961. P. 1, col. 1.
10. Walsh, Bryan. *Op. cit.* P. 393.
11. Torres, María de los Angeles. *Op. cit.* Pp. 6-22.
12. *Ibid.* Pp.70-84.
13. Saxon, Wolfgang. "Polita Grau, 84: Headed Effort on Behalf of Cuban Children." *New York Times,* March 25, 2000.
14. Torres, María de los Angeles. *Op. cit.* Pp. 89-93.
15. Lopez-Fresquet. Rufo. *Op.cit.* Pp. 45-46.
16. Torres, María de los Angeles. *Op. cit.* Pp. 88-121.
17. Candy Sosa appears in the documentary film produced by Estela Bravo, which is available in both English and Spanish. See for example: http://es-telabravo.com/press/index.html. Last Accessed on July 7, 2014.

18. Dr. Juan Clark was a Cuban sociologist who has done extensive work on the issue of the living conditions in Cuba and the Cuban refugees. The issue of the comprehensive student record is detailed in his book *Cuba: Mito y Realidad. Saeta Ediciones.* Miami, Florida. 1990. P. 226-230. Dr. Clark appeared at the Operation Peter Pan 50th Anniversary Reunion, where he also explained the fact that a *patria potestad* law was not needed in a totalitarian state.

Chapter 5

1. Conde, Yvonne M. *Operation Pedro Pan.* Routledge, New York. Pp. 57-70.
2. "U.S. Breaks Diplomatic Relations with Cuba and Advises Americans to Leave Island: Eisenhower Cites 'Vilification" by Castro. U.S. Will Help Evacuate Its Citizens Living in Cuba." *New York Times,* Jan. 4, 1961. P. 1, col. 4-7.
3. Conde, Yvonne M. *Op. cit.* Pp. 47-56.
4. Walsh, Bryan. *Op. cit.* P. 397.
5. Torres, María de los Angeles. *Op. cit.* P. 80.
6. "Castro Shipping Reds New Cargo-Cuban Children." *The Voice,* Jan. 27, 1961. P. 1, col. 4-5.

Chapter 6

1. During the struggle against the Batista dictatorship, the *Directorio* organized several student strikes. Jose Antonio Echevarria was the leader of the *Directorio* at the time and the strikes involved university students. During this phase of the struggle against Castro's totalitarian dictatorship, the *Directorio* organized students' strikes to protest the incarceration of many students and the execution of Julio Yebra Suarez. See the article: Hendrix, Hal. "Catholic Pupils Strike in Cuba." *Miami News,* Jan. 26, 1961. P. 2A, col. 2.
2. "*Clausrada 'La Quincena' por Milicias de Cuba*." *The Voice,* Jan. 20, 1961. P. 25, col. 1-3.
3. Hart Phillips, Ruby. *The Cuban Dilemma. Op. cit.* P. 293.
4. Personal communication with my father.
5. Personal communication with Jos Sanz, who served under Col. Martin Elena in Matanzas in the early 1950s.

Chapter 8

1. Walsh, Bryan. *Op. cit.* P. 387.
2. *Ibid.* P. 390.
3. *Ibid.* P. 397.
4. All files of Operation Pedro Pan and the Program for Unaccompanied Cuban Children are in the custody of a special section at Barry University in Miami Shores, Florida. Presently, individual files are only accessible by the individual whose records are in that particular file. The process to review a file is rather convoluted. It requires that a letter be sent to Catholic Charities of the Archdiocese of Miami. Someone from that office collects the requested file at the Barry University Library. Then the interested party is notified to go to the main office of Catholic Charities and review, under the supervision of someone appointed to oversee the process, the file requested.
5. Walsh, Bryan. *Op. cit.* P. 411.
6. McNally, Michael J. *Op. cit.* Pp. 112-126.
7. *Ibid.* Pp. 78-79.
8. These are some of the post-graduate theses on the general subject of Operation Pedro Pan and Father Bryan Walsh:
9. Goyos, J.M." Identifying Resiliency Factors in Adult 'Pedro Pan' Children: a Retrospective Study." Ph.D. Dissertation, 1997. Barry University.
10. Schlise, Suzane. "The Cuban Refugee Child: A Study in Parent-Child Separation." M.S.W. Dissertation. 1971. Barry University.
11. McNally, Michael J.T. "Cross in the Sun: The Growth and Development of Catholicism in South Florida, 1868-1968." Ph.D. Dissertation. 1982. Notre Dame University.
12. Bruquetas, María B. "Monsignor Bryan Walsh and Operation Pedro Pan: Catholic Social Justice in Action." M.A. in Theology Dissertation, 2002. Barry University.
13. Tyhurst, Libuse. "Displacement and Migration: A Study in Social Psychiatry." *The American Journal of Psychiatry,* Feb. 1951. Pp. 561-568.

Chapter 9

1. Mc Nally, Michael J. *Op. cit.* Pp. 16-20.
2. Quote from St. Augustine Record was obtained from Bishop Kenny 50th Anniversary Alumni Bulletin.

Chapter 10
1. Ramirez, José Ignacio. *Op. cit.* Pp. 140-155.

Chapter 11
1. The speech pronounced by Father Cistierna was transcribed from the film *The Lost Apple*. It is accessible on YouTube.
2. Conde, Yvonne M. *Op. cit.* Pp. 220-229.
3. Aglio. Thomas. *Op. cit.* Pp. 5-6.
4. Mehrabian, A., and M. Piercy. "Differences in Positive and Negative Connotations of Nicknames and Given Names." *Journal of Social Psychology.* 2001. Vol. 133(5). Pp. 737-739.

Chapter 14
1. Lopez-Fresquet, Rufo. *Op.cit.* Pp. 147-156.
2. Carroll, Wallace. "Kennedy Warns Khrushchev on Cuba After Russian Vows Help to Castro: Migs and Tanks Attack Beachhead." *New York Times,* April 19, 1961. P. 1, col. 4-7.
3. "Statement by Premier Khrushchev." *New York Times,* April 19, 1961. P. 1, col. 7.
4. Szulc, Tad. "Anti-Castro Units Land in Cuba: Report Fighting at Beachhead. Rusk Says U.S. Won't Intervene." *New York Times,* April 18, 1961. P. 1, col. 4-7.
5. Thomas, Hugh. *Op. cit.* Pp. 1370-1371.
6. Szulc, Tad. "Rebels Hopeful: Heartened by Speech by President, They Expect New Drive." *New York Times,* April 21, 1961. P. 1, col. 4.
7. Eire, Carlos. *Op. cit.*
8. Torres, María de los Angeles. *Op. cit.* Pp. 122-142.
9. Southworth, George. "23 Americans Sign Up for Invasion to Cuba." *Miami Herald,* Dec. 24, 1960. P. 3, col. 1.
10. Szulc, Tad. "Castro Resumes Talk of Invasion. He Warns 50,000 Militia to be Ready to Meet Aggression from U.S." *New York Times,* March 28, 1961. P. 10, col. 1-2.
11. Carroll, Wallace. "Kennedy Tells Khrushchev U.S. Won't Tolerate Outside Intervention in Cuba." *New York Times,* April 19, 1961. P. 12, col. 1-4.

Chapter 16
1. Finney, John J. "President Orders Cuba Refugee Aid." *New York Times,* Feb. 4, 1961. P. 1, col. 2.

2. Papanek, Ernst, and E. Linn. *Op. cit.* Pp. 63-76.
3. Asimov, Isaac. *Soviet Science Fiction.* Collier Books, New York. 1962

Chapter 19

1. "U.S. and Cuba Sign Treaty Abrogating Platt Amendment." *New York Times,* May 30, 1934. P. 11, col. 2.
2. University of Miami Cuban Heritage Collection. Review of materials on record under Operation Pedro Pan.
3. Eder, Richard. "Cuba Shuts Borders to Exchange Pesos." *New York Times,* Aug. 6, 1961. P. 1, col. 4.

Chapter 21

1. "Actions by the Americans. Punta del Este, Uruguay." *New York Times,* February 1, 1962.
2. Fillyaw, Marjorie. "'Unite in God to Fight Communism,' Bishop Boza Tells Latin America." *The Voice, Diocese of Miami Paper,* February 2, 1962. P. 1.
3. Aglio, Thomas J. "Recollections of Shared Struggles at Camp St. John 1962-2012." Booklet distributed by Mr. Aglio at the 50th Anniversary of Operation Pedro Pan reunion in Miami Beach, Florida. Several copies of the booklet are kept at the Pedro Pan Collection at Barry University Library, Miami Shores, Florida.
4. Aglio, T. *Ibid.*
5. Aglio, T. *Ibid.*

Chapter 22

1. Papanek, Ernst, and E. Linn. *Op. cit.* Pp. 13-32.
2. Father Bryan Walsh appears in the documentary film produced by Estela Bravo, which is available in both English and Spanish. See for example: http://estelabravo.com/press/index.html. Last Accessed on July 7, 2014.
3. Papanek, Ernst, and E. Linn. *Op. cit.* Pp. 217-237.
4. Masud-Piloto, Felix. *Op. cit.* Pp. 32-43.
5. "13 Million for Operation Zapata." *Washington Post,* April 29, 1961.
6. Lagarreta, Dorothy. *Op.cit.* P. 102.
7. Papanek, Ernst, and E. Linn. *Op. cit.* Pp. 115-119.

Chapter 23

1. NPR reported on April 8, 2015 on poll based on 1,200 in-person interviews conducted by Bendixen & Amandi and commissioned by Fusion and Univision. The poll found that 80 percent of the Cubans polled in the island held a positive view of President Obama. Only 17 percent held a negative view of the American President. On the other hand, 48 percent held a negative opinion of President Raul Castro and 50 percent held a negative view of Fidel Castro.

2. The poll also found that Cubans on the island were optimistic that a new, warmer relationship with the United States would lead to political and economic change in Cuba. Cubans also expressed widespread dissatisfaction with the current situation on the island.

3. Valladares, Armando. *Against All Hope*. New York. Encounter Books. 2001.

4. Moses, Catherine. *Real Life in Castro's Cuba*. Wilmington, DE. Scholarly Resources Inc., 2000.

Index

The New York Times 5, 12, 14, 15, 197, 350, 351, 352, 353, 354, 356, 357, 359, 360
Torreira Crespo, Ramón xv, xvi, 349
Torres, María de los Angeles xv, 129, 349, 352, 356, 357, 359
Trujillo, Rafeal Leonidas, 15
Tuberculosis 4, 106, 164
U.S. Air Force 119, 120, 124, 126, 169, 171, 195
U.S. Immigration and Naturalization Service 252, 273
U.S. Naval Base at Guantanamo 273
U.S. State Department xiii, 10, 47, 49, 64, 66, 263, 266
Unaccompanied Cuban Children Program viii, ix, xii, xiii, xiv, 81, 93, 94, 117, 140, 150, 161, 165, 175, 177, 180, 196, 205, 208, 236, 241, 245, 251, 277, 283, 285, 286, 289, 300, 312, 316, 318, 322, 323, 324, 325, 337, 358
Uncle César 138, 140
Uncle Emilio 20, 27, 42, 72, 74, 78, 80, 81, 91, 94, 99, 108, 148, 149, 165, 168, 190, 191, 204, 208, 209, 229, 230, 251, 259, 276, 277, 281, 300, 307
Uncle Ramón 9, 20, 42, 160, 187, 206, 213, 239, 240, 300, 324
Underground 16, 17, 22, 24, 26, 29, 43, 75, 83, 161, 197, 200, 202, 210, 211, 214, 281, 312, 313, 323, 327
Universidad de Villanueva ix, 19, 27, 36, 37, 46, 64, 79, 80, 126, 208
University of Detroit, MI 231, 337
University of Havana 6, 8, 9, 11, 12, 37, 38, 40, 294
University of Miami ix, 35, 154, 236, 271, 277, 284, 294, 301, 303, 306, 337, 339, 342, 352, 360
Urban Reform 56, 58
Urrutia Lleó, Manuel 16, 37
USS Maine 6, 24, 351
varicella 116, 159, 168
Vermont xvii, 205, 237, 238, 248, 251, 252, 253, 261, 262, 274, 275
vigencia 53, 58, 59, 63, 64, 70, 74, 94, 282, 314
Villa Marista 220
Virgin of El Cobre, see Our Lady of Charity
Visa Waiver v, 64, 66, 189, 192, 211, 261, 262, 263, 264, 265, 266, 267, 268, 272, 282, 295, 314, 315, 335
Walsh, Father Bryan 47, 49, 50, 64, 66, 82, 93, 94, 95, 96, 241, 261, 265, 267, 314, 315, 316, 319, 356, 357, 358, 360
War Criminals 33, 40, 41, 43, 75, 322
Webster College, St. Louis, MO 231

Appendix

Cuban adolescents who appeared in the registry of Camp St. John and died prematurely.

Alberto Castro
Ángel Castro
Ivo Fernández
Javier Hernández
Roberto Miquel
Mario Miqueli
Rolando O'Farrill
Jorge Viñas
Wilfredo Zayas

CPSIA information can be obtained
at www.ICGtesting.com
Printed in the USA
BVOW06s1217261217
503675BV00013B/274/P